¶An exposi-

tion of certaine difficult

and obscure wordes, and termes of
the lawes of this Realme, newly set foorth & augmented, both in French and English, for the
helpe of such yonge Studentes as are
desirous to attaine the knowledge of the same. VVhere-
unto are also added
the olde Te-
nures,

New Introduction by
Bryan A. Garner
President, LawProse, Inc.

THE LAWBOOK EXCHANGE, LTD.
Clark, New Jersey

ISBN 978-1-58477-328-3

Lawbook Exchange edition 2004, 2017

The quality of this reprint is equivalent to the quality of the original work.
The irregular pagination is reproduced as it appears in the original work:
Page 141 is misnumbered as 143.
Page 143 is misnumbered as 141.
Page 197 is misnumbered as 187.
Page 209 is misnumbered as 194.
Page 211 is misnumbered as 196.

THE LAWBOOK EXCHANGE, LTD.
33 Terminal Avenue
Clark, New Jersey 07066-1321

*Please see our website for a selection of our other publications
and fine facsimile reprints of classic works of legal history:*
www.lawbookexchange.com

Library of Congress Cataloging-in-Publication Data

Rastell, John, d. 1536.
  [Expositiones terminorum legum Anglorum. English & Anglo-Norman]
  An exposition of certaine difficult and obscure wordes and termes of the
lawes of this realme: newly set foorth & augmented, both in French and
English, for the helpe of such yonge studentes as are desirous to attaine the
knowledge of the same: hereunto are also added the old tenures.
    p. cm.
  Originally published: London: R. Tottelli, 1579.
  ISBN 1-58477-328-6 (alk paper)
  1. Law—England—Dictionaries. 2. English language—Dictionaries—
French. I. Title.

KD313 .R3813 2003
349.42'03—dc21
                                                          2002042760

Printed in the United States of America on acid-free paper

Introduction

Bryan A. Garner

John Rastell (1470?–1536), a printer and barrister of Lincoln's Inn, wrote and then published the first edition of this book in 1527. Originally, it was in Law Latin and Law French. In the second edition of 1530, a parallel English translation was added — perhaps by Rastell's son William (1508?–1565), who had been studying law at Oxford and would soon become a barrister himself. This seventh edition reflects the joint efforts of father and son. A reviser named Paget (a barrister of the Middle Temple) may also have contributed to the work, although it is unclear whether his unacknowledged contributions appeared in this posthumous 1579 edition or in one of the three editions printed in the 1590s.[1]

The Rastells' work is notable in several ways. First, it is a lexicographic landmark because it antedates by 11 years the first general English dictionary, written by Sir Thomas Elyot.[2] Second, for its time it was a sophisticated piece of lexicography that would provide definitions for legal terms in other dictionaries for generations to come.[3] Third, the side-by-side translations marked a typographic innovation

---

[1] See John D. Cowley, *A Bibliography of Abridgments, Digests, Dictionaries, and Indexes of English Law to the Year 1800* lxxxiii (1932).

[2] Sir Thomas Elyot, *The English Dictionarie* (1538).

[3] See De Witt T. Starnes & Gertrude E. Noyes, *The English Dictionary from Cawdrey to Johnson 1604–1755* 35, 40, 49–50 (1946) (noting that John Bullokar [1616], Thomas Blount [1656], Edward Phillips [1658], and Henry Cockeram [1670] borrowed heavily from Rastell — and through the 18th century still other writers borrowed from them).

for dictionary-makers; apart from the typefaces, the columns look surprisingly modern more than 400 years later. Fourth, the dictionary had an extraordinary life through 29 editions that spanned a period of 292 years (the final American edition having appeared in 1819) — a longevity that few if any other lawbooks can rival.

This seventh edition, the last one printed by Richard Tottell of London, incorporated several new features. For the first time, Kentish customs (e.g., *gavelkind*) and various antiquarian civil-law terms appeared. The civil-law additions seem to have been borrowed from the 15th-century legal wordbook entitled *Expositiones vocabulorum*. And with this edition the book took on a new title: *An Exposition of Certain Difficult and Obscure Wordes, and Termes of the Lawes of This Realme*. Earlier editions had all used *expositions* (or the Latinate *expositiones*) in the plural. For example, the sixth edition of 1575 had been called *The Expositions of the Termes of the Lawes of England*. It was not until the sixteenth edition of 1624 that the book became known by the now familiar title: *Les Termes de la Ley*.

Pre-1600 editions of this book are rare. Modern researchers are fortunate that the Lawbook Exchange has made the 1579 edition so broadly available in this handsome reprint.

Dallas, Texas
October 2003

¶An exposi-

tion of certaine difficult
and obscure wordes, and termes of
the lawes of this Realme, newly set foorth & augmented, both in French and English, for the
helpe of such yonge Studentes as are
desirous to attaine the knowledge of the same. VVhere-
unto are also added
the olde Te-
nures.

¶ *In aedibus Richar-*
di Tottelli.

¶ Cum Priuilegio.

Le Table

Le Table.

Le Table.

FINIS.

La table del Tenures.

FINIS.

¶ Abatement of a writ
or plaint.

¶ Abatement de brief
ou plaint.

Abatement of a
writ or plaint,
is whē an acti=
on is brought by writ
or plaint, wherein is
lack of sufficient & good
matter, or els the mat=
ter alleaged, is not cer=
teinly set downe, or if
the plaintife or defen=
dāt, or place, are misna=
med, or if they appeare
variance betwene the
writ and the specialty,
or recorde, or that the
writ or the declaration
be vncerten, or for death
of the plaintif or defē=
dāt, & for diuers other
lyke causes which I
ompt of purpose, for
thereof alone, a man
might make a large dis
course, and I determin
to satisfie you (good
Brother Nicholas)as
wel as I may, with as
much breuitie, and as
litle trouble to my self

Abatement de
brē ou plaint,
est quant vn
action est port per brē
ou playnt , en que
fault sufficient & bone
matter, ou autermenele
matter alleage, nest cer=
teinement alleage, ou si
le plaintife, ou defen=
dant, ou lieu sont mis=
nosme , ou sil appiert
variaunce parenter le
briefe & le specialtie,
ou recorde, ou que le
briefe ou declaration
sont vncerteine, ou pur
mort del plaintife ou
defendāt,& pur diuers
auters semblable causes
qux ieo omise de pur=
pose, car de ceo solemt,
vn poit faire vn grand
discourse, & ieo deter=
mine de satisfier vous
(bon Frere Nicholas)
sibien q̄ ieo poy, oue cy
mult breuity, et cy petit
trouble a moy mesme

A.j.   come

come ieo poy, donques ſur ceux defaultes, le defendaunt poit prie, que le briefe ou plaint abatera, ceſt adire, que le ſuir del plaintife enuers luy ceſſera pur ceſt temps, & que il commencer a auter temps ſon ſuit, & porſ vn nouel briefe ou plaint ſi ſoit iſſint diſpoſe a faire.

as I can, then vppon thoſe defaults, the defendant may pray that the writte or plaint may abate, that is to ſay, that the plaintife ſuit againſt him may ceaſe for that time, and that he ſhall begyn againe his ſuit, & bring a new writ or plaint if he bee ſo dyſpoſed to do.

¶ Abatemſt en terres.

¶ Abatement in landes.

A Batement en terres ou tenements, eſt quſat vn home moruſt ſeiſie de terres ou tenementes, & vn eſtranger, ceſt adire, vn que nad droit entra, en meſmes les terres ou tenements, deuant que le heire faſ ſon entrie, ceſt entrie de le eſtrſager eſt appell vn abatement, & il vn abatour. Mes ſi le heire enter primes apres le mort de ſon auncestor

A Batement in lſands or tenementes, is when a man dyeth ſeiſed of landes or tenementes, and a ſtranger, that is to ſay, one that hath no right entreth into the ſame landes or tenementes, before the heir maketh his entrie, this entrie of the ſtrſager is called an abatement, & he an abatour. But if the heire enter firſt after ꝑ death of his ſunceſtor, and

and the straunger en=
ter vpon the possession
of the heire, this en=
trie of the straunger,
is a disseisine to the
heire.

& le estraunger en-
ter sur le posses-
sion del heire, cest
entrie de le estraun-
ger est vn disseisine al
heire.

¶ Abbot.

Abbot, was the so=
ueraigne head or
chief of those hou=
ses of Popish Reli=
gion, whiche when
they stoode were cal=
led Abbeis, and this
Abbot together wyth
the Monkes of the
same house, who were
called the Couent,
made a corporation.

¶ Abbot.

Abbe fuit le soue-
raigne, head, ou
principall de ceux
measons de Papish re-
ligion, queux quant ils
fuerent, fuerent appell
Abbeis, & cest Ab-
be ensemble oue les
Moignes de mesme le
meason, queux fueront
appel le Couent, font
vn corporation.

¶ Abbettors.

Abbettors are in di=
uers cases diuersly
taken, one kind of ab=
bettors are they that
maliciouslye without
iust cause or desert do
procure other to sue
false appeals of murder

¶ Abbettors.

Abbettors sount en
diuers cases diuers-
ment prise, vn kind de
abbettors sount ceux
que maliciouseinent sā
droitur cause ou desert
prur aus de suer faux
appeales de murder,

ou

ou felony, enfis homes, al entent de troubler, & greeuer eux, & pur fayre eux en enfamye & flaunder.

Abbettors en murder, fount ceux que commaund, procure, counfell, ou comfort auters de murder. Et en afcun cafe, tiels abbettors ferront prifes come principals, & en afcun cafe forfq; come acceffories. Ifsint en auter felonies, et lour prefece a le chofe fait, & lour abféce de la, fait vn difference en le cafe. Il y ad abbettors auxy en Treafon, mes ils font en cafe come principals, car en Treafon il ny ad afcun acceffories.

oʒ felony, againſt men, to the entet to trouble and greue them, and to brynge them into infampe and fclaunder.

Abbettoʒs in murder, are thofe that commaund, pʒocure, counfell, oʒ comfoʒt otheʒs to murder. And in fome cafe, fuch abbettoʒs fhall bœ taken as pʒincipals, and in fome cafe but as Acceffoʒies So in other felonies. And theyʒ pʒefence at the dœde doing, ʒ theyʒ abféce, maketh a difference in the cafe. There are abbettoʒs alfo in Treafon, but they are in cafe as pʒincipals; foʒ in Treafon there are no acceffoʒies.

¶Abeiance.

¶Abeiance.

A Beiance eft quant vn leas eft fait pur terme de vie, le remaynder al droit heires de I. S. le quel
I.S.

A Beyance is when a leas is made foʒ terme of life, the remaynder to the right heires of J. S. which
J.S.

I. S. is lyuing at the tyme of the graunt: Now this graunt of remainder passeth from the grauntor present-lye, yet it vesteth not presently, nor taketh holde in the grauntee, that is to say, the right heire of I. S. but is said to be in Abeiance, or as the Logytiens terme it in power, or in vnderstanding, and as we say in ye clouds. That is to witte, in the consideration of the lawe. That if I. S. dye, leauing a ryght heire lyuing, and ly-uing the lessee for lyfe, then this is a good re-mainder, and now ves-teth and commeth into that right heyre, in such sort, as that hee may graunt, forfait, or otherwise dyspose the same, and ceaseth to be any more in abeyance, for ye there is one now of abilitye to take it

I.S. est en vie al temps del graunt : Ore cest graunt de remayndor passa hors del graun-tour maintenant, yn-core il ne vesta main-tenant, ne prist effect en le grauntee ; cest a-dire le droit heire de I. S. mes est dit deste en abeyance, ou come les Logiciens appell ceo, in potentia, ou in intellectu, & come nous diomus in nubi-bus, cest a scauoir, en le confideration de le ley. Que si I. S. morust, relinquens vn droyt heire en vie, & yiuans le lessee pur vie, don-ques ceo est vn bon re-mainder, & a ore veste & vyent en le dit droit heire, en tiel forte, que il poyt graunt, forfaite ou auterment dispose ceo, & cessa deste ore en abeyance, pur ceo que il est vn a ore de abi-litie pur prender ceo,

A.iij. pur

pur ceo que I. S. est
mort, & ad relinquish
vn droit heire en vie,
le quel ne puit estre
vyuant I.S. car durant
son vie, nul poit pro-
perment este dit son
heire. Item si vn home
soit patron dun esglise
& present auter a ceo.
Ore est le fee en le
person, mes si le per-
son morust, & le es-
glise est deuenus void,
donques est le fee en
abeyance, tanque il
soit vn nouel person
presente, car le patron
nad le fee, mes tan-
tum le droit de presen-
ter, & le fee est en le
encumbent que est
present, & puys son
mort, il nest en ascun
mes en abeyance tan-
que il soit vn nouel in-
cumbent come est a-
uantdit.

because that J. S. is
dead, and hath left a
right heire in lyfe,
which coulde not bee
lyuing J. S. for that
duringe his life, none
could properly be said
his heire. Also if a man
be patron of a church,
and presenteth one to
the same: Now is the
fee in the person, but if
the person dye, and the
church is become void,
then is the fee in abey=
ance, vntill there bee a
new person presented,
for the patron hath
not the fee, but onely
the right to present,
and the fee is in the in
cumbent that is pre=
sented, and after hys
death, it is in no body
but in abeyance tyll
there bee a new in=
cumbent, as is afore.
saide.

¶ A bitherfing.

¶ A bitherfing.

¶ Abith—

A Bithersing (and in some coppes Mis=hersing,) that is to be quite of amercementes befoze whom soeuer of transumption pzo=ued.

A Bithersing (& en ascun copyes Mis=hersing) hoc est quie=tum esse de amercia=mentis coram quibus=cunq; de intransump=tione probata.

¶Abiuration.

¶Abiuration.

A Biuration is an othe that a manne oz woman shall take, when they haue com=mitted Felonie, and flie to the Church oz church yarde foz safe=garde of their lyues, choosing rather perpe=tuall banishment out of the Realme, then to stand to the Law, & to be tried of the felony. And this lawe was instituted by Saynt Edward the Confes=sour a kinge of thys realme befoze the con=quest, & was grounded vpon the law of mer=cie, & foz the loue and

A Biuration est vn seremet, que home ou femme preygnont quant ils ount com=mise Felonie., & fue al Esglise ou Cemi=torie pur tuicion de lour vyes., eslysant pluystost perpetuall banishment hors del Realme, que a estoyer a le ley, & destre trie del Felonie. Et cest Ley fuit institute per Sainct Edwarde le Confessour, vne Roy de cest Realme deuaunt le Conquest, & fuit grounde sur le ley de Mercye, & pur le amour &

A.iiij. re=

reuerence, ſans doubt, que il et auters ſes ſuc-ceſſours porteront al meaſon de Dieu, ou lieu de prayers, & ad-miniſtration de ſon parol & ſacramentes. le quel nous appello-mus le eſgliſe. Mes cōe vnſemely choſe il fuit ou eſt, & come diſ-tant de le nature de le meaſon de Dieu, de faire el vn ſuccouror & defendour de hor-rible murderers & la-rons. Vous poyes conſiderer (frere Ni-cholas) & le meliour quaunt vous penſiſt quid noſtre Sauiour Chriſt diſt, reprehen-dans les Iewes, & perauenture auxy pro-pheſeant de ceo. Do-mus mea domus ora-tionis vocabitur, at vos feciſtis eam ſpeluncam latronum.

reuerence, no doubt, that hee and other hys succeſſoꝛs did beare vn to the houſe of God, oꝛ place of pꝛayer and adminiſtration of hys ſwooꝛd and ſacramen-tes, which wee cal the church. But how vn-comely a thing it was oꝛ is, and how farre from the nature of the houſe of God, to make her a ſuccourer and de-fender of hoꝛrible mur-derers & theeues. You may conſider (bꝛother Nicholas) and the ra-ther when youremem-ber what our Sauy-our Chꝛiſt ſaide, re-pꝛehēding the Iewes, and paraduenture alſo pꝛopheſinge of thys. My houſe ſhalbe cal-led the houſe of pꝛaier, but you haue made it a denne of theeues.

¶Abridgemt de plaint ou demaund.

¶Abridgement of a plaint or demaund.
Abꝛidge

ABridgement of a
plaint oz demaund
is wher one bzin=
geth an Assise, wzitte
of dower, wzitte of
warde, oz such lyke,
Where the wzit is , de
libero tenemento, as in
a wzitte of dower,the
Wzit is , Rationabilem
dotem que eam contingit
de libero tenemento VV.
her husband. And in a
wzitte of Warde the
Wzitte is , Custod' ter-
rarum & hered' &c. And
the plaintyfe oz de=
mandant demaundeth
dyners acres oz par=
cells of lande,and the
tenant pleadeth Non=
tenure oz iointenancy,
oz some other such like
plee , to parcell of the
land demaunded, in a=
batement of the wzit:
then the plaintif oz de=
mandant, may abzidge
hys plaint oz demaund
to that parcel, that is
to say, hee may leaue
that part out and pzay

ABridgement de
plaint ou demãd
est lou vn port
vn Assie, bre de dower
briefe de Garde , ou
tiels semblables , ou
le briefe est, De libe-
ro tenemento,come en
briefe de Dower , le
brief est,Rationabilem
dotem que eam con-
tingit de libero tene-
mento w. son baron.
Et en vn brief de gard,
le bre est , custod' ter-
rarum & hered' &c.&
le plaintife ou demaũ-
dant demaund dyuers
acres ou parcelles de
terre , & le tenaunt
plede Nontenure , ou
iointenancie , ou ascun
auter tiel semblable
plee al parcel del terre
demaunde, en abate-
ment del briefe , don-
ques le plaintif ou de-
mãdant poit abridger
son plaint ou demãd
al cest parcel , cest a-
dire ,il poit omit hors
cest parte , & prie
que

que le tenaunt reſpon-
dera al reſt, a que il ne
ad vncore plede aſcun
choſe . Le cauſe eſt,
pur ceo que en tiels
briefs le certeintie neſt
miſe, le demaund eſt
generalment, de libero
tenemento , & nyent
obſtant le demaundāt
ad abridge ſon plaint
ou demaunde en
part , vncore le briefe
demurre bone , de li-
bero tenemento pur le
reſidue.

that the tenaunt ſhall
aunſweare the reſt to
which he hath not yet
pleded any thing. The
cauſe is , for that in
ſuch writs þ certein=
tye is not ſet downe,
but the demaund run=
neth generally de libe-
ro tenemento , and not=
withſtanding the de=
mādant hath abridged
his plaint or demaund
in part, yet the writte
remaineth good ſtil , de
libero tenemento for the
reſt.

¶Acceptance.

¶Acceptance.

A Cceptance eſt vn
prendrans en bone
gree , & come vn a-
greement a laſcun chos
fait deuant, le quel puit
eſte auoyde & vnfait,
(ſi tiel acceptance nad
eſtre) per luy ou ceux
que iſſynt accepta ,
Sicome pur example,
ſi vn Abbot leſſe terre
de ſon meaſon pur

A Cceptance is a ta=
king in good part,
and as it were an a=
greeing vnto ſome act
done before , which
might haue ben vndon
and auoyded (if ſuch
acceptāce had not ben)
by him or them that ſo
accepted. As for exam-
ple, if an Abbot leaſe
lande of his houſe for
terme

terme of yeares, re=
feruinge rent and dy=
eth), and after an o=
ther is made Abbot,
who accepteth, that
is to fay, taketh or
receyueth the rente
when it is due, and
ought to bee payed:
Now by this accep=
taunce the leafe is
made perfect and good,
which els the Abbot
myght very well haue
auoyded and made
fruftrate. The lyke
law is, if a man and
his wife feifed of land
in the ryght of the
wyfe ioyne and make
a leafe or feoffement
referuinge rent, and
the hufbande dyeth,
fhee accepteth or recei=
ueth the rent, by
which the feoff=ment
or leafe is made per=
fecte and good, and
fhal barre her to bring
her wrytte called Cui
in vita.

ans, referuant rent &
moruft, & puis vn
auter eft fait Abbot,
le quel accepta, ceft
adire, prift ou receiue
le rent quant il eft due
& doit efte pay, ore
per ceft acceptaunce
le leas eft fayt per-
fecte & bone, le
quel auterment le
Abbot puyt affettes
byen auoyde & fayre
fruftrate. Semblable
ley eft, fi vn home
& fa femme feifie de
terre en droyte del
femme. ioyne & font
leafe ou feoffement
referuant rent, & le
baron moruft, el ac-
cept ou receyua le
rent, per quel le fe-
offement ou leafe eft
fait perfect & bone,
& ferra barre a luy
de porter fon bryefe
appelle vne Cui in
vita.

¶ Accef-

¶Acceffories.

ACceffories font en deux fortes, lun ante factum lauter poft factum.

Accefforie ante factum , eft celuy que commaunda ou procura auter de faire vn Felonie , & neft la prefent quant lauter le fait , mes fil foyt prefent , donques il eft auxy principal.

Accefforie poft factum , eft celuy que receyua , fauoura , ou ayda vn felon , conufant del fait que il ad fait.

Auxy vn poit eftre accefforie del acceffory ficome vn felonioufment receyua auter que eft accefforie del felonie , la le receyuer eft vn accefforye .

¶Acceffories.

ACceffozies are in two fozts, the one befoze the offence, the other after the offence is done.

Acceffozie befoze the fact, oz offence, is he that commanndeth oz pzocureth an other to doe felonie, and is not there-pzefent him felfe when the other doth it but if he be pzefent, then he is alfo pzincipal.

Acceffozy after the offence oz fact, is he that recepueth, fauoureth, oz aideth a felon,knowing well of the dæde that he hath done.

Alfo one may be acceffozie to an acceffozy, as if one felontonfly recepue an other that is acceffozie of a felonie, theze the receiuer is an acceffozie.

¶Accion

¶ Accion.

A Ccion is a suite gæuen by the law to recouer a thing, as an action of debte and such like.

¶ Accion est vn suite done per le ley de recouer chose, cõ action de det, & tiels semblables.

¶ Accions personals.

A Ccions personals bee such actions whereby a manne claymeth debt, or other goodes or cattell, or dammage for them, or damages for wrong done to his person.

¶ Accions personals.

A Ccions personals sont tiels actions per queux home claime dette ou auter biens & chateux, ou dammages pur eux, ou damages pur tort fait a son person.

¶ Accion populer.

A Ccion populer is an accion which is gæuen vppon the breach of some Penal statute; which action euery man that wyll may sue for him selfe, and the Quæne, by information or other-wise, as the statute al-

¶ Accion populer.

A Ccion populer est vn action que est done sur le breach dascun Penall statute, le quel action chescun home que voit poyt suer, pur luy mesme & le Roigne, per infor-mation ou auterment, come le statute allow,

lowe, & le cafe requif.
Et de ceux actions il y
ad vn infinite number,
mes vn put example
eft, quant afcun del iu-
rie que font impanell
& iure, de paffer enter
partie & partie indif-
ferentment, prift afcun
chofe de lun part ou
auter, ou de ambideux
parties pur lour verdict
dire al ceo part, don-
ques afcun home que
voit deins le an pro-
cheine enfuant le of-
fence fair, puit fuer vn
briefe, appell Decies
tantum enuers luy, ou
ceux que iffint pryft
pur lour verdict dyre.
Et pur ceo que ceft
action neft done al
vn home fpecialment,
mes generalment al
afcune les people del
Roygne que voit fuer,
il eft appell vn action
populer.

loweth and the cafe
requyreth. And of
thefe actions there bee
an infinite number, but
one for example is,
when any of the iurie
that are impanelled &
fworn to paffe betwen
party and party indif-
ferently, do take any
thing of the one fide or
other, or of both par-
ties, to fay their ver-
dicts on that fide: then
any man that wil win
the yeare next follow-
inge the offence made,
may fue a writ called
Decies tantum agaynft
him or them that fo
did take to geeue their
verdict, & becaufe that
this action is not gee-
uen to one man fpecy-
ally but generally to
the Queenes people
that wyll fue, it is
called an action po-
puler.

¶ Actions reals,   ¶ Actions reals.

Acti-

Actions reals, bee such actions where by the demaundaunt claymeth title to any landes or tenementes, rentes, or common, in fee simple, fee taile, or for terme of life.

Acions reals, sont tiels actyons per queux le demaundant clayme title a ascun terres ou tenementes, rentes, ou common, en fee simple, fee taile, ou pur terme de vie.

¶Accorde.

¶Accorde.

Accord is an agree=ment betwene two at the least, eyther to satisfie an offence, that the one hath made to the other. Or els it is a contract with diuers articles to bee done, some on the one part, and some on the other, where there shalbe one thinge for an other &c. The firste is, when a manne hath done a trespas, or such like vnto an other for the which hee hath agreed with hym, satisfied and contented hym, with some recompence alreadie executed and

Accorde est vn a-greement parenter deux al meins, ou pur satisfier vn offence, que le vn ad fait al auter. Ou il est vn contract, oue diuers articles dée fait, ascun sur le vne part, & ascuns sur le auter, lou il serra Quid pro quo &c. Le primer est, quaunt vn home ad fait vne trespasse ou tiel sem-blable al auter pur le quel il ad agree oue luy de satisfier & con-tent luy, oue as-cune recompence a ore executed, & fait

fait en fait. Et pur ceo que cest recompence est vn pleine satisfaction pur le offence, il serra vn bone barre en le ley si lauter voyt suer arrere vn accion pur mesme le trespas. Le auter est, quod I.S lessa vn chamber pur ans al H.G. & il est ouster agree parenter eux, que le dit H.G. serra al boorde oue le dit I. S. & pur le dit chamber & boorde il payera al dit I. S. vn certeine summe &c. cest vn contract & accorde oue articles en ambideux partes.

done in deede. And be cause that this recompence, is a full satisfaction for the offence, it shalbe a good barre in the law, if the other should sue againe any action for the same trespas. The other is, when as I. S. letteth a chamber for yeres to H. G. & it is farther agreed betwene them, that the said H. G. shal be at boorde with the said I. S. and shal for the same chamber and boorde pay to the sayd I. S. a certein summe &c. this is a contract & accorde, with articles on both sides.

¶Acquital.

ACquital est, quant il y ad seigniour, mesne, & tenaunt, & le tenaunt tient de le Mesne certeyne terres ou tenementes en frankalmoygne,

¶Acquital.

ACquital is where there is Lorde, mesne, and tenant, and the tenant holdeth of the Mesne certeyne landes or tenementes in frankalmoygne, frank-

frankmariage oʒ ſuch lyke, and the meſne holdethe ouer alſo of the Loʒd paramount, (oʒ aboue him. Nowe ought the meſne to ac= quite oʒ diſcharge the tenant of all and eue= ry manner of ſeruice, that any other ſould haue oʒ demaunde of hym concernynge the ſame landes oʒ tene= mentes, foʒ that the tenaunt muſt doo his ſeruice to the meſne onely, and not to dy= uers Loʒdes foʒ one tenement, oʒ parcel of lande. The ſame laſe is ſhere there is loʒd, meſne, and tenant, as afoʒeſayde, and the meſne graunted to the tenant (vppon the te= nure made betſeene them) to acquite, and dyſcharge hym of all rentes ſeruyces, and ſuch lyke. This diſ= charge is called acqui= tall.

frankemariage, ou tiels ſemblables. Et le meſ= ne tyent ouſter auxy de le ſeignior paramõt (ou de haut luy.) Ore doit le meſne acquit ou diſcharge le tenant de tout & cheſcũ ma= ner de ſeruice, que aſcun auter voet a= uer ou demaunde de luy concernaunt meſ= mes les terres ou tene= ments. pur ceo que le tenant doit faire le ſer= uice a le meſne tant ſolement, & nemy al diuers ſeigniours pur vn tenement, ou par= cell de terre. Meſne le ley eſt, ou il eſt ſeig= nior, meſne, & t, come auauntdit, & le meſ= ne graunta al tenaunt (ſur le tenure fait pe= renter eux) pur ac= quiť, & diſcharger luy de toutes rentes ſer= uices & tyels ſem= blables. Ceſt dyſ= charge eſt appell ac= quitall.

Ac=

¶Acquitance.

ACquitance eſt vn dyſcharge en eſ-cript, dun ſumme de money, ou auter dui-tye, quel doit eſte pay ou fait, Sicome vn ſoit oblyge de payer money ſur vn obly-gation, ou rent reſerue ſur vn leas, ou tyel ſemblable, & le par-tye a que le money, ou duety doit eſte pay, ou fait, ſur le reſceit de ceo, ou ſur auter agreement perenter e-ux ewe, fait eſcript, ou bill de ſon maine en dyſcharge de ceo, teſtemoynaunt que il eſt paye, ou auter-ment content, & pur ceo acquite, & diſ-charge luy de ceo, le quel acquitaunce eſt tyel diſcharge & barre en le ley, que il ne poit demaund & reco-uer meſme le ſume ou duity auterfoites, con-

¶Acquitance.

ACquitance is a diſ-charge in writing, of a ſumme of money, oz other duetie which ought to bee payde, oz done. As if one be bounde to pay money vppon an obligation, oz rent reſerued vp-pon a leaſe, oz ſuch like, and the partye to whom the money, oz duety ſhoulde bee payed, oz done, vp-pon the reſceit there-of, oz vppon other a-greement betwene the had, maketh a writ-ting, oz bil of his hand, in diſcharge thereof, witneſſing, that hee is payed, oz otherwyſe contented, and there-foze doth acquite, and diſcharge him of the ſame, which acquitãce is ſuch a diſcharge and barre in the law, that hee cannot demaunde, and recouer that ſume oz duety againe, con-trary

trarp thereuntó if hee   tra a ceo, ſil poet mon-
can ſhew y̾ acquittáce.   ſtre lacquitance.

¶Addicions.   ¶Additiõs.

ADdicyon is that, that is geuen vnto a man, but chiefely to the defendaunt, in actyons where proces of outlawrie do lie, as in det, and such like. ouer and besides hys proper name and sirname that is to say to shewe of what estate or degree, or mysterye hee is, and of what Towne or Hamlet or County.

Additions of Estate are these, yeoman, gentleman, Esquire, and such like.

Addityons of degree are those that we cal names of dignitye, as knight, Earle, Marques, and Duke.

Additions of mistery

ADdityon eſt ceo, que eſt done al home, mes princypaiment al defendant en actions, ou proces de vtlagary giſt, come en dett, & tiels ſemblables, ouſter ſon proper noſme & ſirnoſme, ceſt adire pur monſtrer de quel eſtate, ou degree, ou miſtery il eſt, & de que ville, ou hamlet, ou countie.

Additions de eſtate ſount ceux, yeoman, Gentlehome, Eſquier, & tiels ſemblables.

Additions de degree ſount ceux que nous appellomus noſmes de dignitie, come Chiualer, Coũtee, Marques, & Dux.

Addicions de miſtery
B.ij.   ſount

fount ceux, Scriuener,
Painter, Mason, Car-
penter, Tailer, Smith,
et iſſint touts auters de
ſemblable nature , car
miſtery eſt le craft ou
occupation, per q̄ hom̄
gaine ſon liuing.

Addicions de villes,
come Sale, Dale,& i-
els auters , & iſſint de
les auters.

Et lou vn home
ad houſholde en de-
ux lyeux , il ſerra dit
demurſ en ambide-
ux , iſſint que ſon ad-
dicion en vn de eux
ſoffiſt.

Et ceo fuit ordeigne
per vn eſtatute fait en
le primer an de H . 5 .
cap. 5 . al entent , que
vn home ne ſerroyt
greeue ne trouble per
le vtlagarie dun auter,
mes que per reaſon de
le certayne addicion ,
cheſcun home puit eē
certeynement conus ,
& portera ſa burden
demeſne.

are ſuche , Scryue-
ner, Painter, Mason,
Carpenter, Tayler,
Smith, ꝗ ſo all other
of like nature, for mis-
tery is the craft or oc-
cupatiō, wherby a mā
getteth his liuinge.

Addicions of tow-
nes, as Sale, Dale,
and ſuch, and ſo of the
reſt.

And where a man
hath houſhold in two
places , he ſhalbe ſaid
dwellinge in both of
thē, ſo that his addici-
on in one of them doth
ſuffice.

And this was or-
dayned by a Statute
made in the firſt yere
of H.5. cap. 5. to the
intent that one man
ſhoulde not bee gꝛæ-
ued noꝛ troubled by
the vtlary of an other,
but that by reaſon of
the certeine addicion,
euery man myght bee
certeinly knowne, and
beare his own burden.
Adiour-

Adiournement.

ADiournement is
when any Court
is dissolued, and
determyned, and as=
signed to bee kept a=
gaine at an other place
or time.

¶Adminiſtratour

ADminiſtratour is
hee to whome the
ordinary commit=
teth thadminiſtration
of the goods of a dead
man, for defaut of an
executour, and an acti=
on ſhal lie againſt him
and for him as for an
executour, & he ſhalbee
charged to the value of
the goods of the dead
man & no further, if it
be not by his own falſe
plee, or for that that
he hath waſted y goods
of the dead, but if thad
miniſtratour die, hys
executours be not ad=
miniſtratours: but it
behoueth y Ordinaſie

¶Adiournement.

ADiournement eſt
quant aſcun court
eſt diſſolue, &
determyne & aſsig
ne deſtre garde arre-
re al auter lyeu. ou
temps.

¶Adminiſtratour.

ADminiſtratour
eſt celuy a que
lordinary com-
mitt ladminiſtratyon
des biens la mort pur
defaut de executours,
& actyon gyſt vers
luy & pur luy come
pur executour, & ſer-
ra charge iſques al
value des byens le
mort & nient ouſter,
ſil nı ſoyt per ſon fa-
ux ple, ou pur ceo
que il ad waſte les
byens le mort. Mes
ſi le Adminyſtratour
deuie, ſes executours
ne ſount Adminiſ-
tratours, mes co-
uyent al Ordinarye

B.iij. de

de committ nouel ad-
miniſtration , mes ſi
vn eſtraunge que neſt
adminiſtratour ne ex-
ecutour priſt les by-
ens le mort, & mini-
ſtr̄ de ſon tort demeſñ,
il ſerra charge & ſue
come executour &
nemy come admini-
ſtrator in aſcñ acc' que
eſt port vers luy per
aſcun creditours. Mes
ſi lordinarie fayt vn
briefe ad colligen-
dum bona defuncti ,
ceſtuy que ad tyel let-
ter neſt Adminiſtra-
tour , mes lact̃ on
gyſt vers Lordinarye
auxy byen come ſil
priſt les byens en ſon
mayne demeſne ou
per le maine daſcun
ſon ſeruaunt per aſ-
cun auter commaun-
dement.

to commit a newe ad-
miniſtration , but if a
ſtraunger that is not
Adminiſtratour nor
executoure take the
goodes of the dead and
minyſter of hys owne
wronge , hee ſhalbe
charged and ſued as
an executour & not as
adminiſtratour in any
action that is brought
againſt hym by any
creditour . But if the
ordinary make a letter
ad colligendum bona de-
fucti, he that hath ſuch
a letter is not Admy-
niſtratour, but the ac-
tion lyeth againſt the
Ordinary, as wel as if
he tooke the goodes to
his owne hande , or
by the hande of any of
hys ſeruauntes by a-
ny other commaunde-
ment.

¶Actes.
ACtes de parliament
ſont leis poſitiue ,
que conſiſt de deux

¶Actes.
ACtes of parliament
are poſitiue lawes
which conſiſt of two
partes

partes, that is to say,
of the wordes of the act
& of the sence thereof,
& they both ioined to=
gether make the lawe.

partes.s. de les parols
del acte , & del sense
de ceo , & ils ambi-
deux ioint en semble
font le ley.

¶Admiral.

ADmirall is an offi=
cer vnder ÿ Queene
that hath auchoritie,
vpon the sea onely, to
see the nauie repaired,
& maintained, to sup=
presse, and chase away
robbers, and rouers
and to deale in mat=
ters betwœne party,
and partie, concerning
thinges done there,
and for that purpose
hath his court called
the Admiralty: yet he
may cause his Citati=
on to be serued vppon
the lande, and take the
parties body, or goods,
in execution vpon the
lande. And also he hath
cognisāce of the death
or mayhem of man cō=
mitted in any great

¶Admiral.

ADmirall est vn of-
ficer south le Roy-
gne, que ad auctho-
ritie sur le meere tan-
tum , pur voyer le
nauie repaire et maint
pur suppresse & chase
de hors estumeurs de
meere , & de faire
en chose perenter par-
tye & partye , con-
cernaunt choses fayt
la , & pur cest pur-
pose il ad son court
appell le Admiral-
tye , vncore il po-
et causer son Cita-
tyon deste serue sur
le terre , & prender
le corps del partye ,
où byens en execu-
tion sur le terre. Item
il ad cognis. del mort
ou mayhem dun hom
fait en ascun graunde

B.iiij.   niese

niefe fleetant en graud riuers en le terre de-baſe les ponts de eux procheyne al meere. Auxi pur arreſt niefes en les graunde ſtrea-mes pur les viages del Roygne & Realme, & ad iurifdiction en les diftes ſtreames du-raunt ms les viages.

¶Aduowſon.

ADuowſon eſt lou vne home & ſes heires, ount droit de preſent lour clerke al Ordinarye, al vn per-ſonage, ou auter eſ-piritual benefice quant il deuient voide. Et celuy que ad tiel droit de preſent, eſt appell Patron.

¶Age prier.

AGe prier eſt quat action eſt porte vers lenfaunt de terre,que il ad per diſ-cent, la il mra la mat-ter al court, & prier.

ſhip fleetinge in great riuers in the land be-neth the bridges of ÿ same next the ſea, alſo to arreſt ſhips in the great ſtreames for the vyages of the Queene and Realme, and hath iurisdiction in the said ſtreames duringe the same viages.

¶Aduowſon.

ADuowſon is where a man, & his heires haue right to preſent their Clerke to the or-dinarye, to a perſo-nage, or other ſpiri-tuall benefice when it becommeth void. And hee that hath suche right to preſent,is cal-led patron.

¶Age prier.

AGe prier is when an action is brought agaynſt an infaunt ,of landes that he hath by difcent, there he ſhall ſhewe the matter to the court,and ſhal pray that

that the action shall a-
bide till his ful age of
one and twenty yeres,
and so by award of
the court, the suit shal
surcesse: But in a writ
of Dower and in As-
sise, & also in such ac-
tions where the infant
cometh in of his owne
wrong he shal not haue
his age.

Also note well, that
there be many diversi-
ties of ages, for þ lord
shal haue ayd of his te-
naunt in socage for to
marrye his daughter
when the daughter of
the Lorde is of the age
of vij. yeres, and also
aide for to make hys
sonne & heire knight,
when he is of the age
of vij. yeres.

Also a woman which
is maried at the age of
ix. yeres if her husbad
die seysed, shall haue
dower and not before
nine yeres.

Also xiiij. yeres is the

que laction demurra
tanque a son pleyne
age de xxj. ans, & is-
sint per agarde de
court le suit surcesse-
ra : mes en briefe de
dower &cen assise, &
auxy en tyels actions
ou lenfaunt vyent
eyns de son tort de-
mesne il nauera sa
age.

Auxy nota que
sount plusours diver-
sities de ages . Car
le Seignior auera ayde
de son tenaunt in so-
cage pur sa file ma-
ryer quaunt le file le
seigniour est del age
de vij. ans . Et auxy
ayde pur faire son
fites & heire chiualer
quaunt il est dage de
septe ans.

Auxy femme que
est espouse al age de
ix. ans, si son baron
murrust seisi auera do-
wer & nemy deuant
ix ans.

Auxy xiiij. ans est
lage

lage de feme quel ne ſerra en garde ſi el fuit de tyel age al temps de mort ſon aunceſtour , mes ſi el fuit deyns age de xiiij. ans & en garde ſon ſeigniour , donques el ſerra en garde tanque al age de xvj. ans, & auxy xxj. ans eſt lage de heire male deſtre en garde & apres hors de garde, & auxy il eſt lage de male & female de ſuer ou deſte ſue des terres que ils ont ou clame per diſcent, & de faire touts manners contracts & bargaines, & nient deuat: mes ſi tiel enfant deins age de xxj. ans done ſes biens, & le donee eux priſt, il poet auer vn action de treſpas, mes auterment il eſt ſil deliuer eux.

¶Agreement.

AGreement eſt en cõ mañ deſine ou ex-

age of a woman ꝥ ſhe ſhal not be in warde if ſhe were of ſuch age at the time of the death of her aunceſter. but if ſhe were within the age of xiiij. yeares and in warde of the lord, the ſhe ſhalbe in ward till the age of xvi. yeres & alſo xxi. yeares is the age of ꝥ heire male to be in warde, & after that out of warde, & alſo it is the age of male and female to ſue & to be ſued of landes which they haue or claime by diſcent and to make al maner of contractes & bargains & not before: but if ſuch an infaunt within the age of xxi. yeres geue his goods, & the donee take them, he may haue an action of treſpas, but otherwiſe it is if he deliuer them him ſelfe.

¶Agreement.

AGræmt is after this ſorte defined or expounded

pounded in Master Plowdens Commentaries : Aggreamentum is a worde compounded of two wordes namely of Aggregatio, and Mentium, that is to saye agreement of mindes, so p agremēt is a consent of mindes in some thinge done, or to be done, and by drawynge together of the ij. wordes Aggregatio, and Mentium, and by the hastye and shorte pronouncinge of them, they be made one word to witt, Aggreamentum, which is no other thing, then a ioining, putting, cupling, and knitting together of ij. or moe mindes in any thinge done, or to be done. See after in Testament.

And this agreement is in 3. maners. The j. is an agremt executed

pounde en Master Plowdens Commentaries : Aggreamentum est vn parol compounde de deux parolx, cestassauoir, de Aggregatio, & mentium, cest a dire agreement de ments, issint que agreament est aggregatio ment, in re aliqua facta, vel facienda: Et per le contractiō de les deux parolx. Aggreg. & mentium, & per le correpc & briefe perlance de eux, ils sont fait vn paroll cestassauoir, Aggreamentum, le quel nest auter chose que vn vnion, collec, copulation, & coniunction de deux ou plusours mentes en ascun chose fayt, ou deste fait. Voies apres en Testament.

Et cest agrement est en iij. maners. Le prim est vn agreemt execuc

en fait al commence-
ment. Le feconde eft
vn agreement puis vn
acte fayt per auter, &
eft vn agreement auxi.
Le tierce eft vn agre-
ment execuf ou defte
fait en temps vncore
a vener . Le primer,
que eft vn agreement
execuf en fait al com-
mencement , eft tyel
de que mencion eft
fait en le ftatute de
25. E. 3. cap. 3. de
pannis, en le quart fta-
tute que dit, que les
biens & chofes acha-
tes per foreftallers que
de ceo ferrount at-
taintes, foient forfaites
al Roygne , fi le a-
chaf ent vft fait gree
al vendour , en quel
cafe, ceft parol (gree)
que eft autrement ap-
pell agreement , fer-
ra entende agreement
execute. s. payement
pur les chofes . Le fe-
cond maner de agree-

all ready , at the bee-
ginning. The feconde
is an agreement after
an act done, by an o-
ther and is an agree-
ment executed alfo.
The third is an agre-
ment executorie or to
be done in time yet to
come. The firft, which
is an agreement exe-
cuted already at ye be-
ginning, is fuch where
of mencion is made in
the ftatute of 25. E.3.
ca. 3. of clothes, in the
4. ftatute which faith,
that ye goods & things
bought by foreftallers
being therof attaited,
fhalbee forfayt to the
Queene, if the buyer
haue therof made gree
wyth the feller , in
which cafe, this word
(Gree) which is other-
wife called agrement,
fhalbe vnderftood agre
ment executed, ye is pai-
ment for ye things. The
fecond maner of agre-
ment

ment, is where one both a thinge, or acte, and an other agrees or assentes thereto afterwarde, as if one do a disseisin to my vse, and after I agree to it, now I shall bee a disseisour from the beginninge, and such agreement is an agreement after an act done.

The thirde agreement is when bothe partyes at one tyme are agreed, that such a thinge shalbee done in tyme to come, and this agreement is executorie, in as much as the thing shalbe done after, and yet there, their mindes agreed at one time, but because the perfourmance shalbee afterwarde, and so the thing vpon which the agreement was made remaynes to be done, that agreement shall bee sayde executorye. And that the statute

ment, est lou vn fayt vn chose ou acte, & vn auter agree ou assent a ceo apres, come si vn fayt disseysin a mon vse, & apres ieo agree a ceo, ore ieo serra disseysour ab initio, & tiel agreement est vn agreement puis vn act fayt.

Le tierce agreement est quaunt ambideux partyes a vn temps sount accordes que tyell chose serra fayt en temps a vener, & ceo agreement est executorye entaunt que le chose serra fayt apres, & vncore la, lour mients accorde a vn temps, mes entaunt que le perfourmaunce serra apres, & issynt le chose sur que lagreement fuit fait remaine a faire, ceo agreement serra dit executorye. Et ceo le statute de

de 26. H. 8. cap. 3.
proue, ou il dit que
chescun vicar person
& tyels &c. deuaunt
lour actuall possessi-
on ou medlinge oue
les profittes de lour
benefice, satisfiera,
content &c. ou a-
greera a payer al vse
le Roygne, les pri-
mer fruites &c. & si
ascun tyel person, vi-
car, &c. enter en
actuall possession &c.
ceo agreement est de-
ste intende xecuto-
rie come le common
vsage proue, car est
vse, que il oue vn
ou deux oue luy faief
deux vel trois obliga-
tions pur ceo, deste
pay en certeine iours
apres. Et cest agree-
ment executorie est
deuide en deux points,
vn est agreement ex-
ecutorye, que est cer-
teyne al commence-
met, coe est dit darraiñ
deuant del prim fruits.

of 26. H. 8. cap. 3.
doth proue, where it
sayth, that every vi-
car, person, and such
lyke &c. before their
actuall possessyon or
medling with the pro-
fits of their benefice,
shall satisfie, content
&c. or agree to pay to
the vse of the Queene,
the first fruits &c. and
if any such person, vi-
car &c. enter in actu-
al possession &c. this
agreement is to be vn-
derstode executory as
the common vse proues,
for it is vsed, that hee,
with one, or ij. with him
doe make two or three
obligations for it, to
bee payed at certayne
dayes after. And this
agreement executory,
is deuyded in two
pointes, One is an
agreement executory,
which is certeyne at
the beginning, as is
sayde laste before of
the first fruits.

The

The other is, where the certeinty doth not appeare at the first, and the parties are agreed, that the thinge shalbe perfourmed, or payed, vppon the certeinty knowen. As if one sell to an other, al his wheat in such a tasse in his barne vnthreshed, and it is agreed betweene them, that he shal pay for euery bushel xij. d. whe it is threshed cleaned & measured.

¶Aide.

Aide is when tenant for terme of life, tenaunt in dower, tenant by curtesie, or tenant in taile after possibilitye of issue extinct is impleded, then for that that they haue noe estate but for terme of lyfe, they shal pray in ayde of him in the reuersion, and proces shall bee made by

Lauter est, lou le certeintye nappiert al primes, & les parties sount accordes que le chose serra perfourme. ou pay sur le certeintye conus, come si vn vender al auter tout son wheat en tiel taffe en son barne nyent threshe, & il est agree perenter eux, que il payera put chescun bushell xij. d'. quaunt il est threshe cleane & measure.

¶Ayde.

Aide est quaunt tenant a terme de vie, tenát en dower, tenant per le curtesie, ou tenaunt en taile, apres possibilitye dissue extincte, est impled', donques pur ceo que ils nount que estate pur terme de vie, ils prayeront ayd de cestuy en le reuersion & proces serra fayt per briefe

briefe vers luy, de veñ & pleder oue le tenaunt en defence del terre fil voyle, mes il couyent que ils accorde en plee, car fils vary, le plee le tenaunt ferra prñe, & donques leyde pryer eft en vayne: mes fil ne vyent al feconde briefe, le tenaunt refpondera fole. Auxy tenaunt a terme dans, tenaunt a volunt, tenaunt per Elegit, & tenaunt per ftatute merchaunt, aueront ayde de ceftuy en la reuerfion, & le feruaunt & baylie de lour Mafter quaunt ils ount fayt afcun chofe loyallment en le droit lour mafter, aueront ayde.

Ayde de Roy eft en femble cafe come eft dit deuant de commen perfon, & auxy en plufours auters cafes

wꝛitt againft him, to come & plede with the tenant in the defence of the land if he will, but it behoueth that they agree in the plee, foꝛ if they vary, ꝑ plee of the tenaunt fhalbe taken & then the ayde pꝛaier is void, but if he come not at the fecond wꝛit, then the tenant fhall aunfwere fole. Alfo tenant foꝛ terme of yeres, tenant at will, tenant by Elegit, and tenant by ftatute merchaunt, fhall haue aide of him in the reuerfion, and the feruaunt and baily of their mafter when they haue done any thing lawfully in the ryght of their mafter, fhal haue ayde,

Ayde of the kinge is in lyke cafe as it is fayd befoꝛe of a common perfon, and alfo in many other cafes where

Where the kinge may haue losse, although that the tenant be tenant in fee simple hee shall haue aide, as if a rent bee demaunded against the kinges tenaunt which holdeth in chiefe; hee shal haue ayde, and so hee shall not haue of a common person.

lou le Roy puit auer perde, coment que le tenaunt soit tenaunt en fee simple, il auera ayde, Come si vne rent soit demaunde vers tenaunt le Roy, que went en chyefe, il auera ayde, & issint nauera de auter person.

Also where a Citie or Boroughe hath a fee ferme of the kinge, and any thing bee demaunded against them whiche belongeth to the fee ferme, they shal haue aide for the losse of the king.

Auxy lou vn City ou Boroughe ad vn fee ferme del Roy, & ascun chose est demaud vers eux que apperteyne al fee ferme, ils auerount aide pur le perde le Roy.

Also a man shal haue ayde of the king in the steede of voucher. Also the kinges Bailife, the collector and purueyour shall haue aide of the kinge, as well as the officers of other persons.

Auxy home auera ayde de Roy en lieu de voucher. Auxy le Bailife, Collectour & purueyour del Roy auerount ayde del Roy, auxibyen côe les officers de auters persons:

¶Alyen.

¶Alye 1.
C.j.   Alyen

ALien eft celuy que pere & il mefme fueront ambideux nee hors del legeaunce le Roigne, & fi tiel a-lien, nefteant vn ene-mie del Roigne, mes vn alien amy, vient & demurre cy en Engle-terre & ad iffue, ceft iffue neft alien mes Anglois. Ifsint fi vn Anglois ala oufter le mere oue le licence del Roygne, & la ad iffue, ceft iffue neft a-lyen.

ALien is he whofe father & him felfe were both borne out of the Queenes legeance, and if fuch an alien beeing none of the Queenes enemies but an alyen friende, come and dwel here in England & haue iffue, this iffue is no alyen but English. So if an English man go ouer the Seas with the Queenes licence, and there hath iffue, this iffue is no alien.

¶Alienation.

ALienation idem eft quod alienum fa-cere, de alter, ou mitte le poffefsion de ter-re, ou auter chofe de lun home al auter.

ALienation is as much to fay, as to make a thing an other mans, to alter or put the poffeffion of lande or other thinge from one man to another.

¶Ambidexter.

AMbidexter eft ce luy, que quant v_

AMbydexter ys he, that when a mat=

matter is in suit bee=
twene men , taketh
money of the one side
and of the other, either
to labo2 þ suit, o2 such
like, o2 if he bee of the
iury, to say his verdict

matter est in suite part-
enter homes , prist
money de lun part &
del auter, ou pur labor
le suit, ou tiels sembla-
bles, ou sil soit del iurie
pur dire son verdict.

¶Amendement.

A Mendement is ,
when errour is in
the p2ocesse, the Iusti=
ces may amende it af=
ter iudgement. But if
there be errour in gee=
ning of iudgemēt, they
may not amend it, but
the party is put to his
w2it of Erro2. And in
many cases where the
default appeareth in þ
clerk that w2iteth the
reco2d it shalbe amen=
ded: but such thinges
as come by info2mati=
on of the partie, as the
towne, misterie, & such
like, shal not be amen=
ded, fo2 he must info2m
true vpon his peryl.

¶Amendement.

A Mendement est ,
quant errour est en
le proces, les Iustices
poient ceo amender a-
pres iudgement. Mes si
error soit en iudgemēt
done, ils ne poyent a-
mender ceo, mes le
partie est mise al briefe
de Error. Et in plusors
cases, lou le defaut ap-
piert en le clerk que es-
criera le record, il serra
amend: Mes tiels cho-
ses que vient per infor-
mation del party, come
le ville, misterie, & hu-
iusmodi , ne serra a-
mende , car il doit en-
former veray a son
peril.

¶Amercement.

¶Amercement.

A Mercement plus propermēt est ceo en vn court barō, leete ou lavvday, ꝗl en vn court de record detiant Iustices est appel vn fine, & est vn penaltie assesse per le homage pur vn offence fait encounter mesme le court, come pur defaut de suit de Court, ou pur non amending de ascun chose ꝗ il suit appoint de redresser per certeine temps al darrein court iour deuant, ou pur tiel semblable cause.

A Mercement most ꝓperly is that in a Court Baron, leete oꝛ lawday, which in a Court of Recoꝛde befoꝛe Iustices is called a fine, and it is a penaltie assessed by the homage foꝛ an offence done agaynst the same court, as foꝛ lacke of suit of Court, oꝛ foꝛ not amending of some thing that he was appointed to redꝛesse by a certeine time at the laste Court day befoꝛe, oꝛ foꝛ such lyke cause.

¶ Amercement royal.

¶ Amercement royal.

A Mercement royal est quant vn vycont, coroner, ou auter graunde Officer del Roigne est amercie per les Iustices pur son misdemeaning en le office.

A Mercement royal is when a Shirif, coꝛoner, oꝛ other suche Officer of the Queene is amerced by the Iustices foꝛ hys abuse in the office.

¶ An, iour, & wast.

¶ An, iour, & wast.

In

AN, iour, & waſt is a foꝛfaiture when a man hath cōmitted petit Treaſon, oꝛ felony, and hath lands which hee holdeth of ſome common perſon which ſhalbe ſeiſed foꝛ the Queene, & remain in her hāds by ẏ ſpace of one yere & a day next after ẏ attainder, and then ẏ trees ſhalbe digged vp, ẏ houſes ſhalbe raſed & pulled downe, & the paſtures & meadowes eyꝛed & plowed vp, a thing the moꝛe to græue the offendoꝛs, & terrifie other to fal into the like, in ſhewing how the law doth deteſt their offence, ſo farre foꝛth as that it doth execute iudgemēt & puniſhment euen vp on their dum & deade thinges.

AN, iour et waſt, eſt vn forf. quant vn home ad fait petit Treaſon, ou felony, & ad terres queux il tient de aſcũ common perſon, queux ſerra ſeiſie pur le Roigne, & remaine en ſa maynes per le ſpace dè vn an & vn iour p̄cheyn aps le attainder, & donques les arbres ſerront defoſſe, les mealōs ſerꝫ raſes, & les paſtures et prees aires & plowed, Vn choſe le plus degreuer le offendors, & terrifie auters de fall̃ en autiel, en demonſtrans coment le ley deteſtꝛ lour offence, cy auant, iſſint que il execute iudgemēt & puniſh-ſur lour mute & moꝛꝫ choſes.

¶Annuitie.

ANnuitie is a certein ſumme of money graūted to aꝫ

¶Annuitie.

ANnuitie eſt vne certein ſumme dè argent grāt al vn

C.iiĵ.   auter

auter en fee ſimple,fee taile,purterme de vie, ou pur terme de ans.a receyuer del grauntour ou ſes heires,iſſint que nul franktenement eſt charge de ceo.

other, in fœ ſimple, feꝛ taile,foꝛ terme of life, oꝛ foꝛ terme of peres, to receiue of the grañ̄ toꝛ oꝛ his heires, ſo that no fœ is charged there with.

¶Appeale.

A Ppeale eſt lou vn ad fait murdr,robberie,ou felonie, donques la feme ceſty que tue auera vn action de appeal vers le murderer, mes ſil nad femme donques ſon prochein heire male auera le appeale a aſcun temps deins lan & iour apres le fact . Et auxy ceſty que eſt iſſint robbe auera ſon appeal deins meſme le temps. Et ſi le def. foit acquite il recouera damages vers lappellour & labbettours, & ils auerount le empriſonment dun an , & ferront fine al Roy .

¶Appeale.

A Ppeal is where one hath done murder, roberp oꝛ felonp,then the wife of him that is ſlain ſhal haue an accion of appeale againſt þ murderer : but if hee haue no wife, then his next heire male ſhall haue the appeale at anpe time within the pere and dap after the deede. And alſo he that is ſo robbed, ſhal haue his appeal within the ſame time,& if the def. be acquited he ſhal recouer damages againſt the appelloꝛ,& thabettoꝛs, & thep ſhal haue the impꝛiſonment of a pere, & ſhall make fine to the king.

An

In Appeale of Mai=
hem is in maner but
an action of trespas,
foz he shal recouer but
damages.

Vn appeale de Mai-
hem nest en man̄ fors-
que action de trespas,
car il ne recouera fors-
que damages.

¶Appellant.

APpellant is the
plaintif in þ appeal

¶Appellant.

APpellant est le
plaintif ē le appeal

¶Appellour.

¶Appellour.

APpellour oz appzo-
uer, is he who hath
committed some felony
which hee confesseth,
and now appealeth oz
appzoueth, that is to
say, accuseth other
that were coadiutozs,
oz helpers with hym,
in doing the same, oz
other felonies, whych
thing he wil appzoue,
& therefoze is called in
latin Pzobator.

APpellour ou ap-
prouer est cesty q̄
ad fayt ascun felonye,
le quel il confesse et a
ore appeal, ou approue
cest-adire, accuse au-
ters que fueront coad-
iutors ou helpers oue
luy en feasans de ceo,
ou auters felonies, le
quel chose il voit ap-
prouer, & pur ceo est
appel en latine Pro-
pator.

¶Appendāt & appurtenāt

Appendant et ap-
purtenant.

APpendant et appurte-
nāt are things that
by time of pzescriptiō

APpendāt & appur-
tenant, sōt choses q̄
per tēps de p̄scription,
ont

C.iiij.

ont belong,pertein, &
fónt ioiñ al auter prin-
cipal chofe ouefq; quel
ils paffont, & va come
acceforie al mefme
principal chofe, p yer-
tue de ceux paroiles
Pertinentijs: come terr
aduowfons,commons
pifcaries , chimynes ,
courtes, & diuers tyels
femblables al vne
manour,meafon,office
ou tiels auters.

haue belonged, pertei-
ned, and are toyned to
another principal thig
with which they paffe
and goe as acceffaries
to the fame principal
thinge , by bertue of
thefe wordes Pertinen-
tijs: as land, aduowfos
commons , pifcaries ,
wayes, courtes, & dy-
uers such lyke, to a
manour, houfe, office,
oz such other.

¶Apporcionment.

¶Apporcionment.

APporcionment eft
vn deuiding en
partes dun rent (le
quel eft deuydable) &
nient entier ou whole,
& entant que le chofe
pur le quel,ou hors de
que il fuit defte pay,eft
feperate & deuyde , le
rent auxy ferra deuy de
ayant refpecte a les
partes . Sicome vn hõe
ad vn rent feruice iffu-
aunt hors de terre,
& il purchafe parcel

APporcionment is
a deuydinge into
partes of a rent
(which is deudable s
not entier oz whole,)
and foz fo much as the
thing foz which,oz of
which it was to be
paied,is feperated and
deuided , the rent alfo
fhalbe deuided,hauing
refpect to þ partes. As
if a mã haue a rẽt fer-
uice iffuing out of lãds
& he purchafeth parcel
of

of the lande, the rent ſhalbe appoꝛcioned according to the value of the lande.

So if a man hold his lande of an other by Homage, Fealty, Eſcuage, and certeine rent, if the Loꝛde of whom the lande is holden purchaſe purcell of the lande, the rent ſhalbes appoꝛcioned.

Alſo if a man lett landes and goodes foꝛ yeares reſeruing rent, and after a ſtraunger recouereth the lande, then the rent ſhalbee appoꝛcioned, becauſe the goodes are not recouered, but reinapne. And ſo it is it but part of the lande bee recouered the rent ſhal bee appoꝛctoned, that is to ſay, deupded, and the leſſee ſhall pay, hauinge reſpect to that which is recouered, and to that which

de le terre, le rent ſerra apporcion, accordaunt al value del terre.

Iſſint ſi home tyent ſon terre dun auter per Homage, Fealty, Eſcuage, & certein rent, ſi le ſeignior de que le terre eſt tenus, purchaſe parcel de le tert, le rent ſerra apporcion.

Item ſi home leſſz terres & biens pur ans reſeruant rent, & apres vn eſtraunger recouer le terre, donques le rent ſerra apporcion, pur ceo que les biens ne ſont recouer mes remaine. Et iſſint eſt ſi forſque parte del terre ſoyt recouer, le rent ſerra apporcion, ceſt adire deuyde, & le leſſee payera, ayaunt reſpecte a ceo que eſt recouer, & a ceo que ore

ore remayne en fes
maines , accordant al
value.

Mes vn rent charge
ne poit efte apporcion,
ne chofes que font en-
tier . Sicome vn tient
terres per feruyce , de
payer a fon feigniou r
annuelment a tiel feaft
vn Chiuall vn Efper-
uer, vn rofe, vn chery,
ou tiels femblables ,
La fi le feigniour pur-
chafe parcel de la terre,
ceit feruice eft tout ale,
pur ceo que vn chiual,
efperuer, vn rofe , vn
cherie, & tyels auters,
ne poyent efte deuide,
feuer, ne apporcyon
fauns dammage al en-
tiertie .

yet remaines in hys
handes , accoding to
the value.

But a rent charge
can not be apporcio=
ned, noz thinges that
are entier . As if one
hold ld by feruice to
pay to his lord perely
at fuch a feaft a hozfe,
a hauke , a Rofe , a
Cherry oz fuche like.
There . if the Lozde
purchafe parcel of the
lande, this feruice is
gone altogether , be=
caufe a Hozfe , a
hauke , a Rofe , a
Cherry , and fuch o=
the , can not bee deui=
ded , fenered , noz
appozcioned without
hurt to the whole

¶Appropriations.

APpropriations fu-
eront quant ceux
meafons de le Ro-
mifh Religion, & ceux

¶App ropiation.

APpropyyations
were when thofe
houfes of the Ro=
mifh Religion,& thofe
th=

religious perſons, as Abbottes, Priours, and ſuche lyke, had the aduowſon of a= nye Parſonage to them, and to their ſucceſſours, and ob= tayned lycence of their holie father the Pope, that they them ſelues and their ſuc= ceſſours from thence forth ſhould bee par= ſones there, and ſerue the cure. And ſo at the beginnynge ap= propⱬpations weare made onelye to thoſe perſons ſpiritual that could miniſter the ſa= craments and ſay de= uyne ſeruice, as Ab= bottes, Pⱬyours, Deanes, and ſuche lyke: After by lyttle and little, they were enlarged and made to other, as namely to a Deane and Chap= ter, whych is a bodye coⱬpoⱬate, conſyſtinge

religious perſons, come Abbes, Priours, & tiels temblables, ount le aduowſon de aſ= cun Parſonage, al eux & a lour ſuc= ceſſoures, & ob= teyne licence de lour Saint Peere le Pape, que ils meſmes & lour ſucceſſours, de ceo en auaunt, doy= ent eſte perſones la, et ſeruer le cure. Et iſſint al commence= ment, appropriaty= ons fuerount faytes ſolement a ceux per= ſones ſpiritualls, que puiſſoient miniſter les ſacramentes & faire deuyne ſeruice, come Abbes, Priours, Deans, & tiels ſem= blables: Apres per petite & petite, ils fuerount enlarge & fait as auters, ceſtaſ= ſauoir, al Deane & Chapter, ql eſt corps corporate, conſiſtant de plusors , quel corps ensemblement ne puissoit dire dyuine seruyce. Et que pluis fuit al Nunnes, que fueront priorefses de afcun Nunrie , quel fuit chose horrible , entaunt que ils ne puifsoient minister sacramentes , ne precher ,ne dire al Parochians deuyne seruice .

Et tout ceo fuit sur pretence de Hospitalitie , & mayntenaunce de ceo . Et de supplyer les dyts defectes, vn Vycar fuit deuyse , quel serroit deputie al Priores, ou Deane & Chapiter , & auxy al darreine al dits Abbes & auters, adire deuyne seruyce, & il aueroit forsque petit porcyon , & ils as q̃ le apppriatiõs fueront fayt , reteignount le graunde reuenne., & fesoyent

of manie, which bodie togéther , coulde not say deuine seruice, and what moze was to Nunnes that were Pzozefses of some Nunrie , which was a wicked thinge , in so much as they could neither minister Sacraments noz pzeach, noz say deuine seruyce to the Parishioners. And al this was vppon pzetence of hospitalitie, and mayntenaunce thereof . And to supply these defects a Uicar was deupled, who should be deputy to the Pziozes, oz to the Deane and Chapter, and also at the last to the saide Abbots & others, to say deuine seruice, & should haue foz his laboz but a little pozcion, & they to whom the appzopziation was made, should retaine the great reuenues, and they dyd

sso

nothinge foʒ it , by meanes whereof hoſpitalitye decayed in the place where yt ought to haue bene chiefely maintepned , namely in the parpſhe where the benefyce was , and were the pʒofites did growe , and ſo it contynueth to this day , to the great hynderaunce of learning, the impoueriſhment of the Myniſterie , and the infamie of the Goſpel and pʒofeſſoʒs thereof.

ryens pur ceo , per quel meanes hoſpitalitie fuit decay en le lieu ou il doit eſtre chiefement garde, noſment en le Paryſhe ou le benefice fuit , & ou les profites creſſoyent, & iſſint il contynue tanque a ceſt iour, al graunde hynderaunce de learning, le empoueriſhment de le Myniſterie , & le infamye de le Goſpell, & profeſſours de ceo.

¶ Approuement.

¶ Approuement.

APpʒouement, is where a manne hath common in the Loʒdes waſte ground, and the Loʒd encloſeth part of the waſt foʒ him ſelfe, leaninge neuer the leſſe ſuſfycient common ,

APprouement , eſt lou home ad common en le waſte terre del ſeigniour, & le ſeignyour encloſe part del waſt puʒ luy meſme , relynquant nient obſtaunt ſufficient common ,

oue

oue egreſſe & regreſſe pur les' commoners. Ceſt encloſure eſt appell approuement.

with egreſſe and regreſſe foz the commoners : This encloſinge is called apzouement.

¶Arbitrement

Arbitrement.

ARbitrement eſt vne award, determynation, ou iudgement, quel pluſours font al requeſt de deux partyes al meines, pur & ſur aſcun dett, treſpas, ou auter controuerſye ewe parenter les dits parties. Et eſt appell en latine Arbitratus, & arbitrium, & ils que font le awarde, ou arbiterment, font appel Arbitri, e Englois Arbitrator.

ARbitrement is an awarde, determinatyon, oz iudgment, which one, oz moe, maketh at the requeſt of two parties at the leaſt, foz, and vppon ſome debt, treſpas, oz other controuerſie, had betwene the ſaid partis. And this is called in latine Arbitratus, and arbitrium, and they that make the awarde oz arbitrement, are called Arbitri, in Englih Arbitratozs.

¶Arr eſt.

¶Arreſt.

ARreſt eſt quaunt vne eſt priſe & reſtrayned de

ARreſt is when one is taken and reſtrayned from his

his lybertye . none
shall bee arrested for
debt, trespas, detynue,
or other cause of ac=
tyon , but by bertue
of precept , or com=
maundement out of
some court. But for
treason, felony, or bre=
kinge of the peace, e=
nery man hath aut=
thority to arrest with
out warrant or pre=
cept, and where one
shall bee arrested for
felony , it behoueth p
there hath bene some
felony done, and that
he be suspected of the
same felony, or other=
wise he may haue a=
gainst him that so dyd
arrest him, a writte of
false imprysonment.

son libertie, nul serra
arrest pur debt, tres-
pas, detinue, ou auter
cause de actió, mes per
vertue dun precept, ou
commaundement hors
de ascun Court. Mes
pur Treason, felonye,
ou debruser de peace,
chescun home ad auc-
thoritie de arrester sans
garraunt ou precept.
Et ou vn serra arrest
pur felonie, il couient
que ascun felony soit
fait, & que il soit sus-
pecte de mesme le fe-
lony , ou autermenr
il poit auer enuers luy
que issint luy arrest,
vn briefe de Faux im-
prisonment.

¶Arrerages.

ARrerages, are du=
eties behinde vn=
payed after the
daies & times in which
they were due, and

¶Arrerages.

ARrerages , sount
dueties arrere niét
pay apres les iours
& temps, en quel ils
fuerount dues , &
doyent

doyent auer efte payes
foyent il rent de ma-
nour, ou afcun auter
chofe referue.

ought to haue bene
paied, whether they be
rent of a mannour or
any other thinge re=
ferued.

¶ Affets.

¶ Affets.

ASfets eft en deux
forts, lun appell
affets per difcent,
lauter affetts enter
maines. Affets per
difcent eft, lou vne
home eft oblige en vn
obligation & moruft
feifie de terres en fœ
fimple queux difcende
a fon heire, mes il ne
fift executors, ou fil fait
execuitours, ne relin-
quifh fufficient byens
pur difcharger ceft ob-
ligation, donques ceft
terre ferra appell af-
fets, ceft adire fuffici-
ent de payer ceft det,
& per ceft meanes
le heyre ferra charge
cy auant q̃ le terr̃ ifsint
a luy dyfcende voyle

Afets is in two
fortes, the on
called affets per dif
cent, the other affets enter maines. Affets per
difcent, is where a man
is bound in an obliga=
tion and dieth feifed of
landes in fœ fimple,
which difcende to hys
heire, but maketh no
executors, or if hee
make executors lea=
ueth not fufficiet gœdz
to difcharge this obli=
gation, then this land
fhalbe called Affets,
that is to fay, enough
or fufficient to pay the
fame det, and by that
meanes the heire fhal=
bee charged, as fawe
as the lande fo to
hym dyfcended fown
ftretch:

ſtretche: But if hee haue alyened befoȝe the obligatyon be put in ſuite, hee is dyſcharged.

Alſo when a man ſeiſed of landes in tailé, oȝ in the right of hys wife, alieneth the ſame with warrantie, and hath in value as much lād in fee ſimple which diſcedeth to his heire, who is alſo heire in taile, oȝ heire to the woman: Now if the heire after the diſceaſe of his auncestoȝ bȝing a wȝit of Formedon, oȝ ſur Cui in vita foȝ the lande ſo alyened, then hee ſhal bee barred by reaſon of the warrantye and the lande ſo dyſcended, which is as much in value as that that was ſold, and ſo thereby he hath receiued no pȝeiudice, and therfoȝe this land is called Aſſetes per diſcent.

ſtretche. Mes ſil ad alyen deuaunt que le obligation ſoit myſe en ſuite, il eſt diſcharge.

Auxy quaunt vn home ſeyſie de teȝe en tayle, ou en droit de ſa femme, alyen ceo oue garrantie, & ad en value tant terre en fee ſimple que diſcende a ſon heire, que eſt auxy heire en tayle ou heire al feme, ore ſi le heire apres le mort ſon aunceſtour port vn briefe de Formedone, ou ſur Cui in vita, pur le terre iſſint alien, donques il ſerra barre per reaſon del garrantye & le terre iſſint dyſcend, que eſt taunt en value come ceo que fuit vende, & iſſint per ceo il nad receyue aſcun preiudice, & pur ceo ceſt terre eſt appell aſſetes per diſcent.

Aſſets enſ maines, eſt quant vn home endet come deuat eſt dit, ſait executors, et relinquiſt a eux ſuffic' de paier, ou aſcun commoditie, ou profit eſt venus al eux en droit lour teſtator, ceſt appel aſſets en lour mains.

¶Aſsignee.

ASſignee eſt celuy a que vn choſe eſt appoint, ou aſsign deſte occupy, pay ou fait, & eſt touts foites tiel perſon, que occupy ou ad le choſe iſsint aſsignee en ſo droit dem, et pur luy meſme. Et de aſsignees il y ſont ij. ſorts noſmes Aſsignee en fait, & aſsignee en ley. Aſsignee eſt fait eſt quant vn leas eſt graut al vn & a ſes aſſ. ou ſas ceux parols, aſsignees, & le grauntee done graunt, ou vend' le dit leas al auter, il eſt ſon aſsignee en fait.

Aſſets enter maines, is ſwhen a man indebted as before is ſayde, maketh executours and leaueth to the ſufficient to pay, or ſome commodity or profit is come to the in right of their teſtatour, this is ſaid aſſets in their handes.

¶Aſsignee.

ASſignee is hee to ſwhom a thing is appointed, or aſsigned to be occuppyed, payed, or don, & is alſwaies ſuch a perſo ſwhich occupieth or hath þ thing ſo aſsigned in his owne right, & for him ſelfe. And of aſsignees there be ij. ſortz. Namely aſsignee in deede, & aſsignee in law, aſsignee in deed is ſwhe a leas is graunted to a ma & to his aſsignees or ſwout thoſe ſwordes, aſsignees & þ grauntee giueth, grauteth, or ſelleth þ ſam leas to an other, he is his aſsignee in deede.

Aſsigne

Assignee in law is euery executor named by the testator in hys testament, as if a leas be made to a man and to his assignees (as is aforesaid) and he maketh his executors & dieth without assignement of the leas to any other, now the executors shall haue the same leas because they are his assignees in law, & so it is in diuers other like cases.

¶Attainder.

Attainder is a conuiction of any person, of a crime, or fault, whereof he was not conuicte before, as if a man haue committed felony, Treason, or such like, and thereof is endicted, arrained, & founde gilty, and hath iudgement, then he is sayd to bee attainted, & this may be ij. waies the one vpon apparance, the other vpon default

Assign en ley est chescun executour nosme per le testatour en son testament, Sicome vn leas soit fait al vn hom & a ses assignees (sicome est auantdit) & il fait ses executors & morust sauns assignement del leas al ascun auter: Ore les executors auera mesme le leas pur ceo que ils sount ses assignees en ley. Et issint est en diuers auters semblables cases.

¶Attainder.

Attainder est vn conuiction dascun person dun crime, ou faut, dount il ne fuit conuicte deuaunt: Sicome vn home fait felony, treason, ou tiels semblables, & de ceo est endict, arr, & troue gilty, & adiudge, donques il est dit deste attaint. Et ceo poet este deux voies, lun sur appar, lauter sur def.

Le attainder fur ap-
parance eft per con-
feſsion , battaȝle ou
verdicte. Le attainder
fur default eft per pro-
ceſſe.

The attainder vppon
apparaunce is by con-
feſſion, Battaiie, oȝ
verdict. The attainder
vppon defaulte is by
pȝoceſſe.

¶Auerment.

¶Auerment.

A Verment eft lou
vn home plede vn
plee en abatement de
briefe, ou barre dacti-
on quel il diſt, il eſt
priſt de prouer come
le court voit agarde,
ceſt offer de prouer
ſon plee, eſt appell vn
auerment.

A Uerment is where
a man pleadeth a
plœ in abatement of
the wȝitt oȝ barre of
the action which hee
ſayth hee is ready to
pȝoue as the court wil
awarde : this offer to
pȝoue his ple is called
an auerment.

¶Auer peny.

¶Auerpeny.

A Verpeny hoc eſt
quiet eſſe de di-
uerſis denarijs pro
aueragijs domini Re-
gis.

A Uerpeny that is
to bœ quite of di-
uers ſummes of
money foȝ the kinges
auerages.

¶Auncien demeſne.
A Vnc’ demeſne, ſont
cerť tenures tenus
de ceux manors queux

¶Auncien demeſne.
A Uncien demeſne, are
certein tenures hol-
den of thoſe manoȝs ỹ
were

were in the handes of Saint Edwarde the confessour , and the which hee made to be written in a booke called Domes day , sub titulo Regis, and all the landes holden of the sayd manours be auncyen demesne, and the tenauntes shall not be impleaded out of the sayd manours, and if they bee , they may shewe the matter, and abate the writte, but if they aunswere to the writte, and iudgement bee geuen , then the lads become frank fee for euer. Also the tenauntes in auncien demeane bee free of tolle for all thinges concerninge their sustenaunce and husbandry in ancien demesne, and for such landes they shal not be put or impanelled vppon any inqueste. But al y lads in auncyen demeane

fuer' en les maynes de Saint Edwarde le confessour,& les queux il fist escryer en vn liuer appell Domes day , sub titulo Regis , & toutes les terres tenus del dyt mannours sount auncien demesne , & les tenauntes ne serrount implede hors del dit mannours, & sils sont ils poyent monstre le matter, & abater le briefe, mes sils rnd' al briefe et pled & iudgment don,donques les terres sount deuenus frank fee a touts iours. Auxi toutes tenaunts en auncyen demesne sount franke de tolle pur toutes choses concernant lour viand' & husbandry in aunci-en demesne , & pur les terres ils ne serrount mis ne impanel sur ascun enqueste. Mes toutes les terres en auncien demesne queux sount en mains le roy sont franke fee, & pledable al commen ley . Voyes plus apres en le tytle Sokmans.

that are in the kings handes bee frankefee, and pleadable at the common inlwe. See moze after in the tytle Sokemans.

¶Auowrie.

AVowrye est lou vn prist distres pur rēt ou auter chose,& lauter sua Repleuin,donques celuy que auoit prise, iustifiera en son plee pur quel cause il le prist , & issint auowa le prise, & ceo est appell son auowrye.

¶Auowrie.

AUowzye is where one taketh a distres foz rent oz other thing and the other sueth a repleuin, then he that hath taken it,shal iustifie in his plee foz what cause he toke it and so auowe the takinge,and that is caled his auowzye.

¶Baile.

BAile est quaunt vn home est prise, ou arrest pur felony, suspicion de felony, endicte de felonye , ou en ascun tyel case, issint que il est restrayne de son libertie.Et esteant per la ley baylable offer suerty al eux q̃ ont au-

¶Baile.

BAile is when a man is taken , oz arrested, foz felony, suspition of felony, endicted of felony, oz any such case. so that he is restrayned of his lybertye: And bæinge by lawe baileable offreth suerty,to those y̆ haue au-
thozity

thozity to baile hym
which fuerties are
bounde foz him to the
Queenes vfe in a cer=
taine fumme of money
oz bodye foz bodye,
that he fhall appeare
beefoze the Iuftices
of Gaole deliuery at
the next feffions &c.
Then vpon the bonds
of thefe fuerties, as
is afozefaide, he is
bailed, that is to fay,
fett at libertye, vntil
the day appointed foz
his apparance.

¶Bailement

BAilement is a delp=
uery of things (whe
ther it it be of wzy=
tinges, goodes, oz
ftuffe) to an other,
fome times to be rede=
liuered backe to the
bailoz, that is to fape,
to him p fo deliuered it
fometimes to p vfe of
p baily, p is to fay of
him to who it is delp=
uered, & foetims alfo it
is deliuered to a 3.pfon

thoritie a luy bayle,
les queux fuerties font
oblige pur luy al vfe
le Roigne en vn cert
fumme del money, ou
corps pur corps, que
il apperera deuaunt
les Iuftices de gaole
deliuery al procheine
Sefsion &c. Donques
fur les bondes de ceux
fuerties, come eft a-
uauntdit, il eft baile,
ceft adire, mife al li-
berty tanque le iour
appoint pur fon ap-
parance.

¶Bailemnet.

BAilement eft vn de-
liuerye de chofes
(foyent ils de efcripts,
biens, ou ftuffe) al
auter, afcun foits defte
redeliuer erer al bay-
lour, ceft adire, al ce-
luy que ifsint delyuer
ceo, afcun foites al
vfe del baily, ceft adire,
de luy a que il eft de-
liuer, & afcun foites
auxi defte deliuer ou-
ftera vn tierce perfon.

D.iiij.   Ceft

Ceſt deliuere eſt appel vn bailement.

¶Bailife.

BAilife eſt vn of-ficer que apperti-ent al vn manor, pur order le huſban-dry, & ad aucthoritie, de paier quitrents iſſu-ants hors del mañ,ſuc cide arbres,repairer les meaſons, faire pales, haies,diſtreiñ auers ſur le terre, & diuers tiels ſemblables . Ceſt of-ficer eſt celuy , que les auncyent Saxons ount appel vn Reeue: car le noſme (Baylife ne fuit donques conus enter eux : mes vient eins oue les Normãs, & eſt appell en latyn, villicus.

¶Bakberinde theefe.

BAkberind Theefe eſt vn laſ que eſt priſe oue le man-ner ceſt adire, ayant ceſt troue ſur luy (eſ-teauɪ t purſue oue le

This deliuery is cal-led a bailement.

¶Bailife.

BAilife is an offi-cer that belongeth to a mannour to order the huſbandry, and hath aucthorytye, to paye quitrents iſ-ſuing out of the man-nour,fell trees,repaire houſes, make pales, hedges,diſtrain beaſts vpon the ground, and diuers ſuch like.This officer is hee whome the auncient Saxons called a Reeue:foȝ the name (Baylife) was not then knowne a-monge them:but came in with the Noȝmãs, and is called in latin villicus.

¶Bakberinde theefe.

BAkberind Theefe, is a theefe that is taken with þ ma-ner,þ is to ſay,hauing that found vppon him (being followed tõ the hue

hue and crie) which he hath stollen whether it bee money, linnen, woollen, or other stuffe but it is moste properlye sayed when hee is taken, carryinge those thinges, that hee hath stollen in a bundel, or fardel, vpon his backe.

¶Bargaine & sale.
BArgaine and sale, is when a recompence is geuen by both the partyes to the bargayne. As if one bargaine and sell his land to another for money. Here the lande is a recompence to him for the money, and the mony is a recompence to the other for þ land, and this is a good contract and bargaine, and fee simple passeth, notwithstanding he doth not saye, to haue and to holde the lande to him and to his heires.

¶Bargaine & sale.
BArgayne & sale, est quaunt vn recompence est don per ambideux les parties al bargaine. Come si vn bargayne & vender son terre al auter pur argent. Icy le terre est vn recompence a luy pur largent, & le argent est vn recompence al auter pur le terre, & cest vn bone contract & bargayne, & fee simple passa nient obstaunt il ne dyt; a auer & tener le terre a luy & a ses heires.
Et

Et per tiel hargayne & ſale, terres poyent paſſe ſauns liuery de ſeiſin, ſi le bargaine & ſale ſoyt per fayt endent, ſeale, & enrolle, ou en le countye ou le terre giſt, ou en vn des courtes del Roygne de recorde al weſtminſter deins vj. moyes procheyne apres le date de meſme le eſcript endent accordaunt al ſtatute en ceſt caſe fayt en le 27. Ann. de H. 8. cap. 16.

And by ſuch a bargain and ſale, landes maye paſſe without lyuerye of ſeiſin, if the bargain and ſale be by dæd indented, ſealed, and inrolled, either in þ county where the land lyeth, oꝛ in one of the Queenes courtes of Recoꝛds at Weſtminſter, win vj. moneths next after the date of the ſame wꝛitinge endented accoꝛding to þ ſtatute in that behalfe made in the 27. yeare of H. 8. ca. 16.

¶Barre.

¶Barre.

BArre eſt quaunt le defendant en aſcun action plede vn plee que eſt ſuffycient reſpons, & ceo adnul laction del pleintife a touts iours.

BArre is when the defendant in any action pledeth a ple which is a ſufficient anſwere and that deſtroieth the action of the plaintife foꝛ euer.

¶Baſtarde.

¶Baſtarde.

BAſtarde eſt celuy que eſt nee daſcuꝑ fée

BAſtard is he that is boꝛne of any womā not

not maried so that his father is not knowen by ye order of the law, & therefore he is called the child of the people. But by the law spiritual if one get a childe vpon a woman which childe is borne out of wedloke, and after hee marry ye same woman, thē such a child shalbe said mulier & not bastarde. But by the law of England it is a bastarde: & for that cause when such special bastardye is alleaged, it shalbe tried by ye coūtrey and not by the Byshoppe. But generall bastardye alleaged shall bee tried by the certificat of the Bishop.

And if a woman be great with childe by her husband who dieth & she taketh an other husbād, & after ye child is borne, this childe shalbe said the child of

nient espouse, issint que son pere nest conus per order del ley, & pur ceo il est dyt filius populi, mes per la ley spirituall si vn engender vn infaunt sur ascun femme que infaunt est nee hors del espouselles, & puis il marry mesme la femme : donques tiel enfaunt serra dyt mulyer & nemy bastarde, mes per le ley Dengleterre il est bastarde, & pur ceo quāt tyel especyall basterdye est alleage, il serra trye per payes, & nemy per Leuesque, mes generall bastardye serra trye per certificatyon del Euesque.

Et si vn femme soyte grosse de infaunt, per son baron, que morust & el prist auter baron, & apres lenfant est nee, cest serra dyt lenfaunt
le

le primer baron. Mes
si el fuit pryuement
infeint al temps del
mort fon primer ba-
ron, donques il fer-
ra dit lenfaunt le fe-
conde baron, fed que-
r:, & voyes loppy-
nion de Thorpe 21.
E. 3. 39.

Auxy fi vn home
prent feme que foyt
groffement infeint per
afcun auter que ne
fuit fon baron , &
puis lenfaunt eft nee
deins les efpoufels,
donques il ferra dyt
lenfaunt le baron mef-
que il fuit nee forf-
que vn iour apres
les efpoufelles folemp-
nife.

¶Battaile.

BAttaile eft vn aun-
cient triall en no-
ftre ley que le defen-
daunt en vn appeale
de felonie poit eflier,
ceftaffauoir , a com-
batour oue lappellant
pur proofe fil foyt

the firfte hufbande.
But if fhee were pri-
uely wyth childe at
the time of þ death of
her firft hufband, then
it fhalbe faid þ child of
þ fecõd hufbãd, but en-
quire farther, and fee
the opinion of Thorpe
21. E. 3. 39.

Alfo if a man take
a wife which is great
with childe by an o-
ther that was not her
hufband, and after the
childe is borne within
the efpoufels , then
hee fhal bee faide the
childe of the hufband,
though it were borne
but one day after the
efpoufels folempny-
fed.

¶Battaile.

BAttaile is an aun-
cyent tryal in our
law, which the defen-
daunt in an appeale of
felony may choofe, that
is to fay, to fight with
the appellaunt , for
proofe whether he be

cui-

culpable of the felony
oz not : which com=
bate if it fall out so
wel on the part of the
defendant,that he doe
banquiſhe the appel=
lant,he ſhal go quite,&
barre him of his appel
foz euer. But if one be
indicted of felony, and
an appell is bzought
vpon the ſame indicte=
ment, there the defen=
daunt ſhall not wage
battayle. Battaile al=
ſo may be in a wzit of
right.

¶Bigamy.

BIgamy was a coũ=
terplea (deuiſed at
the Councel of Lions
vpon miſlike of ſecond
mariage)to be obiected
whẽ p pzifoner demaũ
deth the benefit of the
Clergie, to wit hys
bæk,as namely to ſay,
that he which demaũ
deth the pziuiledge of
the clergy, was mari=
to ſuch a woman, at

culpable del felonye
ou non : quel com=
bate ſil ſucceds ſi bi=
en del part le defen=
daunt que il vanquiſh
lappellant , il alera
quite , & luy barre=
ra de ſon appelle a
toutes iours . Mes ſi
vn ſoyt endite de fe=
lonye & vn appelle
eſt porte ſur meſme
lendictement , la le
defendaunt ne gage=
ra battayle . Battaile
auxy poit eſtre en vn
briefe de droit.

¶Bigamy.

BIgamy.fuit vn coñ=
terplea (deuiſe al
Councell de Lyons
ſur miſlike de ſeconde
mariage) deſte ob=
iecte quaunt le bene=
fite del Clergie, ceſt=
aſſauoire , ſon lyuer
come noſment a di=
re , que il que de=
maunde le priuiledge
del Clergy , fuit mar=
rye a tyel femme en
tiel

tiel lieu deins tiel di-
oces , & que el est
mort , & que il ad a-
pres marrie vn auter
femme deins mesme
le dioces , ou deins
ascun auter dioces, &
issint Bigamus : Ou
sil nad este forsque vn
temps marrie , don-
ques adire que el,que
il ad espouse est , ou
suit vn viefe, cest a-
dire le réliste dun ti-
el &c. Le quel chose
serra trye per Leues-
que de le dioces ou
le espousals sount al-
leage. Et esteaunt is-
sint certifie per Leues-
que, le prisoner per-
dera le benefite del
clergie : Mes al cest
iour per force de le
Acte fait en Anno 1.
Ed.6 . cap. 12 . cest
nul plea , mes que il
poet auer son Cler-
gie ceo nyent obs-
taunt.

Issint est Brooke ti-
tulo Clergie plac' 20.

such a place win such a
dioceste, & that shee is
dead, and that he hath
since maried an other
woman , within the
same dioces, or within
some other dioces, and
so is Bigamus. Or if
hee haue bin but once
maryed,then that is to
say that shee whom he
hath maried,is or was
a widowe , that is to
say the left woman of
such a one &c. which
thinge shalbee tried by
the Bishoppe of the
Dyocesse , where the
maryages are allea-
ged . And beinge so
certyfied by the By-
shoppe , the prisoner
shall loose the bene-
fite of the clergie.But
at this day, by force
of the act made in An-
no 1.E.6.cap.12.this
is noe plea, but that
he may haue his Cler-
gie y notwithstanding.

Soe is Brooke ti-
tulo Clergie Placito 20.

to the same purpose. And hereuppon, if you be desirous (Bro-ther Nicholas) to see what reasons they haue that perswade a-gainst seconde marry-ages, reade, amonge manye other, Fraun-ches Petrach of Reme-dies for both fortunes the first booke & lxxvj. Dyalogue intituled of seconde marriage, which booke nowe of late our brother ma-ster Thomas Twyne hath verye well and with good grace (as they that can iudge do say) translated out of latin into Englishe, & most aptlye called it Phisicke against for-tune.

al mesme purpose. Et sur ceo, si vous estis desirous (Frere Nicho-las) de voyer queux reasons ils ount q̃ per-svvade enuers secunde Espousels, lege enter diuers auters, Fraun-ches Petrarche de Re-medijs vtriusque for-tunæ le primer lyuer & lxxvj. Dialogue entituled de secund' nuptijs, quel lyuer ore tarde nostre frere Mr Thomas Twyne ad byen & oue bone grace (come ils que poyent Iudger dy-ount) translate hors de latine en Eng-lois, & moult apt-ment appell ceo Phi-sicke encounter for-tune.

¶Blodewit.

BLodewit, that is to be quite of amerce-ments for blodshedding & what pleas are hol-den in your court you

¶Blodewit.

BLodewit, hoc est quietũ esse de amer-ciamentis de sanguine fuso, & que teneantur placita in curia vestra
&

& habeatis amercia-
menta inde proueni-
entia quia (wit) Ag-
glic', eſt miſericordia
latine.

ſhall haue the Amerce-
mentes thereof coming
becauſe (wit) in En-
gliſh is Miſericordia,
latine.

¶Boote.

BOote eſt vn vyel
paroll & il ſignifie,
helpe ſuccour, ayde,
ou aduauntage, &
eſt communemt ioint
oue vn aut' parol, que
ſignification il augmet
come ceux Brigboote,
Burghboot, fireboote,
hedgeboote, plowe-
boote, & diuers tiels
ſeblables, pur queux
ſignifications, voyes
en lour proper titles.

¶Boote.

Boote is an old woꝛd,
& ſignifyethe helpe
ſuccour, ayde, oꝛ
aduauntage, and is
commoly ioyned with
an other woꝛd whoſe
ſignification it doth
augmét, as theſe bꝛig-
bœt, burghbœte, fire
bœte, hedgbœt, plow-
bœte, & diuers ſuch
like, foꝛ whoſe ſigni-
fications, looke in their
pꝛoper titles.

¶Brodehalpeny.

BRode halpeny (en
aſcūs copies Bord-
halbenye) hoc eſt
quietum eſſe de qua-
dam conſuetudine ex-
acta pro tabulis le-
uatis.

¶Brodehalpeny.

BRodehalpeny (in
ſome copies Boꝛd-
halbeny) that is
to bœ quite of a cer-
teyne cuſtome exacted
foꝛ ſettinge vp of ta-
bles.

¶Burg.

¶Brugbote.

¶Brugbote.

BRugbote (and in
some copies Brige
bote .) that is to bee
quite of gæuing aybe
to the repayringe of
bꝛidges.

B Rugbote) & en as-
cuns copies Bridge
bote) hoc est quietum
esse de auxilio dando
ad reficiendum pon-
tes.

¶Burgbote.

¶Burghbote.

B Urghbote, that is
to bee quite of gæ-
uing aybe to make a
Boꝛough, Castel, Ci-
tie, oꝛ walles thꝛowen
downe.

B Vrghbote, hoc est
quietum esse de
auxilio dando ad faci-
endum Burgum , cas-
trum , Ciuitatem, vel
muros prostrata.

¶Burghbrech.

¶Burghbrech.

B Urghbꝛech, that is
to be quite of tres-
passes done in Citie oꝛ
boꝛough agaynst the
peace.

B Vrghbrech, hoc est
quietu esse de trãs-
gressionibns factis in
ciuitate vel burgo con-
tra pacem.

¶Burgh English.

¶Burgh English.

B Urgh English, oꝛ
boꝛough english, is
a custome in some aun-
cient Boꝛough, that if

B Vrgh English , ou
borough english est
vn custome en vn ãci-
ent Borough , que si
        E.j.   vn

vn home ad iſſue dy-
uers ſites & moruſt ,
vncore le puiſne ſites
ſolement enheritera &
auera touts les terres
& tenementes , que
fueront al ſon pere ,
de que il moruſt ſey-
ſie deyns meſme le
burgh per dyſcēt, come
heire a ſon pere , per
force del cuſtome de
meſme le burgh.

a man haue iſſue dy-
uers ſonnes and dieth,
yet the yongeſt ſonne
onely ſhall enheryte
and haue all the lands
and tenementes that
were hys Fathers,
whereof he dyed ſey-
ſed within the ſame
burgh by diſcent, as
heire to his father, by
force of the cuſtome of
the ſame boꝛough.

¶Burglarie.

Burglarie eſt quant
vn debruſe & en-
ter en le meaſon dun
auter en le nuit , oue
felonious intent , de
robber, ou occider, ou
de faire auter felonie,
en queux caſes nyent
obſtant il ne emport
riens , vncore il eſt fe-
lonie , pur que il ſerra
pendue . Auterment
eſt ſil ſoit en le iour, ou
que il debruſe le mea-
ſon en le nuit , & ne
entra pas en ceo a ceſt
temps

¶Burglarie.

Burglarie is when
one bꝛeaketh and
entreth into the houſe
of another in the night
with felonious intent
to robbe oꝛ kill , oꝛ to
do ſome other felonie,
in whiche caſes al-
though he carie away
nothing, yet is it felo-
nie , foꝛ which he ſhal
ſuffer death . Other-
wiſe it is if it be in the
day time , oꝛ that yee
bꝛeak the houſe in the
night , and enter not
therein at that time.
But

But if a seruant wil conspire wyth other men to robbe his Mafter, and to that intent he openeth hys Mafters doores or wyndowes in the nyght for them, and they come into the house by that way, thys is Burglarye in the ftraungers, and the feruant is a theefe but no burglar. And this was the opinion of the Right worfhipful Syr Roger Manwoode Knight, moft worthy Lord chiefe Baron of the Efchequer, at the Quarter Seffions holden in Canterburie in Ianuarie laft 1579. 21. Elizabeth.

Mes fi vn feruant voile conspire oue auters de robber fon Mafter, & a cel entent il ouert les doores & fenefters de fon Mafter en le nuit pur eux , & ils vient en le meafon per ceft voye, ceft Burglarie en les eftraungers, & le feruant eft vn laron , mes nemy burglar. Et ceo fuit le opinion de le Right worfhipfull Sir Roger Manwood Chyualer , plus digne feigniour chiefe Baron de le Efchequer , a le Quarter Seffions tenus en Caunterburie en Ianuarie darreyne. 1579. 21. Elizabeth.

¶Caruage.

Caruage , that is to bee quyte if the kinge fhal taxe al hys lande by Carues,

¶Caruage.

Caruage, hoc eft quietum effe fi dñs Rex talliauerit totá terram fuam per carucas. E.ii.   Nota

Nota que vn carue de terre eſt vn plow lãd.

Ɲote that a carue of land is a ploꝟ land.

¶Ceſſion.

CEſſion, eſt quant vn eccleſiaſtical perſon eſt cree Eueſq;, ou quãt vn perſone dun parſonage priſt vn auter benefice ſãs diſpenſation, ou autermẽt niẽt qualified &c. En ambydeux caſes, lour primer benefices ſont deuenus voide, & al ceux que il ad que ſuit cree Eueſque, le Roigne preſentera pro illa vice, quicunque ſoit patron de eux. Et en lautꝛ caſe le patron poit preſenter.

¶Ceſſion.

CEſſion, is ꟺhen an eccleſiaſtical perſon is created Biſhop, oꝛ ꟺhen a Parſon of a parſonage taketh another benefice ꟺythout diſpenſation, oꝛ otherꟺiſe not qualified &c. In both caſes, theyꝛ firſt benefices are become voide, & to thoſe that he had ꟺho ꟺas created biſhop, the Ɱ. ſhal pꝛeſent foꝛ ꝑ time ꟺhoſoeuer be patron of them. And in the other caſe, the patron may pꝛeſent.

¶Challenge.

CHallenge, eſt lou Iurours appearont pur trier vn iſſue, donques ſi aſcun des parties, ſuppoſont que ils ne ſont pas indifferent,

¶Challenge.

CHallenge, is ꟺhere Iurours appeare to trie an iſſue, then if anyei of the parties ſuppoſe that they are not indyfferent, they

they may there chal-
lenge and refuse them.

There be diuers chal-
lenges , one is chal-
lenge to the array, the
other to the polles.
Challenge to tharray
is when the panell is
fauourably made by
the Sherife or other
Officer. Challenge by
the polles , are some
principal, and some by
cause as they call it.
Principall is when
one of the Iurors is
the sonne, brother , or
cosin, to the plaintyfe
or defendant or tenant
to him, or that he hath
espoused the daughter
of the plaintife , & for
those causes hee shalbe
withdrawen.

Also in a plee of the
death of a man, and in
euery other action real
& in actions personal,
if the debt or damages
amount to xl. Markes
it is a good challenge,
that he cannot dispede

la ils poyent eux chal-
lenge & refuse.

Il y ad diuers chal-
lenges, vn est challenge
al array , lauter a les
polles. Challenge al
array est quant la pa-
nell est fauorablement
fait per le Vicont, ou
auter Officer. Chal-
lenge per les polls sont
ascuns principall, &
ascun per cause, come
ils appel ceo. Princi-
pall est quant vn des
Iurours est le fites,
frere , ou cosine al
plaintife ou defendant
ou tenaunt a luy , ou
que il auoit espouse la
file le pleintife , & pur
ceux causes il serra re-
trahit.

Auxy in plee de le
mort de home , & en
chescun action real, &
en actions personel, si
le dette ou dammages
amount a xl. Markes,
il est bon challege que
il ne puit dyspender

E.iij.   xl.

xl.s. per an de frank-
tenement.

Challenge per cause,
est ou le partie alleage
vne matter que nest
princypall challenge ,
come que le fites dun
des Iurours ad espouse
la file le plaintife , &
donques conclude , &
pur ceo il est fauoura-
ble , quel serra trie per
auters del enquest, si il
soit fauorable ou in-
different, & si ils diont
que il est fauourable
& nemy indifferent ,
donques il serra treit ,
auterment il serra iure.
Auxy vn felon que est
arraigñ, puit challenge
xx. Iurors peremptorie
sauns ascun cause , &
ceo est in fauorem vi-
te, & taunt que il voyle
oue cause , mes don-
ques il serra trie si pur
tiel cause il soit indif-
ferent ou nemy.

¶ Champertours.

xl. s. by the yeare of
freeholde.

Challenge by cause,
is where the partye
doth alleage a matter
which is no principall
challenge, as that the
sonne of one of the iu-
rors hath espoused the
daughter of the plain-
tife, & then he doth co-
clude, & therefore he is
fauorable, whych shal
be tried by others of
thenquest, whether he
be fauorable or indif-
ferent, and if they say
that he is fauorable &
not indifferent, the he
shalbee drawen out ,
otherwise he shalbee
sworne. Also a Felon
that is arraigned may
challenge xx. Iurours
peremptorie without
any cause, and that is
in fauor of life: and as
many as he will wyth
cause, but the it shal be
tried if for such cause
he be indifferet or not.

¶ Champertours.
Cham-

Hampertors be they that moue plees and suites, oz cause to bee moued by their owne, oz others pzocuremēt, and sue them at their owne costes to haue part of the lande, oz gaines in variance.

Hampertors sount ceux que moue plees & suites, ou cause deste moue per lour, ou auters procurement, & sue a lour costages et charges demesne, pur auer part del terre, ou gaines en variance.

¶Charge.

¶Charge.

Harge is where a man graunteth a rent out of his groūd, and that if the rent be behinde, that it shal be lawfull foz him, hys heyzes and assygnes to distreine tyll the rent be paide, this is called a rent charge. But if one graunt a rent charge out of the lande of an other, and after purchase the lande, the graunt is voyde.

Harge est lou vne home graunta vn rent issuant hors de son terre, & que si le rent soit arrere, que list a luy, ses heyres & assignes a distrainer tanque le rent soit pay, cest appell vn rent charge. Mes si vn graunt vn rent charge hors del terre vne auter, & puys purchase le terre, le graunt est voyde.

¶Charters of landes.   ¶Charters de terres.

E.iiij.   Char-

CHarters de terres, ſont eſcripts, faites, euidences, & inſtruments, fait de vn home al auter, ſur aſcun eſtate conueyed, ou paſſed perenter eux de terres ou tenements monſtrans les noſmes, lieu, et quantity del terre, le eſtate, temps, et maner del feſance del ceo, les parties a le eſtate deliuer et priſe, les teſtemoynges preſent al ceo oue auters circumſtances.

CHarters of landes, are writings, dedes euidences, and inſtruments, made from one man to an other vpon ſome eſtate conueyed oʒ paſſed betwene thē, of landes oʒ tenemēts, ſhewing the name, place, & quātity of the land, the eſtate, time, & maner of þ doing thereof, þ parties to þ eſtate deliuered & taken, þ witneſſes preſent at the ſāe w other circumſtāces.

¶ Chattels.

¶ Chattels.

CHattels ſont en ij. ſorts, ceſt adire, chatels Reals, & chatels Perſonals. Chatels Reals ſount leaſes pur Ans, gardes, & a tener a volunt.

Chattells Perſonals ſount toutes moueables biens, come argent, plate, biens del meaſon, chiualles,

CHattels are in two ſoʒts, that is to ſay chatels reals, & chatels perſonals. Chatels reals, are leaſes foʒ yeares, wardes, and to holde at will &c.

Chattels perſonalʒ are al moueable goods as Money, Plate, houſhold ſtuffe, hoʒſes kyne, byne, co2ne, and suche like.

vaches, blees, & tyels semblables.

¶ Childewite

¶ Childewitt.

Childewitte, that is that you may take a fine of your bondswoman defiled, & begotten w childe w= out your licence.

Hildwitt, hoc est, Quod capiatis ger-summam de nati-ua vestra corrupta & pregnata sine licentia vestra.

¶ Chimin.

¶ Chimin

Chimin is the hye way where euery man goeth, which is called via regia, and yet the Kinge hath no other thinge there but the passage fo2 him & his people, fo2 the fre holde is in the Lo2de of the soile, and all the p2ofit growinge there as trees, and other thinges.

Hymin est le haut Voye ou chescun home passa, que est appel via regia, et vn-core le Roy nad auter chose la, forsq; le pas-sage pur luy & pur so people, car le frankte-nement est le seigny-ors del soile, et toutes les profits crescents la come arbres & auters choses.

¶ Thinge in action.

¶ Chose inaction.

Thinge in action, is when a manne

Hose en action est quant vn home ad

ad cauſe, ou poit por̃ vn action pur aſc' duty due a luy,come vn ac‑ cion de det ſur vn ob‑ ligac' , annuyty, rent, couenant,garde, byẽs, treſpas ,ou tiels ſem‑ blables,et pur ceo que ils ſont choſes de quex vn home neſt poſſeſſe, mes pur recouerye de eux ,eſt miſe a ſon ac‑ tyon, ils ſount appell choſes in actyon.Et ti‑ els choſes en action,q̃ ſount certaine,le roign poit graunt, & le grā‑ tee poit vſer vn actyon pur eux en ſon noſme demeſne tantſolement: Mes vn common per‑ ſon ne poit graunter ſon choſe en acc' ne le roigne meſma ne poit graũt ſa choſe in action le q̃l eſt vncertein, cõe trñs,et tiels ſemblables

hath cauſe , oʒ may bʒinge an actyon foʒ ſome dutye due to him as an actyon of debt vpon an oblagation, annuity.rent ,couenāt warde, gꝏdes, treſpas oʒ ſuch like. And bee= cauſe they are thinges whereof a man is not poſſeſſed, but foʒ reco= uery of them is dʒiuē to his actyon,they are called things in actiō, & thoſe things in acti= on that are certeine, the Queene may grāt and the grauntee may vſe an action foʒ them in his owne name on= ly. But a commō per= ſon can not graunte hys thinge in actyon, noʒ the Queene her ſelfe can not graunt her thinge in actyon which is vncerteyne, as treſpas & ſuch like.

¶Circuit de action. ¶Circuit of action .

Circuit de actyon eſt quant vn action eſt

Circuite of actiō is when an actyon is rightly

rightly brought. for a dutye: but yet about ye bushe as it were. for ye it might aswel bene otherwise aunswered, and determined, and ye suite saued, and bee=cause that the same action was moze then nædefull, it is called circuite of actyon. As if a man graunt a rent charge of x.li. out of his mannour of Dale, and after the graun=tee disseise the graun=tour of the same Ma=nour of Dale. and hee bzingeth an assise and recoucreth the lande, and xx.li. dammages. Which xx.li. bæynge paied, the grauntee of the rent sueth his ac=tyon foz x.li. of his rent due duringe the time of the disseison, Which if no disseisine had ben, he must haue had. This is called cir=cuit of actiõ because it might haue bē shoztly

droitturalment port pur vn duetye, mes vn-core circum le bushe come semble : pur ceo que il poct sibien estre auterment respondu et determine & le suite saue, & pur ceo que mesme le actyon fuit pluys que besoigne, il est appell Circuit del actyon. Come si vn home graunt vn rent charge de x.li. hors de son manour de Dale, & puis le grauntee disseisist le grauntour de mesme le manour de Dale, & il port vn Assise, & recouer le terre, & xx. li. dam-mages, le quel xx. li. esteant paye, le graun-tee del rent sue son ac-cyon pur x.li. de son rent due durannt le teps de le disseisin, le ql si nul disseisin adee, il doit auer ewe. Cest appell circuit de acty-on, pur ceo que il poit aũ estre plus briesemēt res-

respondue, car ou le grauntour doit receiue xx.li. damages, & pay x.li. rent, il puyt auer resceiue forsque le x.li. tantsolement pur les damages, & le grauntee puit auer recoupe & tenus arrere le auter x.li. en ses maines per voy de detayner pur son rent, & issint per ceo puit auer saue son action.

aunswered, for where as the grantor should receiue xx.li. damages, and pay x.li. rent, hæ might haue recepued but the x.li. onely for the damages, and the grauntæ myght haue cut of and kept backe the other x. li. in hys handes by way of detainer for his rent, and so there by, mought haue saued his action.

¶Clayme.

CLaime est vn challenge per asc' home del propertie ou ownership dun chose que il nad en possession, mes que est detaine de luy per tort.

¶Clayme.

CLaime is a challenge by any man of the property or ownershippe of a thinge which he hath not in possession, but which is withholden from him wrongfully.

¶Clergie.

CLergie est vn auncient libertie del esglise Papisicke, le quel ad auxy este confirme

¶Clergie.

CLergie is an auncient lybertie of the Popish church, which hath also ben cōfirmed with

with vs in dyvers Parliamentes. And it is when a Priest, or one within holie Orders (as they terme it) or any other what soeuer, in whom is no impediment or impossibilitie to be a Priest, is arraigned of felonie or such like before a temporall Judge &c. and the prisoner prayeth his Clergie, that is to say, to haue hys booke, whych is as much as if he desyred to bee dismissed from the Temporal Judge, and to bee deliuered to the Ordinarie to purge hymselfe of the same offence. Thys priuiledge at the first was not so generall, in respect of the parties that should take benefite thereby, as it afterwarde became to bee, for at the beginnyng, beeynge a Popishe inuention,

oue nous en dyuers Parliamentes. Et est quant vn Prester, ou vn deins holie Orders (come ils appell ceo,) ou ascun auter quicunque, en que est nul impediment ou impossybilitye deste vne Prester, est arraigne de felonye ou tiels semblables, deuaunt vne Temporall Iudge &c. & le prisoner pria son clergie, cest adire, pur auer son Liuer, quel est a taunt, sicome il vst prie deste dysmissed del temporal Iudge, & deste deliuer al Ordinarie de purger luy mesme del mesme offence. Cest Priuyledge al primer ne fuit cy generall, in respect del partyes que prendra benefite per ceo, come il apres druient. Car al commencement esteant vn Papishe inuention,

les

les patrons de ceo fue-
ront mult parcial, &
ne voyllent que afcun
prendroit commoditie
per ceo , mes lour Pa-
piftical Prefters fole-
ment,et tiels queuxfu-
erount deins Orders ,
come eft auantdit. Et
ceo commence enter
eux, pur part per lour
graund fuperbitie,dif-
dayning defte fouth le
obedience de lour na-
tural Royes & tem-
porall correction , &
pur part de policie, pur
hont ne le male man-
ners de lour fpiritualtie
doyent vener al ouert
view & examination
del laitie, (come ils
diftinguifh eux ,) &
nul meruayle , car
deins vn petite de les
primer ans del raigne
le Roy H.le feconde ,
le Clergie del Realme
ad commyt plus que
vn cent feueral Mur-
ders fur fes fubiectes ,
come le Roye fuit

the Patrons therea
were very parcial,ant
woulde not that any
fhould reape commodi-
tie thereby , but their
popifh Priestes onely
and fuch as were with
in Orders, as is afore
faide. And this arofe
amonge them , partly
through their greate
pryde, difdaining to be
vnder the obedience of
their naturall kinges
and temporal correcti-
on ; and partly of po=
licie, for fhame left the
lewde maners of their
fpiritualtie , fhoulde
come to the open biew
and examynation of
the laitie, (as they dif=
tinguifh them) and no
meruail at al,for with
in a few of the fyrft
yeares of king Henry
the feconds raigne,the
Clergy of the Realme
had committed aboue
one hundrede feuerall
murders vpon his fub=
iectes,as the king was
cer=

certeincly infoʒmeᴅ, besiᴅes many robbe= ries anᴅ other outra= ges, foʒ remeᴅie where of, oʒᴅer was ta= ken by the kinge, his Mobilitie, anᴅ wyth much a ᴅoe the Cler= gie confenteᴅ thereto, that if any clerke from thence foʒth commit= teᴅ felony oʒ Trea= fon, he ſhoulᴅ firſt be ᴅegraᴅeᴅ, anᴅ after= warᴅe ᴅeliuereᴅ to the lay power, there to receiue as to his of= fence belongeᴅ ꝛc. at the laſt in fauour of life, (a thinge to bœ ſhewed indifferentlye towarᴅs al mankinᴅ) anᴅ foʒ the loue of learning, it was gra= teᴅ to all men that coulᴅe reaᴅe, though they weare neyther Pʒieſtes, noʒ within oʒᴅers. Anᴅ since in Parliamet maᴅe bpon gœᴅ consiᴅerations, it hath bene reſtrayneᴅ

certeinement enforme, oufter mult robberies & auters outrages, pur remedie de quel, orᴅer fuit evve per le Roy, ſon nobilitie, & oue graund faire le Clergy confent a ceo, que ſi afcun Clerke de ceo en auaint, comytte Felonie ou Treaſon, il doyt prymer eſte degrade, & apres de= lyuer al Lay power de receyuer la come a ſon offence appient &c. al darreyne en fauour de vie, (vn choſe de eſte extende endyffe= rentment al cheſcun homes,) & pur le a= mour de eruᴅicion, il fuit graunt al cheſ= cun home queux puiſ= ſent lieſer, non ob= ſtaunt ils ne fue= rount Preſters, ne deyns Orders. Et puys en Parli= ament fait fur bone confyderations, il aᴅ eſte reſtraygne &

& repeal en dyuers ca-
fes, côe in wilful mur-
der , burglarie,& tiels
auters.

and taken away in di-
uers cafes, as in wil-
full murder, burglary,
and fuch others.

¶Clerke attaint.
¶Clerke conuict.

¶Clerke attaint.
¶Clerke conuict.

CLerkes font en ij.
fortes, ceft adire,
Clerkes attaint , &
clerks conuict. Clerke
attaint eft ceftuy que
pria fon Clergie apres
iudgement fur luy don
de le felonie,& ad fon
clergie allow, tiel clerk
ne poit faire fon pur-
gation.

CLerkes are in two
fortes , that is to
fay , Clerkes attaint,
and Clerkes conuict.
Clerke attaint is he
whiche prayeth his
clergie after iudgemêt
gyuen vpon him of the
felony , and hath hys
clergie allowed, fuch a
clerke may not make
his purgation.

Clerke conuict eft
ceftuy que pria fon
clergie deuant iudge-
ment done fur luy de
le felony,& ad le cler-
gie a luy graunt , tyel
clerke poit fayre fon
purgation.

Clerke conuict is he
whiche prayeth hys
clergie before iudge-
ment geeuen vpon him
of the felonie, and hath
his clergy to him grâ-
ted, fuch a clerke may
make his purgation.

¶Colour.
COlour eft vn fay-
ned matter, le ql le

¶Colour.
COlour, is a fayned
matter which the
defen-

defendaunt oz tenant
vseth in his barre
when an acyon of
trespas, oz an assise is
bzought against him,
in which hee gyueth
the demaundaunt oz
pleintife a shew at the
first sight that he hath
good cause of acyon
wherein troth it is no
iust cause, but onely a
coloz & face of a cause:
And it is vsed to y in-
tent that the determi-
nation of the acyon
should be by the Iud-
ges, and not by an ig-
nozaunt Iury of xij.
men. And therefoze a
colour ought to bee a
matter in law oz doubt-
ful to the commō peo-
ple, as foz example. A.
bzings an assise of lād
against B. & B. saith
that he himselfe dyd
let the same lād to one
C.foz terme of life, &
afterward did graunt
the reuersion to A.
the demaundaunt, and

defendaunt ou tenant
vse en son barre, quant
vn action de trespas,
ou vn assise est port
enuers luy, en le quel
il done le demaun-
daunt, ou pleintyfe
vn shewe, prima fa-
cie que il ad bon cause
de action, ou en ve-
ritie il nest iust cause,
mes tauntsolement vn
colour, ou visour
dun cause. Et il est
vse al entent que le
determination del ac-
tion doet este per les
Iudges, & nemye
per vn ignoraunt Iu-
rie de xij. homes. Et
pur ceo vn colour do-
et este vn matter en
ley, ou difficult al
lay gentes, com : pur
example. A. port vn
assise de terre enuers
B. & B. dit que il
mesme lessa mesme le
terre al vn C. pur
terme de vie, & apres
graunt le reuersion al
A. le demaundant, &

F. j. puis

puis C . le tenaunt pur terme de vie moruſt , apres que deceaſe A . le demaundaunt claymaunt le reuerſion per force del graunt (ou C. le tenaunt pur vye ne vnques atturne) entra, ſur que B. entra, enuers que A. pur meſme entre port ceſt aſſiſe &c. ceſt vn bon colour , pur ceo que le ley gentes penſant, que le terre voyle paſſe per le graunte ſauns atturnement, ou en fayt il ne voyle paſſe &c.

Auxy en vn action de treſpas , coloure doet eſte donc , & de eux ſount vn infinit number , vn pur examble : En vn action de treſpas pur priſell de auers del pleintyfe , le defendaunt dit , que deuant le pleintife riens auoit en eux , il meſme fuit

after C . the tenaunt fo₃ terme of lyfe died, after whoſe deceaſe A. the demaundant claymyng the reuerſion by fo₃ce of that graunt (whereto C.the tenãt fo₃ lyfe did neuer atturne)entred, vppon whom B . entred, againſt whõ A.fo₃ that entre b₃inge₃ this aſſiſe &c. this a good colour becauſe the common people think that the lande wil paſſe by the graunt without attournement, where in dæde it wyll not paſſe &c.

Alſo in an action of treſpas colour muſt be geuen,and of them are an infinite nũber, one fo₃ example: In an action of treſpas fo₃ takinge away of the playntifes beaſtes, the defendaunt ſayth,that beefo₃e the pleyntife had anye thynge in them,hee himſelfe was
poſ=

possessed of them as of
his proper goods, and
deliuered them to A.
B. to redeliuer them
to him againe whē &c.
and A. B. gaue them
vnto the plaintife, and
the pleintif supposing
the propertie to be in
A. B. at the tyme of
the gift, tooke them, &
the defendaunt tooke
them from the pleyn-
tif, whereupon þ plain
tife bringeth an action
this is a good colour,
and a good plea.

possesse de eux come
de ses proper biens,
& eux deliuer al A.
B. pur eux rebayler
a luy quando &c. &
A. B. eux dona al
plaintife, & le plain-
tife suppose le pro-
pertye destte en A
B. al temps del done,
prist eux, & le de-
fendaunt eux reprist
del pleintife, sur que
le pleyntife port lac-
tyon, cest vn bone
colour & vn bone
plea.

¶ Colour of office.

¶ Colour de office.

Colour of office, is
alwayes taken in
the worst part, & sig-
nifieth an act euel don,
by the countenance of
an office, and it bea-
rethe a dissemblynge
face of the right office,
where as the office is
but a baile to the fals-
hode and the thinge

Olore officij, est
toutes dites prise in
malam partem,& sig-
nifie vn acte male-
ment fait per le coun-
tenaunce de vn of-
fice, & il port vn dis-
simulant vysage del
droit office, ou le of-
fice nest.que vegle del
fauxytie & le chose
est

F.ij.

eſt grounde ſur vice, &
loſtice eſt com̄ vn ſha-
dowe al ceo.

Mes Ratione offi-
cij, & virtute officij,
ſount pryſes toutes
foytes in bonam par-
tem, & lou le office eſt
le iuſt cauſe del choſe,
& le choſe eſt pur-
ſuant al office

is grounded vpon vice
& the office is as a ſha-
dowe to it.

But by reaſon of ꝑ of-
fice, & by vertu of ꝑ of-
fice are taken alwaies
in the beſt part, and
where the office is the
iuſt cauſe of the thing,
and the thing is pur-
ſuing to the office.

¶ Colluſion.

Olluſion eſt lou
vn action eſt port
vers vn auter perſon
agreement demeſne, ſi
le pleintyfe recouer,
tiel recouerie eſt dit
per colluſion : & en
aſcuns caſes le collu-
ſion ſerra enquyre,
come en vn Quare
impedit, aſſiſe, & tiels
ſemblables : Mes en
auowrie, ne en briefe
dentre, ou aſcun ac-
tyon perſonall, le
colluſion ne ſerra en-
quire.

¶ Colluſion.

Olluſion is where
an action is brought
againſt another by his
owne agreement, if the
plaintife recouer, then
ſuch recouery is cal-
led by colluſion : and
in ſome caſes the col-
luſion ſhall bee enqui-
red of, as in a Quare
impedit, an aſſiſe and
ſuch like : But in a-
nowry, no2 in a w2it
of entrie, o2 any acti-
on perſonal, the collu-
ſion ſhal not be enqui-
red.

Com-

COmmon law, is for the most part taken 3. waies, first for the lawes of this Realme simply without any other lawe, as customary lawe, Ciuil law, Spirituall lawe, or whatsoeuer els lawe ioyned vnto it, as whē it is desputed in our lawes of Englande, what ought of right to bee determyned by the common lawe, and what by the spirituall lawe, or Admirales Court, or such lyke.

Secondly it is taken for the kings courtes, as the kinges Bench, or common place, onelye to shewe a difference betweene them and the base courtes, courtes barons, countie courtes, pipowders, and such like, as when a plea of lande

COmmon ley, ē pur le pluis part prise 3. voyes. Primerment pur les leyes de cest Realme simply sauns ascun auter ley, come customarie ley, Ciuil ley, Spirituall ley, ou quecunque auter ley ioyne al ceo. Come quant il est dispute en nostre leyes dengleterre, quid doet de droit este determine per le common ley, & quid per le spirituall ley, ou le Court del Admirall, ou tiels semblables.

Secondariment il est prise pur les courtes le roy, cōe le bank le roy ou cōmon place, tantsolemt pur mr̄ vn différéce penr̄ eux & les basecourts, cōe customarȳ courts, courts barons, coūty courts, pipowders, et tiels sebla-bles, cōe qhit vn ple d'tr̄

F.iij. eſt

eſt remoue hors de aū-
cien deſm pur ceo que
le terre eſt franke fee,
& pledable al com-
mon ley, ceſt adire en
le court le roy, & ne-
my en aūcien demeſn,
ou en aſcun auter baſe
court.

Tiercement, & plu-
is vſualment, per le
common ley eſt en-
tendue, tiels leys que
fuerent generalment
priſe, & tenus pur ley,
deuaunt que aſcun eſ-
tatute fuit fait pur al-
ter ceo, come pur ex-
ample. Tenaunt pur
vie, ne pur ans, ne
fuerent deſte puniſhe
pur feſaunce waſt al
common ley, tanque
le ſtatute de Gloceſ-
ter cap. 5. fuit fait le
quel done vn actyon
de waſte enuers eux:
mes tenant per le cur-
teſie, & tenant en do-
wer, fuerount puni-
ſhable de waſt al com-
mon ley ceſt adire, per

is remoued out of aū-
cient demeſne, becauſe
the lande is franke fæ
and pleadable at the
cōmon law, that is to
ſay in the kings court,
and not in aūncien de-
meſne, oʒ in any other
baſe court.

Thirdly and moſte
bſually by the cōmon
law is onderſtood, ſuch
lawes as were gene-
rally taken and holden
foʒ lawe befoʒe aꝝe
ſtatute was made to
alter the ſame: as foʒ
ʒxample. Tenaunt foʒ
lyfe, noʒ foʒ yeares,
were not to be puny-
ſhed foʒ doing waſt at
the common lawe, tyl
the ſtatute of Gloceſ-
ter. cap 5. was made
which doth gæue an
action of waſt againſt
them: But tenant by
the curteſie, and te-
naunt in dower, were
punyſhable of waſt,
at the common lawe,
that is to ſaye, by
the

the vſuall, and cōmon receiued lawes of the realme, befoze the ſaid ſtatute of Glotester was made.

le vſuall, & common receiued leyes del realme, deuaunt le dyt ſtatute de Gloceſter fuit fait.

¶Common.

¶Common.

COmon is the right that a man hath to put his beaſtes to paſture, oz to vſe & occupy the ground that is not his owne.

And note ÿ there be diuers comons, that is to ſay cōmon in groſſe, cōmon appendant, cōmon appurtenant, and common beecauſe of neighbourhood

Common in groſſe is where I by my deede graūt to another that he ſhall haue common in my lande

Common appendant is where a mā is ſeiſed of certaine land, to the which he hath cōmo. in anothers grounds, al they that ſhall bee

COmon eſt le droit que home ad de mitter ſes beaſts a paſture, ou de vſer & occupier le terre que neſt ſon proper ſole.

Et nota que ſont diuers commons.s.common in groſſe, common appendant, common appurtenaunt, & common per cauſe de viſinage.

Common in groſſe eſt lou ieo per mon fayt graunt a vn auter que il auer comon in materre.

Common appendant eſt lou home eſt ſeyſie de certeyne terre, aque il ad common in auter ſoile, & routs ceux que ſerront

F.iiij. ſeiſie

The expofition of

feifie del dyt terre a-
uerount le dit com-
mon folement pur ce-
ux beftes que compeft
fa terre a que il eft ap-
pendaunt except oy-
fons, chiuers, & por-
ceaux.

Et toutes iours ceft
commen eft per pre-
fcription, & de com-
mon droit, et il eft ap-
pendaunt al terre era-
ble folement, & ne-
my al auter terre ou
meafon.

Common appur=
tenant eft in mefme le
maner come common
appendant, mes eft o-
uefque touts manners
des auers cibien pur-
ceaux, chiuers & ti-
els femblable come
chiuals, vaches boefes,
berbits, et tiels q̃ com-
pefter le terre. Et tiel
cõmon poit efte fait a
ceft iour, & poit efte
feñe del t̃re a que il eft
appurtenãt, mes iffint
ne poit cõmon appéd'.

feifed of that land, that
haue the faid common
only foz thofe beaftes
which compefte that
lande to which it is
appendaunt excepting
Gœfe, Gootes, and
hogges.

And alwayes this
cõmon in by pzefcrip-
tion and of common
ryght, and it is ap-
pendaunt to erable
lande onely, and not
to any other lande oz
houfe.

Common appurte-
nant is in the fame man-
ner as cõmon appen-
dant, but it is in al mã-
ner of beaftes, as well
hogges goates & fuch
like, as hozfes, kine,
oxen, fheepe & fuch as
compeft the grounde.
And fuch cõmon may
bee made at this day,
and may bee feuered
from the lãd to which
it is appurtenaunte,
but foe cannot com-
mon appendaunt.
                 Com=

Common by cause of neighbozhod, is where the tenaunts of two lozds which be seysed of two townes where one lyeth nighe another, & euery of them haue vsed from y time whereof no mind runneth, to haue comē in y other towne, with all maner of beasts cominable.

But the one may not put his cattel in y others ground, foz soe they of y other towne may distraine thē damage fesaunt, oz may haue an action of trespas, but they may put them into their owne fœldes, and if so they stray into y fœlds of y other town, they there ought to suffer them. And the inhabitāts of y one town ought not to put in as many beastes as they will, but hauing regard to y inhabitants of the other

Common pur cause de visinage, est lou les tenants de deux seigniours que sount seisies de deux villes dont lun gyst pris lauter, & chescun de eux ont vse de temps dount memorye ne courte de auer commen en auter vylle ouesque toutes beastes cominable.

Mes lun ne poyt mitt ses auers en le terre lauter, car la ceux de lauter vylle poyent eux distr. ne dammage fesaunt, ou auer actyon de trespas, mes ils eux mittera en lour camps demesne, & sils estraye en les camps del auter vylle, ils la doyent eux sufferer. Et les inhabytauntes de lun ville ne misteront eins tauntes come ils voile, mes-aiant regard al franktefir del inhabitants de lauer ville

ville, car auterment
il ne ſoit bone vy-
cinytye , ſur que
tout ceſt matter de-
pend.

toꝛne, foꝛ otherwiſe
it were no good neigh
bourhoode, vpō which
all this matter doth
depend.

¶Condition.

¶Condytion.

COndition ē vn reſ-
traint ou bridel an-
nexe & ioine al
choſe, iſſint que per le
non performance &
feſans de ceo le party
al condicion receuera
preiudice & perde , &
per le performāce &
faire de ceo , com-
modytye , & auaun-
tage.

COndition is a reſ-
traint oꝛ bꝛidle ā-
nexed , and ioyned
to a thinge, ſo that by
the not perfoꝛmance
oꝛ not doinge thereof,
the party to the condi
cion ſhall receiue pre-
iudice and loſe, & by
the perfoꝛmance and
doopnge of the ſāe cō-
modity & aduantage.

Et touts condicions
ſont ou conditions ac-
tuall & expreſſe, quex
ſont appell condic' en
fait, ou us ſont icondy-
cyons implicite ou
tacite , & nient ex-
preſſe, les queux ſont
appells conditions en
ley.

And all condityons
are either condityons
actuall and expreſſed,
which be called con-
ditions in deede, oꝛ els
they bee conditions
implyed oꝛ couert &
not expꝛeſſed, which
are called conditions
in law.

Auxy touts condy-
cyons ſount ou condic

Alſo al condytions
are either conditions
            pꝛece-

precedent and goinge before the estate & are executed oʒ eis subsequent, and following after the estate and executoʒte.

The condition pʒecedent, dotʒ gaine and gett the thinge oʒ estate made bpon condition by the perfoʒmance of the same.

The condition subsequent, wtʒ keepe & continue the thinge oʒ estate made bppon condition by the perfoʒmance of ẏ same

Actuall and expʒessed condition, which is called a condition in deede: is a condityon knitt and annexed by expʒesse woʒdes to the feoffement, leas, oʒ graunt, either in wʒitinge oʒ without wʒitinge, as it ʒ enfeoffe a man in landes reseruing rēt to be paied at such a feait bpon condition ẏ if ẏ feoffee

precedent & vaont deuaunt lestate & sount executed, ou subsequent & veniens apres lestate & executorye.

Le condicyon precedent, fait gaine, & obtaine le chose ou estate fait sur condycyon per le performance de mesme.

Le condicion subsequent fait garde, & continue le chose, ou estate fait sur condytyon per le performance de ceo.

Actuall & expresse condition que est appell vn condicion en fait. est vn condicion knitt & annexe per expresse parolx al feffment, leas, ou grant, ou en escript, ou sauns escrypt: Sycome ieo enfeoffe vn home en terres reseruaunt rent destre payed a tvel feast sur Condicion que sile feoffee
fayle

faile de payement al iour, que donques il serra loyal pur moy de reenter.

Conditions implicite ou tacite, & nient expresse queux sount appelle condic' en ley, sont quant vn hõe grãt al auter le office deste gard dun parke, Seneschal, Bedle, bailife, ou tiels semblables, pur terme de vie, & nyent obstant que la ne soit ascun condicyon expresse en le graunt, vncore le ley perle couertment dun condicion le quel est que si le grauntee ne execute pas touts pointes appertenant al son office per luy mesme ou son suffic' depute, donques il serra loyall pur le grauntor denõ et disch. luy de son office. Cõdityon precedent & vaant deuant est quãt vn leas est fait al vn pur vie sur condicion

faile of payment at the day, that then it shall be lawfull for me to reenter.

Condition implyed or couert and not expressed which is called a condition in law, is when a mã graunteth to one the office to be keeper of a parke, stewarde, Bedle, bailife, or such like, for terme of life & though there bee no condition at al expressed in the graũt, yet the lawe speaketh couertlye of a condityon, which is that if the grauntee do not execute all points appertepninge to his office by himselfe or his sufficyent deputye, then it shall bee lawfull to the grauntour to enter and discharge him of his office. Condition precedent and goinge before is when a leas is made to one for life bpon condition that

that if the lessée for life, will paie to the lessor xx.li. at such a day, þ thē he shal haue fee simple: here þ condicion precéeds & goeth béefore the estate in fée simple, and vppō the performance of þ condycion, doth get and gaine the fée simple. Condition subsequent and followinge after, is when one graunts to I.S. hys manor of Dale in fée simple, vpon condityon, that þ grauntée shal pay to him at such a day xx.li.or els þ his estate shal cease, here þ conditiō is subsequēt & following the estate in fée simple, and vpon the performance thereof, doth kéepe and continue the estate.

que si le lessée pur vye voile paie al lessour xx.li. a tiel iour, que donques il auera fee simple: Icy le condicyon preceeda & va deuaunt le estate in fee simple, & sur le performnce de le condicyon, gaiñ & gett le fee simple. Condicion subsequent et veniens apres est quant vn grãt a I.S. son manour de Dale en fee simple sur condicion, que le grãtee paiera a luy a tyel iour xx. li. ou auterment que son estate cessera. Icy le Condicyon est subsequent & sequens le estate en fee simple, & sur le Performaunce de ceo fait, garde & contynue lestate.

¶Confiscate goods.

¶Confiscate biens.

Onfiscate goodes are goods to which

Onfiscate biens sōt byens as queux
le

le ley entitle le Roy-
gne, quant ils ne sont
pas clayme per ascun
auter . Come si home
soyt endite que il fe-
lonisement emblea les
byens de I . S . lou
en veritye ils sount
ses biens demesne, &
ils sount myses en
court vers luy come
maineur, & donques
il est demaunde que il
dit al mesmes les by-
ens, & il eux denie,
ore per cest denyer de
eux, il perdra ceux bi-
ens , coment que a-
pres il soyt acquyte
del felonye, & issint
en auters semblables
cases.

¶Contract.

COntracte est vn
bargeine ou co-
uenaunt per enter ij.
parties , ou vn chose
est done pur auter que
est appelle quid pro
quo, come si ico vende

the lawe intitleth the
Queene, when they
are not claimed by any
other. As if a man bee
indited that he feloni-
ously stole the goods of
I. S. where in truth
they are hys owne
goodes , and they are
brought into the court
against him as a mai-
neur, & then is deman-
ded, what he sayth to
those goods, and he de-
nieth them, nowe by
this denying of them,
hee shall loose those
goods, although that
afterwarde he be ac-
quited of ye felony, and
soe in other lyke ca-
ses.

¶Contracte.

COntracte is a bar-
gaine or couenaunt
betweene two parties,
where one thinge is
geeuen for an other
which is called quid
pro quo, as if I sell
my

my horſe foz money, oz
if I couenant to make
you a leaſe of my man=
noz of Dale in conſi=
deration of xx.li. that
you ſhal giue me, theſe
are good contracts be=
cauſe there is one thig
foz an other, But if
a man make pzomyſe
to mee that I ſhall
haue twentye ſhyl=
inges, and that hee
wil be debtour to mee
thereof, and after I
aſke the the xx.s.and
hee wil not deliuer it,
yet I ſhal neuer haue
any action to recouer
this xx.s.foz that, that
this pzomiſe was no
contracte but a bare
pzomyſe, and ex nu-
do practo non oritur ac-
tio: but if any thinge
were geuen foz the xx.
ſhillinges though it
were not but to the
value of a peny, then
it had ben a good con=
tracte.

mon chiual pur argent
ou ſi ieo couenaunt de
faire leaſe a vous de
mon mañ de Dale en
conſideration de xx.li.
que vous dones a moy
ceux ſont bone con-
tractes, pur ceo que il
ad vn choſe pur au-
ter, mes ſi vn home
fayt promiſe a ɯoye
que ieo auera xx.s.&
que il voyle eſte det-
tour a moy de ceo,&
puis ieo demaunde le
xx. s. & il ne voyle a
moy delyuer, vncore
ieo nauera iammes ac-
tyon pur recouer ceſt
xx. s. pur ceo que
ceſt promys ne fuyt
contracte, mes nu-
dus pactus, Et ex
nudo pacto non ori-
tur actio, mes ſi aſ-
cun choſe fuyt done
pur le xx. s. meſque il
ne fuit forſque al va-
lue de vn denier,don-
ques il fuit bone con-
tracte.

¶Conu-

¶Conuſance. ¶Conuſance.

COnuſance de plee eſt vn priuyledge que vn Cytye ou ville ad del graunt le roy, de tener plee des touts contractes, & des terres deins le precinct del franchiſes : Et quant aſcun home eſt impleded pur aſcun tiel choſe en le court del Roy, les Maiors, ou Bailifes de tyels franchiſes, ou lour at-tournies poient dema-under conuſance del plee, ſcilicet que le plee & le matter ſerra pled & determine deuant eux

Mes ſi le Court al VVeſtminſter ſoit loi-allment ſeiſye del plea deuaunt que conuſce ſoyt demaunde, don-ques ils ne auerount conuſaunce pur ceſt ſuite , pur ceo que ils ount negligent-ment ſurceaſſe lour

COnuſance of plee, is a pꝛiuiledge that a citie oꝛ Towne hath of the kinges graunt to holde plee of al contractes , and of landes within the pꝛecin̄g of the fran-chiſe: and when anye man is impleaded foꝛ any ſuch thinge in ꝑ Court at Weſtmū-ter: the Maioꝛ and bailifes of ſuch fraun-ches oꝛ theyr attur-ney may aſke conu-ſance of the plee, ꝑ is to ſay, ꝑ ꝑ plee & ꝑ mat ter ſhal be pleded & de-termined befoꝛe thē.

But if the Court at Weſteminſter bæ lawefullye ſeiſed of the Plæ , bæfoꝛe Conuſaunce bæ de-maunded, then they ſhall not haue Co-nuſance foꝛ that ſuit, becauſe they haue neg-ligētly ſurceſſed their tyme time of demaunde, but this shalbe no barre to them to haue conusace in an other action, for they may demaunde conusance in one action, and omit it in an other action at theyr pleasure.

And note that conusance lyeth not in prescription, but it behoueth to shew ye kinges letters.

temps de demaunde, mes ne serra barre al eux dauer conusaunce en auter action, car ils poyent demaunde conusance en vn action, & omitte ceo en auter action a lour pleasure.

Et nota que conusace ne gist en prescription, mes ils couient monstr letters le Roy.

¶Corodie.

Corodie, was a reasonable allowance of Meat, bread, drink, money, clothing, lodging, and such like sustenance, which of common right euery foundor of Abbeies, Priories, Nunries, & other houses of religion, had in the same house, whe any were standing, for his father, brother, cosine, or other man that hee woulde appoynt

¶Corodie.

Corodie, fuit vn reasonable allowance de Meat, pane, boyer, argent, vestamentes, lodges, & tiel sustenace que de common droyt chescun foundour de Abbeis, Priories, Nunries, & autets measons de Religion papisticke ount in mesme les measons quant ils fueront: pur son pere, frere, cosine, ou auter home que il voit,

G.j.   prendroit

prendroit ceo , fil fuit vn meafo de Moignes, & fil foit foundor dun meafon de Nunnes ou muliers , donques ceo pur fa mere , foer, cofine, ou auter mulier, que il voile direct al ceo,& touts iours ceft Prouifo fuit ew , que il que ad corodie en vn meafon de Moignes, ne doit mitter vn feme de prender ceo. Ne ou corodie fuit due en vn Nunrie , la il ne fuyt loyal de appointer vn home de receyuer ceo, car en ambideux cafes, tiel prefentation fuit defte reiect.

Et ceft Corodie fuit due fibien al vn common perfon que fuyt foundour, ficome ou le Roy mefme fuyt foundour. Mes ou le meafon fuit tenus en frankealmoygne , la le tenure mefme fuit vn difcharge de Corodie encounter touts

fhould take it , yf it were a houfe of Monkes , and if hee were foundor of a houfe of Nunnes or women, then the fame for hys mother, fifter, cofin, or other woman that he would direct thither, and alwaies this was prouided for, ꝑ he that had corodie in a houfe of Monkes, might not fend a woman to take it. For where corodie was due in a Nunrie, there it was not lawfull to appoint a man to receiue ꝑ fame , for in both cafes, fuch prefetacion was to be reiected. And this Corodie was due as well to a common perfon ꝑ was foudor, as where ꝑ the king him felf was foudor. But where ꝑ houfe was holden in frankalmoigne, ther the tenure it felfe was a dyfcharge of Corodye agaynfte all men.

men. Except it were afterward charged voluntarily, as whē the king would sende hys writ to the Abbey for a Corodie for such a one whom they admit, there the house should bee charged for euer, whether þ king were foundor or not.

¶ Crowner.

CRowner is an auncient officer of trust and of great authoritie, ordeyned to bee a principall conseruator, or keeper of the peace, to beare recorde of the plees of the Crowne, and of his owne sight, and of dyuers other thynges inanye in number &c. But at thys day, eyther the authoritye of the Coroner ys not so great, as in foretime yt was, where by

---

homes. Sinon q̄ il fuit apres charge voluntaryment, come ou le Roy voit mister son briefe al Abbey pur vn Corodie, pur vn tyel, le quel ils admit, la le measō doit este charge a toutes iours, si le Roy soit foundour ou nemy.

¶ Coroner.

COroner est vne auncient officer de trust, & de graunde aucthoritie, ordeyne deste vne princypall conseruator, ou gardeine de la peace, a porter record des plees del Corone, & de son view demesne, & de diuers auters choses, mult en number &c. Mes al cest iour, ou le aucthoritie de le Coroner nest cy graunde, sicome en auncyent temps il fuit, per que
G.ij.   loffice

loffice neſt ewe en ſẽ-
blable eſtimacion. Ou
auterment le viſcount
& ils que ont auctho-
rity de elect le coroner
ne ſont cy careful ſi-
cõe ils doient eſtre en
lour election , & pur
ceo il eſt a ore tantoſt
deuenus arere al meſ-
mè le point, que il fu-
it en temps le Roye
Edwarde le primer,
quaunt ceſt eſtatute
ſequens fuit fayt. Pur
ceo que petit Gentts
& meins ſages ſoyent
eſlyeus ore de nouell
communement al of-
fice del Coroner, &
meſtyer ſerroyt que
prodes homes, loyalx,
& ſages ſe entermel-
lent de cel office. Pur-
uiew eſt, que per touɼ
les counties ſoient eſ-
lyeus ſuffiſants homes
Coroners, des pluys
loyals & plus ſages
Chiuàlers & cæteɼ. Et
nyent obſtaunt le let-
ter de ceſt eſtatute

the office is not had in
like eſtimacion : Oɹ
els the Sherife and
thoſe that haue auc=
thoɹitye to chooſe the
Coɹoner are not ſo
careful as they ſhould
bee in theyɹ electyons
and therefoɹe , it is
nowe almoſt come a=
gaine into that plight
that it was in Kynge
Edwarde the firſtes
daies, when this ſta=
tute followinge was
made : Foɹaſmuch as
meane men and vn=
diſcrœte nowe of late
are commonly choſen
to the office of coɹoner
where it is requiſite
that wiſe men, lawe=
ful and able ſhould oc-
cupy ſuch offices: It
is pɹouided p̃ thɹough
al Shires ſufficient
men ſhould be choſen
to bœ Coɹoners out
of the moſt wiſe and
diſcrœteſt Knyghtes
&c. And although the
lettter of this ſtatute

beɜ

bee not precislye ob-
crued:yet at the least
the entent should be
followed as nigh as
mought be, that for þ
befault of knights ge-
tilmen furnished with
such qualities as the
statute setteth downe
(of which sort there
be many) might bee
chosen : with thys
addicyon that they bee
vertuous , and goode
knowne Christians.

ne soyt precisément
obserue , vncore al
meines le entent doyt
estre sequer , cy pres
come poit , que pur
le default des Chy-
uallers , Gentle hões
furnished oue tyells
qualytyes , sycome le
estatute myse (de que
il y ad dyuers) poy-
ent estre eslieu , oue
cest addicion , que ils
soient vertuous,& bõe
conus Christians.

¶Corporatyon.

¶Corporation

COrporation ys a
permanent thinge
that may haue suc-
cession : And is an
assembly and ioyning
together of many into
one felowshippe, bro-
therhoode and minde,
whereof one is hedde
and chiefe, the rest are
the bodye : and thys
hedde and bodye knytt
together make the cor-
poration.

COrporation est vn
chose permanent, q
poit auer successi-
on : Et est vn assem-
blye & ioyninge en-
semble de diuers en
vn felowshippe , fra-
ternitye , & ment , de
que vn est le Test &
Principall , les auters
sont le corps , & cest
Test & corps ioynt
ensemble sount le cor-
poration.

G.iij.　　　Et

Et de corporations afcuns fount appells fpiritualls , & afcuns temporalls , & de ceux que fount fpy-ritualls , afcuns fount Corporations de mort perfonns en ley , & afcuns auterment , & afcuns fount per auc-thoritye del Roy fole-ment , & afcuns ount eftre dun myxt auc-thoritye. Et de ceux queux font temporall afcuns fount per auc-thoritye del Roigne auxy , & afcuns per le common ley del Realme.

Corporation fpyri-tuall , & de mort per-fons en ley , eft lou le Corporatyon confift dun Abbe & Couent & ceux ount lour cō-mencement del Roye, & le Home de Rome quaunt il y ad a fayre cy.

Corporation fpiryt & dable perfons ē ley

And of Corporaty-ons , fome are called fpirituall , and fome temporal, and of thofe that are fpirituall, fome are corporations of deade perfonnes in lawe , and fome other wyfe , and fome are by the auchorytpe of the kynge oneiye, and fome haue bene of a myxt authorytpe, and of thofe that are Temporall , fome are by the auchorytpe of the kynge alfo , and fome by the Com-mon lawe of the Realme.

Corporatyon fpiri-tual and of dead per-fons in lawe, is where the corporatyon con-fifteth of an Abbot & Couent, and thefe had begynning of þ king and the man of Rome when hee had to doe here.

Corporatiō fpiritual & of able perfōz in law
15

is where the corpora-
tion consisteth of a
Deane and chaptier
and this corporaton,
had beginninge of the
Kinge onely.

Corporation Tem-
poral by the Kinge is
where there is a ma-
ior and comminaltye.

Corporation tem-
porall, by aucthoritye
of the common lawe
is the assemblye in par
liament, which con-
sisteth of the Queene
the hedde of the Cor-
poraion, and of the
Lords spirituall and
temporal, and the cō-
mons of the realme, ƥ
body of ƥ corporatyō.

est lou le corporation
consist dun Deane &
Chapiter, & cest cor-
poration ad cōmence-
ment del Roye sole-
ment-

Corporation tem-
poral per le roy est,
lou est vn maior &
comminalty.

Corporation tem-
porall, per authory-
tye del common ley,
est le assemblye en
Parliament, le quel
consist del Roigne, le
teste del corporation,
& del seigniors spiry-
tualls & temporals, &
de les commons del
Realme, le corps del
Corporation.

¶Bodyes politike.   ¶Corps politike.

BOdies politike are
bishops, abbots, pri-
ors, deanes, person of
a churche & such like
which haue successiō.

COrps politike sont
euesques, abbes, pri
ors, deanes, person dun
esglis, et tiels seblables
qux ont succession.

¶Coruption of blood.   ¶Corruption de sague
                                                   G.iiij.   Cor-

Corruption de ſangue, eſt quant le pere eſt attaint de felonīe ou treaſon, donques ſon ſangue eſt dit deſte corrupt, per reaſon de quel ſes enfants ne poyent eſte heires a luy, ne a aſcun auter auncester. Et ſil fuit noble ou gentle home deuant, il & touts ſes enfants per ceo ſount faits ignoble & vngentle, ayant regarde al nobilitie ou gentrie que ils claime perlour pere, quel ne poit eſte ſane arrere ſans aucthoritye del Parliament.

¶Couenant.

Couenant eſt vn agreement fait par enter ij. perſons, lou cheſcun de eux eſt tenus al auter, de performer certein couenants pur ſon part.

¶Couerture.

Corruption of blood is when the father is attainted of felonie oz treaſon, then his bloode is ſayd to be cozrupt, by meanes whereof his chyldzen cannot bee heires to him noz to any other aunceſtoz. And if he were a noble man oz gentleman befoze, he and all hys chyldzen thereby are made vnnoble and vngentle, hauing regarde to the nobilitie oz gentrie ỹ they claim by their father, which cannot bee made whole againe without aucthozity of parliament.

¶Couenant.

Couenant is an agreement had betwene two perſons, where euery of thē is bounden to the other, to perfozme certein couenants foz his part.

¶Couerture.

C Ouerture, is when a man & a woman are maryed together: Now the time of the continuaunce of thys marpage betwen them is called couerture, and the wyfe is called a woman couert.

C Ouerture, eft quát vne home & vne femme font efpoufe: Ore le temps de le continuaunce de ceft mariage parenter eux, eft appell couerture, & le femme eft appell vn femme couert.

¶Couin.

¶Couin.

C Ouin is a secrete affent, determined in the hartes of two or more, to the preiudyce of any other. As if a tenaunt for terme of life, will secretly confpire with an other, that the other fhall recouer agaynft the tenaunt for lyfe, the lande which hee holdeth &c. in preiudice of hym in the reuerfion.

C Ouin eft vn fecrete affent, determyne en les cuers de deux ou plufours, al preiudice dun auter . Come fi tenaunt pur terme de vie, voile fecretement confpire oue vn auter, que le auter recouera vers le tenaunt pur vie, le terre que il tyent &c. en preiudice de celuy en le reuerfion .

¶Counterplee.

¶Counterplee.

C Ounterplee , ys where one bringeth an

C Ounterplee , eft lou vne porte vn

vn action , & le te-
naunt en son respons
& plee vouch ou ap-
pell pur ascun home
pur garraunt son title,
ou prayer aide de au-
ter que ad meliour es-
tate , come de cesty en
la reuersion , ou vn es-
traunge al action vy-
ent & prayea deste
resceiue de sauer son
estate : si le demaun-
dant replye a ceo &
monstre cause que il
ne doit tiel home vou-
cher , ou que il ne doit
de tiel home aide auer,
ou que tiel home ne
doit este resceiue , cest
plee est appel vn coun-
terplee.

an action , and the te-
naunt in hys aun-
swere and plee , vou-
cheth oz calleth foz a-
nie manne to warrant
his title , oz prayeth
in ayde of an other,
which hath better es-
tate then hee , as of
hym that is in the re-
uerlion , oz if one that
is a straunger to the
action, come & pray to
be receiued to saue his
estate, if the demaun-
dant reply thereto,and
shew cause that hee
ought not to bouch
such one,oz p he ought
not of such one to haue
aide, oz that such one
ought not to be recey-
ued,this plee is called
a counterplee.

¶Cinque Portes.

¶Cinque Portes.

Cinque Portes ,sont
certeyne Hauen
villes, cinque in num-
ber, as queux ad este
graunt longe temps

Cinque Portes, bee
certeyne Hauen
Townes,fiue in num-
ber , to whiche haue
bene graunted longe
since

since, many liberties,
(that other Po2te
Townes haue not,)
and that first in the
tyme of king Edward
called the Confessour,
(who was befo2e the
Conquest,) and hath
bene encreased synce
chiefly in the dayes of
the ij. Edwardes, the
first and second (since
the Conquest) as ap-
peareth in the Booke
of Domesday , and o=
ther olde Monuments,
which in this wo2ke
bœing to long to cyte,
I meane B2other N.
to omit, and set you
here downe the Copie
of an auncient reco2de
in French, which the
wo2shipful our louing
and very good father,
Master Iohn Twyne of
Caunterbury gaue me
out of his booke called
w. Biholt, sometyme
a Monke of þ Abbey
of saint Augustines,
where in yon shall
learne

passe multes liberties,
(que auters port villes
nont) & ceo primer-
ment en le temps del
Roy Edwarde appell
le confessor (que fuit
deuant le Conquest)
& fueront encrease a-
pres, & ceo especial-
ment en les iours de les
deux Ed. le primer &
second, (apres le con-
quest) come appiert en
le Liure de Domesday
& auters viels Monu-
ments , queux en cest
Liure esteants haut te-
dious de citer , ieo en-
tende frere N. de omit
& mise vous cy le co-
pie de vn auncient re-
corde en Frankcois, le
quel le VVorshipfull ,
nostre louing & bone
pere, Mounsier Iohn
Twyne de Caunter-
burie done a moy hors
de son Liure , appell
VV . Biholt , ascune
temps vn Moygne de
le Abbey de S. Augus-
tines , en que vous
scauois

fcauoies que fuer aun-
cientment accompt le
Cinq; Portes , & lour
members, queux fer-
uices ils deuoyent, ou
lour court doit efte te-
nus, deuant que, & de
queux chofes ils poy-
ent tener plee, oue tiels
femble digne defte co-
nus, & per ceo vous
entendes auxy que le
viel rude verfe fayt
faux nofme de les v.
Portes, en nofment eux
folonque ceft maner.
Douer, Sandwicus,
Rye, Rumney, Frig-
mareuentus. Douer,
Sandwich, Rye, Rum-
ney, VVinchelfey, que
eft entende Frigmare-
uentus &c. quel Re-
corde ieo voile englois
fibien come mon pe-
tite fcience en ceft viel
French voile done a
moy conge, & ifsint
il eft.

¶ Ceux fount les
chiefe villes des cin-
que Portes.

learne which were af-
ciently accompted the
fyue Poztes, and their
members, what ferui-
ces they owe. where
their Court ought to
be kept, befoze whom,
and of what matters
they may hold plee, ti
fuch like, wozthy to be
knowen, & therby you
fhall perceiue alfo that
the old rude verfe doth
falfely name the fiue
Poztes, in recknyng
the vp after this fozt.

Douer, Sandwicus,
Rye, Rumney, Frig-
mareuentus. Douer,
Sadwich, Rie, Rum-
ney, winchelfey, which
is ment by Frigmare-
uentus, &c. which Re-
cozde J will Englifh
as well as my fmall
fkil in the old French
will gæue me leaue, &
thus it is.

€ Thefe are the
chiefe townes of the
fyue Poztes.
                    I. Hal-

1 Haſtinge.
2 Romney.
3 Heth.
4 Douer and
5 Sandwich.
The Members of the Porte of Haſtinge are theſe.
1 Peueneſe.
2 Bolewareheth.
3 Petite James.
4 Bekeſborne.
5 Greneth.
6 Rye and
7 winchelſe.

Some adde to theſe the Seaſhoze in Sefforde, Hydeney, and Nozthy.

The chiefe Port of Haſtinge, wyth the members afozeſayde, ought to finde to the kinge frō yere to yere, if næde bee vpon the Sea xxj. Ships, that is to ſay, the Cowne of Haſting iij. ſhipps, Peueneſe one ſhippe, wolewozchery & Petite Jhamme one ſhip, Bekeſburne one ſhip,

1 Haſtinge.
2 Romeney.
3 Heth.
4 Douer &
5 Sandvvich.
¶ Les Members del Port de Haſting ſount ceux.
1 Peueneſe.
2 Bolewareheth.
3 Petite Iames.
4 Bekesborne.
5 Greneth.
6 Rye &
7 VVinchelſe.

Aſcuns adde a ceux le mere bank en Sefforde, Hydeney, & Northye.

Le chiefe Port de Haſting oue les members auantdits, deuyent trouer au Roy de an en an, ſi meſtyer ſoit per mere vynt & vn neſes, ceo eſt a ſcauoir, la ville de Haſtinge iij. neſes, Peueneſe vn neſe, woleworchetie & Petyte hamme vne neſe, IBekesborne vn neſe,
Greneſhe

Greneſhe ij . homes , oue deux armours oue ceux de Haſting . La ville de Rye v . ı efes , la ville de VVinchelſe x.nefes.

La members del Porte de Romenal ſont ij.

1 Vieu Romenal,&
2 Lyde.

Aſcuns adde al ceux Prormhel , Oſwarde-ſtone, & Denge Mar-reis. Komeny oue les auauntdyts members deuient a Roy, come auant eſt dit 5 . nefes, dount Lyde doit vn neſe .

Le Port de Hethe oue ſon member VVeſt-Hethe deuient trouer 5 .nefes au Roy , come auant eſt dit.

Les members de le Port de Douer ſount ceux .

1 Folkeſtone, &
2 Feuerſham.

Aſcuns adde Mere-gate &c.

Greneſhe ij. men with two armours , wyth them of Haſting. The Towne of Rye fiue ſhippes, the Towne of Winchelle x.ſhips.

The members of the the Port of Romeney are ij.

1 Olde Ronney &
2 Lyde.

Some adde to theſe Pzozmhell, Oſward-ſtone, & Denge Mar-reis. Romeney wyth the afozeſaid members oweth to the king, as is befoze ſaid 5.ſhips, whereof Lyde oweth one ſhip.

The Port of Hethe with his member weſt Hethe, ought to finde 5. ſhippes to the king, as is afozeſaid.

The members of the Porte of Douer are theſe.

1 Folkeſtone, &
2 Feuerſham.

Some adde Mere-gate &c.

This

This port of Douer, with the aforesaide members, ought to finde to the kinge xxj. ships, y is to say, Douer 19. ships, Folkestone one ship, & Feuersham one shippe.

The members of the Port of Sandwiche are these.

1 Stoner.
2 Fordwich.
3 Dale.
4 Seire.

Soc abe Reaculure.

This port of Sandwich, with the members aforesaide, ought to finde in the kinges seruice, as is before saide 5. shippes.

Summe lvij. shipps.

When the Kinge would haue hys seruice of the aforesayde shipps, they shall haue xl. dayes summons, & they shall finde to the king in euery ship xx. men, & the Master wel

---

Mesme cel Port de Douer, oue les auantdits members, doyent trouer au Roy xxj. nefes, ceo est a scauoir, Douer 19. nefes, Folkstone, vn nefe, & Feuersham vn nefe.

Les Members del Port de Sandwith sont ceux.

1 Stoner.
2 Fordwich.
3 Dale.
4 Seire.

Asc' adde Reaculure.

Mesme cel port de Sandwich oue les mēbers auauntdits doyt trouer en seruice le roy come auant est dit v. nefes.

Summe lvij. niefes.

Quant le Roy voudra au:r son seruice des auantdits niefes, ils auerount xl. iours de summons, & ils troueront au roy en chescum niefe xx. homes, & le Master byen arme,

arme, & byen attier pur fayre le ſeruice le Roy.

Et irront les nefes en proper coſtages des cinque Portes la ou eux ſerront ſummons. Et quant les nefes ſerront la venus, eux demurront xv. iours en ſeruyce le Roy al proper coſtages des cinq; Portes. Et apres les xv. iours paſſes ils demurront au coſtages le Roy, ſil en ad a faire.

Le Maſter de la nefe prendra le iour vj. deniers. Le Conſtable vj. deniers, & cheſcun des auters Mariners iij. deniers.

Et eſt a ſcauer, que le court de Shipway que eſt chiefe Court des cinque Portes, ou cheſcun Maior de cheſcun port, ou 12. 10. 6. ou 4. & le Maior de cheſcun port, ſicome eux per letters de

armed, and well appoynted to doe the kinges ſeruice.

And the ſhippes ſhall go at the pzoper coſtes of the Cinque Pozts, thyther whether they ſhalbee ſummoned. And when the ſhipps are thither come, they ſhal continue xb. daies in the kinges ſeruice, at the pzoper coſtes of the b. pozts. And after the xb. dayes are paſt, they ſhalbe at þ charges of the K. if he haue any thing foz thẽ to do. The Maſter of þ ſhip ſhall take bi. d. a day. The Conſtable bi. d. & euery of the other mariners iij. pence.

And it is to be knowen, that the court of Shipway, which is þ chief court of the fiue Poztes, where euery Maioz of euery pozt, oz 12.10.6.oz 4. & the Maioz of euery pozt, as they by letters of
the

the warden of þ Cinque portes haue hym summoned, and as the port is greater or lesser , without essoyne ought to come, ought to be summoned by the letters of the sayde warden to al the portz that ought to doe sute there.

And the summons ought to be vpon sute made to summon any commynaltie to aunswere to any of any plee, contayning 40. dayes from the day of the recepte of the Letters of the sayde warden.

And the foresayde Court ought to bee summoned chiefely for Treason done against the kinge or kinges: for counterfaitinge of the kinges seale : or of his money, for treasure founde vnder the groud: For the kings seruice denied, or with

le gardeyne des Cinke portes ount estre summonus, & sicōe le port est greind' ou meinder sans essoigne doit vener , doit estre summonus per letters del dit gardeyne a toutes les portes que illonques suit deuient enuoies.

Et doit la summons a la sute fere & a summounder ascun communaunt a responder a ascun, de ascun plee conteyner quaraunte iours del iour de la resceyte des letters le dit gardeine.

Et lauauntdir court doyt estre summons princypalment , pur Treason fayt encounter le Roy ou Royes, pur fausure de scale le Roye , ou de sa money , pur treasure troue de southe le. terre , pur seruyce le roy dedist, ou detenue,

H.j.　　　nue,

nue , pur faux iudge-
ment pur aſcun com-
munant rendu.

Et nul cõmunaunt
al aſcũ plee vers meſ-
me la comunàt meſne
reſpond' ne doit, ſorſ-
que a la court auãtdit.

Et plee illonques
meſne vers aſcune
baron des Cinkes
portes challenge per
le baylife de cel port
de que baylie meſne
le baron eſt , doyt
eſtre aiournee dekes
al porte dount ycel
baron eſt , ſil ne ſoit
de treſpas fayt au roy,
pur ceo que les dites
Barons ount cony-
ſaunces de touts ma-
ners de plees fors
pris plees de Coro-
ne . Et quant que ce-
ux Barons aue'ount
de fayles endroyture
fayre . Le dyt Gar-
deyne a la pleynt de
celuy a que ils aue-
rount defayles de
droyture entrant yeel

holden,foz falſe Judg-
ment giuen by any co-
munaltie.

And no commoner
to any plea agaynſt
him bzought ſhal aun-
ſwere but at the court
afozeſaid.

And plees there had
againſt any Baron of
the Cinque pozts be-
ing challenged by the
Bailyfe of the ſame
pozt of which the ſaid
Baron is:ought to be
adiourned vnto the
pozt, wherof the ſame
Baron is, (if it be not
foz treſpas done a-
gainſt the kinge) be-
cauſe that the ſayde
Barons haue cony-
ſaunce all manner of
pleas except pleas of
the Crown. And whē
thoſe Barons haue
fayled to doe ryght:
The ſaid warden at
the complaynt of him
to whome they haue
fayled to doe ryght,
ſhall goe to the ſame
pozt

port to do right, as is contained in the charter.

Moreouer, the aforesaid court ought not to be holden from the feast of the natiuity of saint Mary, vntil the feast of saint Andrew, becaufe of the martes of Germany.

Also when the Barons of the Cinque ports are in the kings seruice vpon the Sea, or at the kings summons, or at the kings commaundement.

Furthermore, it ought not to be holden but one day.

And one Essoine onlie lyeth in the aforesayde Court in euery plea.

Of sute no Essoine lieth, as is before said, and therefore if the maior, who becaufe of sickenesse or other sodeyne infirmytye cannot come thither,

port a droyture faire ficome il est contenue en la chartre.

Ouftre ceo la auauntdit court ne doit estre tenue de la feast del Natiuitie de saint Marie iefques a la feast de Saint Andrewe pur les faires de Germañ.

Ouster ceo quaunt les Barons des Cinke portes fount en le feruice le roy fur meere, ou a la fûmons le roy, ou al maundement le Roy.

Ouster ceo ne doit pas tenue forsque per vn iour.

Et vn effoign tantfolement gist en le auauntdit Court en chefcun plee.

De fuit nul Effoigne gyst ficome il est auauntdyt, & pur ceo si le Maior que de langour ou enfermere fudeine illonques venir ne purr,

H.ij.   auter

auter purra a cel iour
ſon lieu tener, iſſint
ne pur taunt que re-
torne ſoit fait per ſon
bailiſe.

Ne auters princy-
pallement deuient eſtř
charges de aſcū iudge-
ment rendu en m̄ la
court, forſq; ceux noſ-
mes queux per les bai-
liffs illonqs ont eſtre
retornes &c.

Ouſter tout ceo,
prouiſion de niefs &
homes come eſt auāt-
dit, ieo aye view en
vn auter record(brief-
ment eſcript) que cheſ-
cun niefe doyet auer
vn garſon, que la eſt
appell vn Gromet.
Iſſint que en ſomme
les cinque ports ſont
charges oueſques 57.
niefs,1197.homes,&
57.garſons ou Gro-
metts.

¶Damage feſans.

D Amage feſans eſt
quant les beaſts
dē eſtrāger ſout

an other may at that
daye keepe his place,
ſo notwithſtandinge
p̄ returne be made by
his bailiſe.

For others princi-
pally ought to be char
ged of any iudgement
giuen in the ſame
court but thoſe names
who by the Baylifes
there haue bœne re-
turned.

Biſides all thys,
prouiſion of Shippes
and men, as is afore-
ſaide: I haue ſœne in
an other record(ſhort-
lye written) that e-
uerye Shippe ought
to haue a boye, which
there is called Gro-
met: ſo that in ſume
the Cinque portes are
charged with 57 ſhipz
1197. men, and fif-
tye ſeuen boyes, oz
Gromets.

¶Damage feſans.

D Amage feſans,
is when a ſtran-
gers beaſtes are

in an other mannes grounde, without auc thoritie of the lawe, oz lycence of the tenaunt of the ground, and there doe fæde, treade, oz otherwise spoyle the Cozne, grasse, woods, oz such like : in which case the tenant whom they hurt, may therefoze there take, distrain, & impounde them, as wel if it be in þ night, as in the day tyme. But in other cases as foz rent and seruices and such like, none may distreyne in the night season.

auters terres, sauns aucthoritye del ley ou lycence del Tenaunt de la terre, & la man-ger treade, ou auter-ment spoila les blees grasse, boyes, ou ty-els semblables, en ql case le Tenaunt que ils issint dammage, poyt pour ceo la pré-der, dystraine et im-pounde eux, cybyen sil soit en le nuict co-me en la iour. Mes en auters cases, co-me pur rent et seruy-ces & tyels sembla-bles, null poit dys-traynor en la nuict temps.

¶Danegelde.

¶Danegeld.

Danegeld, that is to be quitt of a certaine custome which hath runne sõe times, which þ danes did leuye in Eng-glande. This beganne first

Danegeld, hoc est quietum esse de quadam consue-tudine quæ cucurrit a-liquo tempore, quam quidem Dani leuaue-runt in Anglia. Ceo cõmence prim

H.iij.   en

en temps le Roy. E-
theldred que esteaunt
en graunde distresse
per le continuall im-
uasion de les Danes,
pur purchaser paxe
fuit compelle de char-
ger son paies & peo-
ple oue importable
paiments: car il primer-
ment done al eux v. se-
uerall payes 113000.
li. & puis graunt al
eux 48000.li. annu-
alment.

¶Deane & Chapter.

DEane & chapter
est vn corps cor-
porate spirituall, con-
sistant de plusours a-
ble persons en ley,
come nosement le
deane (que est le prin-
cipall) & les Pre-
bendes: & ils ioynt
font le corporation.
Et sicome cest corpo-
racion poient ioynt-
ment purchase tres &
tents al vse de lour esgl'

in kinge Etheldreds
daies, who being sor
distressed by the con-
tinuall inuasion of the
Danes, to purchase
peace was compel-
led to charge hys
countrey and people
wyth importable pay-
mentes: for hee first
gaue them at v. seue-
rall paies 113000.li.
and afterward graun-
ted them 48000.li.
yerely.

¶Deane and Chapter.

DEane and chapter
is a body spiritu-
all corporate, consis-
ting of many able per-
sons in law as name-
ly the deane (who is
the chiefe) and the
prebendes, & they to-
gether make the cor-
poratyon. And as
this corporation may
ioyntly purchase lads
and tenementes to the
vse of their Church
and

and ſucceſſours: Doe
likewiſe euery of thē
ſeuerally maye pur=
chaſe to the vſe of
hym ſelfe and hys
heires, as wee daylie
ſee them doe moſt a=
bundantly.

& ſucceſſours : Aſint
auxi cheſcun de eux
ſeueralment p̱ cet pur-
chaſe al vſe de luy &
ſes heires,come nous
iournalment voiomus
eux faire mult abun-
dantment.

¶Declaration.

Declaratyon is a
ſhewinge forth in
writing , of the griefe
and complaynt of the
demaundant or plein=
tife againſt the tenant
or defendant, wherein
he ſuppoſeth to haue
receiued wrong. And
this declaratiō ought
to be plaine & certeine,
both becauſe it impea=
cheth the defendant or
tenant, & alſo compel=
leth him to make aun=
ſwere thereto.

¶Declaration.

Eclaration eſt vn
monſtrance en eſ-
cript de le griefe &
complaint dē le de-
maundaunt ou plein-
tife, enuers le tenaunt
ou defendaunt , en
que il ſuppoſe de a-
uer receyue tort. Et
ceſt declaratyon, doit
eſte playne , & cer-
teyne , pur ceo que
il impeach le defen-
daunt ou tenaunt , &
auxy chaſe luy reſ-
ponder.

¶Defendant.

Defendaunt is hee
that is ſued in an

¶Defendant.

Efendant eſt ce-
luy que eſt ſue en
action

action perfonall, & il
eft appel ter.ant en ac-
tion reall.

actyon perfonal, & he
is called tenant in an
action real.

¶Demaines.

¶Demaines.

DEmaines, ou de-
mefnes,e le princi-
pall manor place del
fnr, que il & fes aun-
ceftours, ount ewe de
temps hors de me-
mory en lour maines
demefne, & ount oc-
cupie ceo, enfemble
oue toutes edefices &
meafons quecunque,
& auxy les prees paf-
tures,boies,terres erra-
rable, & tyels fem-
blables appartainaunt
a ceo.

DEmaines, oz de-
mefnes,is the lozds
chpefe mannoz place,
which he and his aun-
ceftoures haue from
tyme out of mynde,
kepte in their owne
handes, and haue oc-
cupped the fame,toge-
ther with al buildings
& houfes whatfoeuer,
alfo the meadowes,
paftures, woodes, er-
rable lande, and fuch
like, belonging there-
unto.

¶Demaundant.

¶Demaundant.

DEmaundaunt eft
celuy que fue ou
complayne en action
reall pur title de ter-
re,et il eft appel plein-
tife en vn affife &
en vn actyon perfo-

DEmaundant is he
that fueth oz com-
playneth in an acty-
on reall, foz tytle of
land, and he is called
plaintyfe in an affife,
and in an action perfo-
nall

well as in an action of dette, trespas, disceit, detinue, and such other.

nell cōe en action de det, trespas, disceit, detinue, & tiels sembla-bles.

¶Halfe bloode.

¶Demy sancke ou sangue.

HAlfe bloode, is when a manne maryeth a wife, and hath issue by her a sonne, and shee dyeth, and then hee taketh an other woman, and hath by her also a sonne. Now these two sonnes are after a sort Brothers, or as they are termed, halfe Brothers, or Brothers of the halfe bloode, that is to say brothers by the Fa-thers side because they had both one father, & are both of his bloude and not brothers at all by the mothers side, nor of bloodde ne kinne that way, & therefore the one of them can-not be heire to other,

DEmy sancke, est quant vn hōe ma-ry vn feme, & ad issue per luy vn fites, & el morust, & donques il prist vn auter feme & ad per luy auxi vn fits, Ore ceux deux fites sount solonque vn maner freres, ou cōm ils sount appels, de-my freres, ou freres del demy sanke, cest adire frere per le part del pier, pur ceo que ils ount ambideux vn pier, & sount ambi-deux de son sangue, & nemy freres per le part le mere, ne de ascun sancke ou clime cest voye, & pur ceo lun de eux ne poet este heire al auter,

car

car il que voile clay-
me come heire al vn
per dyscent , doyte
este dentyer sancke a
luy de que il claime.

foz hee that wil claime
as heire to one by dis
cent , must bee of the
whole bloode to him
from whome he clay=
meth.

¶Demurrer.

¶Demurrer.

DEmurrer est quant
ascun actyon est
port, & le defendaunt
plede vn plee a que
le pleintife dyt que
il ne voyle respon-
der , pur ceo que il
nest sufficient plee in
le ley , & le defen-
daunt dyt al contra-
rye que il est sufficy-
ent plee , cest doubt
del ley est appelle vn
demurrer.

DEmurrer is whē a
ny actiō is bzought
and the defendaunt
pleadeth a plee , to
which the playntyfe
sayth that hee wil not
aunswere , foz that,
that it is not a suffy=
cient plee in the lawe,
and the defendaunt
sayth to the contra=
ry , that it is a suffi=
cient plee , this doubt
of the lawe is called
a demurrer.

¶Denizen.

¶Denizen.

DEnizen est Iou
vn alyen deuy-
ent le subiecte del
Roygne, & obteine,
sa letters patentes, pur

DEnizen is where
an alien becommeth
the Queenes subiecte
and obtayneth her let=
ters patentes to en=
                    inne

toye all p̃iuiledges as
an Engliſhman. But
yet notwithſtanding,
hœ ſhall paye cuſto=
mes and dyuers o=
ther thinges as aly=
ens dꝏ &c.

enioer toutes priuy-
leges con e vn Ang-
loyes. Mes vncore ni-
ent obſtaunt, il payera
cuſtomes , & diuers
auters choſes come a-
liens font.

¶Deodande.

¶Deodande.

DEodande is when
any man by myſ=
foztune is ſlaine by an
hozſe oz by a cart, oz
by anie other thinge
that moueth, thē this
thing that is cauſe of
his death, and which
at the time of the miſ=
foztune mꝏued, ſhall
bœ foʒfayte to the
Quœue, and that is
called deodande, and
that perteyneth to the
Quœenes Almener foʒ
to dyſpoſe in almes
and in dœdes of cha=
ritie.

DEodande, eſt quāt
aſcun home per
miſfortune eſt tue per
vne chiuall , ou per
charet , ou per au-
ter choſe que mo-
uet, donques cel choſe
que eſt la cauſe de
ſon mort , que all
temps de la myſfor-
tune moua , ſerra for-
fayte al Roygne, &
ceo eſt appell Deo-
dande , & pertayne
al Almener le Roy-
gne pur diſpoſer in
almes & actes de cha-
ritye.

¶Depar-

¶Departure de fon plea ou matter.

¶Departure from a plea or matter.

DEparture de fon pł a, ou matter, eſt lou vn home plede vn plee en barre, & le pleyntife replye a ceo, & il apres en fon reioynder plede ou monſtr̄ auter matter contrary a fon primer plea en barre, ceo eſt appelle vn departer de fon barre &c.

DEparture from his plæ oz matter, is where a man pleadeth a plæ in barre, and the pleyntyfe replyeth thereto, and hæ after in hys reioynder pleadeth oz ſheweth an other matter contrarye to hys firſt plæ, that is called a departer from his barre ⁊c.

¶Departure in difpite del Court.

¶Departure in difpite of the Court.

DEparter in dyſpite del court, eſt quaunt le tenaunt ou defendaunt appeare all action porte enuers luy, & ad iour ouſter en meſme le terme, ou eſt demaund apres fauns iour en meſme le terme, & ne appeare, mes fait defaute, ceſt vn de-

DEparture in dyſpite of the court, is when the tenaunt oz defendāt appeareth to the action bzought againſt him, and hath a day ouer in þ fame terme, oz is called after without daye in the fame terme,⁊ doth not appeare, but makes defaut, this is a departure

parture in dispite of
the court, & therefoze
he shatbe condempned.

parture in despite del
court,& pur ceo il ser-
ra condempne.

¶Deputie.

¶Deputy.

DEputie, is he y̆ oc=
cupieth in an other
mans right, whether
it bee office oz any o=
ther thing els and his
fozf. oz misdemeaner
shall cause the officer,
oz him whose deputie
hee is to loose his of=
fice oz thinge. But a
man cannot make his
deputie in al cases, ex=
cept the graunt so bee
as if it bee with these
oz such lyke wozdes,
to exercise oz vse by
himselfe oz his suffi=
cyent deputye: oz if
the wozdes goe fur=
ther by himselfe oz
his deputye, oz the
deputye of his deputy
then hee may make a
deputy, and his depu=
tie also may make a de-
putie,els not.

DEputie, est celuy
que occupya en
auter droit,soit ceo of-
fice, ou ascun auter
chose, & son forfay-
ture, ou misdemeaner
causef lofficer, ou ce ·
luy que deputy il est
de pard' son office ou
chose. Mes vn ne poet
faire son deputye en
toutes cases, nisi le
graunt soit issint si-
come il soit oue ce-
ux ou tyels sembla-
bles parols: exercen-
do per se vel suffici-
entem depuf suum,ou
si les parols va oustre,
per se vel deputaf su-
um,aut deputaf depu-
tati, donques il poet
faire vn deputy,& son
deputy auxi poet faire
vn deputy, auterment
nemy.

¶Deua-

¶Deuaſtauerunt.

Deuaſtauerunt bona teſtatoris, eſt quant les executors voile deliuer les legacies que lour teſtatour ad done : ou fayre reſtitution pur torts faits per luy, ou paye ſes detts due ſur contractes, ou auter dettes ſur ſpecyaltyes, que iours de paiment ne ſount vncore venus &c. Et ne garde ſufficyent en lour maines, pur diſcharger tyells dettes ſur ſpecyaltyes que ils ſount compellable preſentment per la ley de ſatisfier, donques ils ſerrount conſtrain de payer de lour byens demeſne ceux dutyes, le quel al primer per le ley ils fueront compelles de paiyer, accordant al value de ceo, que ils deliueront ou paye ſãs compulſió, car tiels paimẽts

¶Deuaſtauerunt.

Deuaſtauerunt bona teſtatoris, is when Execut ours wyl deliuer the legatyes that their Teſtatour hath geeuen, oʒ make reſtytutyon foʒ wʒõges dõe by him, oʒ pay hys det due vpon cõtracts oʒ other detes vpõ ſpecialties, whoſe dayes of paymentes are not yet come &c. And keepe not ſufficiẽt in their hãds to diſcharge thoſe detes vpon ſpecyalties that they are commeilable pʒeſently by y law to ſatiſfie : Then they ſhall bee conſtrayned to paye of theyʒ owne goodes thoſe dutyes, which at the firſt by the law they were cõpelled to pay : accoʒdinge to the valu of y that they deliuered oʒ paied without cõpulſion : foʒ ſuch paimẽtes
of

of dettes oz deliuerp of legacies, as is afoze=said, befoze dets paied vpõ specialties, whose daies of paimēt ar al=ready come: are accõp=ted in the law a wast=tinge of þ goods of the testatoz, as much as if they had giuen thē a=way ihout cause, oz sold them, & cõuerted them to theyr owne vse.

¶Deuise.

DEuise is where a man in his testa=ment gœueth oz bequeaeth hys gœdes oz his landes to an o=ther after his decease.

And where such de=uise is made of gœdes, if the executours will not deliuer the gœdes to the deuisee, the de=uisee hath no remedye by the comon law, but it behoueth hi to haue a citacyon against the

de detts, ou deliuerie de legacies, come est auauntdit, deuaunt detts paies sur especy-altyes, q̄ iours de pay-ment sont a ore venus, sount accompt en le ley, vn vastant des bñs del testatour, cy tant, come si ils ad done eux sauns cause, ou vende eux, & con-uert eux a lour propet vse.

¶Deuise.

DEuise est lou vn home en son tes-cament done ou graunt ses biens ou ses terres a vn auter apres son decease.

Et lou tiel deuise est fayt des byens, si les executours ne voylent delyuer les byens a le deuisee, le deuisee nad remedye per le common leye, mes il couyent de auer vn Cytatyon vers les exe-

executours le teſtatour dappearer deuaunt lordinarye de monſtrer pur quoy il ne perfourmer le volounte le teſtatour, car le deuiſee ne poet prender le legacye & luy meſme ſeruer, mes il doet eſte deliuer a luy per les executours.

Et ore al ſine de monſtre a vous (frere Nicholas) quaunt les leyes de ceſt Reahne, & les ſapyent dyſcreete Iudges de ceo, queux ſount les interpreters de le ley, ount fauour voluns & teſtamentes , & iſſint deuiſes en yeldinge al eux tyel reaſonable conſtruction, come ils penſant poet byen agreer oue les mentes de les mortes , conſiderantes que voluns & teſtamentes ſount pur le plus part,& per common entendmēt,

executoʒs of the teſtatoʒ, to appeare befoʒe the Oʒdinary to ſhew why hee perfourmeth not tye will of the teſtatour, foʒ the deuiſee maye not take the legacye and ſerue himſelfe, but it muſt be deliuered to him by the executoʒs.

And here to the ende to ſhewe you (Bʒother Nicholas) howe much the lawes of this Realme, and the wiſe diſcreet Iudges of the ſame, who are the interpʒeters of the lawe , doe fauour willes , and teſtamentes , and ſo deuiles in yelding to thē ſuch a reaſonable conſtructyon , as they thinke might beſt agree with the mindes of the dead , conſideringe that willes and Teſtamentes are foʒ the moſt part, and by common intendement made

made when the testa-
tor is now very sicke,
weake, & past all hope
of recouerie, for it is a
receiued opinion in the
countrey amonge most
that if a man should
chaunce to be so wyse,
as to make his will in
his good health when
he is stronge, of good
memorie, hath time &
leasure, & might aske
counsell if any doubt
were of the learned, þ
then he should not liue
longe after, and there-
fore they deferre it, to
such time, when as it
were moze conuenient
to apply them selues,
to the dysposicion of
their soules, then of
their landes oz goodes,
except it were, that by
the fresh memozie, and
recital of them at that
time, it myght bee a
cause to put them in
minde of some of their
goodes oz lands false-
ly gotten, and so moue

fait quant le testatour
est ore en graund lan-
gour, feble, & passe
tout sperans de reco-
uerie, car il est vn opi-
nion en le payes enter
le greinder numbers,
que si vne home per
chaunce soit cy sapient,
come de faire son vo-
lunt en son bone sane,
quant il est stronge, de
bone memorie, ad tēps
& oportunitie, & poit
demād counsel si ascun
dout soit de le learned,
que donques il ne doit
vyuer long apres ceo,
& pur ceo, ils ceo de-
ferre, tanꝗ tiel temps,
quant il soit plus con-
uenient de applier eux
mesmes a le disposicion
de lour almes.ꝗ de lour
terres & biens, sinon ꝗ
il soit, ꝗ per fresh me-
morie & recital de eux
a cest temps, il poit estꝵ
vn cause de mise eux
en ment, de asc'de lour
biens, ou terres fauxm̄t
purchase, et issint moue

eux al reſtitucion &c.
Et a ceſt temps le eſ-
cripture de tiels voluts
ſont cōmunemt cōmit
al miniſtr̄ del poch ou
al aſcun auter plus ig-
norant que luy, ſil poit
eſtr̄, que ne ſcauoit qux
parolx ſount neceſſarie
pur faire vn eſtate en
fee ſimple, fee taile, pur
terme de vie , ou tyels
ſemblables, preter dy-
uers auters miſchiefes.
Ieo voile pur ceo miſe
a vous cy aſcuns de
ceux caſes queux ſont
plus common en les
bouches de les igno-
rant homes,& portont
per le ſapient interpre-
tacions de les Iudges,
come eſt auantdit, vn
larger & plus fauora-
ble ſence en voluntes q̄
en faites . Et pur ceo
primerment, ſi vn de-
uiſe al I.S. per ſon vo-
lunt,toutz ſes terres &
tenementes , icy non
ſolement tout ceux ēres
que il ad en poſſeſſion

them to reſtitution
&c. And at that tyme,
the penninge of ſuch
willes,are commonly
committed to the Mi-
niſter of the pariſh, oz
to ſome other moze ig-
nozant then he,it that
may be,who knoweth
not what wozdes are
neceſſarie to make an
eſtate in fee ſimple, fee
taile,foz terme of lyfe,
oz ſuch like , beſides
many other miſchiefs.
I will therefoze ſett
you here downe ſome
of thoſe caſes that are
moſt common in igno-
rant mens mouthes, a
do carie by the wiſe
interpzetacions of the
Judges, as is afoze-
ſaid,a larger and moze
fauozabie ſēce in wils
then in deedes : firſt
therefoze if one deuiſe
to J.S. by his will,
all his landes and te-
nements ,here not on-
ly al thoſe lands that
bee hath in poſſeſſion

Ds

do paſſe, but alſo thoſe that he hath the reuerſion of, by vertue of theſe wordes tenements.

And if lands be deuiſed to a man to haue to him for euermore, or to haue to him and his aſſignes, in theſe two caſes the deuiſee ſhall haue a fee ſimple. But if it be gæuen by feffement in ſuch maner, he hath but an eſtate for terme of life.

Alſo if a man deuiſe his lande to another, to gæue, ſell, or doe therewith at his pleaſure or will, this is fee ſimple.

A deuyſe made to one & to his heires males, doth make an eſtate taile, but if ſuche wordes bee put in a dæde of feoffement, it ſhalbe taken in fee ſimple, becauſe it doth not appeare of what bodye the heyres

paſſont, mes auxy ceux de que il ad le reuerſion, per vertue de ceux parolx tene-ments.

Et ſi terres ſont deuiſe a vn home, a auer a luy imperpetuum, ou a auer a luy & a ſes aſſignes, in ceux deux caſes le deuiſee auera fee ſimple, mes ſi ſoit done per feoffement, en tiel maner il nad forſq; eſtate pur terme de vie.

Auxy ſi vn home deuiſe ſes terres al auter, pur doner, vend', ou faire de ceo a ſon will & pleaſure, ceſt fee ſimple.

Vn deuiſe fait al vn & a ſes heires males, fait vn eſtate taile, mes ſi tiels parolx ſont miſe en vn fait de feoffement, il lerra priſe en fee ſimple, pur ceo que il nappyert de que corps les heyres

I. ij.   males

males ſerra ingendre.

Si terres ſount done perfaytal I. S. & a les heires males de ſon corpes &c. que ad iſſue file, que ad iſſue fites & moruſt, la le terre reuertera al donour, & le fitts del file nauera ceo, pur ceo que il ne poyt a luy meſme conueyer per heyres males Car ſa meere eſt vn obſtacle a ceo, mes auterment eſt de tyel deuiſe, car la le fites del file ceo auera rather que le volunt ſerra voide.

Si vn deuiſe al Enfant in ventre matris ſuæ, ceſt bone deuiſe, auterment eſt per feoffement, grant, ou done. Car en ceux caſes yl doyet eſtre vn del habylytye pur prendre maintenaunt, ou auterment il eſt voide.

Vn deuiſe fait (en

males ſhalbe begotté.

If lands be geué by deed to J. C. & to the heirs males of his body &c. who hath iſſu a daughter, who hath iſſue a ſone, and dieth, there the land ſhal returne to the donor, and the ſone of the daughter ſhal not haue it, becauſe he can not conuey hi ſelf by heirs males for his mother is a let therto: but otherwiſe it is of ſuch a deuiſe, for there the ſone of ÿ daughter ſhal haue it rather then the will ſhall be voide.

If one deuiſe to an Enfant in hys mothers bellye, it is a goode deuiſe, otherwiſe it is by feoffement, graunt, or gift, For in thoſe caſes there ought to bee one of habylytye to take preſently, or otherwiſe it is voide.

A deuiſe made (in
fee

fee simple)without ex-
preffe words of heires
is good in fee simple.

But if a deuife bee
to I.N.he fhall haue
the lande but for term
of life,for thofe words
will carry no greater
eftate.

If one wil that his
fone I.fhall haue his
land after the deathe
of his wife, here the
wife of the deuifonr
fhall haue the lande,
firft for terme of her
life. So likewife if a
man deuife his goodes
to his wife, and that
after the deceafe of his
wife, his fonne and
heire fhall haue the
houfe where þ goodes
are,there þ fonne fhal
not haue the houfe du-
ring the life of þ wife,
for it voth appeare that
his intēt was, þ hys
wife fhould haue the
houfe alfo for terme of
her life,not with ftan-
ðig it were not ðeuifeð

fee fimple)fans expffe
parols del heires,eft bõ
en fee fimple.

Mes fi vn deuife
foit al I.N.il auera les
terres forfq; pur terme
de vye, car ceux polx
ne voilent porter grein
der eftate.

Si vn voile que fon
fits I. auera fon ter-
re poft mortem fon
feme , icy le femme
de le deuyfour a-
uera le terre primes
pur terme de fa vye.
Iffynt fi home deuife
fes byens a fa feme,
& que apres le de-
ceafe de fon femme,
fon fites & heyre a-
uera le meafon ou
les byens fount, le
l: fits ñauera le mea-
fon duraunt le vye
de le femme , car il
appyert que fon in-
tent fuyt , que fa
feme doyet auer le
meafon auxy , pur
terme de fa vye , niet
obftát il ne fuit deuife

I.iij. a

a luy per lexpreſſe pa-
rollx.

Sy vn deuiſe ſoyt
al I. N. & a les
heires femals de ſon
corpes ingendres : a-
pres le deuiſee ad iſ-
ſue ſites & file &
moruſt , icy le file
auera le terre , & ne-
my le ſits , & vn-
core il eſt plus digne
perſon , & heire al
ſon piere , mes pur
ceo que le volunt del
mort eſt , que le file
doyet ceo auer , ley
& conſcience voet
iſſint auxy. Et en
ceſt point les heathen
fuerount precyſe, co-
me appyert per ceux
verſes de Octauius
Auguſtus que Dona-
tus report il feſoyt
apres que Virgil a ſon
mort donoit com-
maundement que ſes
lyuers doyent eſtre
combure, pur ceo que
ils fuerount imperfect,
& vncore aſcuns per-

to her by expꝛeſſe
woꝛdes.

If a deuiſe be to I.
N. and to the heires
females of his boꝺye
begotten: after the de-
uiſe hath iſſue a ſone
and a daughter and
dieth, here the daugh-
ter ſhal haue the land,
and not the ſonne, and
yet he is the moſt woꝛ
thy perſon, and heire
to his father, but be-
cauſe the will of the
deade is, that þ daugh-
ter ſhoulde haue it,
law and conſcience wil
ſo alſo. And here-
in the verye heathens
were preciſe , as ap-
peareth by thoſe ver-
ſes of Octauius Auguſ-
tus , which Dona-
tus repoꝛtethe , he
made after that Uir-
gil at his death, gaue
commaundement that
his bookes ſhoulde be
burnte , becauſe they
were imperfecte, and
yet ſome perſwa-
ded

ded that they shoulde
be saued as in deed
they happily were, to
whom he aunswered
thus: but faith of law
must neds be kept:, &
what last wil doth say

And what it doth
commaunde be done,
ẏ neds we must obay.

¶Discent.

Discent is in two
sortes, either lini-
al or collateral.

Liniall discent, is
whē ẏ discent is con-
ueied in ẏ sāe line of ẏ
whole blood, as grand-
father, father, sonne,
sonns sonne and soe
downeward.

Collateral discent,
is out in an other
branche from abue, of
the whole bloode, as ẏ
graundfathers bro-
ther, fathers bro-
ther, and so downe-
warde.

¶Disclaimer.

suadount que ils doy-
ent estre saue, come en
fait ils happiment fu-
eront a que il res-
pond issint.

Sed legum seruanda
fides, suprema volūtas

Quod mandat, fieriq;
inbet, parere necesse
est.

¶Discent.

Discent est in ij.
sorts, ou linial, ou
collateral.

Linial discent, est
quaunt le discent est
conuey en mesme le
lyne dentier sanke, co-
me aile, peere, fits, fits
del fits et issint de-
bassa.

Collateral discent
est dehors en yn au-
ter braunche dehaut,
dentier sank, come le
frere del aile, frere
del pere, & issintde-
bassa.

¶Disclaimer.

I, iiij.　Dis-

Diſclaymer, eſt lou le feigniour dyſtrayne ſon tenaunt, & il ſua Repleuin , & le feignyour auowa le priſel , per reaſon que il tient de luy , ſi le tenant dit que il diſclaim de tener de luy, ceſt appel vn diſclaymer,& ſi le feigniour ſur ceo port briefe de Droit ſur diſclaymer , & il ſoit troue encounter le tenaunt, il perdera le terre.

Diſclaymer , is where the Lozde diſtraynethhys tenãt, & he ſueth a Repleuin & the Lozd anoſweth þ taking by reaſon that he holdeth of hym, if the tenant ſay that hæ diſclaymeth to hold of him , thys is called a diſclaimer,& if þ Lozd therupon bzing a wzit of right ſur diſclaimer & it be founde agaynſt the tenaunt , hæ ſhall loſe the lande.

¶Diſmes.

¶Tythes.

Diſmes ſont deuides en trois ſortes,noſment , Predial diſmes, Parſonall diſmes , & Mixt diſmes.

Predial diſmes ſount diſmes , que ſont pay de choſes queux vient de le terre ſolement , come feine , fruites del arbors , & tiels ſemblables.

Perſonal diſmes ſont

Tithes are in thzæ ſoztes deupded, to witte,Pzedyal tithes Parſonal tithes , and Mixt tithes.

Pzediall tithes , are tithes that be paied of thinges that come of the grounde onely , as Cozne , Haye , fruites of træs , and ſuch like.

Parſonal tithes, are tithes,

tithes that bee payed
of such profits as come
vp the labour and in-
dustrie of a mans per-
son, as by buying, sel-
ling, gaines, of mar-
chandise, and of handy
craftes men, labou-
rers, & such as worke
for hyer, as Carpen-
ters, Masons, and
such like.

dismes que sont payes
de tiels profites que
veigne per le labour &
industrie del person
dun home, come per
emption,& vendicion,
gaine de marchandize,
& de manuell craft
homes, laborers,& ti-
els q̄ labor pur salarye,
cõe carpenters,masons
& tyels semblables.

Mixt tithes are the
tythes of Calues,
Lambes, Pigges,and
such like,that encrease
partly of the grounde
that they be fed vpon,
and partly of the kee-
ping,industrie,& dili-
gence of the owner.

Mixt dismes, sont les
dismes de vitels, agnes,
porcels,et tiels sembla-
bles,que encrease part-
ment del terre,sur que
ils sont depastures, &
partment del gardians
endustrie, & diligence
del owner.

¶Disperagement.

¶Disperagement.

Disperagement, is
a shame, disgrace,
or billany done by the
Gardein in Chiualry,
to his ward in chiual-
rie, (which in olde
time was as much to
say as a Gentleman)

Disperagement, est
vn honte,disgrace,
ou villanie fait per le
gardein en Chiualrie,
al son garde en chiual-
rie(quel en auncient
temps fuit taunt adire
come vn Gentlehome)
este-

esteant deins age, per reafon de marriage. Come quaunt le gardein marrie fon ward deins age de xiiij. ans, & deins tiel temps que Il ne poit confent al marriage, al vn nefe, ou al file dun que demurt en vn Borough, (que eft defte entende tiels que peres profeffe maincraftes, & tyels bafer art es de emption & vendicion pur gayner lour viuer per ceo) ou al vn que ad forfque vn pee, ou vne main, ou eft decrepite, ou deforme, ou ayant horrible difeafe, come le leproffe, les pockes des franks, falling ficknes, ou tiels femblables, ou marie luy a vn feme que eft paffe lage defant, & diuers tiels auters, donquos fur le complaint fait per les amyes de tiel heire, le feigniour ou gardeine perdera le gardifhip, &

being within age, vp reafon of marpage. As when the Gardeine doth marrie his ward within the age of xiiij. yeares, and within fuch time that he cannot confent to marryage, to a bondwoman, or to the daughter of one that dwelt in a borough, (which is to bee vnderftcode fuche whofe fathers profeffe handycraftes, & thofe bafer artes of buyng & fellinge to gett theyr lyuing by) or to one that hath but one fcote or one hand, or is lame or deformed, or hath fome horrible difeafe, as the leprofie, French pockes, falling ficknes or fuch like, or marieth him to a woman that is paft child bearing, and diuers fuch other: then vpō p complaint made by the friendes of fuch heire, p Lord or garden fhal lofe p wardfhip, &

the

the profits during the
nonage of the heire,
for the shame done vn-
to hym.

les profites durant le
nonage de le heire,
pur le honte fayt a
luy.

¶Disseisine.

¶Disseisine.

Disseisin is when a
man enters into
any lands or tenemēts
where his entre is not
lawful, & putteth him
out ẏ hath the freehold

Isseisin est quant
vn home enter en
ascū terres ou tenemts
lou son entre nest pas
congeable, & oulta ce-
luy ǧ ad le frankfent.

¶Disseisin vpon disseisin.

¶Disseisin sur disseisin.

Disseisin vpon dys-
seisin, is when the
disseisor is disseised by
an other.

Isseisin sur dissei-
sin est, quaunt le
disseisour est disseisi per
vn auter.

¶Disseisour and disseisee.

¶Disseisour & disseisee

Isseisour, is hee
which putteth a-
ny man out of his land
without order of the
law, and disseisee is he
that is so put out.

Disseisour est celuy
que mist ascune
home hors de son terre
sauns order de ley, &
disseisee est celuy ǧ est
issint mis de hors.

¶Distresse.

¶Distresse.

Distres

Istres est la chose que est prise & distreine sur ascun terre pur rent arere, ou pur auter duetie, ou pur tort fait, coment que le propertie del chose soit perteygnant al estraunge, mes si sount beastes que perteignāt a vn estranger, il couient que sont leuant & couchant sur le terre. s. que les beastes auoyēt este sur le terre per certeine space que ils ount eux bien repose sur la terre, ou auterment ils ne sount distraynable. Et si vn dystreine pur rent ou auter chose sans cause loyal, donques le party greeue auera vn Repleuin sur suerty troue de pursuer son action, & auera la distresse a luy rede-lyuer.

Mes sont diuers choses que ne sont distrey-nable, cestassauoir, le robe de auter home

Istres is the thing which is taken and distreined vpō any lād foȝ rēt behind, oȝ other duitie, oȝ foȝ hurt don, although ꝑ the ꝓꝑer-tie of ꝑ thing belōgeth to a strāger, but if they be beastes that belong to a straunger, it beho-ueth that they be le-uant and couchant vp on the same ground, ꝑ is to say, ꝑ the beasts haue ben vpon ꝑ groūd certein space that they haue them selfe well rested there, oȝ els they bee not distreynable. And if one distrain foȝ rent oȝ other thinge without cause lawful, then the party grœued shall haue a Repleuin vpon suertie found to pursue hys action, and shall haue ꝑ distres to him deliuered againe.

But there be dyuers thinges which bee not distrainable, ꝑ is to say an other mans gowne in in the house of a Tailor, or cloth in ye house of a Fuller, shereman, or weyuer, for that, that they bee common artificers, and that the common presumption is, that such thinges belong not to the Artificer, but to other persons which put the there to be wrought.

Also vittaile is not distraynable, nor corne in sheeues, but if they be in a cart, for that, that a distres ought to be alway of such thinges whereof the sherife may make Repleuin, and deliuer againe in as good case as it was at the time of the takinge.

A man may distraine for homage, and fealty and escuage, and other seruices, & for fines & amerciamentes which be assessed in a Leete, but not in a Court baron. And also for

en le meason de vne Tayler, ou drape en le meason dun Fuller, shereman, ou weyuer, pur ceo que ils sount common artificers, & que le common pre-sumption est, que tiels choses ne perteygnent al artificer, mes al auters persons q̃ les mittont la a ouerer.

Auxy vittaile nest pas distreynable, ne blees en garbes, sinon que ils sont en vn chareot, pur ceo que distres couient este touts foits de tiel chose, dont le vicount puit faire Repleuin, & redeliuer en auxy bone case que il fuit al temps del prisel.

Auxy home puit distraine pur homage de son tenaunt, pur fealtie & escuage, & auters seruices, et pur fines & amercemts q̃ sõt assesso en vn leete, mes ney en court bar. Et auxy pur dam-

dammage feafant . s .
quāt il troue les beafts
ou biens dun auter,fe-
fant tort ou incum-
brant fon terre . Mes
home ne put diftraine
pur afcun rēt ou chofe
due pur afcun terre ,
mes fur mefme la terre
que eft charge ouefque
ceo,mes en cafe lou ieo
veigne a diftreyner, &
lauter voyant mō pur-
pofe , chafe les beaftes
ou port le chofe de
hors,al entent que ieo
ne prendra pur diftres
fur le terr,donques ieo
puiffe bien purfue , &
fi ieo le prift mainte-
nant en le haut chy-
min,ou en auter foile,
la prifel eft loyal,auxi-
bien la come fur la terř
charge,a quecunque la
propertie des byens
font. Auxy pur fines et
amerciaments que font
affeffe en vn leete , vn
puit tours foits pren-
der les biens celuy que
eft iffint amerce , in

dammage fefant , that
is to fay,ſohen he kn=
deth ꝑ beaſts oꝛ goods
of any other , doinge
hurt oꝛ cumbꝛing his
grounde. But a man
may not diſtrain foꝛ a-
ny rēt oꝛ thing due foꝛ
any lād, but bpon the
faine lād ꝑ is charged
thereſwith,but in cafe
ſwhere J come to dif-
trein,e ꝑ other fæing
my purpofe,chafeth ꝑ
beaſts, oꝛ beareth the
thingout to the intent
ꝑ J ſhall not take it
foꝛ a diftres bpon the
ground, then J may
ſwel purfu,e if J take
it pꝛefētly in the high
ſway oꝛ in an others
ground,the taking is
laſwfull afſwell there
as bpon the land char-
ged to ſwhom foeuer
ꝑ ꝑperty of ꝑ goods be
Alfo foꝛ fines e amer=
ceamēts ſwhich be af-
feffed in a læt,one may
alſway take ꝑ goods of
hi ꝑ is fo amerced, in
ſwhofe

wose grounde soeuer
they bee with in the
Iurisdiction of the
Court as it is sayde.
And when one hath
taken a distresse, it be=
houeth hym to bringe
it to the cōmon pound
oz els he may keepe it
in on others grounde
so that he geue notice
to the party , that
hee (if the distresse
bee a quicke beast)
may geue to it foode,
and then if the beast
dye foz default of foode
hee that was distrei=
ned shall bee at ye losse
and then the other
may distraine againe
foz the same rent oz
duptye.

But if hee bzinge
the distresse to a holde
oz out of the County,
that the Sherife may
not make deliuerances
bppon the Repleuin,
then the party bpon ye
returne of the sherife,

quecunq; soile que ils
sont deins la iurisdic-
tion del Court vt di-
citur. Et quant vn ad
prise vn distres , il co-
uient a luy de amesner
a le common pounde,
ou auterment il puyt
garder en auter soyle,
issint que il done no-
tyce al partie , que il
(si le distresse soyt
vyue beaste,) puyt
doner a luy vyand,
& donques si le beast
murrust pur default
de vyand , celuy que
fuit distrayne serra a
le parde , & don-
ques lauter puit dis-
trayne auterfoits pur
mesme le rent ou
duetie.

Mes fil amesna le
distresse a vn forselet,
ou hors del countie ,
que le vicount ne puit
byen faire deliuerance
sur Repleuine, don-
ques la partie sur le re-
returne de vicount
auera

auera vne briefe de
VVithernam, direct al
vicount que il preygne
taunt de fes beaftes, ou
taunt des biens lauter
en fa garde, tanque il
ad fait deliuerance de
la primer diftres.

Auxy fils fount en
vn forfelet ou chateau,
le vicont puit prender
oue luy le povver del
County, & abater le
chaftel. Come ap-
piert per le Statute
weftmonafter. 1. cap.
17. Ideo vide Sta-
tutum.

fhall haue a vvritte of
vvithernam, directed
to the Sherif, that he
take as many of hys
beaftes, or as much
goodes of the other in
his keeping, tyll y hee
hath made deliuerāce
of y firft diftres. Alfo
if they be in a forfelet
or caftell, the Sherife
may take with him y
power of the county,
& beat downe y caftel.
As it appeareth by y
Statute weft. 1. cap.
17. Therefore looke
the Statute.

¶Diuorce.

¶Diuorce.

Iuorce, if fint appel
de diuorcium, ve-
niens del Verbe di-
uorf, que fignifie pur
retorner arrere, come
quant vn home eft di-
uorze de fon femme,
il luy retorne arrere al
fa pere, ou auter a-
mies, ou al lieu ou il
luy ad, & per tiel

Iuorce, fo called
of diuorcium, com-
ming of y verbe diuoro
which fignifieth to re-
torne backe, as when a
man is deuorced from
his wife, he retorneth
her backe home to her
father, or other frinds,
or to y place frō whēce
he had her, & by fuch
de-

dynozce the maryage
is defeated and vn=
done.

diuorce le maryage
est defeate & dif-
troye.

¶Donor,& donee.

¶Donor & donee.

Donoz is he which
giueth lands oz te=
nements to an other in
taile, and he to whom
the same is so giuen,is
called donee.

Onour est celuy
que done terres
ou tenementes al au-
ter en taile, & celuy a
que il est done, est ap-
pell donee.

¶Double plea.

¶Double plee.

Double plæ,is where
the defendaunt oz
tenaunt in any action,
pleadeth a plæ in the
which ij . matters bee
compzehended , and e=
uery one by himselfe
is a sufficyent barre oz
aunswere to the acty=
on, then such a double
plæ shall not be ad=
mitted foz a plæ ex=
cept one depende vpon
an other, and in such
case if hee may not
haue the last plæ with
out the first plæ then

Ouble plee,est lou
le defendaunt ou
tenaunt en ascun ac-
tion plede vn plee ,
in que ij. matters sont
comprehendus,et chef-
cun per luy mesme est
vn sufficient barre ou
respons al action ou
matter de barre, don-
ques tiel double plee
ne serra admit pur ple,
sinon que vn depend
sur lauter , & in tyel
case , sil ne puit auer le
darraine plee , sauns
le primer plee , don-
K.j. ques

ques tiel double plee
ferra bien fuffer.

fuch a double plee fhall
be wel fuffered.

¶Droit.

¶Right.

DRoyt eft lou vn
ad chofe que fuit
toll de auter per tort,
come per difleyfin,
ou eiectement, ou
tyels femblables, &
le challenge ou claim
que il ad, que auoyt
le chofe, eit terme
droit.

Right is where one
hath a thinge that
was taken from an o-
ther wrongfully, as by
difleifine, or puttinge
out, or fuch like. And
the challenge or claime
that hee hath, who
fhould haue the thing
is called right.

¶Droit dentre.

¶Right of entrie.

DRoit dentrie, eft
quaunt vn feyfie
de terre en fee, eft de
ceo diffeifi: Ore le dif-
feife ad droit dentre
en le terre, & poet
quaunt il voyle, ou il
poet auer briefe de
droyt enuers le dyf-
feifour.

Right of entrie, is
when one feifed of
lande in fee, is thereof
diffeyfed: Nowe the
diffeifee hath right to
enter into the lande, &
may fo do whe he wil:
or els hee may haue a
writ of right againft
the diffeifour.

¶Dures.

DVres e lou vn hõe
eft garde in prifon

¶Dures.

DUres is where one
is kept in pryfon,

o₂

oz reſtrained from his
liberty contrary to the
ozder of the lawe, and
if ſuch a perſon ſo bee=
ing in dures make any
eſpecialty oz obligati=
on by reaſon of ſuch
impziſonment , ſuch a
dœde is voide in the
lawe: and in an action
bzought vpon ſuch an
eſpecialty, he may ſay
that it was made by
dures of impziſonmēt,
but if a man bœ arreſ=
ted vppon any action,
at the ſuit of an other;
thoughe the cauſe of
the action be not gœd
noz trewe, if he make
any obligatyon to a
ſtraunger bœinge in
pziſon by ſuch arreſt,
yet it ſhall not be ſaid
by dures, but if hœ
make an obligatyon
to him at whoſe ſuite
he was arreſted to bœ
diſcharged of ſuch im=
pziſonment, thē it ſhal
be ſaid dures.

ou reſtreyne de ſon li-
bertie contrary al or-
der del ley , & ſi tyel
perſon iſſint eſteant ,
fayt in dures aſcun eſ-
pecialtie, ou obligati-
on. ꝑer reaſon de tyel
empriſonment,tiel fait
eſt voyde en le ley: &
in action port ſur ti-
el eſpecialtie , il puit
dire que il fuit fayt
per dures de ſon im-
priſonment : mes ſi
home ſoyt arreſt ſur
aſcun actyon al ſuite
dun auter , meſque le
cauſe del actyon ne
ſoyt bone ne voyer,
ſil fayt aſcun obly-
gation a vn eſtraunge
eſteant in priſon pur
tyel arreſte , vncore
il ne ſerra dyt per
dures , mes ſil fait ob-
lygation a luy a que
ſuite il fuit arreſt de
eſte dyſcharge de tyel
impriſonment , don-
ques il ſerra dyt du-
res .

K.ij. Eire

¶Eire Iuſtices.

EIre Iuſtices, ou Iti-
nerant, come nous
appelle eux, fuerount
Iuſtices que vſe de
equitare de lieu al li-
eu , per tout le Re-
alme , pur adminiſter
Iuſtice.

¶Embraſour ou em-
braceour.

EMbraſour ou Em-
braceour, eſt celuy
que quaunt vn matter
eſt en tryall perenter
partie & partie, vyent
al barre oue vn del
partyes (ayant re-
ceiue aſcun rewarde
pur iſſint faire) &
parle en le caſe , ou
priuement labour le
iury ou ſtat la pur ſur-
ueier ou ſuruiew eux,
pur ceſt meanes de
mitter eux en pauour
& doubt del matter.
Mes homes que ſont
erudite en le ley,poi-
ent parle en le caſe

Eire Iuſtices.

EIre Iuſtices , oʒ
Itinerant as we
cal them, were Iuſty-
ces that vſed to ryde
from place to place
thʒough out the Re-
alme , to adminyſter
Iuſtice.

¶Embraſour or Embra-
ceour

EMbraſour oʒ Em-
bʒaceour,is he that
when a matter is in
trial betwene partye
and partye commeth
to the Barre wyth
one of the parties (ha-
uinge receyued ſome
rewarde ſoe to doe)
and ſpeaketh in the
caſe, oʒ pʒiuely labo-
reth the Iurie,oʒ ſtan-
deth there to ſuruey,
oʒ ouerloke the, there-
by to put the in feare
and doubt of the mat-
ter . But men that are
learned in the lawe,
may ſpeake in the caſe
foʒ

foz their fee, but they may not laboz the Iu= rye, and if they take money so to doe, they also are embzasozs.

pur lour fee, mes ils ne poient labour le Iurie & sils preigne mony a issint faire, ils auxi sont embrasors.

¶Encrochment.

Encrochment is said when the Lozd hath gotten seisin of moze rent, oz seruices, of his tenaunt, then of ryght is due, oz ought to bee payed oz done vnto him: As if the tenaunt holdeth is land of his Lozde by feal= tie and ij.s. rent yere= lye, And nowe of late tyme, the Lozde hath gotten seisin of iij.shil= linges rent, oz of ho= mage oz Escuage, oz such like, Then thys is called an Encroch= ment of that rent oz seruice.

¶Encrochment.

ENcrochment est dit quaunt le seigny= our ad happa seisin de plus rent ou seruices de son tenaunt que de droit est due, ou doet este pay ou fait a luy: Come si le tenant ty= ent sa terre de son seigniour per fealty & ij.s. rent annuelment. Et ore de tardife tēps, le seigniour ad hap= pa seysin de iij.s. rent, ou de homage, ou es= cuage, ou tyels sem= blables, donqs cest ap= pel vn Encrochment de cest rent, ou ser= uice.

¶Enheritance.

ENheritance.is such estate in landes, oz

¶Enheritance.

ENheritaunce est riel estate en terres ou

re=

tenementes, ou auters chotes, que poyent efte enheryte per le heire, foit ceo de eftate, en fee fimple, ou taile per difcent de afcun de fes aunceſters, ou per fon purchafe demefne.

Et enheritaunce eft deuide en deux forts, ceftaffauoir. enherytaunce corporate, & enheritance encorporate.

Enheritance corporate fount mefuages, terres, prees, paftures, rentes, & tiels femblables, que ount fubftance en eux mefnes, & poyent contynuer tout remps. Et ceux font appell chofes corporall.

Enheritaunce incorporate, fount aduowfons, villeins, voies, commons, Courts, piſcaries, que fount ou poient efte appendaunt, ou appurte-

tenementes, oz other things, as may be inherited by the heire, whether it be of eſtate in fee ſimple, oz taile, by dyſcent from any of hys Aunceſters, oz by hys owne purchaſe.

And Enheritaunce is deuyded into two fortes, that is to fay, enheritance cozpozate, an enheritãce incozpozate.

Enheritaunce cozpozate are meſuages, lands, meadowes, paſtures, rentes, and ſuch like that haue ſubſtance in them ſelues, and may haue contynuance alwaies. And theſe are called cozpozall thinges

Enheritance incozpozate, are aduowſons, villaines, waies, commons, Courtes, fiſhinges, and ſuch like that are, oz may be apendant, oz appurtenan-

raunt to inheritances corporate.

nants a enheritaunces corporate.

¶Equitie.

EQuitie is in two sortz, differing much the one from the other, & are of contrary effectes, for the one doth abridge, diminish and take from the letter of the lawe. The other doth inlarge, amplifie & adde thereunto.

The first is thus defined, Equitie is the correction of a law generally made, in that part wherin it faileth, which correction of the generall wordes, is much vsed in our law. As if for example, when an act of parliament is made, that whosoeuer doth such a thing, shalbe a felon, & shal suffer death: yet if a madde man, or an infant of yonge yeres that hath no dyscretion, doe the same, they

¶Equitie.

EQuity est en deux maners, dyuers. moult lun del auter, & sount de contrary effectes, car lun abridge, diminishe, ou tolle de le letter del ley. Le auter enlarge, amplyfie, & ad a ceo.

Le primer est issint define. AEquitas est correctio legis generatim latæ qua parte deficit, le quel correction del generall parols est moult vse en nostre ley, Sicome pur example, quaunt acte de parliament est fayt, quecunque que fait, tiel acte serra felon, & serra mise al mort, vncore si home de non sane memorie, ou enfaunt de tender age que nad discretion le fayt, ils

K. iiij.   ne

ne ſerront felons , ne
miſe al mort.

Auxi ſi eſtatute fuit
fait que touts persons
que recetteront , ou
doneront maunger
ou boier ou auter
ayde a ceſtuy que fai-
era tyel acte , ſerront
acceſſorye a ſon of-
fence , & ſerrount
myſe al mort ſi ils co-
nuſteront del facte,
vncore lun fait tyel
acte & veigne a ſa
proper feme que ſci-
ant ceo luy reſceiue &
done manger & boy-
er a luy el ne ſerra ac-
ceſſorie ne felon , car
en le generaltye de les
dits parolls del ley
ceſtuy de non ſane
memoria , ne le en-
fant , ne le feme fu-
erounr include in in-
tent. Et iſſint equy-
ty correct le general-
tye del ley en ceux ca-
ſes , & les parolx ge-
nerals ſont per equy-
tie abridge.

ſhal be no felons , nor
ſuffer death therefore.

Also if a ſtatute
were made that al per-
ſons that ſhal receiue,
or giue meate or drink
or other ſuccrour, to
any that ſhal be ſuch
a thinge, ſhal be acceſ-
ſory to his offence, &
ſhal ſuffer death if they
did knowe of the fact,
yet notwithſtandinge
one doth ſuch an act,
and commeth to his
wife, who knowinge
thereof doth receiue
him and giues hym
meat and drinke, the
ſhal not be acceſſory
nor felon , for in the
generaltye of the ſaid
wordes of the lawe,
he that is mad, nor ſ
infant, nor the wife
were included in mea-
ninge. And thus equi-
ty doth corred the ge-
neralty of the law in
thoſe caſes, & the ge-
neral wordes are by
equity abridged.

The

The other equitye is defined after thys sorte: Equity is whē the wordes of the law are effectually directed and one thinge onely prouided by þ wordes of the lawe, to the end that al thinges of like kinde may be prouided by the same. And so when the wordes enact one thinge, they enact al other thinges that are of like degrææ. As the statute which ordeines that in an action of debt against executors, he þ doth apere by distresse shal aunswere, doth extend by equity to adminis-trators, for he of them that doth first apeare by distresse, shal aun-swere by equytye of the sayd acte. Bee-cause they are of like kinde.

So likewise þ sta-tute of Glocest. geues the actyon of wast, and

Lauter equitye est defyned en tyel man-ner: A Equitas est ver-borum legis directyo efficiens, cum vna res solummodo legis ca-uetur verbis, vt om-nis alia in æquali ge-nere eisdem cauea-tur verbis. Et ifsint quaunt les parolx e-nacte vn chose, ils enact toutes auters choses que sont en semblables degrees. Sycome le statute que ordeygne que en' ac-tyon de dett vers ex-ecutours cestuy que vyent per distresse respondera, extende-ra per equytye al ad-mynistratours, car cestuy de eux que vi-ent primes per dis-tresse respondera per equitye del dist acte, Quia sunt in æquali genere

Ifsint le statute de Glocester donē le actyon de VVast & le

le puniſhement de ceo vers ceſtuy que tyent pur vye, ou ans, & per le equitye de ceo home auera actyon de waſt vers ceſtuy que tyent forſque pur vn an , ou demy an , & vncore ceo eſt hors del parolx del eſtatute , car ceſtuy que tient forſque pur demy ann , ou vn an , ne tyent pur ans , mes ceo eſt le entent , & les parolx que enacte lun per equitye enacteront lauter.

the paine thereof , a=gainſt him that holds foʒ life, oʒ yeares, and by the equity of the ſame a man ſhall haue an actyon of waſt a=gainſt him that hol=deth but foʒ one yeare, oʒ halfe yeare, and yet that is without the woʒdes of the ſtatute, foʒ he that holdeth but foʒ halfe a yeare, oʒ one yere, doth not hold foʒ yeres, but that is the meaninge, and the woʒds that enact the one by equitye, enact the other.

¶Eſcape.

¶Eſcape.

Eſcape eſt en deux ſortes, videlicet voluntarye & negligent.

Voluntarie eſcape eſt quant vn arreſta auter pur felonye ou auter crime , & puis luy leſſer aler ou il veult, cē leſſer de luy

Eſcape is in two ſortes , that is to ſay , voluntary, and neglygent.

Voluntary eſcape, is whē one doth arreſt an other foʒ felony, oʒ other crime, & after let teth him go where he wil, this lettig of him
to ꝺꝺꝺ

to gee is a voluntarie escape. And if the arrest of him that escaped were for felonye, then that shal be felony in him that did suffer þe escape, and if for treason, then it shalbe treason in him, and if for trespas, then trespas, & so of other.

Negligent escape, is when one is arrested and after escapes against the wil of him that did so arrest him. and is not freshly pursued and taken before the pursuer looseth þe sight of him, this shal be said a negligent escape, notwithstanding that hee out of whose possession he escaped, we take him after hee lost sight of him.

There is an escape also without arrest, as if a murder be made in the daye, and the murderer be not take, then it is an escape.

aller est vn voluntary escape . Et si larrest de cestuy que escape fuit pur felony , ceo serra dit felony en cestuy que luy lessa descaper , & si pur treason , il serra treason en luy , & si pur vn trespas , donques trns. & sic de singulis.

Neglygent Escape est quant vn est arrest , & puis escape encounter le volunt de cestuy que luy arrest , & ne soit freshment pursue , & reprise deuant que le pursuor perda le view de luy , ceo serra dit negligent escape , non obstaunt que cestuy hors de que possessio il escape luy reprist aps le view perdu.

Il y ad vn escape auxi sauns arrest , come si vn murder soit fayt en le iour, & le murderer ne soyt prise, donques il est escape, pur per que le ville ou le murder fuit fait ſerra amercy,

for the which ꝑ towne where ꝑ murder was done ſhalbe amerced.

¶Eſplees.

¶Eſplees.

ESplees eſt ſicome le ſeiſin, ou poſſeſſion dun choſe, profit, ou commodity que eſt a prender : come dun commen les eſplees eſt le prender del graſſe ou common per les mouthes de les beaſtes que cōmon la : dun aduowſon de prender de groſſe diſmes, dun bois, le vender de bois, dun orchard, le vender de pomes, ou auter fruit creſſants la, dū molin le priſel de toll eſt les eſplees, & de tiels ſemblables.

ESplees is as it were the ſeyſin, or poſſeſſion of a thinge profit, or commodity that is to bee taken. As of a common the eſplees is the takinge of the graſſe or cōmon by the mouthes of the beaſtes that common there: Of an aduowſō the takinge of groſſe tithes: Of a wood, the ſelling of wood, of an orchard the ſelling of Aples or other fruit growinge there : of a mill the taking of toll is the eſplees, and of ſuch like.

Eſſoine.

¶Eſſoine.

ESſoine eſt lou vn action eſt port, & le pleyntife ou defen-

ESſoine is where an action is brought, & the plaintife or defendant

dant may not wel ap-
peare at the day in
court, for one of the
v. caues vnder expres-
sed, then hee shal bee
essoined to saue his de-
faut, whereupon note
well that there bee v.
maner of essoines, that
is to say, essoyne de
ouster le mere, and that
is by xl. daies, the se-
cond essoine is de terra
sancta, and that shalbe
by a yere & a day, and
these two shalbe layed
in the beginning of the
plee. The iij. essoine is
de male vener, and that
shalbe at common daies,
as the action requireth
and this is called the
common essoine. The
iiij. essoine is de malo
lecti, & that is onely in
a writte of right and
there vpon there shall
a writte go out of the
Chauncerie, directed
to the sherife, that hee
shall send iiij. knights
to the tenant to see the

dant ne poit byen ap-
pearer al iour in court
pur vn des v. caues de
south expresses, don-
ques il serra essoyne
de sauer son defaut,
vnd' nota que sount
v. manners de essoi-
nes, cestassauoir, es-
soine de ouster le mere
& ceo est per xl. iours,
Le seconde essoyne
de terra sancta, &
ceo serra pur vn an
& vn iour, & ceux
deux serrount gist al
commencement del
plee. Le tierce essoine
est de male vener, &
ceo serra al commen
iours, come lactyon
require & cest appell
le common essoyne.
Le iiij. essoine est de
malo lecti, & ceo
est solement en briefe
de droit, & sur ceo
issera briefe hors de
chauncerie directe al
vicount que il maund
iiij. Chyualers al te-
naunt de voyer le
tenant,

tenaunt , & ſil ſoyt
malade, de doner a luy
iour apres vn an &
vn iour. Le v. eſſoine
eſt de ſeruice le Roy,
& giſt en toutes acti-
ons forſque en aſſiſe de
nouel diſſeiſin , briefe
de dower , darreyne
preſentmeut, & in ap-
pell de murder , mes
in ceſt eſſoine, il coui-
ent al iour de monſtre
ſon garraunt , ou au-
terment il tornera in
vn defaut ſil ſoyt in
plee reall , ou il per-
dra xx. s. pur le iour-
ney del pleyntife ou
plus per diſcrecion des
Iuſtices , ſil ſoyt en
plee perſonell, vt patet
per ſtatute de Glouc
cap. 8.

tenaunt, and if he be
ſicke , to geeue him a
day after a yere and a
day. The v. eſſoyne is
de ſeruice le roy , and it
lyeth in al actions, ex-
cept in aſſiſe of nouel
diſſeiſin. writ of dower
darreine preſentment,
and in appell of mur-
der : but in thys eſ-
ſoine, it behoueth at
the day to ſhewe hys
warrant, or els it ſhal
torne into a defaut, if
it be in a plee real,or he
ſhal loſe xx.s. for the
plaintifes iorney , or
more by the diſcretion
of the Iuſtices,if it be
in plee perſonall,as it
appeareth by the ſta-
tute of Glouceſter.
cap. 8.

¶ Eſtoppell.

¶ Eſtoppell.

EStoppell eſt quant
vn eſt conclude &
denie en ley de par-
ler encounter ſon act
ou fayte demeſne

EStoppell is when
one is concluded, &
forbidden in lawe to
ſpeake agaynſt hys
owne acte , or deede,
yet,

yea, although it bee to
say the truth: And of
estoppells there are a
great many, one for ex=
ample is, when I. S.
is bound in an obliga=
tion by the name of
Thomas Stile, or a=
ny other name, and is
afterward sued accor=
ding to the same name
put in the obligation,
that is to saye Tho=
mas Stile, Nowe hee
shal not be receiued to
say that hee is misna=
med, but shalbe driuen
to aunswere accor=
dinge to the name put
in the obligation, that
is to saye T. S. for
peraduenture the ob=
ligee did not know his
name, but by the re=
port onely of the obli=
gor himselfe: and in
as much, as he is the
same man that was
bound: he shalbe estop=
ped and forbidden in
law to say the contra=
rie against his owne

nient obstāt il soit pur
dire le veritie. Et de
estoppelles il y ad vn
graunde number, vn
pur example est, quāt
Ioh. Sti. est oblige en
vn oblygation per le
nosme de Thomas
Style, ou ascun au=
ter nosme, & est a=
pres sue accordaunt
al mesme le nosme
mise en loolig. cest a=
dire Thomas style,
ore il ne serra receyue
adire que il est mys=
nosme, mes serra chase
a responder accordant
al nosme mise en lob=
ligatyon, cest adire
Thomas Style, car
peraduenture lobly=
gee ne scauoyt pas
son nosme, mes el re=
port tantsolement del
obligor mesme. Et en=
taunt que il est mes=
me le home que fuit
oblig. il serra estop=
pe & deny en ley,
pur adire le contrary
encounter sor. fayt
demesne,

demeſne , car auter-
ment il puit prend'ad-
uauntage de ſon tort
demeſne, le quel le ley
ne voet ſuffrer vn hõe
de faire.

Auxi ſi le file que
eſt tauntſolement la
lheire ſon pier, voet
ſuer liuerie oue ſa ſoer
que eſt vn baſtard, el
ne ſerra apres receyue
pur dire que ſa ſoer
eſt vn baſtarde, en-
tant que ſi ſa baſtarde
ſoer priſt le moytie
del terre oue luy, il
ny ad remedy per le
ley.

Item ſi vn home
ſeiſie de terre en fee
ſimple, voet prender
vn leas pur ans de
meſme le terre dun eſ-
traunger per fayt en-
dent , ceſt vn eſtop-
pell duraunt le terme
des ans . Et le leſſee
eſt per ceo barre a-
dire le veritie. Car le
veritie eſt, que il que
leſſa le terre nad riens

dæde : for otherwyſe
hee myght take ad-
uantage of hys owne
wronge , which the
lawe will not ſuffer a
man to doe.

Alſo if the daughter
that is onely heire to
her father, wil ſue ly-
uery with her Siſter
that is a baſtarde, ſhee
ſhal not afterward be
receiued to ſay that her
Siſter is baſtarde, in
ſo much that yf her
baſtarde Siſter take
halfe the lande wyth
her, there is no remedy
by law.

Alſo if a man ſeiſed
of landes in fee ſimple,
will take a leaſe for
yeres of the ſame land
of a ſtraunger by dæde
indented, this is an
eſtoppell duringe the
terme of yeares. And
the leſſee is thereby
barred to ſaye the
trouth, for the trouth
is, that he that leſſed
the land had nothing
in it

in it at the time of the leafe made, and that the fee fimple was in him that did take the leafe. But this he fhal not be recepued to fap, till after the peres are determined, becaufe it appeareth that he hath an eftate for peares, & it was hys folip to take a leaf of his owne landes, and therefore fhall thus be punifhed for his folly.

en ceo al temps del leafe fait, & que le fee fimple fuit en luy que prift le leas, mes ceo il ne ferra receyue adyre, tanque apres les ans ferra determine, pur ceo que il appiert que il ad vn eftate pur ans, & il fuit fon folly de prender vn leafe de fes terres demeine, & pur ceo ferra iffint punye pur fon folly.

¶Eftraungers.

¶Eftraungers.

E Straungers are they, that are not parties nor priuies to the leuping of a fine, or making of a deede.

E Straungers font ils que ne font parties ne priuies al fine leuie, ou feafauns dun fait.

¶Eftray.

¶Eftray.

E Stray, is where any beaft or cattel is in any Lordhippe, and none knoweth the owner thereof, then it fhalbe feifed to the vfe

E Stray, eft lou afcun beaft ou cattel eit en afcun feigniorie, & nul conuft le owner de ceo, donques il ferra feifie al oepes

L.j. le

le Roigne, ou le feig-
niour que ad tiel eftray
per graunt le Roygne,
ou per prefcription, &
fi le owner vient et fait
claime a ceo deins vn
an & vn iour, donques
if le reauera paiant put
fon viande , ou auter-
ment apres an, le pro-
pertie de ceo ferra al
feignior, iffint que le
feignior face procla-
mation de ceo , accor-
dant a le ley, en deux
Market villes.

of the Quœne, oz of
the Lozde that hath
fuche Eftray by the
Quœnes graunt, oz
by pzefcription, and if
the owner come and
make clayme thereto,
win a yere & a day, thē
he fhal haue it agayne
paying foz his meat,
oz els after ẏ yere, the
pzopertie therof fhalbe
to ẏ Lozd, fo ẏ the lozd
make pzclamation ther
of accozding to ẏ law,
in ij. Market townes.

¶Excommengement.

¶Excommunication.

EXcommēgement,
eft quant vn home
per iudgement en le
fpiritual Court eft ac-
curfe, donques il eft
difable de fuer afcun
action en le Court le
Roigne, & fil remayne
excommenge xl. iours,
& ne voyle efte iufti-
fie per fon Ordinary,
donques le Euefque
maundera fa letter

EXcommunication,
is when a man by
iudgement in the fpy-
ritual Court is accur-
fed, then he is difabled
to fue any actiō in the
Quœnes court, and if
he remaine excomma-
nicate xl. dayes, and
will not bee iuftified
by hys Ozdinarye,
then the Byfhoppe
fhall fende hys letterꝰ
pa-

patent to the Chaun=
cellor, and thereupon
it shalbe commaunded
to the Sherife to take
the bodie of him that
is accursed, by a writ
called de Excommuni-
cato capiendo, till hee
hath made agreement
with the Church for
the contempte and
wronge, and when he
is iustified and hath
made agreement, then
the Byshoppe shall
sende his letters to the
Queene, certifyinge
the same, and then it
shalbe commaunded to
the Shirife to delp=
uer hym, by a writte
called Excommunicato
deliberando.

patent al Chaunce-
lour, & sur ceo serra
maunde al Vicount,
de prender le corps le
excommengee, per vn
briefe appell de Ex=
communicato capien-
do, iesque il ad fait
gree al esglise, pur le
contempt & tort, &
quaunt il est iustifie &
ad fait gree, donques
Leuesque maundera
sa letter al Roygne
certifient ceo, & don-
ques serra maunde al
Vicount de luy de-
lyuer per vne briefe
appell, de Excom-
municato deliberan-
do.

¶Exchange.

¶Exchange.

Exchange, is where
a man is seised of
certeine lande, and an
other man is seysed
of other lande, if they
by a deede indented,

Exchange, est lou
vn home est seisie
de certeine terre, &
vn auter home est seisie
de auter terre, si ils
per vne fait endent,

L.ij.   ou

ou sauns fait (si les terres sount en vn Countye) exchang lour terres , issint que chescun de eux auera auter terre a luy issint exchaunge en fee , fee taile , ou terme de vye , ceo est appell vn exchaunge & est bone sauns lyuerye & seisine. Et in exchange il couuent que les estates a eux lymitte per le exchange sount egalls, car si vn ad estate in fee in sa terre , & lauter ad estate in auter terre forsque pur terme de vye , ou en taile , donques tyel eschange est void, mes si les estates sont egalle, & ses terres ne sont de egall value, vncore le exchange est bone. Auxi vn eschange de rēt pur terre est bone. Issint exchange inter rēt et comon est bõe, et ceo couiet estre p fait.

or without dede (if þ landes be in one selfe county)exchãge their landes,so that euerye of them shal haue others landes to hym, so exchanged in fee,fee taile, or for terme of lyfe,that is called an exchange , and it is good with out lyuerie and seisine. And in exchange it behooueth that the estats to the limited by þ exchãg w equal,for if one haue an estate in fee in hys lãd,& the other hath estate in þ other land but for terme of life, or in taile,thē such exchange is void, but if the estates bee equall, and the landes bee not of equall value , yet the exchange is good. Also an exchange of rent for landes is good so an exchaunge beetwene rent and common is good and that ought to bee by dede.
And

And it behoueth al=
way that these words
(exchange) be in the
dede, oz els nothinge
paſſeth by the dede,
except that he haue
lyuerie and ſeiſine.

Et il couyent toutes
foites que ceux parolx
(exchange)ſont en le
fait, ou auterment ri-
ens paſſa p le fait ſinó
que il ayet lyuerye et
ſeſin.

¶Execution.

¶Execution.

Execution is where
Iudgement is gœ=
uen in any actyon
that the plaintife ſhal
recouer the lande, the
debt, oz damages, as p
caſe is, and when the
wzitt is awarded to
put him in poſſeſſion,
that is called a wzitte
of Execution, e whē
he hath the poſſeſſion
of the land, oz is pay=
ed of the debt, oz dam=
mages, oz hath the bo=
dy of the defendaunt
awarded to pziſon, thē
hee hath execution;
and if the plee bee in
the County, oz court
baron, oz hundzed, and
they deferre p iudge=

Execution, eſt lou
iudgement eſt dõ
en aſcun action
que le plaintife reco-
uera la terre, le dett,
ou dammages, come
le caſe eſt, & quaunt
aſcun briefe eſt agard
de luy mytter en poſ-
ſeſsion, ceo eſt ap-
pell briefe de execu-
tion, & quaunt il ad
le poſſeſsion de le ter-
re, ou eſt paye del
dette ou dammages,
ou ad le corps le de-
fendant agarde al pri-
ſon, donques il ad ex-
ecution, & ſi le plee
ſoit en coúty ou court
baron, ou hundred, et
ils alyenont le iudge-

L iij. ment

ment en fauour del partie , ou per auter encheafon , donques le demaundant auera briefe de Executione iudicij . Mes en briefe de dette home nauera recouerie de null terre, mes de cel que le defendant auoit iour de iudgement rendue. Et de chateux home auera execution folement des chateux, ǵux il auoit iour de execution fue.

ment in fauour of the partie , oz foz other caufe, then the demã=dant fhall haue a wzit of Executione iudicij . But in a wzit of debt a man fhall not haue recouerie of any land, but of that which the defendãt hath the day of the iudgement yel=ded. And of chattells a man fhall haue exe=cution onelye of the chatels which he hath the day of execution fued .

¶Executour.

¶Executour.

EXecutor, eft quant home fait fon teftament & darrein volunt , & en ceo nofma le perfon que executera fon teftament,donques cefty que eft iffint nofme,eft fon executour , & tiel executour auera action vers chefcun dettour de fon teftatour , & fi le exe-

EXecutoz,is when a man maketh hys teftament and laft wil, and therin nameth the perfon that fhall execute his teftamẽt,then he that is fo named is hys executour, & fuch an executoz fhal haue an action againft eue=rie debtour of his tef=tatour, and if the exe=cutozs

cutours haue aſſetts,
euery one to whom
the teſtatour was in=
debt , ſhall haue an
action againſt the exe=
cutour, if hœ haue an
obligation oꝛ ſpecy=
altie , but in euerye
caſe where the teſta=
tour myght wage his
lawe, no action ly=
eth agaynſt the exe=
cutour.

cutours ad aſſettes,
cheſcun a que le teſ=
tatour fuit endette,a=
uera action vers lexe=
cutours ſil ad obliga-
tion ou eſpecialtie ,
mes en cheſcun caſe
lou le teſtatour puiſ-
ſoyt gager ſon ley,
nul action giſt vers
executour.

¶Extinguiſhment.

¶Extinguiſhment.

EXtinguiſhment, is
where a Loꝛde of a
manoꝛ , oꝛ any other,
hath a rent going out
of lande , and he pur=
chaſeth the ſame land,
ſo that hee hath ſuch
eſtate in the lande as
hœ hath in the rent ,
then the rent is ex=
tinct,foꝛ that , that a
manne may not haue
rent going out of his
owne land.And when
any rent ſhal bœ ex=
tinct, it behouꝛth that

EXtinguiſhment, eſt
lou vn ſeygniour
dun manor, ou aſcun
auter, ad vn rent iſſu-
ant daſcun terre , &
il purchaſe meſme le
terre , iſſint que il ad
tiel eſtate en la terre,
come il auoit en le rẽt,
donques le rent eſt ex-
tinct , pur ceo que vn
ne puit auer rent iſſu-
ant hors de ſon terre
demeſne . Et quaunt
aſcun rent ſerra ex-
tinct , il couyent que

le terre & le rent ſcount
en vn maine , & auxy
que leſtate que il ad
ne ſoit defeaſible , &
que il ad auxy bone
eſtate en le terre, comè
en le rent, car ſil ad eſtate en le terre forſque
pur terme de vie , ou
dans,& ad vn fee ſim-
ple en le rent, donques
le rent neſt extinct,mes
eſt en ſuſpence pur cel
temps, & donques a-
pres le terme le rent eſt
reuyue. Auxy ſi ſoyt
ſeignior, meſne, & te-
nant , & le ſeigniour
purchaſe le tenauncie,
donques le meſnaltie
eſt extinct,mes le meſn
auera le ſurpluſage de
rent, ſi aſcun ſoit come
vn rent ſecke. Auxy ſi
home ad chymin ap-
pendaunt , & puys
purchaſe le terre en que
le chimine eſt , dòn-
ques le chimin eſt ex-
tinct , & iſſint eſt de
vn common appen-
daunt.

the lande and the rent
be in one hande,and al
ſo that the eſtate that
he hath be not defeaſa-
ble , and that he haue
as good eſtate in the
land as in the rent;foz
if he haue eſtate in the
lande but foz terme of
life oz yeares , & hath
a fee ſimple in the rent,
then the rent ys not
extinct, but is in ſuſ-
pence foz that time, &
then after þ terme the
rent is reuiued. Alſo if
there be Lozd, Meſne,
& tenaunt, & the Lozd
purchaſeth the tenan-
cie , then the meſnalty
is extinct , but that
meſne ſhal haue þ ſur-
pluſage of the rent, if
there be any, as a rent
ſecke . Alſo if a man
haue a hygh way ap-
pendant, & after pur-
chaſe the land wherein
the hygh way is, then
the way is extinct,& ſo
it is of a common ap-
pendant.

Extor-

¶Extorcion. ¶Extorcion,

Extorcion is a wrong done by an Officer, as a Maior, Baylife, Sherife, Eschetor, or other officer, by colour of his office, in taking excessiue reward or fee, for execution of hys saide office or otherwise, and is no other thinge in deede then plaine robberie, or rather more odious then robberie, for robberie is apparant, and alwayes hath with it the countenance of vice, but extorcion being as great a vice as robberie is, carrieth with it a countenance of vertue, by meanes wherof, it is the more hard to be tryed, or discerned, and therefore the more odyous, and yet some there be that wil not sticke to stretch their office, credyte, and conscyence, to

Extorcion est vn tort fait per vn Officer, come vn Maior, Bailif, Vicount, Eschetor, ou auter officer, colore officij sui, en prendrans excessiue rewarde ou fee, pur execution de son dit office, ou auterment, & nest auter chose en fait que plain robberie, mes plus odible que robberie, car robberie est apparaunt. & tout temps ad oue luy le countenaunce de vice, mes extorcion esteant cy haut vice come robberie est, port oue luy vn countenaunce de vertue, per reason de quel il est le plus dure deste trie, ou discerne, & pur ceo le plus odible, & vncore ascuns il y ad que ne voylent demurre, mes stretch lour office, credyte, & conscience, pur
pur-

purchaſer money, cibi-
en per extortion, come
auterment , accordant
al diſans de le Poet
Virgil .

Quid non mortalia
pectora cogit , auri ſa-
cra fames .

purchaſe money aſwel
by extoztion as other=
wiſe, accozding to the
ſayinge of the Poet
Wirgil.

What can be tolde? oz
what is y that hunger
ſweete of golde doth
not conſtrayne men
moztal to attempt?

¶Failer de Record.

¶Failing of Record.

FAiler de record, eſt
quant vn action de
treſpas ou tiels ſembla-
bles , eſt port enuers
vn , & le defendaunt
dit, que le plaintife de-
uant ceo, port vn ac-
tion pur meſme le treſ-
pas en auter Court, &
recouer damages &c.
Et demaunde iudge-
ment del Court ſi a-
uera arrere ceſt action
&c. Et le plaintife dit
nul tiel recorde , ſur
que le defendaunt ad
iour done a luy, pur
ameſner eins le record,

FAiling of Recozde,
is when an action
of treſpas oz ſuch like
is bzought againſt one
and the defendant ſay=
eth , that the plaintif
befoze thys bzought
an action foz the ſame
treſpaſſe in an other
court, e recouered dā=
mage ec. And demaū=
deth iudgement of the
court, if he ſhal againe
haue this action ec. e
the plaintif ſaith there
is no ſuch recozd, wher
vpon the defendaunt
hath a day gyuen him
to bzing in the recozd,
                        at

at which day he say=
leth, oz bzingeth in
suche a one, as is no
barre to this action,
then he is said to faile
of his recozde, & there
vpon the plaintife shal
haue iudgement to re=
couer &c.

a quel iour il fayle, ou
amesne eyns vn tiel,
que nest barre al cest
action, donques il est
dit de fayler de Re-
corde, & sur ceo le
plaintife auera iudge-
ment de recouer &c.

¶Deede.

¶Fait.

*D*Eede is a pzoofe
and testimonie of
the agreement of the
partie whose deede it
is, to the thinge con=
tayned in the deede, as
a deede of feoffement
is a pzoofe of the ly=
uerie of seisin: foz the
lande passeth by the li=
uerie of seisine, but
when the deede and the
lyuerie are ioyned to=
gether, that is a pzoofe
of the liuerye, and
that the feoffour is
contented, that the
feoffee shall haue the
lande.

F Ait est vn proue
& testimonie de
le agreement del par-
tie quel fait il est, al
chose contayne en le
fait, come vn fait de
feoffement est vne
proue del liuerie de
seisine, car le terre
passa per le liuerie de
seisine, mes quant le
fait & le liuerye est
ioynt ensemble, cest
vn proue del liuerie,
& que le feoffour
est contente que le
feoffee auera le terre.

And note that all

Et nota que toutes
faits

faits ſount ou indent, de q̃ il ad deux , trois , ou pluſors,come le caſe require,de que le feof-for,grauntor, ou leſſor ad vn, le feffee, graun-tee,ou leſſee, vn auter, & peraduenture aſcun auter perſon auxy vn auter &c . ou auter-ment ils ſont faits pol, ou ſingle, & forſque vn, le quel le feoffee , grauntee , ou leſſee ad &c.

Et cheſcun fait con-ſiſt de trois principal choſes (& fils troys ne ſount ioyne enſemble, il neſt perfect fait de lyer les parties,) noſ-ment, eſcripture, ſigil-lation,& deliuerie.

Le primer point eſt eſcripture, per que eſt declare les noſmes del parties al fait , lour habytacion , lour degrees , le choſe graunt,ſur queux con-ſiderations, leſtate li-mit , le temps quant

dædes are either inde-ted,whereof there be two,three, oz moze as the caſe requireth , of whiche the feoffour, grautoz, oz leſſoz hath one,the feffæ,grauntæ, oz leſſæ an other , and peraduenture ſome o-ther bodie alſo ano-ther &c. oz els they are poll dædes oz ſingle, e but one,which the fef-fæ, grauntæ , oz leſſæ hath &c.

And euery dæde con-ſiſteth of iij. pzincipall points , (and if thoſe iij.be not ioyned toge-ther , it is no perfect dæde to binde the par-ties)namely, wziting, ſealing,and deliuery.

The firſt point is wziting , whereby is ſhewed the partyes names to the dæde, their dwelling places, their degræs,the thing graunted, vpon what cōſiderations, theſtate limitted, ÿ time when
it

it was graunted, and
whether simply or vp=
pon condicion, wyth
other such like circum-
stances. But whether
the parties vnto the
deede, writ in the ende
their owne names, or
set therto their marks
(as it is commonlye
vsed,) it maketh no
matter at all (as I
thinke)for that is not
ment where it is said,
that euery deede ought
to haue wryting.

The second poynt is
sealinge, which is a
farther testimonie of
their consents to that
contayned in the deede
as it appereth by these
wordes. In witnesse
whereof &c. alwayes
put in the later end of
deedes,without which
woordes the deede is
insufficient.

And because we are
about sealing and sig=
ning of deedes, it shal
not be amisse (brother

il fuit graunt , & si
simplement , ou sur
condicion , oue auters
ticls semblables cir-
cumstances. Mes si les
parties al fait,escript en
le fine lour nosmes de-
mesne , ou mise a ceo
lour markes (come il
est communement vse)
il ne fayt ascun matter
(come ieo suppose,)
car ceo nest entende
ou il est dit, que chescu
fait couient de auer es-
cripture.

Le second point est
sigillation, que est plus
testimonye de lour
consents al ceo con-
tayne en le fait, come
appiert p ceux parolx.
In cuius rei testimo-
nium &c.toutes foits
mise en le fine de faits,
sauns queux parolls ,
le fait est insufficy-
ent.

Et pur ceo que nous
sumus en sigillation &
signing de faits, il ne
serra de hors (frere
Nicho-

Nicholas) icy a mõ-
ftre a vous , pur le
amoure de antiquy-
tye , le manner del
figning & fubfcribing
de faites en noftre
aunceftors les Saxons
temps , vn fafhion dif-
ferent de ceo que nous
vfe en ceux noftre
ioures , en ceo que
ils a lour faites fub-
fcribe lour nofmes,
(communement ad-
dinge le figne del
crole) & en le fine
mife vn graund num-
ber des teftimonyes,
nient vfant a cel temps
afcũ maner de figil. Et
nous a ceft iour pur
plus fuerty , auxibien
fubfcribe noftre nofm
(nient obftãt c' neft
mult neceffary cõe ieo
ay deuãt dit) mife nře
figlis,& vfe le aid des
teftmoignes auxy.

Ceft prim fafhion
ont continuance per
tout tanque al tempes
del conqueft per les

Nicholas) here to
fhewe you , foz anti=
quities fake, the ma=
ner of figninge and
fubfcribinge of dedes,
in our aunceftours þ
Saxons times , a fa=
fhion differen: from þ
wee vfe in thefe our
daies,in this that they
to their dedes fubfcri-
bed their names(com=
monlye addinge the
figne of the crofe) and
in the end did fett
downe a great num=
ber of witneffes , not
vfinge at that time a=
ny kinde of feale. And
wee at this day foz
moze fuerty,woth fub=
cribe our names (al=
though that bee not
verye neceffarye as I
haue afozefayde) put
to our feales , and
vfe the helpe of tefty=
mony befides.

That fozmer fafhi=
on contynued through
out, vntill the time
of the conqueft by the
Noz=

Normans, whose ma= | Normans, que maners
ner by litle a litle at $ | per petit et petit al dar
légth preualed amógst | rain preuaile ent nous
vs, for the vrst sealed | Car le primer charter
Charter in Englande | sigil en Angliterre est
is thought to be that | pense destre ceo del
of kinge Edward the | roy Edw. le confessor
confessor to $ abbey of | al abbey de westm,
Westm: who (beinge | que (esteaunt educate
brought vp in Nor= | en Normandy) port
mandy) brought into | en cest Realme ceo, et
this realme that, and | ascun auter de lour
for other of their gui= | guyses oue luy. Et
ses with him: And af= | apres le venians de
ter the comminge of | Guillyam le Conque-
Williã $ conqueror, $ | rour, les Normanes,
Normanz liking their | estemans de le cus-
owne coütry customs | tome de lour payes
(as naturally all na= | (come naturalment
tions to) reiected the | toutes nacyons font)
maner that they foüd | reiecte le manner
here, and reteneb their | que ils trouont cy, &
owne, as Ingulphus $ | reteignount lour pro=
Abbot of Croilande, | per, come Ingulphus
who came in with the | le Abbott de Crove-
Conquest witnesseth | lande, que vyent
sayinge: The Nor= | eins oue le Conquest,
mans we change the | testymoigne, dicens,
makinge of writings | Normanni cheiro-
which were woont | graphorum confec-
to bee firmed in Eng= | tionem, cum crucibus
lande withe Crosses | aureis
of

aureis,& alijs fignacu-
lis facris,in Anglia fir-
mari folitam, in ceræ
impreffionem mutant,
modumque fcribendi
Anglicûm reijciunt.
Mes nient obftant ceo
ne fuit fait toùt al vn
temps , mes il encreaft
& vient eins per cœ-
teine fteps & degrees,
iffint que primes &
pur vn feafon le Roy
folement, ou vn peu
auters de le nobilitie
oufter luy, vfe de fi-
giller. Donques le no-
ble homes pur le plus
part, & nul auters, quel
chofe vn home poyt
veyer en le Hiftorie dé
Battel Abbey, ou Ri-
chard Lucy chiefe Iuf-
tice de Engleterre , en
le temps del Roy Hen-
rye le fecond, eft report
de auer blame vne
meane fubiect , pur
ceo que il vfe vn priuat
figilf quant ceo pertain
(come il dit) al Roy
& Nobilitie folement.

of Golde , and other
holie fignes, into the
printing ware, & they
reiect alfo the manner
of the English wry-
ting . Howbeit this
was not done all at
once, but it encreafed
and came forwarde by
certeine fteps and de-
grees, fo that firft and
for a feafon, the kinge
onely , or a fewe other
of the Nobilitie be-
fides him vfed to feale.
Then the Noble men
for the moft part, and
none other , whiche
thinge a man may fe
in the Hiftorie of
Battel Abbey, where
Rycharde Lucy chief
Iuftice of Englande,
in the time of kyng
Henry the feconde is
reported to haue bla-
med a meane fubiect,
for that he vfed a pry-
uate feale, when as
that pertained (as he
fayde) to the kinge
and Nobilitie onely.

It

At which tyme also (as I. Rosse noteth it) they vsed to ingraue in their seales, their owne pictures, & coū= terfaits, couered with a long coate ouer their Armours. But after this the Gentlemen of the better sort tooke vp the fashion, and bee= cause they were not al warriours, they made seales ingrauen wyth their seuerall Coates, or shyeldes of armes, for difference sake. as the same authour re= porteth. At the length, about the time of king Edwarde the thirde, seales became very co mon, so that not onely suche as bore armes vsed to seale but other men also fashioned to them selues signets of their owne deuyse, some takinge the let= ters of their owne names, some flowers, some knottes and flo=

Al quel temps auxy (cōe Iohn Rosse note ceo) ils vse de ingraue en lour sigils, lour pic- tures demesn, & coū- terfaits, couer oue vn lōge tunicle sup lour Armours. Mes apres ceo les Gentlehomes del meliour sort prist le fashion, & pur ceo q̃ ils ne fueront toutes guerrours, ils fesoient sigilles engraue oue lour seuerall coates, ou shieldes de armes, pur difference. come m̃ le authour report. All darraine, al temps del roy Edwarde le tierce, sigils fuerount mult common, issint que non solement tiels que portant armes, vse de sigiller, mes auter: homes auxy fesoyent al eux mesines, signets de lour deuise demes- n, ascuns prentirans les letters de lour nos- mes demesne, ascuns fiores, ascuns & flo-rifhes, afcun aues, ou beaftes , & afcuns auters chofes , come nous ore vncore iournalment voier en vfe. Afcuns auters maners de figillation ouster ceux ad eftre oier enter nous , come nofment ceo del Roy Ed. le iij. per que il done, Al Norman le hunter le hopp , & le hop ville oue toutes les bounds vpfide down, Et en teftmoigne que il foit veray, il morde le cere oue fon fonge dent.

Le femblable de cē (frere Nicholas) noftre reuerende & bone piere , enter auters antiquities pur ma purpofe, monftre a moy en vn lofe chart, mes non moult auncyentment efcript , & pur ceo il voile , que ieo efteema de ceo come ieo penfe bien, il fuit come enfuift.

rifhes, fome birdes, oʒ beaftes, and fome other thinges , as wee now yet daily behold in vfe. Some other maner of fealinge be= fides thefe haue bene hearde of amonge vs, as namely that of king Edward the thirde by which hee gaue to Norman the hunter, the hop and the hop= towne , with all the bofides vpfide towne, and in witneffe that it was footh , hee bitt the waxe with hys foʒe tooth.

The like to this (Bʒother Nicholas) our reuerend and good father , amonge other antiquities feruinge my purpofe , fhewed me in a lofe paper, but not very auncientlye wʒiten , and therefoʒe he willed me to efteme of it as I thought good, it was as fol= loweth.

I willyam Kinge geue to thee Powlen Royden, my hop and my hoplandes , with the wountes vp and wowne , from heauen to earth , from earth to hell , for thee and thine to dwel,from me and mine, to thee and thine,for a tow and a brode arrow, when J come to hunt vppon yarrow. Jn witnesse that this is sothe , J bite this waxe with mye tooth , in presēce of Magg , Maude, and Margerye , and my thirde sonne Henrye.

Also that of Alberic de Weer , conteyning the donation of Hat= field to the which hœ affixed a short blacke hafted knife , like vn= to an olde halfepenny whittle , insteede of a scale , with diuers such like. Bnt foe per aduenture wil thinke that

Ieo Guilliam King done a vous Powlen Royden, ma hop & ma hop terres , oue toutes les bounds vp & downe , de cœlo al terre,de terre ad infern,pur voy & vestres a demurrer , de moy & mes,al toy & vestres,pur vn ark & vn brode sagit quant ieo veigne pur hunter sur yarrow , en teste-moigne que ceo est veray,ieo morde cest cere oue mon dent,en la presence de Magg, Maude , & Marge-rye , & mon tierce fits Henry.

Item ceo de Alberic de Veer, conteignant le donation de Hat-field,al quel il fixe vn curt noier haft cul-tell semblable al vn veel demy.denier whit-tle,en steed de vne si-gil,oue diuers tiels se-blables.Mes asc' perad uenture voilent pense que

que ceux fuerount re-
ceiue en common vſe
& cuſtome, & que ils
ne fuerount les de-
uiſes & pleaſures dun
peu ſinguler perſons,
tyels ne ſount meines
deceiue , que ils que
penſont cheſcun char-
ter & eſcript que nad
ſigille annexe , deſte
cy auncyent come le
conqueſt, lou (en ve-
ritie) ſigillation ne fuit
communement vſe tá-
que al temps del roy
Edwarde le iij . come
ad eſte dit.

Le tierce poynt eſt
deliuerie, quel nyent
obſtaunt il ſoyt myſe
darraine , neſt le me-
inſt, car apres que vn
fait ſoit eſcript , & ſi-
gil , ſil ne ſoit dely-
uer, tout le reſidue eſt
a nul purpoſe.

Et ceſt deliuery doit
eſte fait per le partye
m , ou ſon ſufficyent
garrant, & iſſint il luy
liera quecque eſcript,

that theſe were recei-
ued in common vſe &
cuſtome, and that they
were not rather ẏ de-
uiſes & pleaſures of a
few ſinguler perſons,
ſuch as are no leſſe de-
ceiued, then they that
deme euery charter &
wꝛitinge that hath no
ſeale annexed, to be as
auncient as the Con-
queſt, whereas in dede
ſealinge was not com-
monly vſed, til ẏ time
of Kinge Edward the
third, as hath bene al-
ready ſaide.

The third point is
deliuerye, which all-
though it be ſet laſt,
is not the leaſt, foꝛ af-
ter that a dede be wꝛi-
ten, and ſealed, if it be
not delyuered al the
reſt is to no purpoſe.

And this deliuerie
ought to be done by ẏ
party him ſelfe, oꝛ his
ſufficient warraunt,
and ſo it ſhall bynde
him, whoſoeuer wꝛote

oꝫ

or sealed the same, and by this last acte the dede is made perfecte accordinge to the intent and effect thereof and therefore in deeds the deliuerie is to bee proued &c. So thus you see, that writinge and sealinge without deliuerie, is nothinge to purpose. That sealinge and deliuerie where there is no writinge, worketh nothinge, nor writinge and deliuery without sealinge also maketh no dede. Therefore they al ought iointlye to concurre to make a perfect dede, as is before saide.

ou sigille ceo, & per cest darrayne acte, le fait est fait perfect accordaunt all entant & effecte de ceo, & pur ceo en faits le deliuery est deste proue &c. Issint poies veier que escript, & sigillation sauns deliuerye est a nul purpose. Que sigillation & deliuerie, lou nest ascun escripture worke nul chose, Ne escripture & deliuerie sauns sigillation auxy, fayt nul fayt. Et pur ceo ils tout doyent iointment concurre pur faire vn perfecte fait, come est auauntdyt.

¶Farme or ferme.

¶Farme ou Ferme.

Farme or ferme, is the chiefe mesuage in a billage, or towne, and therto beelonging great demeasnes of al sortes, and hath bene

Farme, ou ferme, est le chief mesuage en vn village, ou towne, & a ceo appurtenaunt graunde demeasnes de toutes sorts, & ad este

M.iij.   vse

vfe defte leffe pur tme de vie, ans, ou a volunt.

Item le rent que eft referue fiir tiel leas, ou femblables, eft appell, farme,ou ferme.

Et farmour, ou fermour, eft celuy que occupya le farme, ou ferme ou eft leffee de ceo.

Auxi en afcun lieus, & counties, chefcun leffee pur vie, ans, ou al volunt, nyent obftaunt il foit dun petite cottage, ou meaf. en appel farmor, ou fermor.

Et nota, que ils fount appels farmes, ou fermes, del Saxon paroll, Feormian, que fignifie pur feede, ou render victuall. Car eft auncyent temps, lour referuations fuer cybien (ou pur le plus part) en victuall come argent, tanque al darraine, & ceo

bfed to be let for terme of lyfe, yeares, or at will.

Also the rent that is referued bpon fuch or like leafes, is called farme, or ferme.

And farmor, or fermour is hee that occuppeth the farme, or ferme, or is leffee thereof.

Also in fome places, and countics euery leffee, for life, yeres, or at will, although it be of neuer fo fmal a cottage or houfe, is called farmor, or fermour.

And note, that they are called farmes, or fermes, of the Saxon worde Feormian, which fignifieth to feede, or yelde victuall. For in the auncient time, their referuatiõs were as well (or for the moze parte) in victualles, as money, bntil at the laft, and that chiefely

chiefely in the tyme
of Kinge Henry the
first (by agreement)
the reseruation of bic=
tualles , was tour=
ned into ready mo=
ney , and so hitherto
hath continued among
most men.

principalment en le
temps del Roy Hen-
ry le primer (per a-
grement) le reseruaciõ
de victuals , fuerount
conuert en redy ar-
gent,et issint vncore ad
continue enter plures
homes.

¶Fee farme.

¶Fee farme.

FEe farme is when
a tenaunt holdeth
of his lord in fee sim-
ple , payinge to him
the value of halfe , or
of the thirde,or of the
fowerth part or of o=
ther part of the land,
by the yeare. And hee
that holdeth by fee
ferme , ought to doe
no other thinge then
is conteyned in the
feoffement , but one=
ly fealtie, for that be=
longeth to al kinde of
tenures.

FEe ferme,est quant
vn tenaunt tyent
de son seigniour en
fee simple rendaunt
a luy le value del moi-
tie , ou de tierce par-
te ou quater par-
te , ou de auter par-
te del terre, per an,
& que tyent en fee
ferme ne doyt faire
auter chose mes si-
come est copteyne en
le feoffement forsque
fealtie , car ceo ap-
pent a toutes maners
tenures.

¶Feoffement.

¶Feoffement.

M .iiij Feoffe-

FEoffement eft lou vn done terre a vn auter en fee fimple, & il delyuer feyfin & poffeffion del terre, ceo eft vn feoffement.

FEffement is where a man geueth lands to an other in fee fimple, and delyuereth feifin and poffeffion of the lande that is a feoffement.

¶Feffor & feffee.

¶Feffor, and Feffee.

FEoffour eft celuy que enfeoffe, ou fait feoffement al auter de terres ou tenemēts, en fee fimple. Et feffee eft celuy, que eft enfeoffe, ou a que le feoffement eft iffint fait.

FEoffor is he that infeffeth, oʒ maketh a feoffement to an other of landes, oʒ tenementes, in fee fimple. And feoffee is hee, who is infeffed, oʒ to whōm the feoffement is fo made.

¶Fireboote.

¶Fireboote.

FIreboote eft neceffarie boys pur arder, quel per le comon ley, leffee pur ans, ou pur vie, poyt prender en fon terre, nient obftaunt il ne foit expreffe en fon leas, & nient obftaunt il foit vn leas per parol tantū

FIreboote is neceffary wood to-burne, whiche by the common lawe, leffee foʒ yeres, oʒ foʒ life, may take in his grounde, although it bee not expʒeffed in his leafe: and although it bee a leafe by woʒde onely with

without writynge.
But if hee take more
then is needeful, he shal
be punished in wast.

ſauns fayte . Mes ſi¹
priſt plus que beſoi-
gne , il ſerra piunye
en waſt.

¶Fledwite

¶Fledwite.

Fledwite, that is to
bee quyte from a-
mercements when an
outlawed fugitiue cō-
meth to the kinges
peace of hys owne
will , or beinge ly-
cenced.

FLedwite , hoc eſt
quietum eſſe de a-
merciamentis   cum
quis vdagatus fugi-
tiuus veniat ad pa-
cem domini Regis
ſponte , vel licentia-
tus.

¶Flemeſwite.

¶Flemieſwite.

Flemeſwite, that is,
that you may haue
the cattel, or amerce-
ments of your man or
fugitiue.

FLemeſwite , hoc eſt
quod habeatis cat-
talla ſiue amerciamē-
ta hominis veſtri fu-
gitiui.

¶Fletwit.

¶Fledwit.

Fletwit (or Flit-
wit) that is to bee
quite from contention
and conuicts, and that
you maye haue plea
thereof in your court

FLedwit (ou Flit-
wit) hoc eſt quie-
tum eſſe de contenti-
oue & conuictis, &
quod habeatis placi-
tū inde in curia veſtra,
&c

& amerciamenta, quia (flit) anglice ē Tēfone gallice.

and the amercements, for (Flit) in Englifh is Cenfone in french.

¶Forftall.

¶Forftall.

FOrftalle, hoc eft quietum effe de a- merciamentis & cat- tallis arreftatis infra terram veftram, & a- merciamenta inde pro uenientia.

FOrftall, that is to bee quite of amer- cementes and cattels arrefted within your lande, and the amer- cements thereof com- ming.

¶Foreftaller.

¶Forftaller.

FOrftaller eft celuy que achate blees, auers, ou auter mar- chandize quecunque eft vendible, per le chi- min quant il vient al markets, faires, ou tiels femblables lieus defte vend' al entent que il poet vender ceo auter- foits al vn plus haut & chare price, en pre- iudice & dammage de le common weale & people &c.

Le penaltie pur ceux

FOrftaller is he that buieth Corne, Cat- tell, or other Mar- chaundize whatfoe- uer is falable, by the way, as it commeth to markets, faires, or fuch like places to bee fold to the intent that he may fel the fame a- gaine at a more high and deere price in pre- iudice and hurt of the common wealth and people &c.

The paine for fuch

as are conuiæ thereof ec. is the first tyme, a= mercement, and losse of the thing so bought, the seconde time iudg= ment of the pillozye: The third time impzi= sonment and Raun= some : The fowerth time abiuration of the towne ec.

queux sont conuict de ceo &c . en le primer téps amercement, & le parde del chose issint achat . Le second téps iudgement de pillory. Le tierce temps im- prisonment & raun- some . Le quater temps abiuration del ville &c.

¶Franches Royal.

¶Franches Royall.

FRanches Royal, is where the Queene graynts to one and to his heires, that they shalbee quite of tolle. oz such like.

FRaunches Royall , est lou le Roygne graunt al vn & a ses heires que ils serrount quite de tolner, vel hu- iusmodi &c.

¶Free mariage.

¶Frankemariage.

FRee maryage , is when a man seised of landes in fee simple, gyueth it to an other man, and to his wyfe (who is the daughter Sister oz otherwise of kinne to the donoz) in free mariage, by vertue

FRankemariage, est quaunt vn home seisie de terres en fee simple done ceo al auter home & a sa fee (que é file, soer, ou au- terment de kynne al donour,) en franke- mariage , per vertue
de

de queux parolx ils
ount vn eſtate en ſpe-
cyall taile, & tien-
dra le terre del do-
nour quit de toutes
manners de ſeruices
tanque le 4. degree
ſoit paſſe, accountants
eux meſmes in le pri-
mer degree, ſinon
fealtye, queux ils fi-
eront, pur ceo que il
eſt incydent a toutes
tenures forſque frank-
almoigne. Et tiel
done poit eſtre fayt
cybien apres mariage
ſolempniſe, come de-
deuant. Et home po-
it doner terres al ſon
fits in frankemariage
cibien come a ſa file,
per le opinion de maſ-
ter Fitzherbert en ſon
briefe de Champerty
H. Mes il appiert au-
terment en maſter Li-
tleton, et en maſter
Brook tiſ Frankma-
riage P. 10. Et iſsint
il fuit. tenus clere en
Graies Inne en lent

of which words they
haue an eſtate in ſpe-
cyall tayle, and ſhall
hold the lande of the
onour quite of al ma-
ner of ſeruyces vntil
the fowerth degree be
paſt accomptinge the
ſelues in the firſt de-
gree except fealtye,
which they ſhall be
becauſe it is incy-
dent to all tenures ſa-
uinge free almes. And
ſuch gift may be made
as wel after mariage
ſolempniſed as before.
And a man may geue
landes to hys ſonne
in free mariage, as
well as to hys daugh-
ter by the oppnyon
of Maſter Fitzherbert
in hys wzitt of cham-
pertye. H. But it
appeareth otherwyſe
in Maſter Lyttleton,
and in Maſter Brooke
titulo Frankemarry-
age Placito decimo. And
ſo it was holden clere
in Graies Inne in let
An-

Anno 1576.18.Eliz.
by the right woꝛſhip=
full maſter Rhodes the
reader there.

Anno 1576. 18.Eli.
per le droit worſhipful
maſter Rhodes donꝗs
lector la.

¶Freeholde.

FReeholdis an eſ=
tate that a mann
hath in landes oꝛ
tenementes,oꝛ pꝛofite
to be taken in fee ſim=
ple,taile,foꝛ terme of
his owne life , oꝛ foꝛ
terme of an others life
And vnder that,there
is no free hold:foꝛ he ꝑ
hath eſtate foꝛ peares
oꝛ holdeth at wil hath
no free hold:but they
are called chattels.

And of free holdes
there are two ſoꝛtes
that is to ſay,freehold
in deede, and freeholde
in lawe.

Freeholde in deede,
is when a mann hath
entred into landes ,oꝛ
tenementes , and is
ſeaſed thereof really,
actuallye, and in deede

¶Franktenement

FRanktenement ē
vn eſtate que hōe
ad en terres , ou
tenementes,ou profit
a prendre, en fee ſim-
ple , taile ; pur terme
de ſon vie demeſne,
ou pur terme dauter
vye.   Et ſouth ceo il
neſt   franktenement,
car il que ad eſtate pur
ans, ou tient a volunt
nad aſcū franktenemē
mes ils ſōt appel chatt̄.

Et de franktenemr̄ts
il y ad deux ſorts, ceſt
aſcauoir , franketenāt
en fait,& franktenant
en ley.

Franktenaunt en
fait,eſt quant vn hom
ad entred en terres on
tenementes,& eſt ſei-
ſie de ceo , reallment
actualment,& en fayt,
ſicome

Sicome le pier ſeyſie de terres ou tenements en fee ſimple deuie, & ſon fites enter en eux come heire a ſon pier, dōques il ad vn frank-tenemēt en fait perſon entrie.

Franktenement en ley, eſt quaunt terres ou tenements ſont diſcend' al vn home, & il poet enter en eux quāt a luy pleſt, mes nad vncore fayt ſon entrie en fait, come en le caſe auauntdit, ſi le pier eſteaunt ſeiſie de terre en fee ſimple deuie ſeiſie, & ils dyſcende al ſon fits, mes le fites nad vncore enter en fait en eux, ore deuaunt ſon entrie, il ad vn franktenēt en ley.

As if the father ſeiſed of lands oz tenements in fee ſimple dieth, and his ſonne entreth into the ſame, as heire to his father, then he hath a freehold in deede by his entry.

Freeholde in lawe, is when landes oz tenementes, are dyſcended to a man and hee may enter into them when he woil, but hath not yet made his entry in deede, as in the caſe afozeſaid, if the father beinge ſcyled of landes in fee ſimple die ſeiſed, and they diſced to his ſonne, but the ſonne hath not yet entred into thē in deede, nowe beefoze his entrie hee hath a freehold in lawe.

¶Freſhſuite.

¶Freſhſuit.

FRreſhſuit, eſt quant vn hōe é robbe, &

FReſhſuit, is when a man is robbed, and the

the partye so robbed,
followeth the felon
immediatlye, and ta=
keth him wyth the
manner, oz otherwise,
and then bzingeth an
appeale against him &
doth conuince him of
the felony by verdict,
which thinge beinge
inquyred of foz the
Queene and found, the
party robbed shal haue
restitutiõ of his goods
againe.

Also it maye bee
sayde that the partye
made freshesuite al=
though he take not the
theefe presently, but
that it be halfe a yere,
oz a yeare after the
robbery done, befoze
hee bee taken: if so bee
that the partye rob=
bed do what lyeth in
him, by dylygent in=
quiry and searche to
take him, yea, and al=
though hee bee taken
by some other body,

le partye issint robbe,
pursua le felon im-
medyatement, & luy
pryst oue le man-
ner, ou autrement,
& donques port vn
appeale enuers luy,
& luy conuynce del
felonye per verdicte,
le quel chose este-
aunt enquire par le
Roygne & troue, le
partye robbe auera
restitucion de ses by-
ens arr'.

Item il poet este dit
que le partie fait fresh-
suite, nient obstaunt il
ne prist le felon pre-
sentment, mes que
il soit demy an, ou
vn an apres le robbe-
rye fait, deuaunt que
il soit prise, si soyt issint que le party robbe
fayt taunt que en luy
est, per diligent en-
quiry, & searche de
luy prender, nyent
obstaunt que il est
prise per vn auter hõe,
vn→

vncore ceo ferra dit
bone freſhſuit.

Et iſſint freſhſuite
eſt quaunt le ſeigni-
our vient pur diſtreig-
ner pur rent ou ſer-
uice, & le owner des
beaſtes fait reſcous,
& enchaſe eux en auſ
terre que ne tenus del
fñr, & le ſeigñ enſuer
preſentment,& repriſt
eux, cē appel freſhſuit.
Et iſſint en auter ſē-
blables caſes.

¶Gager de deliueráce.

GAger de delyue-
raunce eſt, lou vn
ſua repleuin des byens
priſe, mes il nad de-
liuere des byens, &
lauter auowa, & le
pleintife monſtrē que
le defendaunt eſt vn-
core ſeyſie &c. &
pria que le defen-
daunt gagera dely-
ueraunce, donques
il mettera eyns ſuer-
tie ou pledge pur rede-

yet this ſhal be ſaide
treſheſuite.

And ſo freſhſuit is,
when the loꝛd com-
meth to diſtreine foꝛ
rent oꝛ ſeruice, and þ
owner of the beaſtes
doth make reſcous, ē
dꝛiueth them into o-
thers groũde that is
not holden of the loꝛd,
and the loꝛd followeth
pꝛeſently and taketh
them, this is called
freſh ſuit, and ſo in o-
ther like caſes.

¶Gager of deliuerãs.

GAger of deliuerans
is where one ſueth
a repleuin of goodes
taken, but he hath not
delyuery of the goods,
and the other auow-
eth, and the plaintife
ſheweth that the de-
fendant is yet ſeiſed
ēc. and pꝛaieth that þ
defendant ſhall gage
the deliuerance, then
he ſhal put in ſuertye
oꝛ pledges foꝛ þ rede-
liuē

liuerance, and a wryt shall go foorth to the Sherife for to redeli-uer the goodes &c. But if a man claime proper-tie, he shal not gage þ deliuerance. Also if he say that the beasts bee dead in the pound, hee shal not gage &c. Also a man shall neuer gage the deliuerance before that they be at issue, or demurrer in the lawe.

liuerance, & briefe is-sera al vicont pur rede-liuer &c. Mes si home claime propertie, il ne gagera deliueraunce. Auxy si il dit que les auers sount mortes en le pounde, il ne gage-ra &c. Auxy home ne gagera iammeis le deliueraunce auaunt que ils sount a is-sue, ou demurre en ley.

¶Warde.

¶Garde.

Warde, is when an infant whose aun-cestor held by knights seruice, is in the ward or keeping of the Lord of whom those landes were holden. And if the tenant hold of dy-uers Lordes dyuers landes, the Lord of whom the land is hol-den by prioritie, that is to say, by the more ylder tenure, shal haue

Garde, est quant vn enfant que aunce-stour tient per seruyce de chiualrie, est en le garde & custodie de le seigniour de que ils fueront tenus. Et si le tenaunt tient de diuers seigniors dyuers terres, celuy seigniour de que il tient per prio-ritie, cestascauoier, per le plus auncy-ent Tenure, auera la garde del enfant, mes si vn tenure soyt auxy auncient que le auter, donques celuy que primes happa le garde del corps, gardera ceo, mes en ceo case, chescun seigniour auera le garde del terre que est tenus de luy, mes si le tenaunt tyent del Roigne en chiefe, donques le Roigne per sa prerogatiue auera le garde del corps & de tout le terre que est tenus de el, & de chescun auter seigniour.

the wardshippe of the infant, but it one tenure be as olde as the other, then he that first happeth to haue the warde of the body shal keepe it, but in that case euery Lord shall haue the warde of the land that is holden of him, but if the tenant hold of the Queene in chiefe, then she by her prerogatiue shal haue the ward of the bodie, and of al the land that is holden of her, & of euery other Lord.

¶ Gardeine.

¶ Wardeine.

Gardeine plus properment est celuy que ad le gard ou custodie dun heire, & de terre tenus per seruice de chiualrie, ou de vn de eux a son vse demesne durant le nonage del heire, et deins cest teps ad le bestowing del corps del heire,

Wardein most properly is he that hath the wardship or keeping of an heire, & of lande holden by knightes seruice, or of one of them to his owne vse, during the nonage of the heire, & with that time hath the bestowing of the bodie of the heires

to

in marpage at his ple=
fure, without difper=
agement.

And of Wardeines
there be ij.fo2ts, name
ly, gardein in ryght, &
gardein in dæde.

Gardein in right is
he that by reafō of his
feignio2ie is feifed of
the wardfhip o2 kæ=
ping of the lande, & of
the heire, during the
nonage of the heire.

Gardein in dæde, is
where the Lo2d after
his feifin, as afo2efaid,
graunteth by dæde o2
wythout dæde, the
wardfhip of the land,
o2 of the heire, o2 of
both to an other, by
fo2ce of which graunt
the grauntee is in pof=
feffion, then ys the
graūtæ called gardein
in dæde.

And this gardein in
dæde may graunt the
heire to another alfo,
but that other is not
p2opcrly called garden

en mariage al fon vo-
lunt fauns difperage-
ment.

Et de gardeins il y
ad ij. fortes nofmemt,
gardeiñe en droit, &
gardeine en fait.

Gardein en droit, eft
celuy que per reafon
de fon feigniorie eft
feifie del gardfhip ou
cuftodie del terre, et
del heire, durant le no-
nage del heire.

Gardeine en fait, eft
lou le feigniour apres
fon feifin, come auant-
dit, graunta per fait, ou
fans fait, le gardfhuppe
del terre ou del heire,
ou dambideux a vne
auter, per force de
quel graunt, le graun-
tee eft en poffeffion,
donques eft le graun-
tee appell gardeine en
fait.

Et ceft gardeine en
fait poit graunt le heire
al auter auxy, mes ceft
auter neft proper-
ment appell gardeyne

en fait , car ceo eſt le grauntee del garden en droit ſolement. Et icy poies veier (Frere Nicholas) quel miſerye vient apres ceſt tenure per ſeruice de chiualrye ſi le tenant moruſt relinquens ſon heire deins age , coment le pouer infant poet eſtre toſſe , & tumble , choppe , & change , et achate & vende ſemble al vn male chiual en Smith-field,et que plus eſt,il ſerra marry a que pleſt ſon garden,de que en-ſuiſt mult male.

in dede foʒ that is the grauntee ot the Gar-den in rigʒt onꝑly,and here ꝑou may ſæ(bʒo-ther Nicholas)ſhat miſerꝑe folloſeth ꝑ tenure bꝑ knigʒtes ſeruice if the tenaunt dꝑeth leauinge hꝑs heire ſithin age,hoſ the pooʒe childe may bæ toſſed , and tum-bled,chopped and cha-ged, ſougʒt and ſold like a Jade in Smith fielde , and that moʒe is married to ſhom it pleaſeth his garden, ſhereof enſue manꝑ euells.

¶Garniſhement.

¶VVarninge.

GArniſhement eſt quant vn action de detinue des char-ters eſt port vers vne & le defendant dit que les charters fuerount deliuer a luy per le plaintife,& per vn au-ter,ſur certeine condi-

VVArning is ſhẽ an action of de-tinue of charters is bʒougʒt againſt one,⁊ the defendant ſaieth,ꝑ the charters ſere de-liuered to him bꝑ the plaintife,and bꝑ an o-ther vpõ certein condi-tions

tions, and praiethe þ the other may be war= ned to pleade with the plaintife whether the conditions be perfo2= med o2 noe, and there= vpon a w2ite of Scire facias ſhall goe fo2the againſt him. And that is called warninge.

tions, & pria que lau= ter ſoit garnie de plea= der oue le plaintiſe ſi les conditions ſount perimplyes ou nemy, & ſur ceo vn briefe de Scire facias iſſera vers luy. Et ceo eſt ap= pel vn garniſhement.

¶Gauelate.

¶Gauelate.

Gauelate, is a ſpecy= all and auncyent kinde of Ceſſauit vſed in Kent where þ cuſ= tome of Gauelkinde continueth: whereby the tenant ſhal fo2fait his landes and tene= ments, to the lo2d of whom they are holden if he withd2awe from his lo2de his due rets and ſeruices, after thys manner as fol= loweth.

Gauelate, eſt vne ſpeciall & auncy= ent kinde de Ceſſa= uit vſed in Kent ou le cuſtome de Gauel= kinde continue, per quel le tenant fo2fe= tera ſes terres & tene= ments al ſeignior de que ils ſount tenus, ſil detaine de ſon ſeigni= our ſes due rentes & ſeruyces, ſolon= que ceſt manner que enſuiſt.

If any tenaunt in Gauelkinde, with= holde hys rent, & his ſeruices of þ tenemēt

Si aſcun tenaunt en Gauelkind retayne ſa rent, & ſes ſeruy= ces de le tenement

N.iij.   que

que il tient de fon feig-
niour, querge le feyg-
niour per agarde de fa
Court, de iij. femaines
en trois femaines , de
trouer diftreffe fur cel
tenement , iefque a le
quart court ,a toutfoit
per tefmoigneages; Et
fi dedeins cel temps ne
troue diftreffe en cel
tenement , per queux
il puiffe fon tenaunt
iuftifer . Donq; a la
quart court foit agarde
que il preigne cel tene-
ment en fa maine , en
nofme de diftreffe, auxi
come boefe ou vache,
& le tient vn an & vn
iour , en fa maine, fans
maine ouerer , deyns
quel terme , fi le te-
naunt vyent , & rend
fes arrerages , & fayt
reafonables amendes
de la deteyner , adonc
eit , & ioife fon tene-
ment, ficome les aun-
ceftours & luy a-
uaunt riendront . Et
fil ne vient deuaunt

Which hee holdeth of
his lozd, let the Lozde
feeke by the awarde of
his Court from thze
weekes to iij. weekes,
to find foe diftres bp̃
the tenements bntil þ
iiij. court , alwaies ẏ
witneffes. And if win
that time , he can finde
no diftres in that te-
nement , whereby hee
may haue iuftice of his
tenaunt. Then at the
fowerth court let pt
be awarded, that hee
ſhal take that tenemẽt
into his hande , in the
name of a diftres, as if
it were an oxe oz a cow
& let him kept it a yere
& a day in his hand w-
out manuring it : win
which terme if the te-
naunt come & pay hys
arrerages,& make rea-
fonable amendes foz þ
witholding,then let him
haue & enioy his tene-
ment as his aũceft ozs
& he befoze held it:& if
he do not come befoze
the

the yeare and the day paſte, then let the Lord goe to the next Countie court wyth the witneſſes of hys owne Court, and pronounce there this proceſſe, to haue further witneſſe,and by the aſwarde of hys Court, (after the Countie court holden) he ſhall enter and manure in thoſe lands and tenements as in his owne. And if the tenaunt come afterwarde, and will rehaue his tenements,& hold them as he did before, let hym make agreement wyth the Lord,according as it is aunciently ſaid.

Hath he not ſince any thing gyuen, nor hath he not ſince any thing paid: Then let hym pay fyue pounde for hys were er before hee beecome tenaunt or holder againe.

le an & le iour paſſes donc auaga le ſeyg-niour al procheyne Countie Court ſuyant oue teſmoygnes de ſa Court , & face la pronouncyer cel proceſſe pur teſmoynage auer , & per a-garde de ſa Court(apres ceo countie tenue) entra & meynouera en cels terres & tene-mentes , ſicome en ſon demeſne . Et ſi la tenaunt vyent a-pres , & voyle re-auer ſes tenementes, & tener ſicome il fiſt deuaunt , face gree al ſeygniour , ſicome il eſt auncyentment dyſt.

Neghe ſith ſeldo, & ghe ſith geld , & v. pound for the wer , er he become heal-der.

Il y ad afcuns copies que ad le primer Verfe iffint efcript.

Nifith yelde, and ni-fith gelde.

Et auters iffint.

Nighefith yelde, and nighefith gelde.

Mes ceux ne differ en fignification, auter co-pies ont ceo folonque ceft fort.

Nigond fith felde, & nigond fith gelde.

Ceftafcauoir, payera il nouies foits, & no-uies foits repay.

¶Gauelkinde.

G Auelkinde eft vne cuftome annex & currant oue terres en Kent appel Gauelkind terres tenus en aunci-ent Socage tenure. Et eft penfe per les eru-dite en Antiquities, defte appell Gauel-kinde de Gyue al kin, ceft adire a toutes les kynne en vne lyne,

There bee some copies that haue the firft Uerfe thus written.

Nifith yelde, and nifith gelde.

And others thus.

Nighefith yelde, and ni-ghefith gelde.

But thefe differ not in fignification, other coppyes haue it after this fort.

Nigondfith felde, and nigondfith gelde.

That is to fay, let him ix. times pay, and ix. times repay.

¶Gauelkinde.

G Auelkind is a cuf-tome annexed, and going with landes in Kent called gauelkind landes, holden by auncient Socage tenure, And is thought by y skilfull in Antiqui-ties, to be called Ga-uelkind of Gyue al kyn, y is to fay, to all the kindred in one line

ac-

according as it is vsed among the Germans, from whom we Englishmen, and chiefly of Kent come. Or els it is called Gauelkind of gyue all kinde, that is to say, to all the male children, for kinde in Dutch signifyeth a male childe. And dyuers other like coniectures are made by the of the name (Gauelkind) which I omyt of purpose for shortnes sake, because that here you looke (Brother Nicholas) as you desired me, y̆ I should speak somewhat largely concerninge other more nædeful matters for your purpose, which you ar deurous to know as touching Gauelkind lãds, both because you were born in Kẽt, & also are most abyding there, & therefore you thinke to bæ ignorant of y̆ maners

accordant come est vse enter les Germans, de que nous Anglois, & especielment de Kent venimus. Ou il est appell Gauelkinde, de gyue al kinde, cest a-dire al touts les males, car kinde en Dutch signifie vn male. Et diuers auters semble coniectures sount fait per eux de le nosme (Gauelkinde) le quel ieo omitte de purpose pur breuitie, pur ceo que cy vous expectes (Frere Nicholas) si-come vous moy re-quirast, que ieo escri-uera largement con-cernaunt auter plus needefull matter pur vostre purpose, queux vous desirast de sca-uoir, concernant Ga-uelkind terres, & pur ceo que vous fues nee en Kent, & auxy es plus demurraunt la, & pur ceo vous pen-ses, patriæ res nescire
de-

dedecus.

Pur ſatisfier voſtre demaunde en ceo : Ieo aye pur ceo myſe pur vous cy les auncyent cuſtomes de Kent, ſicome ils fueront verament & carefully de puiſne temps publie oueſque aſcuns caſes ſur eux collecte hors del ceux Liuers , que font aſcun mencion de ceo , quel voit ieo penſe ſatisfier voſtre deſire a-large . Et primerment vous ſcauoies que ceux Gauelkinde cuſtomes, ſont de bon antiquitie port eins cy per les Saxons, Intes , & Angles Germans, de que nous Anglois diſcende (come eſt auantdit) & fueront per eux vſe, & relinquy cy , & iſſint continue en force, tanq; Guilliam Duke de Normandie Conquer tout Engl, (Kent tantſolement forſpris)

oz cuſt. of your natiue cōtry were a foul thīg

To ſatiſſie your requeſt in this : I haue therefoze ſet you here doſone , the auncyent cuſtomes of Kent, is they haue very truely & carefully of late bē publiſhed, tō ſome caſes vpon them, gathered out of thoſe bookes that make any mēction hereof, ſohich ſoyll I think contēt your deſire at full. And firſt you muſt knoſo , that theſe Gauelkind cuſtomes are of good antiquitie , bzought in hither by the Saxons, Intes , and Ingles Germans, from ſohom ſoe Engliſhmen dyſcend (as is afozeſaid) & ſoere by them vſed, & left here, & ſo continued in fozce , vntyll Willyam Duke of Nozmandie , conquered all Englande, (Kent onely excepted)
ſohich

which he had by com=
poſicion & not by con=
queſt. And in this cō=
poſycion the valiant
Kentiſhmen obtayned
a graunt of the conty=
nuation of their cuſ=
tomes of Gauelkinde,
which euer ſince they
haue vſed in the ſame
countrey, & thus they
are as folloſweth.

¶The Cuſtomes of Kent

Theſe are the vſa=
ges & cuſtomes, the
which the comminalty
of Kent claymeth to
haue in the tenements
of Gauelkind, & in the
men of Gauelkind, al=
loſwed in Eire befoꝛe
John of Berwicke &
his Compainions the
Juſtices in Eire m
Kent, the xxj. yere of
king Edw. the ſonne
of king Henrie.

That is to ſay, that
all the bodies of Ken=
tiſhmen be fꝛee alſwell

le quel il auoit per cō-
poſicion, & nemy per
conqueſt. Et en ceſt
compoſicion les vali-
ant Kentois obtayne-
roit vn graunt de le
continuation de lour
cuſtomes de Gauel-
kind, le ql touts temps
puis ils ount vſe en
meſine le pais, & ils
ſont come enſuiſt.

¶Les Cuſtōes de Kēt.

Ces ſont les vſages
& les cuſtomes, les
queux le comminaltie
de Kent claimant auer
en tenements de Ga-
uelkinde, & en g ntes
Gauelkindeis, allowes
en Eire Iohn de Ber-
wicke & ſes compa-
nions les Iuttices en
Eire, en Kent, le
xxj. an le Roy Ed-
warde, ſites le Roy
Henrie.

Ceſtaſcauoir, que
touts les corps de Ken-
teis, ſoient franks auxy
come

come les auters frankes corps Dengleterre.

Ceſt choſe ad eſte puis confeſſe deſte ve-ray, come il appiert en 30. E. 1. in Fitzher-bert Titulo Villenage placito 46. Ou il eſt tenus ſufficient pur vn home de auoyder lob-iection de bondage, a-dire que ſon pere fuit nee en Kent, mes ſil voit ſeruer en ceſt caſe adire, que il meſm fuit nee en Kent, il eſt (pur bone cauſe) deſte doubt.

2 Et que ils ne duiſ-ſent le Eſcheatour le Roy eſlier, ne vnques en nul temps ne feſoy-ent. Mes le Roy pre-igne ou face prender, tiel come luy plerra, de ceo que ſoit miſtier a luy ſeruer.

3 Et que ils puiſſent lour terres & lour te-neméts done & vend, ſans conge demaunder

as the other free bo-dyes of England.

This thing hath ben ſince confeſſed ſo be true, as it appeareth in 30. E. 1. in Fitzherbert titulo Villenage pla-cito 46. Where it is holden ſufficient for a man to auoyde the ob-iection of bondage, to ſay that hys father was borne in Kent. But whether it wyl ſerue in ye caſe to ſay, ye him ſelfe was borne in Kent, it is (for good reaſon)to be doubted.

2 And ye they ought not the Eſchetour of the king to choſe, nor euer in any time dyd they. But the kings ſhall take or cauſe to be taken ſuch a one as it ſhall pleaſe him, to ſerue him in ye which ſhalbe needefull.

3 And that they may their lands & their te-nements gyue and ſel, without licence aſked
of

of their Lordes : Sa=
uing vnto the Lordes
the rents & the serup=
ces due out of the same
tenements.

4 And that all, and
euery of them, may by
writ of the king, or by
plaint,pled for the ob=
tayning of their right,
aswell of their Lordes
as of other men.

5 And they claime al
so,that the comminaltie
of Gauelkinde menne
which hold none other
then tenements of ga=
uelkind nature, ought
not to come to the com=
mon summons of the
Eire,but onely by the
Borsholder,& iiij.men
of the Borough . Ex=
cept the townes which
ought to aunswere by
xij.men in the Eire.

The like to this pri=
uiledge is enioyed at
this day in the She=
rifs Lathe,where ma=
ny whole borows , be
excused by the onely

a lour seigniors : Sa-
ues a seignorages les
rents & les seruic' dues
de mesmes les tene-
mentes.

4. Et que touts, &
chescun puissoit per bf
le Roy , ou per plaint,
plede pur lour droyt
purchaser , auxy byen
de lour seignorages ,
come des auters gets.

5 Et clayment auxy,
que la comminalf de
Gauelkindeis , que ne
tenent mes que tene-
méts Gauelkindeis,ne
deuient vener a le
commune summons
del Eire , mes que per
Borgesaldre , & iiij.
homes de la Borough,
hors prise les vylles ,
que deuient responder
per xij. homes en le
Eire .

Le semble du cest
priuiledge est enioy a
cest iour en le Lathe
del Vicont, ou diuers
entyer Borowes sount
excuse p le tantsolemt
appa-

apprāēce dū Borgefal-
der , & deux,quatuor
ou fixe auters enhabi-
bitants. Borſholder eſt
iſsint nofme de les
Saxon parolx Borher
ealdor,ceſt adire,le pl⁹
auncient ou eigne de
les pledges.

6 Et claiment auxy
que ſi nul tenant en
Gauelkinde foit at-
taint de felony,per que
il ſuffre iudgement de
mort,eit le roy toutes
ſes chateux , & ſon
heire maintenant aps
ſa mort foit enhery é de
touts ſes terres et te-
nementes que il tient
en Gauelkinde en fee,
& en heritage , &
les tiendra per mef-
me les feruyces & cuf-
tomes , ſicome ſes aū-
ceſtors les tiendront
dount eſt diſt en Ké-
toes.

appearance of a Bor-
ſholder, and two, fow-
er, or fixe other of the
inhabitants. Worſhol-
der is ſo named of the
Saxon wordes Bor-
her ealder , that is to
ſay, ÿ moſt auncient or
elder of the pledges.

6 And they clayme
alſo, that if any tenāt
in gauelkind bee at-
tainted or felonye, for
the which he ſuffereth
iudgement of death,
the kinge ſhal haue al
his goods, ¢ his heire
forthwith after hys
death ſhal be enherita-
ble to al his landes ¢
tenemts which heheld
in Gauelkind in fe,
¢ inheritance: And he
ſhal hold them by the
ſame ſeruices ¢ cuſ-
tomes, as his aunce-
tors helde thē: where-
vpō it is ſaid in kētiſh

Ye fader to ye bogh,
Ye fonne to ye plogh
Mes ceſt rule tient

The father to the bough,
And the fon to ÿ plough.
But this rule holdeth
(iij)

in case of felonye, and of murter onelye, and not in case of treason at all : And it holdeth also in case wher the offendour is iustified by order of lawe and not where he withdroweth him selfe after the fault committed, and wil not abide his lawfull trial. And because that this custome shal not be construed by equity but by a straight and literal interpretacion : it hath therefore beene doubted, whether the brother or uncle shall have the aduantage thereof, because the woords extend to the same onely.

See 22. E. 3 . abridged by master Br. tit Custome 54.

7 And if he haue a wife, forthwith to be endowed by the heire, if he be of age, of the one halfe of al § lands and

en case de felonye & de murder solement , & nemy en case de treason. Et il tyent auxy en case ou le offendour est iustised per order del ley , & nemy ou il ne sustrey apres le fact fayt , & ne voet permitter son loyal triall. Et pur ceo que cest Custome ne serra construe per equytye , mes per vn stricte & lyteral enterpretation , il ad estre doubt pur ceo, si le frere , ou vncle auera le aduauntage de ceo , pur ceo que les parollx extende al fits solement.

Vide 22. Ed 3.abridge per Mr Brooke tit Custome 54.

7 Et sil eyt femme maintenant soit endowe per le heire, sil soit dage de la moity , de touts les terres, &

& tenements que fon baron tient de Gauel-kind en fee: A auer & a tener folonque la forme defouthdit. Et de tiels terres le Roy ne auera an ne waft, mes tantfolement les chateux, ficome il eft auantdit.

Le femme ne perdra dower pur le default defa baron, mes en tiel cafe ou le heire perdera fon enheritaunce pur le offence de fon pere. 8.H.3.

8 Et fi vl Gauel-kindeis pur felony, ou pur ret de felonie, fe futhtrey de la pais, & foit en countie demád come il appent, & puis vtlage, ou fil fe myft en feint Efglife, & for-iure la terre & le Re-alme, le Roy auera le an & le waft de fes terres, & de toutes fes tenements, enfemble oue touts fes biens & chateaux.

and tenements which her husband helde of Gauelkind nature in fee: To haue & to hold accoroing to the forme hereafter declared, and of such lands the king shal not haue the yere, nor wast, but onely goods, as is before said

The wife shall not lose her dower for the defaut of her husband, but in such case where the heire shal lose his inheritace for the offence of his father. 8.H.3.

And if any man of Gauelk. either for felonie, or for suspicio of felony, withdraw himout of the countrey, & be demaded in the couty as he ought, & be afterward vtlawed, or put himself into holy church, and abiure the land, & the Realme, the king shal haue the yere & the wast of his lands, & of al his tenemetz, together with his goodes & chattels.

He

So that after the yere and the day, the nexte Lord, or Lordes, shall haue their Eschetes of those landes, and tene=ments, euery lord that which is immediatly holden of him. So is it holden in the bookes 8. E. 2. abridged by master Fitzh. tit Pre=scription 50. et 22. E. 3. abridged by master Brooke titulo Custome 54.

9 And they clayme also, that if any te=naunt in Gauelkind die, & be an inheritor of landes, and tenements in Gauelkind, that all his sonnes shall part that inheritance by e=qual porcions.

10 And if there bee no heire male, let the partition be made be=tweene the females, euen as betwene bro=thers. But the statute of Prærogatiua regis ca. 16. sayeth, That the

Issint que apres lan, & le iour, le plus pro=cheine seigniour, ou seignioures eynt lour eschetes de cels terres, & tenements, chescun seigniour ceo que de luy est tenus sauns men. Issint il est tenus en le liuers. 8. E.2.a-bridged per Master Fitzherb. tit Prescrip-tion 50. Et 22. E.3. abridged per Mr Bro. tit Custome 54.

9 Et claimant auxi, que si ascun tenant en Gauelkinde murt, & soit enheritor de ter-res & de tenements en Gauelkinde, que touts ses fites partent cel heritage p nouels por-cions.

10 Et si nul heire male ne soyt, soyt la partyc' fayt enter les females, sicome entres les freres. Mes le Statute de Prærogatiua Regis capitulo 16. dit, que

O.j. fæfœmiæ non participabunt cum maſculis , que eſt deſte entende, de tiels que ſont en e-quall degree de kinred come freres,& ſo-ers, come en ceſt ix. & x.deuiſion. Car ſi vn home ad iſſue iij. ſits, & le eigne ad iſſue vn file , & moruſt en le vie ſon peere , & le pere deuy:En ceſt caſe le file ioynera oue les deux auters freres ſa vncles , pur ceo que el neſt en equall de-gree oue eux,come ſa peere fuit, que heire nient meins el doet de neceſſitie eſte.

11 Ft la meſuage ſoyt auxy enter eux departye , mes le Aſ-tre demurra al pu-ne & puneè , & la value ſoyt de ceo ly-uere a cheſcun des parceners de cel he-rytage a 40 . pees de cel Aſtre , ſi le tenemente le puet

females , ſhall not departe with the males, which is to be vnder-ſtoode, or ſuch as bœ in equal degrœ of kinred as brothers & ſiſters, as in this ix.and x.de-uiſion . For if a man haue iſſue in ſonnes,& the eldeſt haue iſſue a daughter, and die in the life of his father, & the father dyeth. In this caſe the daughter ſhal ioine w the two other brethren her vncles, for the ſhœ is not in equall degrœ with them, as her father was,whoſe heire neuertheleſſe ſha muſt of neceſſity be.

11 And let the meſſu-age alſo be departed be-twene them, but the Aſ-ter ſhal remaine to the yongeſt ſonne or daugh-ter,& be the value there-of deliuered to each of the parceners of the heritage,from xl. fœte from that Aſtre , if the tenement will ſ
ſuf-

suffer.

By this wozde (Aſ=
tre)is ment)as is cō=
ceyued) eyther the
hall oz cheefe roome of
the houſe, eyther elſe
the wel foz water, oz
the ſouth ſide of the
buildinge, foz (Aſtre)
being founded with=
out (ſ) may come of
the latin wozde Atri-
um, which ſignyfieth
a hall, oz of Hauſt-
rum, which betoke=
neth the bucket of a
well.oz of Auſtrum,the
ſouth ſide , euery of
which haue their par=
ticuler commodityes
aboue the reſt of the
houſe oz tenement, Oz
otherwiſe being foun=
ded with (ſ) it may
bee deduced from the
french wozd (Aſiſter)
by contractyon (Aſ=
tre)which is as much
as a ſite, oz ſituation,
and with the article
(le) befoze it (Leſ-
ter) a churchyarde, oz

suffrer.

Per ceſt parol (Aſ-
tre) eſt ment (come
eſt coniecture) ou le
aule, ou principal lieu
del meaſon , ou au-
terment le well 'pur
ewe, ou le ſouth parte
del edifice car (Aſ-
tre) eſteatint founde
ſauns (ſ) poit vener
del latin paroſt Atri-
um que ſignifie vn
aule, ou de Hauſtrum
que betoken le buc-
ket dun well, ou de
Auſtrum le ſouth ſide,
Cheſcun de que ount
lour particuler com-
modities deuaunt les
autres del meaſon ou
tenement. Ou auter-
ment eſteaunt founde
oue (ſ) il poet eſtre
deduce de le frenche
paroll (Aſiſter) per
contraction (Aſtre)
que eſt taunt , come
ton ſite , ou ſituaty-
on, & oue le article
(le) deuant ceo (Leſ-
ter) vn cimitory , ou

O.ij.   court

court enuiron vn mea-
son. Mes al cest iour il
nad tiel regarde fayt
en le particyon , mes
solement considerati-
on ewe, que les partes
ms soient equal & in-
different.

12 Et donques le
eisne frere eyt la pri-
mer election , & les
auters apres per de-
gree.

13 Ensemt de mea-
sons que serrount tro-
uets en tyels mes-
suages , soyent de-
partie entré les heires
per ouell porcyons,
cestassauoir per pees
sil est mistier , Saue
le Couert del Astre,
que remeynt al pu-
ne , ou al punee , si-
come il est auaunt-
dist . Issint neque-
dount que le pune
face reasonable gree
a ses parceners de le
parte que a eux ap-
pent , per agarde de
bon gents.

Court about a house.
But at this day there
is noe suche regard
made in the particion,
but only consideration
had , that the partes
them selues be equall
indifferent.

12 And then let the
eldest brother haue the
first choyse , and the
others afterward ac-
cording to'their degre

13 Likewise of hou-
ses which shalbe found
in such messuages, let
them bee departed a-
mongst the heires by
equall porcions, that
is to weete , by fote
if neede bee, Sauinge
the Couert of the Is-
ter which shal remain
to the yongest sonne,
or daughter , as is be-
foresayd. So neuer-
thelesse,that y yongest
make reasonable a-
meds to his parceners
for the part which to
them belongeth,by the
award of good men.

14 And

14 And of the afore-said tenemēts, where-of one onely suit was wont to be made be-fore time, be there not by reason of the parti-cion but one sole suite made, as it was before accustomed, but yet let al the parceners make contribucyon to the parcener which ma-keth the suit for them.

15 In lyke sort let þ goods of Gauelkind persons be parted into iij partes, after the fu-nerals and the debtes payed. if there be law-ful issue on liue, so þ the dead haue one part, and his lawful sonnes and daughter an other part, and the wife the iij.part.

Where it is sayde here, that the dead shal haue one part, it is mēt for performance of his legacies by his execu-tours if he make a tes-tament, or by the dis-

14 Et les auauntdits tenementes dount vn sole sute tauntsole-ment soleit estre fait auaunt, ne soyt per la reason de la partici-on fors vn soule sute fait sicome soleyt a-uaunt, mes tam soutes les parceners facent contributyon a celuy que face le suite pur eux.

15 Ensement seint les chateux de Ga-uelkindeis parties en iij. parts apres les exe-quies & les dets ren-dues, si il y eit issue mulier en vie, issint quel al mort eyt l i vn parte, & les fites & les files-muliers lauter parte, & la feme la iij. parte.

Ou il est dit cy, que la mort eit vne par-te, il est entende pur parformaunce de de ses legacyes per ses executours sil fait tes-tament, ou per le dis-

cretion del ordinarie ſil
deuy inteſt.

16 Et ſi nul iſſue
mulier en vye ſoit,
eit la mort vne moi-
tye , & la femme
en vie lauter moitye.
Meſme le order de
que le cuſtome cy
parle en le 15 . &
16. diuiſion , eſt al
ceſt iour obſerue en
la Citie de Londres
et en meſme effèct ſu-
it en auncient temps
vſe per tout le realme.
Car il eſt euident , &
per le ley del Roye
Canutus, per maſter
Glanuill , per les pa-
rolx de magna Char-
ta capite 18.per mſ
Fitzh . en ſon natura
breuium en le briefe
de rationabili parte
bonorum fo.122 L.
que la feme et enfants
ad lour reaſonable pts
del biens per le com-
mon ley del realme &
que le commen leye
fuit iſſint , il appiert

cretion of þ ordinary
iſſue dye inteſt.

16 And if there be no
lawfull iſſue on lyue,
let the dead haue the
one halfe, & þ wife
liue þ other halfe. The
ſelfe ſaine order þ the
cuſtome here ſpeaketh
of in þ 15.& 16. diui-
ſion, is at this day ob-
ſerued in the citye of
London, and the ſame
in effect was longe
ſince vſed throughout
the whole Realme.
For it is euident both
by the law of Kynge
Canutus, by maſter
Glanuil, by þ words
of Magna Charta ca:
18.by maſter Fitzh.
in his natura breuiſ in
the writ De rationabili
parte bonorum fol.122:
L. That the wife
and children had their
reaſonable partes of
the goodes by the com-
mon lawe of þ realme
and that þ common law
was ſo, it appeareth
alſo

also in 30.E.3. 25.
& 21. 30.H.6. And it
was said for law M).
31.H.8. abridged by
M.Br.tit Rationabili
pre bonorñ, pl.6. that it
hath bene often put in
vre as a common law, &
neuer demurred vpon
and therefore it see=
meth that it is com=
mon law, howsoeuer
it came to passe at
length that it was
admitted for law, but
in such countries onc=
ly, where it was con=
tinued by daily vsage,
and that al the writts
in the register de rati=
onabili parte bonorum,
haue mencion of the
special custome of the
shire, in which the
party is demaunded,
and so in the book 28.
H.6.4. But as at
this daye partition of
chatteiles is not b=
sed through out the
whole realme, though
in the meane tyme it

auxy en 30. E.3. 25.
& 21. 30.H 6. Et
fuit dit pur ley M. 31.
H.8, abridge per mas
ter Brooke titulo, Ra
tionabili parte bono
rum, placito 6. que eeo
ad estre sepe mise in
vre come vn common
ley, & nunquam de
murre, & ideo videtur
que eeo est common
ley, per que mains que
cunque il vient al dar
rain q il fuit admit pur
ley mes in tiels catries
solement, ou il fuit cō
tinue per continual v
sage, & que toutes les
briefes en le Regiiter,
de Rationabili parte
bonorum, ount men
cyon del special Cus
tome del county en
que le party è demaūd
& issint est le lyure 28
H.6.4. Mes come
al cest iour partycy
on de chattels nest vse
per tout le entier realm
nyent obstaunt en
le meane temps il

　nad

nad perd le force del
cōmon ley cōe multes
penſe, & come poet
eſtre collect per le o-
pinion auauntdiſt te-
nus pur ley Anno 3 1.
H.8. iſſint il eſt, cōe
aſcuns ſuppoſe, vaniſhe
ouſtrement hors de
vre deins ceſt coun-
trie de Kent auxy.

17 Et ſi le heire, ou
les heires, ſoit ou ſoi-
ent deins le age de
15. ans, ſoyt la
nourture de eux baile
per le Seigniour al
plus procheyne del
ſanke, a que lenhe-
ritage ne puet deſcen-
dre, iſſint que le ſeig-
niour pur le bayle rien
preigne.

18 Et que il ne ſoit
marrye per le ſegni-
our, mes per ſon vo-
lunte demeſne, & p
le counſell de ſes amies
ſil veult.

19 Et quaunt cel
heire ou ceux heires,
ſot de plein age de 15.

hath not loſt the form
of common law as ma-
ny thinke, and as may
be gathered by the o-
pinion aforeſaid hol-
ten for law anno 31.
H.8. So is it as ſome
thinke, baniſhed quite
out of all vre within
this countrie of Kent
alſo.

17 And if the heire
or heires, ſhal be vn-
der the age of 15. pere
let the nurture of the
be committed by the
lorde, to the next of þ
bloud to whom the ē
heritance can not diſ-
cend, ſo that the lord
take nothinge for
the committing there
of.

18 And let not the
heire be married by þ
Lord but by his owne
will, and by the ad-
uiſe of his friendes if
hee will.

19 And when ſuch
heire, or heires, ſhall
come to the age of 15.
yeares

yeares, let their lands
and tenementes be de=
liuered vnto them to=
gether w their goodes
and profits of the sse
landes, remaininge a=
boue their reasonable
sustenaunce : of the
which profites and
goodes, lett hym bee
bounde to make aun=
swere which had the
educatyon of the heire
or els the Lorde, or
hys heires which cō=
mitted the same edu=
cation.

The lord ought to
take good heede , that
he credit not the cus=
todye to anye person
that shall not bee able
to aunswere there=
fore. For if the heire
to his ful age of 15.
yeares shal come to þ
lords court , and de=
maund his enheritāce
although the Lorde
may distreine the gar=
den to yeld his accōpt
(as it appeareth 18.

ans, soient a eux lour
terres & lour tene-
mentes lyueres, ensem-
blement oue lour cha-
teux , & oue les en-
prouementes de cels
terres , ouster reaso-
nable sustynaunce: de
quel enprouement, &
chateux , soyt tenu
a respondre celuy que
de luy auera le nur-
ture , ou le seigny=
our , ou ses heires ,
que cel nurture auera
baile.

Le seigniour doyet
bien consider , que il
ne credit pas le custo-
dy al ascun person, q
ne serra able a respon-
der pur ceo. Car si le
heire al son pleine age
de xv. ans , vyen-
dra al Court del seig-
niour & demaund son
enheritance, nient ob-
stant le seignyour po-
et distreigne le Gar-
den pur faire accōpt
(come il applert 18.

E.2.

E. 2 , Auowry 220)
vncore en defaut de
fon abilitie, le feyg-
niour mefme, & fes
heires,demſt charge al
le heire pur cco : Mes
ico ne oyer, q̃ les feig-
niors priſt fur eux a cẽ
iour de commit le cuf-
rodie de ceux enfants,
mes que ils relinque
cco ouſtrement al or-
der de proch. de amie,
peraduenture pur a-
uoid le daunger en
que ils font,fils enter-
medle come eſt auãt-
dit.

20   Et cco fet aſſa-
uoir , que del heure
que ceux heifs en Ga-
uelkinde foyent , ou
ount paſſe le age de
xv . ans , lyſt a eux
lour terres ou tene-
mentes doner & ven-
der , a lour volunte,
Saues les feruices au
chefcun feigniourages
come il eſt deuaunt
dyt.

   Nient obſtant q̃ ceſt

E.2. Auowꝛy 220.)
yet in default of his a-
bilitie, the Loꝛde him
felfe , and his heires,
remaine charged to the
heire foꝛ the fame: But
I do not heare, that
the Loꝛdes take vpon
them at this daye to
commit the cuſtody of
thefe infants,but that
they leaue it altoge-
ther to the oꝛder of þ
next of kyn,peraduen-
ture to auóid the dau-
ger in which they are,
if they intermedle as
is afoꝛefaid.

20 And this is to bæ
vnderſtood,þ from fuch
time as thofe heires in
Gauelkinde be of , oꝛ
haue paſſed the age of
15.yeres, it is lawful
foꝛ them, their landes
oꝛ tenements, to giue
and fell at their plea-
fure , Sauinge the
feruices to the chiefe
loꝛdes , as is befoꝛe-
faid.

   Although that this
cuſ-

custome enable ẏ heire to make away hys landes and tenementes very soone, namely at the fiftenth yere of his age, by meanes wherof it might be thought vnreasonable in gy= uing such scope and li= berty to so yong yeres, yet vpon the good con= sideration thereof it may appeare, that the custome it selfe doth reasonably and care= fully prouide in the behalfe of the heire for so much as it licenceth him at that yeares not to geue his landes, for that hee might do for nothinge, but to geue and sell hys landes, which it meaneth hee should not do without sufficient recompence. Such like interpreta= tion, the common law also seemeth to make of this custome both by the opinion of Va= uisour ẻ Keble. 5. H. 7.

custome enhable le heire pur faire alicna= tion de ses terres & tenements mult soone, nosment al 15. an de sa age, per meanes de que il puit este pense nient reasonable pur doñ tiel scope & ly= bertie al tiels iune ans, vncore sur le bon con= sideratyon de ceo il poet appeare, que le custome m fait reaso= nable & carefull pro= uision en le behalfe del heire, entaunt que il luy licence a tiel ans, non pur doner ses ter= res, car ceo il poet faire pur nul chose, mes pur doner & vender ses terres, le quel il entende il ne doet faire sauns sufficient recompence. Sem= ble interpretation le common ley auxi sem= ble de faire de cost custome, & per lop= pinion de Vauisour & Keble 5. H. 7.

31.

31.et 41.queux diont
que il fuit adiudge que
vn releas fait per tyel
enfant fuit voide, per
le ſentence del lyuer
21.E.4.24. ou il eſt
dit,que vn enfaunt ne
poet declare ſon vo-
lunt ſur tyel feoffe-
ment. Et per le iudg-
ment de Hank.11.H.
4.33. que auxi tient,
que vn garrantie, ou
graunt dun reuerſion
fait a tyel age, fuit a
nul purpoſe, nyent
obſtaunt vn leas oue
releas puit paduen-
ture eſte bone per le
cuſtome, pur ceo que
il amounta a vn fe-
offement. Et il neſt
bone que ceſt cuſtõe
doet eſte conſtrue per
equitie, entaunt que
il neſtoit oue aſcun e-
quitie denabler vn en-
fant de petit diſcreti-
on, & meines experi-
ence,pur vend'ſon ter-
res, & non pur pur-
uiew que ceo, q̃ il doit
auer Quid pro quo, &

31.& 41.Who ſaid,that
it was adiudged that
a releas made by ſuch
an enfant was voyde,
by the ſentence of the
booke 21. E. 4. 24.
Where it is ſayd, that
an infant cannot de-
clare his wil vpõ ſuch
a feoffement. And by
the iudgment of Hank
11.H.4.33. Who alſo
held, that a warranty
oʒ graunt of a reuerſi-
on made at ſuch age,
was to no purpoſe at
all,although a leaſe w
releas might hapely be
good by y̆ cuſtõe, be-
cauſe y̆ amoũteth to a
feffemẽt. And it is not
fit y̆ this cuſtõe ſhould
bee conſtrued by equi-
tye, foʒ as much as it
ſtandeth not with any
equitie, to enable an
infant, of little diſ-
cretion, and leſſe ex-
perience, to ſell hys
land, & not to pʒouyde
withal that he ſhould
haue Quid pro quo, and
ſome

some reasonable recompence for the same: for that were not to defend the pupil & fatherlesse, but to laye him wide open to euery slie deceyt and circumuentiō. In which respect, their opiniō is very wel to be liked of, who holde, that if an infant in Gauelkind, at this day will sel at xb. yers of age, these 3. things ought of necessitie to concurre, if he will haue the sale good & effectuall . The first that he be an heire, and not a purchaser of the land that he departeth withall. The seconde that he haue recōpence for it: & the third, that he do it with liuery of seisin by his own hād, and not by warrant of attourney, nor by any other manner of assurance. And these men for proofe of the first & seconde point of their

ascun reasonable recompence pur ceo . Car ceo ne fuit pur defender le pupill & sauns pier, mes pur giser luy ouert a chescun subtile deceyt & circumuention. En que respect , lour opinion est deste bien obserue, que tyent, que si vn enfaunt en Gauelkinde, a cest iour voet vend' al xv .ans de son age, ceux tierce choses doyent de necessytie concurr, si il voet auer le sale bone & effectual . Le primer que il soit vn heire & nemy vn purchasor del terres oue queux il depart. Le second que il ad recōpence pur ceo, & le iij. q il ceo face oue liuery de seisin per son maine dem, et nemy p garr de atturney, ne p ascn aut mañ de assurance. Et ceux hōes pur profe de le primer & second part de lour assertion,

affertion, edifie fur les
parols de ceft cuftome
ou il eft dit, del heure
que ceux heirs Gauel-
kinde font, ou ount
paffe le age de xv. ans,
lift a eux, lour terres
ou tenementes don &
vender, en que les pa-
rols, (ceux heires)ref-
train le infaunt que
vient eins per purch.
Et (doner & vender)
en le copulatiue, de
necefsitie implie vn
recompence, entaunt
que vendere ne poet
efte fine præcio. Et
pur mayntenaunce
del tierce matter, ils
ount fur lour parte,
preter le common v-
fage del paies, le com-
mon ley del Realme,
auxy le quel expound
le parol doner de fig-
nifier vn feoffement,
& le quel non fole-
ment diffallowe de
afcun done fayt per
vn enfaunt, mes auxi
punifhe le prendor en

affertion, do build vpõ
ÿ wordes of this cuftoe
where it is laid from
fuch time as thofe hei-
res in Gauelkind be of
oɀ haue paffed ÿ age of
xv. yeres, it is lawful
foɀ thẽ, their lands oɀ
tenements to giue and
fel, in which ÿ wordes
(thofe heires) to ref-
train ÿ infant that cõ-
meth in by purchafe.
And (giue & fel) in the
copulatiue, do of necef-
fity imply a recõpence,
foɀfomuch as fellinge
cãnot be withoutfome
pɀice oɀ thing giue foɀ
it. And foɀ maintenãce
of the iij. matter they
haue of their part be-
fides the cõmon vfage
of the coũtrey, ÿ comõ
law of the realme alfo,
which expoundeth the
woɀd (giue) to meane a
feffement, & which not
onely difalloweth of
any gift made by an
infaunt, but alfo pu-
nyfheth the taker in
tref-

trespas, vnles he haue it by luery from the infãts owne hands as appeareth in 26. H. 8. 2.9.H.7.24. 18 E.4. 2.22.H.6.3. & diuers other bookes.

21 And if any such tenant in Gauelkinde die, & haue a wife that ouer lyueth him, let that wife by & by bee endowed of the one halfe of the tenements whereof her husbande died seized, and seysed by the heires, if they bee of age, or by the Lordes, if the heire bee not of age, so that shee may haue the one halfe of those landes, & tene= ments, to hold so long as shee keepeth her a widow, or shalbe at= tainted of child birth, after the auncient v= sage, that is to saye, þ if shee whẽ she is deli uered of child, & þ infãt be herde cry, & that the hue & crie. be raised, &

trespas, sinon que il ad ceo per liuerie del maines del enfant côe appiert en 26.H.8. 2. 9.H.7.24. 18.E.4.2. 22.H. 6.3. & diuers auters litiers.

21 Et si ascun tyel tenaunt en Gauelkinde meurt, & eyt femme que suruiue, soit cel feme mainte- naunt dow de la moi- ty des renements dont son baron morust ves- tue, & reysse per ses heires, sils soyent de age, ou per les seig- niours, si les heires ne soyent pas de age, is- sint que el eyt la moity de cels terres & te- nementes, a tener taunt come el se ty- ent veue, ou deienfanter soyt attaint, per le auncyent v- sage, ceo est assauoir, que quaunt el en- faunt, & lenfaunt soit oy cryer, & que le hue & le cry soit leue, &
le

le paies affemble, &
ayant viewe de len-
faunt en cy faunte, &
de la meere:adonques
perde fa dower en-
tierment, & auter-
ment nyent tant come
el fe tyent vidue,dont
ill eft dyt en ken-
teyes.

the country affembled,
and haue the viewe of
the child fo borne,and
the mother : then let
her lofe her dower
wholy, and otherwife
not, fo longe as fhe
holdeth her a widow,
whereof it is fayde in
kentifh.

Se thad fip wende,
fe fip lende.

He that doth wende her,
Let him lende her.

Ceft cuftome ad efte
allowe per la com-
mon ley longe temps
puis, come poet efte
vieu, Prærogatiua re-
gis cap.16. & 2.H.
3. en Fitzherbert tic
Prefcription 59. &c.
Mes il eft vn doubt,
fi vn femme ferra en-
dowe per ceft cuf-
tome, dun poffeffion
en ley, ou nemy, pur
ceo que les parols font
(des tenementes dont
fon baron moruft vef-
tue , & feifie) quel
parol (veftue) enforce

This cuftome hath
bene allowed of,by the
common lawe longe
time fince, as may bee
reade,Prærog. regis cap.
16.& 2.H.3. in Fitz. tit
Prefcription 59. &c.
But it is a doubte
whether a womanne
fhall bee endowed by
this cuftome of a pof-
feffyon in lawe or no,
for that the wordes,
bee (of the tene-
mentes whereof her
hufbande dyed vefted
and feyfed (whych
word,vefted,inforceth
a pof=

a possession in deede & not in law onely. And therfore, if landes in Gauelkind discend to a married man, which dyeth before he make his entrie into ý same. Inquire whether it be the maner to endow his wife therof or no: A woman shal not bee endowed by this custome of a Bailywike, or Faire, or such like profite by the opinion of M. Perkins folio 84. because the wordes of this customarie dower be terres & tenementa, & al customes shall finde a litteral and streyght interpretacion. And where she is to be endowed by this custome she may very well bee endowed of a moitie, to be holden in common with ý heire that enioyeth the other halfe &c. It is a doubt whether that a woman entituled to Dower in

vn possession en fayt, & non en ley solemēt. Et pur ceo si terres en Gauelkind discend al home marry, que morust deuant que il face son ētrie en ceo. Quære si soit le maner dendower sa femme de ceo ou nemy? Vn femme ne serra endow per cest custome, de vn Bailywike, ou Faire, ou tiel semblable profite, per loppinion de M. Perkins sol. 84. pur ceo que les parolx de cē customarie dowr̄ sont terres & tenemts, & touts customes trouera vn litteral et strict interpretacion. Et au el est deste endow per cest custome, el poit byen este endowed de vn moitie, deste tenus en common ouesque le heire, que enioye le auter moytie &c. Il est vne doubt, si vn femme entitle al dower en

P.j.　　Ga-

Gauelkind poit wai-
uer fa dower del moi-
ty folonque ceft cuf-
tome , & port fa ac-
cion deftre endowe
del iij.al common ley,
et iſsint exempt luy m̄
del tout daunger del
cuſtomary condition
ou nemy; Afcuns fu-
eront de opinion que
el eſt al liberty de p̄nd̄
lun,et waiue lauter al
fa pleaſure.Et pur ceo
quære de ceo &c.

22 Et claiment auxy,
que home que prent
femme , que eyt he-
rytage de Gauel-
kinde, & la femme
moruſt auaunt luy,
eyt le baron le moi-
tye de celes terres &
tenementes, taunt co-
me il ſe tyent ve-
uers , dount il mo-
ruſt ſciſie ſauns eſ-
trepement , ou waſt
ou exile fayre , le
quel kil y eyt heire
enter eux ou non. Et
ſil prent auter femme

Gauelkind may wain
her dower of the halfe
after this cuſtome, &
bꝛinge her accion to ꝗ
endowed of the 3.at ꝑ
common law , and ſo
exempt her ſelfe from
al daūger of the cuſto-
mary cōditions oꝛ ꝯꝺ
Some haue bene of o-
pintō that ſhe is at ly-
berty to take one and
refuſe the other at her
pleaſure : & therefoꝛ
inquire thereof &c.

22 And they claime
alſo,that if a manne
take a wife which
hath inheritaunce of
Gauelkind , and the
wife dieth befoꝛe him
let the huſband haue
the one halfe of thoſe
lāds & tenemēts wher
of ſhe dieth ſeiſed ſo
long as he holdeth hi
a widower,wout ꝺo-
ng any ſtrippe,oꝛwaſt
oꝛ baniſhmēt,whether
there were iſſue be-
twene thē oꝛ no. And
if he take ā̃other wife
         let

lett hym loose all.

23. And if any te=
nement of Gauelkind
we escheat (and that
escheat ix to any lorde
which holdeth by fee
of Hawberke, or by
Serieancye)by death
or by Gauelette as
is hereafter sayd, or
be to him rendered
vp by hys tenaunt
which beefore helde
it of him by quitte
claime thereof made,
or yf hys escheate bee
by gauelate as is here
after said, let thys
lande remaine to the
heires vnpartible:and
this is to bee vnder=
stode,where the tenāt
so rendringe, woth re=
tain no seruice to him
selfe,but saueth neuer
p lese to p other lords
their fees, fermes & p
rents whereiw the a=
foresaid tenements of
gauelkind(so rēdred)
were before chargd by
hi or thē which might

trestout perde.

23. Et si ascun tene=
ment de Gauelkinde
eschete (& ceo es=
chete soit a vl seig=
niour que tyent per
fee de Hawberken,
ou per serieancye)per
mort, ou per Gaue=
late sicome il est suis
dit, ou luy sort ren=
due de son tenant que
de luy auaunt le ty=
ent per quit claime
de ceo fait, ou soyt
son escheat per Gaue=
late sicome il est de=
suis dist, remaine cel
terre as heires impar=
tible : Et ceo est as=
cauoire, la ou le te=
nant ensi rendant, nul
seruice retent deuers
se, sauet nequedont
as auters seigniorages
fees,fermes, & les rēts
dont les auandits tene=
ments de gauelkinde
(ensi rendus) a=
uaunt fueroune char=
ges per ceux, ou
per cestuy, que le

P.ij   char-

charger poyēt ou poit.

A tener per fee de Hawberk, ou per Seriantie (s'il soit graunde Seriantie,) & a tener per seruice de Chiualrie . Heahbeony en Saxon, est vn haut defence : & les customes de Normandie appell ceo fiefe ou fee de Haubert, que doit defender le terre per pleine armes, ceo est per chiual, haubert, target, espee, ou helme. Et il consist de 300. acres de terre, que est ceo(com ascūs pense)q̄ nous appellom' vn entier fee de chiualer.

24 Et claymant auxi que si ascun tenant en Gauelkinde retayne sa rent, & son seruyce del tenement quel il tyent de son Seygniour : querge le seygniour per agarde de sa Court, de trois semaines en trois semaines, de trouer distres

charge them.

To holde by fee of Hawbert, or by Seriantie (if it be graunte Seriancie) is to hold by knightes seruyce. Heahbeony in Saxon, is a high defence: and the customes of Normandie called that fief or fee de Haubert, which oweth to defend the lande by full armes, that is, by horse, haubert, target, sworde, or helme. And it consisteth of 300. acres of land, which is the same (as som think) that wee call a whole knightes fee.

24 And they clayme also, that if any tenant in Gauelkinde wythhold his rēt & his seruices of the tenement which hee holdeth of his lord, let the Lorde seeke by the award of his Court from thre weekes to iij. weekes, to finde some distres vpon

vpon that tenement, vntil the iiij. Court, alwayes wyth witnesses. And if within that time, he can finde no distres in that tenement, whereby hee may haue iustice of his tenaunt. Then at the fowerth court let yt be awarded, that hee shal take that tenemēt into his hande, in the name of a distres, as if it were an oxe or a cow & let him kepe it a yere & a day in his hand without manuring it: win which terme if the tenaunt come & pay hys arrerages, & make reasonable amendes for þ wholding, then let him haue & enioy his tenement as his auncestors & he before held it: & if he do not come before the yeare and the day passe, then let the lord goe to the next Countie court wyth the witnesses of hys

sur cel tenement, tanque a le iiij. court, a touts foits per tesmoignages. Et si dedeins cel temps ne troue distresse en cel tenement, per queux il puisse son tenaunt iustiser. Donq; a la quart court soit agarde que il preigne cel tenement en sa maine, en nosme de distresse, auxi come boefe ou vache, & le tient vn an & vn iour, en sa maine, sans maine ouerer, deyns quel terme, si le tenaunt vyent, & rend ses arrerages, & fayt reasonables amendes de la deteyner, adonc eit & ioise son tenement, sicome les auncestours & luy auaunt iendront. Et sil ne vient deuaunt le an & le iour passe, donc ange le seygniour al procheyne Countie court suiant oue tesmoygnes de sa

de fa Court , & face
la pronouncyer cel
proceffe pur tefmoy-
nage auer , & per a-
garde de fa Court (a-
pres ceo countie tenue)
entra & mey nouera
en cels terres & tene-
mentes , ficome en
fon demefne . Et fi
la tenaunt vyent a-
pres , & voyle re-
auer fes tenementes ,
& tener ficon e il fift
deuaunt , face gree
al feygniour , ficome
il eft auncyentment
dyft.

owne Court, and pro=
nounce there this pro=
ceffe , to haue further
witneffe, and ly the a=
warde of hys Court,
(after the Countie
court holden) he fhall
enter and manure in
thofe lads & tenemēts
as in his owne demief=
nes. And if the tenāt
come afterwarde, and
will rehaue his tene=
ments,& hold them as
he did before , let hym
make agreement wyth
the Lord, according as
it is aunciently faid.

Neghe fith felde ? &
ghe fith geld ? & v.
pound for the wer ,
er he become heal-
der.

Hath he not fince any
thing gyuen:nor hath
he not fince any thing
paied ? Then let him
pay fyue pounde for
hys were , before hæ
beecome tenaunt or
holder againe.

Afcuns copies ont les
primer verfes iffint.
Nigond fith felde, &
nigond fith gelde.

Some coppes haue
the firft verfe thus.
Let him ir times pay
and ir, times repay.

Thıs

This cuſtome is tou-
ched by the way by
Maſter Frowick 21.H.7
.15. & by him thought
to be good, but whe=
ther it bee at this day
put in vze, enquyze
further.

25 Alſo they claime
that no man ought to
make an othe vpon a
booke, (neyther by diſ=
tres, noz by the poſwer
of the Lozde, noz hys
Bailife) againſt hys
will, tſout the wzit of
the king (vnleſſe it bæ
foz fealtie to be don to
his Lozd,) but onely
befoze the Cozoner, oz
ſuch other miniſter of
the king, ſ hath royal
poſwer to enquire of
treſpas committed a=
gainſt the Crowne of
our Lozd the king.

26 And they claime
that euery Kentiſhmã
may eſſoine another,
either in the Kinges
court, oz in the coûty,
oz in ſ hûdzeth, oz in ſ

Ceſt cuſtõe eſt touch
per le voy, per Maſter
Frowicke. 21. H.
7. 15. & per luy
penſe deſtre bone,
mes ſil ſoyt a ceſt
iour myſe en vre.
Quære plus.

25 Auxy ils claimẽt
que nul home doyt
ſerement ſur lieur faire
(per diſtreſſe, ne per
poier del ſeigniour, ne
de Bailife) encounter
ſon volunt, ſans briefe
le Roy (ſinon pur fe-
altie eſtre fait a ſon
ſeigniour) meſq; per
deuaunt Coroner,
ou auter myniſter le
Roy, que real powcr
eyaunt de enqúyrer
de treſpaſſc fait en-
counter la Corone
noſter ſeygnyúor le
Roy.

26 Et ils clayment,
que cheſcun Kentois
puit auter eſſoiner
en la Court le Roy,
en Countye, ou en
hundreth, ou en la

court son seigniour, la ou essoigne gist, auxibien de common suit, come de ple.

27 Oustre ceo ils claiment per especial faitle Roye Henrye, piere le Roye Edwarde, que de tenementes que sount tenus en Gauelkinde, ne soit pris battaile, ne graunde assise per duzisme chiualers, sicome aylors est prise en le Realme, ceo est ascauoire, la ou le tenaunt & le demaundaunt tyent per Gauelkinde : mes en lieu de ses graundes assises soient iuries prises per xij. homes tenauntes en Gauelkinde, issint q̃ quater tenauntes de Gauelkinde essient xij. tenaunts de Gauelkind destre iurors.

Et la chartre le roy, de cest especyaltie est en la garde Syr

court of his lord wher essoine lieth, & that aswel in case of commõ sute, as of plee.

27 Moreouer they claime by an especiall dede of kinge Henry, the father of kynge Edwarde, that of the tenementes which are holden in Gauelkinde there shall no battaile be ioined, nor graunde assise taken by xij. knightes, as it is vsed in other places of the Realme : that is to wit, where the tenaunt and demaundaunt hold by Gauelkinde : But in place of these graund assises, let iuries be taken by xij. men beinge tenants in Gauelkinde, so that fower tenants of Gauelkend chose xij. tenants of Gauelkind to be iurors.

And þ charter of þ kinge of this especialty, is in þ custody of Sir John

John of Norwood, the day of S. Elphey in Caunterburye the yeare of kinge Edw. the sonne of kinge Henry the 21.

Iohn de Norwood, le iour Sainct Elphegh en Caunterburye, le an le roy Edwarde le fits le Roye Henrye 21.

These be the vsages of Gauelkind, & of Gauelkinde men in Kent, which were before the conquest, and at the conquest, and euer since til now

Ceux sont les vsages de Gauelkind, et d Gauelkindeis é Kent, que fueront deuaunt le conquest, & en le conquest, et touts heuers iesq; a ore.

The end of the customes

Le fine del customes.

Hauinge thus ended the customes as you see (Brother Nicholas) there remayneth now to be shewed what lands within this country of Kent, bee of the nature of Gauelkinde, and what not.

Ayant issint finishe les customes come vous veies (Frere Nicholas) il demurt a ore destre monstre quel terres deins cest pais de Kent sount del nature de Gauelkinde, & queux nemy.

First therefore, it is to be vnderstanded, that al the lands within this shire which be of auncient Socage tenure (as was said at the beginninge) bee

Primerment pur ceo il est destre entend, que toutes les terres deins cest shire, queux sount de auncyent socage tenure (come fuit dit auant) sont
auxy

auxy del nature de ga-
uelkinde. Et les terres
tenus per auncient te-
nure de feruice de chi-
ualer, font al common
ley, & ne font depar-
tible folonque le or-
der de ceft cuftome,
excepta certeine, queux
efteant tenus de aun-
cient temps per feruice
de chiualer del Arch-
eueſque de Caunter-
burie, font nient ob-
ftant departible, come
il poit appeare per le
Liuer 26.H.8.4. Et
ceo vient per reafon de
vn graunt, fait per le
Roy Iohn, al Hubert
le Archeueſque, le te-
nour de que eft come
enfue.

¶Iohannes dei gratia
Rex Angliæ, Dominus
Hiberniæ, Dux Nor-
maniæ, Aquitaniæ, &
Comes Andegauen,
Archiepiſcopis, Epiſ-
copis, Abbat', Comi-
tbus, Baronibus, Iuſ-
ticiar', Vicecõm, Præ-

also of the nature of
Gauelkind. And the
landes holden by aun-
ciēt tenure of knights
feruice, be at the com-
mon law, & are not de-
partible after the or-
der of thys cuftome,
except certeine whych
bæing holden of olde
time by knightes fer-
uice of the Archbiſhop
of Caunterbury, are
neuer the leffe depar-
tible, as it may ap-
peare by the bœke 16.
H.8.4. And that
grew by reafon of a
graunt made by king
John, to Hubert the
Archbiſhop there, the
tenour of which is as
followeth.

¶John by the grace
of God, king of Eng-
land, Lord of Ireland,
Duke of Normandie,
of Aquitane, and earle
of Angieu: To all
Archbiſhops, biſhops,
Abbots, Earles, Ba-
rons, Iuftices, ſhiriffs
Go-

Gouernours, & Offi=
cers, and all Bailifes,
& al his faithfull sub=
iectes greeting. Know
yee that wee haue gra=
ted, & by this our pre=
sent Charter haue co=
firmed, to our reuerend
& deerely beloued fa=
ther Hubert Archby=
shop of Caunterbury,
and his successors for
euer, ý it shalbe law=
ful for them, to con=
uert those lands which
men of the fee of the
Church of Canterbu=
rie do hold in Gauel=
kind into knights fee.
And that the same bi=
shops and their suc=
cessors, haue the lyke
power and libertie for
euer, ouer those men &
their heires, that shal
holde those landes so
couerted into knights
fee, which the Archbi=
shop hath & his succes=
sors after hi shal haue,
ouer other knights of
the fee of the Church

positis, Ministris, &
omnibus Balliuis et fi-
delibus suis salutem .
Sciatis nos concessisse,
& præsenti Charta
nostra confirmasse ve-
nerabili patri nostro
ac Chfo.Huberto Cá-
tuaf Archiepiscopo,&
successoribus suis in
perpetuum,quod liceat
eis terras ,quas homi-
nes de feodo ecclesiæ
Cantuarien̄ tenent in
Gauelkinde, conuer-
tere in feodo Mili-
tam.

Et quod idem Epis-
copi & successores sui,
eandem in omnibus
potestatem , & liber-
tatem habeant in per-
petuum, in homines
illos qui terras eafdem
ita in feoda Militum
conuersas tenebunt, &
in hæredes eorum
quam Archiepisco-
pus habet,& successo-
res sui post eum ha-
bebunt in alios mili-
tes de feodo ecclesiæ
Can-

Cantuar̅ , & in hære-
des . Et homines illi,
& hæredes eorum,
eandem & omnem li-
bertat'habeant in per-
petuum,quam alij Mi-
lites de feodo eccleſiæ
Cantuar̅ , & hæredes
eorum habent. Ita ta-
men , quod nihilomi-
nus conſuetus redditus
denariof̄ reddatur in-
tegrè de terris ſuis,ſicut
prius,prǫmia, aueragia
& alia operǫ, que ſie-
bant de terris jiſdem,
conuertan̅ in reddi-
tione denariorū equi-
ualentem . Et redditus
ille reddatur , ſicut a-
lius redditus denariof̄.
Quare volumus , &
firmiter præcipimus ,
quod quicquid predic-
tus Archiepiſcopus &
ſucceſſor'ſui poſt eum,
de terris illis in feodo
Militum , ſecundum
præſcriptam formam
conuertendis fecerint
ratum in perpetuum
& ſtabile perma-

of Canterbury & their
heirs.And y̆ thoſe men
& their heires haue the
ſame & al ſuch libertie
foꝛeuer , which other
knights of y̆ fee of the
church of Canterb. &
their heirs haue.Pꝛo-
uided alwaies y̆ neuer-
theleſſe their accuſto-
med rent of pence, be
wholly payed out of
their landes, as befoꝛe
time their giftes, aue-
rages,and other ſerui-
ces which iſſued out of
the ſame lands be con-
uerted into a rent of
pence of like balue , &
y̆ the ſame re̅t be paied
as y̆ other rent of pe̅ce
is. Wherefoꝛe we wil
& ſtraightly co̅maund,
y̆ whatſoeuer y̆ afoꝛe-
named Archbiſhop &
his ſucceſſoꝛs after hi
ſhal do co̅cerning thoſe
lands which are to bæ
co̅uerted into knights
fæ,accoꝛdi̅g to y̆ foꝛme
& maner aboue wꝛitte̅,
abide ratiſied & confir-
     med

med for euer. Forbid-
ding any perso to pre-
sume against the deede
of the Archbishop or
his successors in thys
behalfe. Witnesse E.
Bishop of Ely, & S.
of Bath, G. the sonne
of Peter Earle of
Essex, William Mar-
shall Earle of Pem-
brooke, Ro. of Hare-
court, Garine the sone
of Geralde, Peter of
Stoke, Ri. of Reuers
Rob. of Cateshall,
yeuen by the hande of
S. Archdeacon vnto
willis at Rupem au-
rinall, the iiij. day of
May, the third yeare
of our Raigne.

But for asmuch as it
is disputable, whether
this Charter of King
Iohn, be of sufficient
vertue to chaunge the
nature of Gauel kinde
lande, or no, & for that
the certeintie of the
lands so conuerted in-
to knightes fee, doth

neat. Et prohibemus
ne quis contra factum
ipsius Archiepiscopi,
vel successorum suo-
rum, in hac parte ve-
nire presumat. Teste
E. Eliense, & S. Ba-
thon Episcopis, G.
filio Petri Comite
Essex. VVilhelmo
Mareshallo Comite
Pembrooke, Rob.
de Harecourt, Garino
filio Geraldi, Petro de
Stoke, Rich. de Reue-
rus, Rob. de Tateshal.
Datum per manum S.
Archid. VVilhelmi a-
pud Rupem auriual,
quarto die Maij,
Anno Regni nostri
tertio.

Mes entant que il est
dysputable, si cest
charter del Roy Iohn,
soit de sufficient ver-
tue pur chaunger le
nature de Gauelkinde
terre, ou nemy. Et pur
ceo que le certeinty des
terres issint conuert en
fee de Chiualer, ne
appiert

appiert en aſcun lieu
(ſaue ſolement que en
le lyure de aide leuie
en ceſt com̄. Anno 20
E.3. il eſt quater ou
ſinke temps note,que
certeine terres en Kent
ſount tenus en fee de
Chiualer, per nouam
licétiam Archiepiſcopi)
ceo ſufficera pur ceſt,
& il ſerra proue, que
touts les terres de aun-
cient tenure en ſeruice
de chiualer, ſont ſub-
iect al ordinarie courſe
de diſcent al common
ley.Et ceo poit eſte ſuf-
ficientment fait,& per
les expreſſe parols dun
note en 9.H.3.abridg
per Maſter Brooke tñ
Cuſtomes 57. & en
Maſter Fitzh. ti. Pre-
ſcription 63. Et per le
oppinion del Iuſtices
26.H.8.4. come auxy
per pleine recitall en
le Acte de Parlya-
ment fait 31.H.8.
cap.3. Per quel Sta-
tute, les poſſeſſions

not any where appere,
(ſaue onely that in
the booke of Ayde le-
uied in this ſhire. An-
no 20.E.3. it is iiij.
oz fiue times noted,
that certeine lands in
Kent bee holden in
knightes ſeruice, by
the new lycence graū-
ted to the archbiſhop)
this ſhall ſuffice foz þ,
& it ſhal foilow to be
pzoued, that al þ lāds
of auncient tenure is
knightes ſeruice, bee
ſubiect to the ozdinary
courſe of diſcent at the
comon law. And that
may ſufficiently bee
done both by þ expzeſſe
wozdes of a note in 9.
H.3.abzidged by M.
Brook ti.Cuſtomes 57
& in M.Fitzh. ti. Pze-
ſcription 63. & by the
opinion of þ Iuſtices
26.H.8.4. as alſo by
plein recital in the act
of Parliament made
31.H.8.ca.3.by which
ſtatute,the poſſeſſions
of

of certeyne Gentle=
men there were dely=
uered from this custo=
marie discent , and in=
corporated to the com=
mon lawe , for (a=
mongest other things)
in that acte it is said:
that from thence forth
such their landes shal=
be chaunged from the
sayde custome , and
shall dyscende , as
landes at the common
lawe , and as other
landes beeing in the
said County of Kent,
which neuer were hol=
den by seruice of so=
cage , but alwayes
haue bene holden by
knightes seruice , doe
discende . By which
woordes , it is verye
euident, that the ma=
kers of that estatute
vnderstood al lads hol=
den by knights seruice
to bee of their proper
nature, discendable af=
ter the common law, &
that socag.tenure was

de certeyne Gentle-
homes la fuerount de-
lyuer de cest custo-
marie discent & in-
corporate a le com-
mon ley , car (enter
auters choses ,) en
cest acte il est dyt .
que de cest temps en
auaunt , tyels lour
terres serra chaunge
de le dit custome , &
dyscendera come ter-
res al common ley,
& sicome auters terres
esteant en le dit coun-
tie de Kent, queux ne
vnques fuerount tenus
per seruice de Socage,
mes tout temps ount
este tenus per seruyce
de chiualer , discende .
Per queux parols il est
euident, que les fea-
sours de cest estatute
entendont touts terres
tenus per seruice de
chiualer, destre de lour
proper nature , dys-
cendable solonque le
common ley , & que
Socage tenure fuit
sole-

ſolement le ſubiect, in que ceſt noſtre cuſtome de Gauelkinde diſcent preuayle, & tient lieu.

Mes quant mencion eſt cy fait de Socage,et fee de chiualer, il doit touts foits eſte entende vn tenure longe puis, & de auncient temps continue, & nemy a ore nouelment ou darrainement creat, car iſſint il poit happen auterment, que eſt deuãt report. Come pur example, Si terre auncyentment tenus per ſeruice de chiualrie, vient al maines le Roygne, que apres done cco arrere al vne common perſon, deſte tenus de ſa mannour de Eaſt Grenewich en ſocage, ceſt terre (nient obſtant le alteration del tenure) demurt dyſcendable al eigne ſites ſolement, come il fuit deuaunt, come auxy,

the onely ſubiect, in which thys our cuſtome of Gauelkinde diſcent, preuayled and helde place·

But when mention is here made of Socage & knightes fœ, it muſt alwayes be vnderſtanden a Tenure long ſince, & of aunciēt time continued,& not now newely oz lately created, foz ſo it may fal out otherwiſe then is alreadie repozted. As foz example, It lande aunciently holden by knightes ſeruyce, come to the Quœnes hands,who afterward gyueth the ſame out againe to a common perſon, to bœ holden of, her manour of Eaſt Grenewich in ſocage) this lãd notwithſtãding the alteration of the tenure) remaineth diſcendable to y eldeſt ſonne only, as it was befoz,as alſo in like sort, if lands of aunrient Socage ser-uice come to the Crowne, and bee deliuered out agayne, to bee hol en either of the Queene in Capyte, or by knightes seruice of a-ny manor, it ought to discend accordinge to the custome notwith-standing that the te-nure bee altered, and if this bee true in the graunt of the Queene her selfe: then much lesse may the Archbi-shop by newe creati-on of tenure, make to his tenants any alte-ration of this old cus-tome & maner, For as the pleading is, That the lands aforesaid are of the tenure & nature of Gauelkind, euen so the truith is, the pre-sent tenure onely gui-deth not the discent, but that the tenure & the nature together, doe gouerne it. And

en mesme le manner si terres de auncyent Socage seruice vyent al corone, & soyt delyuer arere, destre tenus ou del Roigne en Capite, ou per seruice de Chiualer de ascun manner, il doit descender accor-dant al custome, nient obstaunt que le te-nure soit alter, & si ceo soyt veraye en le graunt de le Roigne mesme:donques mult meins poit le Archi-euesque per vn no-uel creation de te-nure, faire al ses te-naunts ascun altera-zion de cest viele cus-tome & maner, Car sicome le pleadinge est c, terræ predict sunt de tenuf et natura de Ga-uelkind, issint le ve-rity est que le present tanuf solent ne giude le discent, mes que le tenure et le nature en-seble, gouerne ceo. Et

Q.j. pur

parte le cuſtōe ne po-
et attache,ou auer lieu
en cco que ne fuit pas
deuant en nature ſub-
iecte al cuſtome, ceſt
a dire accuſtomable-
ment departe : Iſſint
ſur lautr̄ part,le prac-
tyſe de le cuſtome,
longe temps conty-
nue ne poet eſte in-
terupt per vn nude
alteratyon de le te-
nure come il fuit te-
nus per les Iuſtices,
Añ 4.& 5.P. & M.
come Iudge Daliſon
ad relinque en report.
Et auxy come il ap-
piert per le liuer 26.H
8.4.ou il eſt dit,que ſi
vn home ſeiſie de Ca-
uelkind terre tenus en
ſocage,fait vn done en
tayle & create vn te-
nure en ſeruice de
chiualer, que vncore
ceſt terre*doyt dyſ-
cend ſolonque le cuſ-
tome, ſicome il fuit
deuant le chaunge de
le tenure.

therfoze,as on the one
ſide , the cuſtome can-
not attache , oz take
holde of that whiche
was not befoze in na-
ture ſubiect to the cuſ-
tome , that is to ſay,
accuſtomably departe
So on the other ſide,
the pzactiſe of the cuſ-
tome,long time conti-
nued, may not be in-
terrupted by a bare al-
teration of the tenure,
as it was holden by
the Iuſtices, Anno 4.
& 5.Phi, & Mary, as
Iuſtice Daliſon hath
left repozted. And al-
ſo as it appereth by the
book 26.H.8.4.where
it is ſaid,that if a man
ſeiſed of Gauelkinde
land holdē in Socage,
make a gyft in tayle
and create a tenure
in knightes ſeruice,
that yet thys lande
muſte deſcende after
the cuſtome it did be-
foze the change of the
tenure.

Mozes

Moreouer, as the chaunge of the tenure cãnot preuaile against this custome: So nei-ther the continuaunce of a contrarye vsage, may alter thys pre-scription. For it is holden 16. E. 3. in Fitz. tif Prescriptyon 52. that albeit the eldest sonne onely hath (and that for many dilcers together) entred into Gauelkinde land, and occupyeth it without any contradiction of the yonger brothers, that yet the lande remay-neth partible betwene them, whesoeuer they wil put to their claime Agaynst which asser-tion, that which is said 10. H. 3. in Fitzh. titulo Prescripcton 64 namely of the issue taken thus. whether the lande were par-ted or no is not great-ly forceable. For al-though it bee so, that the

Oustre ceo, si-come le chaunge de le tenure ne poet pre-uaile encounter cest custom: Isint le con-tiñ dun contrarye v-sage, ne poet alter cest prescription. Car il est tenus 16. E. 3. en Fitzherb. titulo Pre-scription 52. que ni-ent obstaunt le eigne fites solement (ad & per ;diuers discentes ensemble) enter en Gauelkinde terre, & occupie ceo sauns a-cñ cotradiction de les puisnes freres, q vn-core le terre remayne-ra deste part peren-ter eux, quant ils voi-lent faire lour claime. Encont quel assertiõ, ceo que est dit 10. H. 3. en Fitz.tiñ Prescrip-tion 64. nosment de le issue isint prise. Si terra illa fuit partits meens, nest graundmt al purpose. Car nient obstãt il soit isint,q le

O .ij.   terre

terre ne fuit vnques part en fait , vncore ſil demurt partible en na-ture , il poet eſte parte a quel temps occaſion ſerra minyſter . Et pur ceo , en le fourme de pleading vſe a ceſt iour (Quod terra illa a toto tempore &c . partibilis fuit, & par-tita) il eſt pleynement priſe, que le parol(par-tibilis) ſolement eſt de ſubſtance, & que le paroll (partita) neſt forſq parol de forme, & nomy material, ou trauerſable, Veramont iſſint inſeperable eſt ceſt cuſtome de le ter-re en que il obtaine, que vn contrary dyſ-cent (continue en le caſe del Corone meſ-me) ne poet hinder, meſque que (apres tiel temps que le terre re-ſortera arrere al vn common parſon) le former viel cuſtome gouernera ceo. Come

lande were neuer par-ted in deede, yet if it re-maine partible in na-ture , it may bee par-ted whenſoeuer occa-ſion ſhalbe miniſtred. And therefore , euen in the fourme of plea-dinge vſed at this day (That the lande al-waies &c . was par-tible, and parted) it is playnlie taken, that the worde (partible) onely is of ſubſtaunce, & that the word (par-ted) is but a worde of fourme, & not materi-al, or trauerſable at al, yea ſo inſeperable is this cuſtome from the land in which it obtai-neth, ẏ a contrary diſ-cent (continued in the caſe of the Crowne it ſelfe) cannot hinder, but that (after ſuch time as the land ſhall reſorte agayne to a common perſon) the fourmer olde cuſtome ſhall gouerne it. As if if lands of Gauelkind nature come to the Queenes handes by purchase, or by Eschete as holden of her manor of Dale, nowe after her death, all her sonnes shall inherite and deuide them. But if they come to her by forfaiture in treason, or by gift in parlyament, so that her grace is seised of thē in right of the crowne, then her eldest sonne onely (which shalbe kinge after her) shal enioy them, in which case although thoie landes which the eldest sonne (beinge kinge) did possesse, do come to his eldest sonne after him (being king also) and so from one to an other, by sundry discentes, yet the opinion of Sir Anthony Browne was 7. Elizabeth, that if at any tyme after the same

si terres de Gauelkind nature vient al mains le roigne, per purchase, ou per Eschete come tenus de sa mannor de Dale, ore apres sa mort, toutes ses fites enheritera, & deuidera eux. Mes fils veigñ a luy per forfayture est treason, ou per done en parlyament, issint que sa grace est seysie del eux in iure Coronæ, donques sa eygne fites solement (que serra Roy apres luy) auera eux, en quel case, nyent obstaunt ceux terres queux le eygne fites (esteant Roy) ad possesse, vyent all son eygne fites apres luy (esteant roy auxy) & issint de vn al auter per sundrey discentes, vncore loppinion de Sir Anthonie Browne fuit 7. Elizab. que si ascun temps apres, ceux

Q.iij. terres

terres font graunt al vn common perfon, ils reuertera a lour primer nature de Ga-uelkinde, & efte par-tible enter fes heires males, nient obftant que ils ad curre vn contrary courfe, en diuers les difcents de les Royes deuaunt. Mes mult meines po-et le vnitye de pof-fefsyon en le feyg-niourfruftrate le cuf-tome de Gauelkinde difcent come il poet appeare. 14.H.4. en le longe Recordare, abridge per Mafter Brooke titulo Auow-ry 64. & titulo Cuf-tomes 19.

Ore fequitur defte parle come longe ceft cuftome extende luy mefme deins ceft noftre paies de Kent &c.

Il eft commune-ment prife, que le cuf-tome de Gauelkinde

landes be graunted to a common perfon, they fhall reuolt to their former nature of Ga-uelkind and be parti-ble amongft his heires males, notwythftan-dinge that they haue runne a côtrary courfe in dyuers the dyf-cents of the kings be-fore. But much leffe may the vnity of pof-feffion in the Lorde fruftrate the cuftome ot Gauelkynde dyf-cent as may appeare, 14. Hen. 4. in the longe Recordare, a-bridged by Mafter Brooke titulo Auowry 46. and tif Cuftomes 19.

Now followeth to bee fpoken howe farre thys cuftome exten-deth it felfe wythin this our Countrey of Kent &c.

It is commonlye taken that the cuf-tome of Gauelkinde

is general, & spreadeth it selfe throughout the whole Shire into all landes subiect by auncient tenure vnto the same, such places only excepted, where it is altered by act of parlyament. And therefore in 5. E. 4. 18. and 14. H. 4. 8. it is sayd, that the Custome of Gauelkinde is (as it were a common lawe in Kent. And the booke 22. E. 4. 19. affirmeth, that in demaunding Gauelkind lande, a man shall not nede to prescribe in certeyne, and to shew that the Towne, Borughe, or Citye, where the landes be, is an auncient towne, Borughe, or Cytie, and that the custome hath byn there (time out of mynde) that the landes within the same Towne, Borough, or Citie,

est generall, & extend luy mesme per tout le entier countie, en toutes terres subiecte per auncyent tenure al ceo, tiels lieus solement except, ou il en alter per acte de parlyament. Et pur ceo en 5, E. 4. 18. & 14. H. 8. il est dyt que le custome de Gauelkind est (com) vn common ley est Kent. Et le lyuer 22. Edwardi quarti 19. affirme que en demaundaunt Gauelkinde terre, vn home ne besoygne de prescribe en certeyne, & de monstre que le ville, borowe, ou Citie, ou les terres sount, est vn auncient ville, Borowe, ou Cytie, & que le custome ad este la (temps hors de memorie) que les terres deins mesme le vill', borowe, ou Cytie

Q.iiij.   doit

doyt diſcende a touts les heires males &c. Mes ceo eſt ſufficyent de monſtre le cuſtome a large & dedire, que le terre giſt en Kent, & que touts les terres la ſount del nature de Gauelkind. Car vn briefe de Particion de terres en Gauelkinde (Mounſier Littleton dyt) ſerra cy generall, ſicome les terres fuerount al common ley, nyent obſtaunt le declaration doyt ſpecyalment de conteyne mention de le cuſtome del pays. Ceſt vniuerſalitie conſider, & auxy le ſtrict bande (per que le cuſtome eſt cy inſeperably vnite al le terre, que en manner nul choſe forſque vn acte de parliament poet clerement diſſeuer eux) il ſequitur, que nul lyeu, Citie, ville, ou

ſhould diſcende to all the heires males et But that is ſufficient ly inough to ſhew the Cuſtome at large, and to ſay, that the lande lieth in Kent, and that all the lands there be of the nature of Gauelkind. For a writ of particion of landes in Gauelkind) ſaith M. Littleton) ſhall be as generall, as if the lands were at the common lawe, although the declaration ought ſpecyally to containe mention of the Cuſtome of the Countrey. This vniuerſalytie conſidered, and alſo the ſtrayte bonde (whereby the cuſtome is ſo inſerablye knit to the lande, as in manner nothrnge but an acte of Parliament can clerely diſſeuer them) it followeth, that no place Citye, Towne, or

2 5 o:

Bozough within this shire, can bee exempt from this custome although the same hath not at any time byn there put in vze, no moze then the Eldest sonne (in the case beefoze) maye foz the lyke reason vze= scrybe agaynst hys pouger Bzetheren &c.

Thus much beinge spoken touchinge the name, tenure, nature, generalty, and ozder of Gauelkind: it shall nowe bee shewed of what qualitie þ rents, remainders, actions, and such other things (of the which some be issuinge out of these landes, some bee an= nexed vnto them, and some bee raised by rea= son of them) shaibee. And of thē some shall ensue the nature of the land & other some shal kæpe the same courfe that commō lawe hath

Borowwe , deyns cest shire, poet este exempt de cest custome ny= ent obstaunt ceo nad a ascun temps este la mise en vze , nyent plus que le eigne fits (en la case deuaunt) poet pur semble rea= son prescribe encoū= ter les punees fre= res &c.

Cest taunt esteant parle touchaunt le nosme, Tenure, Na= ture, generaltie , & order de Gauelkind: il serra ore monstre de q̄ qualitie les rents, remainders , actions, & tyels auters cho= ses (de que ascuns sount issuant hors de ceux terres, ascuns sōt annexe al eux , & as= cuns sount rayse per reason de eux) ser= ra. Et de eux ascuns ensuera le nature del terre , & auters re= taina mesme le courfe que common ley ad
ap-

appoint . Et pur ceo ſi vn rent ſoit graunt en fee hors de Gauelkinde terre, il diſcendra a toutes ſes males ſicome le terre m̄ ferra come appiert en 14. H.8.5.26.H.8.4.& 4.E.3.

Mes ſi 2 . ioyntenants de terres en Gauelkind graunt vn rēt charge hors de ceo terre al I. S. & a ſes heires, & I.S.moruſt aiant iſſue deux ſites, ceſt rent ne diſcendera al ambideux les ſites del I. S. mes al heire al common ley, pur ceo que le cuſtome eſt en ſuſpence durant le iointur, per le opinion de le droit worſhipfull Chriſtopher Yeluerton Armiger, al ſon lecture en Grayes Inne en lent Anno 1573.

Iſſint ſi vn tenancy ſoit de Gauelkinde

appointed. And therefoʒe if a rent be graũted in fee out of Gauelkinde lande, it ſhal dyſcende to all the males as the lande it ſelfe ſhal d, as appeareth in 14.H.8.5.26. H.8.4.& 4.E.3.

But if ij. iointenãts of land in Gauelkinde grant a rēt charge out of that land to I.S. & to his heires,and I. S. dieth hauing iſſue ij.ſonnes,this rēt ſhal not diſcēd to both the ſonnes of I.S.but to the heire at the common laſo becauſe that the cuſtome is in ſuſpence during the iointure by the opinion of the ryght woʒſhipfull Chʒiſtopher Yeluerton Eſquire , at his reading in Grays Inne in lent Anno. 1573.

So if a tenauncye be of Gauelkynde nature,

nature, yet the rent seruice by which it is holden may discende according to the common lawe, as Ald' and Chart in 7. E. 3. were of opinion.

If a remaynder of Gauelkinde lande bee tayled to the heires males, they altogether shall inherite as Fitzherbert & Norwich. thought 26. H. 8, 4. But that is to be vnderstoode of a dyscent onely, for if landes of Gauelkinde nature be leased for lyfe, the remainder to the ryght heires of John Stile which hath issue foarer sonnes and dyeth, and after the lessee for lyfe dyeth, nowe the eldest sonne onely of John Stile shall haue this lande, for hee is right heire, e that is a good name of purchase 17. H. 8. in Master Brooke tit

nature, vncore le rent seruice per que il est tenus poet discende accordant al common ley, coe Ald' & Chart en 7. E. 3. fueront de opinion.

Si vn remainder de terre en Gauelkinde soit taile al heires males, ils touts ensemble inheritront, come Fitzherbert & Norwiche pensouat 26. H. 8. 4. Mes ceo est deste intende dune discent solement, car si terres de Gauelkinde nature sount lease pur vie, le remainder al droit heirs de Ihon Stile que ad issue quater fits et morust, & apres le lessee pur vie morust, ore le eignee fits solement de Iohn Style auera ceit terre, car il est droit heire, & ceo est vn bon nosm de purchase. 37. H. 8. en Mounsier Brooke tit
Done

Done & Remainder 42. Mes ſi les terres ount eſte done al Iohn Stile pur vie, le remainder al ſon procheine heire male, ceſt ad eſte vn eſtate taile en Iohn Style meſme , & donques le terre doyt auer dyſcende al touts ſes ſits, entaunt que en ceo caſe les parolx (procheine heire male) ne ſcount vn noſme de purchaſe. Mes il fuit graundement doubt 3. & 4. P. & M. (com Iuſtice Daliſon ad report) ſi vn remaynder ſoyt deuiſe per teſtameut (proximo hæredi maſculo) ſi en ceſt caſe le eygne frere ſolement auera ceo, en taunt que (en lentendement del ley, que eſt vn Iudge ſur ſoutes cuſtomes) il eſt le procheine heire male, & pur ceo quere de ceo.

Done & Remaynder 42. But if the landes had bin giuen to John Stile for life, the remainder to hys next heire male , this had bin an eſtate tayle in John Stile him ſelfe, and then the lande ſhoulde haue diſcended to al his ſonnes, in ſo much as in that caſe the wordes (next heire male) bee not a name of purchaſe. Howebeit yt was greatly doubted 3. & 4. Ph. & Ma. (as Juſtice Daliſon reporteth) if a remainder be deuiſed by teſtament (to the next heire male) whether in that caſe the eldeſt brother onely ſhall haue it , in ſo much as (in the vnderſtandinge of the lawe. which is a iudge ouer al cuſtomes) he is the next heire male and therefore inquire of it.

X i

As touchinge vou=
chers,it appeareth 11.
E.4.that al the heirs
in gauelkind shal bee
vouched for the war=
ranty of their aunces=
tor,and not the eldest
onely.But the opiny=
on of master Littleto
li.3.cap.13. and of ye
Iustices 22.E.4. is
clere that the eldest
sonne onely shall bee
rebutted,or barred by
the warranty of the
auncestor:to be short,
the eldest sonne onely
shal enter for ye breach
of a condition , but ye
rest of the brethren
shall be ioined with
him in suinge a writt
of attaint to reforme
a false verdict,or Er=
rour,to reuerse an er=
ronious iudgement,
And they all shall bee
charged for the debt of
their auncestor,if so be
ye they all haue assets
in their hands.But if
the eldest onely haue
assets

Concernaunt vou-
chers,il appiert 11.E.
3.que touts les heires
en Gauelkinde serra
vouche pur le garran-
tye de lour auncestour
& nemy le eigne sole-
ment. Mes le opy-
nion de mounsier Lit-
tleton libro 3.cap.13.
& del iustices. 22.E.4
est clere que le eigne
fits solement serra re-
butt,ou barre per le
garraunty de lour aun-
cestour : Briefement;
le eigne fits solement
entra pur le breache
de vne condition. Mes
les auters de les freres
serra ioine oue luy en
suiant vn briefe de
Attaint pur vne faux
verdict ou Errour, pur
reuerser vne erronius
Iudgement. Et ils
touts serrount charge
pur le debt de lour
auncestour,si ilsint soit
que ils touts ont assets
en lour maines. Mes si
le eigne tatsolement ad

affets demurraunt, & les auters auer aly-en lour partes , don-ques il folement fer-ra charge folonque le opinion del ly-uer 11. E. 3. &c. Et ceft taunt pur ceft part fufficera.

Ore vne vel deux parolx de auters cho-fes confufedment , vncore apperteignant al cel nient obftaunt non tout cye necef-farye pur veftre pur-pofe de eftre conus, come ceux deuaunt dits. Il appiert en vn efcript report a-large de 16. E. 2. que eft auxy en part abridge per mafter Fitzherbert titulo pre-fcription, que il fuit trie per verdict , que nul home doit auer common en terres de Gauelkinde , mes le contrarye eft bien co-nus a ceft iour & ceo en diuers lyeus,mes le

affets remaining, and the refidue haue alie-ned their parts, then he onely fhal be char-ged after the mnde of the booke 11. E. 3. &c . And thus muche for this parte fhall fuffice.

Now a worde or two of other thinges confufedly, yet apper-tayninge to this mat-ter,notwithftandinge not fo neceffarie for your purpofe to be knowen as thofe a-forefaid. It appeareth in a written report at large or 16. Edward 2. which is also part-lye abridged by maf-ter Fitzherbert titulo Prefcription, that it was tried by verdict that no man ought to haue common in lad of Gauelkinde, how beit the contrarye is well knowen at this day, and that in ma-nye places the same
booke

woke faieth, þ the vi=
fage of gauelkinde is,
that a man may law=
fully inchafe,oʒ dʒiue
out into þ high way
to their aduenture , þ
waffs of anye other
perfõ that he fhal find
doinge dammage in
his land,and that hee
is not compellable to
impound them, which
thinge is pʒactifed at
this day.

The parliament 15.
Henrici fexti cap.3.
mindinge to amplifie
the pʒiuiledges of ga=
uelkind, graunted to
the tenants of that
land,exemption in at=
taints,in fuch foʒt as
the inhabitaunts of
auncyent demeane, ꝑ
of the fiue poʒts, bee=
fore had : But with
in thʒee yeares after
hppon complaint of
fome of the Countrye
which enfoʒmed the
parliament houfe that
there was not in the

liuer dit,que le vfage
de Gauelkinde eit,
que vn home poit loi-
alment enchafe , ou
chafe hors en la haut
chimin a lour aduen-
ture , les auers de af-
cun auter perfon que
il trouera dammage
feafauntes en fes ter-
res,& que il neft com-
pellable de impounde
eux,quel chofe ē prac-
tize a ceft iour.

Le Parliament xv.
Henrici fexti capitulo
iij. volens de amply-
fier les priuiledges de
Gauelkinde, graunta
a les tenauntes de
ceo terre exemptyon
en attaintes , en tyel
fort come les inha-
bytauntes de auncy-
ent demefne & les
Cinque portes deuant
ad : Mes deins iij.ans
apres fur complaint de
afcun del pais queux
enfourme le Parly-
ament meafon que
il ne fuit paffē en
lentier

lentyer countye 30. ou 40.perfons,que ti-ent al value de xx.li. terre hors de Gauel-kinde, que en default de auters , & per rea-fon de tiel exemp-tion fuerount conty-nualment moleft per returnes en attaintes, ceft acte fuit tout re-peale.

Le Statute 14.H.8. cap.6. done libertie a chefcun home (ayant haut chimine per fes terres en le weald,que eft worne profounde et incommodious pur paffage)pur mife hors vn auter voy,en afcun tiel auter lieu de fa terre , come ferra penfe conuenient per le view de deux Iuf-tices de le peace, & xij . auters homes de wifedome & dyfcre-tion.

Le general ley fait 35. H. 8. 17. pur le preferuatyon de

whole Shire thirtye or forty perfons, that hold to the balue of xx. pounde lande , out of Gauelkinde , who in default of others, and by reafon of that ex-emption , were conti-nually molefted by re-turnes in Attaintes, that act was vtterlye repealed.

The ftatute 14. H. 8.cap.6. giueth liber-tie to euery man) ha-uinge highwaye tho-rough his land in the welde that is worne deepe , and incommo-dious for paffage) to lay out an other way in some suche other place of hys lande, as shal be thought mete by the biewe of two Iuftices of the peace, and twelue other men of wifdome and difcre-tion.

The generall lawe, made 35.H. 8.17. for the preferuatyon of
Co-

Copises woods tho=
rough out the realme,
maketh plain excepti=
on of al woods within
this weald, vnlesse it
be of such as be cōmon
And here an ende of
this matter; sauing þ
I will make master
Littletons aunswere
to such as happely wil
remaund what reason
this custome of gauel=
kind discēt hath, thus
to deuide land among
al the males contrary
to the manner of the
whole Realme beinds:
The yonger sonnes
(saieth hee) be as good
gentlemen as the el=
der, and they (beinge
a like deere to theyr
common aunceſtour,
frō whom they claim)
haue so much the more
neede of their frendes
helpe as thorough
their minoritye) they
be leſſe abie then the
eider brother to helpe
them selues.

Copeiſes boyes per
tout le Realme fait
plaine exception de
toutes boies deins ceſt
wealde ſinon q̃il ſoyt
de tiels queux ſount
common. Et iſſint vn
fine de ceſt matter,
ſauaunt que ieo voile
faire maſter Littletons
reſpons as tiels que vo=
lent demaunde, quel
reaſon ceſt cuſtome
de Gauelkinde diſ=
cent ad, iſſint pur de=
uide terre enter toutes
les males contra al
manner de tout le
Realme ailors : Les
punees fits (dit il) ſont
auxy graurd gentle-
homes, come le eig-
ner, & ils (eſteants cy
chare a lour common
aunceſtor, de que ils
claime) ount taunt le
plus beſoigne del aide
lour amies, come per
reaſon de lour mino-
ritie, ils ſont meins a-
ble que le eigne frere
pur aider lour meſmes.
R.j.   ¶ Gelde

The Exposition of

¶Gelde.

G Elde, hoc eſt quietum eſſe de conſuetudinibus ſeruilibus que quondam dari cōſueuerunt & adhuc dant, cōe hornegeld & hijs ſimilibus.

¶Gelde.

G Elde, that is to be quite of ſeruile cuſ-tomes ᵂhiche ᵂere ᵂont to bee gæuen, and are yet gæuen, as hoznegeld and ſuch lyke.

¶Grithbrech.

G Rithbrech, hoc eſt pax domini Regis fracta, quia (Grith) anglic' pax Latine.

¶Grithbrech.

G Rithbzech, that ys þ kings peace bzo-ken, becauſe (Gzith) in engliſh is pax in latin.

¶Hangewite.

H Angwite, hoc eſt quietum eſſe de latrone ſuſpenſo ſine iudicio, vel extra cuſtodiam veſtram euaſo.

¶Hangewite.

H Angwit, that is to be quite of a thæfe oz felone hanged ᵗhout iudgement, oz eſcaped out of your cuſtody.

¶Hariot.

H Ariot eſt en deux ſortes, lun hariot cuſtome, lauter Hariot ſeruice.

¶Hariot.

H Ariot is in tᵂo ſoztes, the one ha-riot cuſtome, the other hariot ſeruice.

Hariot

Hariot seruice (some say) is alwaies expressed in a mans graunt, or dede that he holdeth by such seruice to pay hariot at the time of his death), and this hariot is payable after the death of the tenāt in fee simple.

Hariot custome, ys where Hariotes haue bene payed tyme out of mynde by custome. And this may be after the death of tenaunt for life &c. but to speake thereof generally.

Hariot is the best beast (whether it bee Horse, Oxe, or Cow) that the tenaunt had at the tyme of hys death. And may bee eyther seysed , or a distresse taken for it, whether it bee hariot seruice , or hariot custome, to the Lords vse of whom the tenaunt held, by his Baylife, or

Hariot seruice (ascuns diont) est touts foites expresse en le graunt dun home , ou en son fait que il tient per tiel seruice pur payer hariot al temps de son mort. Et cest hariot est payable aps le mort de le tenát en fee simple.

Hariot custome, est lou hariots ount este payes temps hors de memorie per custome. Et ceo poit este apres le mort del tenaunt pur vie &c. Mes a parler de ceo generalment.

Hariot est le meliour beast) soit il Chiual, Boefe, ou vache) que le tenaunt ad a l temps de son mort . Et poit este ou seysie , ou vne dystresse pryse pur ceo , soit il Hariot seruyce ou Hariot custome , al vse del Seygniour de que le tenaunt tyent , per son Baylyfe, ou

R.ij.　　auter

anter officer de son manour.

  Mes de droit le seigniour, ne son officer ne doit prendre hariott, deuant que il soit present al prochein court tenus que le tenaunt est mort, & q̄ tiel beast est due al seigniour pur son harriot.

Haybote, ou Hedgbot

HAybote, ou hedgbote, est necessary stuffe pur faire et améd haies, q̄ lessee pur ás, ou pur vie, de common droit poit prend̄ sur le terre a luy lesse, nient obstant il ne soit expresse en son leas, & nient obstant que il soit vn leas per parolx sans escript.

  Haybote auxy poit estre prise pur necessarye stuffe pur faire rakes, forkes, & tiels semblables instruments oue queux

other officer belonginge to his manor.

  But of right þ lord, nor his officer shoulde not take hariot before it be presented at the next court holden, that the tenant is dead, and that such a beast is due to the Lorde for his hariot.

¶Haybote or hedgebote

HAybote or hedgbot is necessarie stuffe to make & mend hedges, which lessee for yeres, or for life of common right may take vpon þ ground to him leased, although it bee not expressed in his lease, & although it be a leas by wordes without writinge.

  Haybote also may bee taken for neccessarye stuffe, to make Rakes, forkes, and suche like Instrumentes where with
men

men vſe in ſommer to
tedde and make haye:
¶ ſo a leſſee for yeres
toke, and it was al=
lowed hym by his let=
for, the rather as I
ſuppoſe, for that ſuch
inſtruments are com=
monly made of ſlender
vnder wood, which by
the common lawe the
leſſee for yeares maye
cutte and take as is
aforeſaid.

homes vſount en ſum-
mer de tedder & faire
feine. Et iſſint vn
leſſee pur ans pſtaceo,
& fuit al luy allowe
per ſon leſſour, le
rather come ieo ſup-
poſe, pur ceo que ti-
els inſtrumts ſount cõ-
munemt fait de ſlend'
ſubbois, q̃ per le cõmõ
ley leſſee pur ans poit
ſuccider et prender co-
me eſt auauntdiſt.

¶Hidage.

¶Hidage.

Hidage, that is to
bee quit, if y king
ſhal taxe al the lande
by hides.

Note that a hide of
land is a whole plow-
lande. And this kind
of taxinge by hides
was much vſed in
olde tyme, as wel for
prouiſion of armoure,
as payementes of mo=
ney, and that chefe=
ly in king Etheldreds
daies (a kinge in this

Hidage, hoc eſt qui-
etum eſſe ſidomi-
nus Rex talliauerit to-
ta terrã per hidas.

Nota que vn hide
de terre, eſt vne entier
plowland Et cẽ kinde
de taxinge per hides
fuir mult vſe en viel
temps, cibien pur p-
uiſion de armour, cõe
paiments de argent, &
ceo principalmt, en ſs
iours del Roye Ethel-
dred (vn roye en ceſt

R.iij.   payes

pais deuaunt le con-
queſt) que en le an
de Chriſt 1006. q̄nt
les Danes priſte lande
al Sandwich en Kent,
taxe tout ſon terre per
hides en ceſt manner.
Que cheſcun 310.
hides ae terre doient
trouer vne riefe fur-
niſhe , et cheſcū 8 .hids
doient trouer vn iacke
& vn ſallet, pur le de-
fence del realme.

Countrey bfoze the
conqueſt)who in the
yeare of Chriſt 1006.
when as the Danes
landed at Sandwich
in Kent, taxed al hys
land by hides thus.
That euery 310 hides
of lande ſhould finde
one ſhip fozniſhed,and
euery 8 hides ſhoulde
finde one Jacke & one
ſallet, foz the defence
of the realme.

¶Hotchpot.

¶Hotchpot.

HOrchpot, eſt vne
medlinge,ou mix
inge enſemble, & vne
particion de terres dōe
en frankemariage, o-
ueſq; auters ēres en fee
ſimple diſcendus. Cōe
pur example,vn home
ſeiſi de 3 0.acres de ēre
en fee ſimple,ad iſſue
ij.files, & done oueſ=
que vn de ſes files al
vne home que luy ma-
ry, 10 .acres de ceo
terre en fraunkemar=

HOtchpot,is a med
linge , oz mixinge
together,and a parti=
cion of lands giuen in
frankmariage , with
other lands in fee ſim=
ple diſcended, as foz
example,a man ſeiſed
of 30.acres of lande in
fee ſimple hath iſſu ij.
daughters,and giueth
w on of his daughters
to a man that marieth
her p.acres of the ſame
land in frankemarry=
age

age, and dieth seised of
the other 20. acres:
Now if she that is
thus maried wil haue
any part of the xx.a=
cres whereof her fa=
ther died seised: Shee
must put her landes
geuen in frankemar=
riage in hotchpot, that
is to say, she must re=
fuse that gift in frāk=
marriage, and suffer
the land to be cōmixt
and mingled together
with the other lande
whereof her father di=
ed seised, so that an e=
qual diuision may bee
made of the whole be=
twene her and her sis=
ter: and thus for her
x.acres she shal haue
xb.els her Sister wil
haue the xx. acres, of
which their father di=
ed seised.

age, & morust] seisie
de les auters xx.acres:
Ore si el que est issint
marrie voiloit auer
ascun parte de les xx.
acres de que son piere
morust seisie : El do=
it mise ses terres done
en fraunkemarryage,
en Hotchpot, ceo est
adyre, el doyet re=
fuser cest done en
fraunkemarriage, &
suffer le terre de estre
commixt, & mingle
ensemble ouesque le
auter terre de que son
piere morust seisie,
issint que vne equall
diuision poit estre fait
de lentyer perenter
luy & sa soer. Et is=
sint pur sa 10.acres,
el auera xv.auterment
sa soer voit auer les xx.
acres, de que lour pier
morust seisie.

¶Homesoken

¶Homesoken.

HOme soken (or hāe
soken) y is to bee

HOmesoké (on hāe
Soken) hoc est
quie-

K.iiij.

quietum effe de amer-
ciamentis , de ingreffu
hofpiciorum violenter
& fine licentia, et con-
tra pacem domini Re-
gis. Et quod teneatis
placita de huiufmodi
tranfgreffione facta in
curia veftra, & in terra
veftra.

to be quite of amercia-
ments for entring into
houfes violently and
without licence , and
contrarie to the peace
of the king. And that
you holde plea of fuch
trefpaffe done in your
Court , and in your
lande.

¶Homicide ou Man-
flaughter.

¶Homicide or Man-
flaughter.

HOmicide ou man-
flaughter , eft le
occider dun home fe-
lonioufment fans ma-
lice prepenced . Il eft
auxy define iffint. Ho-
micidium eft hominis
occific, ab homine fac-
ta, fi auté a cane, boue,
vel alia re , non dicitur
proprie homicidium ,
dicitur homicidium ab
homine, & cędo, quafi
hominis cędium.

HOmicide or Man-
flaughter, is þ kil-
ling of a man feloniouf-
ly without malice for-
thought. It is alfo de-
fined thus. Homicideis
þ killing of a man by a
man, & if fuch killing
be done by a dogge, oxe
or other thinge , it is
not properly called ho-
micide: for it is called
homicide of a man, & to
kil as þ killing of a mã

¶Hornegelde.

¶Hornegelde.

HOrnegelde, hoc eft
quietum effe de

HOrnegeld , that is
to be quite of a cer-
teine

teine cuſtome exacted
by tailage thozow all
the lande, as of what
ſoeuer hozne beaſt.

quadam conſuetudine.
exacta per tallag. p to-
tam terr̄, ſicut de qua-
cunq; beſtia cornuta.

¶Houſebote.

¶Houſebote.

HOuſebote is neceſ-
ſarie tymber, that
the leſſæ foz yeres, oz
foz lyfe , of common
right may take vppon
the ground, to repaire
the houſes vppon the
ſame ground to hym
leaſed, although it bee
not expzeſſed in y leas.
& although it be a leas
by wozds wout dæde.
But if hee take moze
then is nædefull, hæ
may be puniſhed by an
action of waſt.

HOuſebote eſt ne-
ceſſary timber, que
le leſſee pur ans, ou pur
vie, de common droit
poit prender ſur le
terre, pur repayrer les
meaſons ſur meſme le
terre a luy leſſe, nient
obſtant il ne ſoit ex-
preſſe en le leaſe, &
nient obſtant il ſoyt
vn leas per parolx ſans
fait. Mes ſil priſt pluis
que beſoigne, il poyt
eſte puniſh per vn ac-
tion de waſt.

¶Hundred.

¶Hundred.

HVndzedes weare
deuided by Altred
the king, after that he
had deuided the whole
Realme into certeine
partes oz Sections,

HVndredes fueront
deuiſe per Alfred
le Roy, apres que il
ad deuyde le entyer
Realme en certeyne
partes ou Sections,
le

le quel de le Saxon pa-
rol Scynan , ſignificant
de ſcinder , il terme
Shires (ou ſicome nous
vncore parle) Shares &
portions. Ceux Shires
il auxy enfringe en pe-
tites partes , de queux
aſcuns fueront appeles
Lathes, de le parol Ie-
lapian , que eſt de aſ-
ſembler enſemble, au-
ters Tythinges iſsint
noſme, pur ceo que la
fueront en cheſcun de
eux al number de x.
perſons , de que cheſ-
cun fuit ſuertye &
pledge pur auters bon
behauiour: auters hun-
dredes, pur ceo que ils
conteyne iuryſdiction
ſur vn 100. homes ou
pledges demurrāt per-
aduenture en 2. ou 3.
ou plus paroches , bo-
rowes , ou villes, eſte-
ant & adioynants ny-
ent meins procheyne
enſemble , en le quel
il appoint adminiſtra-
tion de Iuſtice deſtre

which of the Saxon
word Scynan ſignify=
ing to cut , he termed
Shires, or (as we yet
ſpeake,) Shares and
portions . Theſe ſhi-
res he alſo brake into
ſmaller partes, where
of ſome were called
Lathes of the worde
Ielapian , which is to
aſſemble together : o=
thers Tithings ſo na-
med , becauſe there
were in ech of them to
the number of x. per-
ſons, whereof eche one
was ſuertie & pledge
for others good abea=
ring: others hundreds
becauſe they conteined
iuriſdiction ouer an
hundred men or pled=
ges , dwelling perad=
uenture in ij. or iij. or
more Pariſhes , Bo=
roughes , or townes ,
lying & adioyning ne=
uertheleſſe ſomewhat
nere together, in which
he appointed adminiſ=
tration of iuſtice to be

exer=

exercyfed feuerally a=
monge them of ý fame
hundʒed, and not that
one fhould runne out
difoʒderly into an o=
thers hundʒed, lath, oʒ
tithing, where in hee
dwelleth not . Thefe
hundʒedes continue to
this day in foʒce , al=
though not altogether
to the fame purpofe ,
whereunto at the trft
they were appointed,
yet ftill verie nædeful
both in time of peace
foʒ good oʒder of go=
uernmēt diuers wayes
ɛ alfo in warre foʒ cer
teintie of leuping of
men : as els foʒ ý moʒe
readie collectyons of
paymentes graunted
in Parliament to the
kinges ɛ Queenes of
this Realme.

exercife feueralmēt en-
ter eux de mefme le
hundred, & nemy que
lun irra hors diforder-
ment en lauter hun-
dred, lath, ou tything,
en que il ne demurt .
Ceux hundredes con-
tynue al ceft iour en
force , nient obftaunt
non en tout al mefme
le purpofe , pur que al
prymer ils fuerount
ordeyn, vncore a ore
mult neceffarie , & en
temps de peace pur
bone order de gouern-
ment dyuers voyes, &
auxy en guerr̃ pur cer-
teintie de leuying de
homes , come auterm̃t
pur le plus fpedie col-
lections de paymentes
graunt en Parliament
a les Royes et Roignes
de ceft Realme.

¶Hundredum.

¶Hundredum.

Hundʒedum , ý is
to be qupte of mo=
ney oʒ cuftomes to bee

HVndredū, hoc eft
quiet’eſſe de denãr
vel confuetudinib? fa-
cien-

ciendis Prepofitis & hundredarijs.

done to the Gouer=
noꝫ & hundꝛedoꝛꝭ.

¶Ideot.

¶Ideot.

IDeot eſt celuy que eſt vn ſot natural de ſa neyſture , & ne ſca=ꞇoit de accompter ou number xx . d'. ne poit noſmer ſon pere ou mere, ne de quel age il meſme eſt , ou tiel ſemblable playne & common choſes, iſ=ſint que il appiert que il nad aſcun maner de intendement de reaſon ne gouernemẽt de luy meſme, quel eſt pur ſon profite , ou diſprofite &c. Mes fil ad tant en-telligence que il poyt lyer , ou apprender de lyer per inſtruction & information de auters, ou poyt meaſure vn vlne de drape, ou noſ-me les iours en le ſe-maine, ou engender vn enfant, fits ou file , ou tiel ſemblable, per que

IDeot iꝭ he that iꝭ a fꝏle naturally from hiꝭ byꝛth, and know=eth not how to accõpt oꝛ number xx . pence , noꝛ cannot name hyꝭ father oꝛ mother, noꝛ of what age himſelfe iꝭ, oꝛ ſuch like eaſie & common matterꝭ : ſo that it appeareth he hath no maner of vn=derſtanding of reaſon, noꝛ gouernement of him ſelfe , what iꝭ foꝛ hiꝭ pꝛofit oꝛ diſpꝛofite &c. But if he haue ſo much knowledge that he can read, oꝛ learn to read by inſtruction & infoꝛmation of otherꝭ oꝛ can meaſure an Ell of cloth , oꝛ name the dayeꝭ in the wæke, oꝛ begette a chylde , ſonne oꝛ daughter, oꝛ ſuche lyke , whereby
it

it may appeare that he hath some lyght of reason: then such a one is no Ideot naturally.

il poit appere que il ad ascun lumen de reason : donques tyel nest Ideot naturalment.

¶Vnlawfull assemblie.

¶Illoyal assemblie.

VNlawful assemblie, is where people assemble themselues together to do some vnlawfull thing against the peace, although that they execute not their purpose in deede.

ILloyal assemblie est lou people eux assemble insimul, pur faire illoyal chose encounter le peace, nient obstant que ils ne execute lour purpose en fait.

¶Imparlance.

¶Imparlance.

IMparlance is when an action of det, trespasse, or such lyke ys brought against a man & after that the playntif hath counted or declared, the defendant prayeth the Court, that he may haue time to put in his answere, at another day. in the same terme, or in the next terme following,

IMparlance, est quát vn action de dette, trespas, ou tiels semblables, est port enuers vn home, & apres que le plaintife ad count ou declare, le defendant pria le Court que il poit auer temps de mise eins son respons al auter iour en mesme le terme, ou en le procheyne Terme, cest

ceſt ſtay de reſpons eſt appell imparlance.

this ſtay of aunſwere is called imparlance.

¶Impriſonment.

¶Impriſonment.

I Mpriſonment neſt auter choſe forſque le reſtraint del lyberṭie dun home, ſoit ceo en le ouert champ, ou en le Cippés, ou Cage en les eſtreates , ou en le proper meaſon dun home, ſibien come en le common gaole Et en touts ceux lyeux, le partie iſsint reſtrayne eſt dit deſte vn priſoner cy longemēt come il nad ſon libertie frākment de ire a toutes lou il voit, ſans bayle , mainpriſe , ou auter aucthoritie.

I Mpriſonment is no other thing, but the reſtraint of a mans libertie, whether it bee in the open fielde oʒ in the Stockes , oʒ cage, in the ſtreats, oʒ in a mans owne houſe as well as in the cōmon gaole. And in all theſe places þ partie ſo reſtrayned is ſaid to bee a pʒyſoner , ſo longe as he hath not his libertie fraely to go at all times whether hee will , without bayle, maynpʒiſe , oʒ other aucthoʒitie.

¶Infangethefe.

¶Infangethefe.

I Nfangethefe, hoc eſt quod latrones capti in dominico vel in feodo veſtro de latrocinijs conuicti , in

I Nfangethefe , that is that theues taken within your demeſne oʒ fee conuycted of theftes, ſhalbe iudged
in

in your Court.

curia veſtra iudicent.

¶Information.

¶Information.

INformation,for the Quæne is that , which for a common perſon is called a declaration, and is not alwayes done directly by the Quæne, or her Attourney , but rather by ſome other manne, who ſueth or inſourmeth as well for the Quæne , as for hymſelfe vpon the breache of ſome penall law or ſtatute, wherein a penaltie is gœuen to the partie that wil ſue for the ſame, but no action of debt to recouer it, then it muſt be had by information.

INformation, pur le Roigne eſt ceo que pur vn commõ perſon eſt appel vn declaration, & neſt touts foits fait directment per le Roigne,ou ſa Atturney mes per vn aut' home. Quitam pro domina Regina quam pro ſe ipſo ſequitur , ſur le breach de aſcun Penal ley ou ſtatute, en que vn penaltye eſt done al partie que voit ſuer pur ceo , mes nul actyon de dette pur recouer ceo, donques il doyt eſte ewe per Informatyon.

¶Iointure.

¶Iointure.

IOinture is an eſtate and aſſurance made to a woman in conſy=

IOinture eſt vn eſtate et aſſurance fait al vn femme en conſideration

deration de marryage,
pur terme de ſa vie, ou
auterment, ſoit il de-
uant ou apres le mar-
riage . Et ſi ſoit apres
le marriage, donques
el poit a ſa libertie a-
pres le mort de ſon ba-
ron refuſer de prender
ou auer les terres iſſint
aſſure pur ſa ioynture,
& demaund ſa dower
al le common ley. Mes
ſil ſoit fait deuant ma-
riage, donques el ne
poit refuſer tiel ioyn-
ture , ne auer dower
accordant al common
ley , ſinon que quaunt
el port ſa bryefe de
Dower, le defendaunt
plede tiel plee que ne
voile luy barrer de ſa
dower : Donques el
ſerra endow . Sicome
il dit en barre , que ſa
baron ne fuit ſeiſie de
tiel eſtate de quel el
doit eſte endowe , ou
aſcun tiel plee , & ne
monſtre que el ad
vne ioynture fait ,

deration of marryage
foʒ terme of her life, oʒ
otherwiſe, whether it
be befoʒe oʒ atter the
mariage. And if it bee
after the maryage, thē
ſhe may at her libertie
atter the death of her
huſband refuſe to take
oʒ haue the landes ſo
aſſured foʒ her ioyn-
ture , ⁊ demaunde her
dower at the common
law. But if it be made
befoʒe mariage , then
ſhe may not refuſe ſuch
iointure, noʒ haue do-
wer accoʒding to the
common ley, vnleſſe ꝑ
when ſhe bʒingeth her
wʒit of dower, the de-
fendant pleadeth ſuch
a plee ꝑ wil not barre
her of her dower: then
ſhe ſhalbee endowed.
As if he ſay in barre ,
that her huſband was
not ſeſed of ſuch eſtate
whereof ſhe might bee
endowed, oʒ any ſuch
plee, ⁊ doth not ſhew ꝑ
ſhe hath a ioiture made
&c.

&c. and therefore de=
maunde iudgement of
that action, oz iudge=
ment if she shalbe also
endowed, oz any such
like plea &c. and this
was the opinion of the
right wozshipful ma=
ster Biograue at hys
readinge in Grayes
Inne in Sömer An=
no 1576. 18. Elizab.
vppon a bzaunch of
the statute made An=
no 27. H. 8. ca. 10. cö=
cerning iointures and
dowers.

And by him of those
things whereof a wo
man may be endowed,
shee may haue ioyn=
ture as of mynes, bes=
turam terrè, woodes,
Townes, Iles, mea=
dowes, and such like.
Also if an aduowson,
of a reuersion depen=
dinge vppon an estate
foz lyfe, of a windmil,
a high chamber, a rec=
tozie and such other,
and they are called te=

&c . & pur ceo de-
maunde iudg. del ac-
tion ou iudgement si
el serra auxy endowe,
ou ascñ tiel semblable
ple &c. Et ceo fuit lo-
pynion de le droyt
vvorshippefull Master
Brograue al son lec-
ture en Graies Inne
en Sommer Añ 1476
18. Elizabeth, sur vn
braunche del statute
fait Anno 27. H.
8. cap . 10. concer-
naunt Ioyntures &
dowers.

Et per luy de ceux
choses de que vn feme
poit este endowe, el
poit auer vn ioynture,
come de mynes, ves-
turam terre, boyes,
villes, Iles, meadowes,
& tyels semblables.
Item dun aduowson,
dun reuersion depen-
dant sur vn estate pur
vie, dun VVindmill,
vn haut chamber, vn
rectorie & tiels auters,
& ils sount appels te-
nants,

S.j.

naũtes . Item dun
villen, car il eſt here-
ditament.Et de toutes
ceux profit poet vener
al feme. Mes de ceux
choſes de que nul p-
ſitte voet vener , mes
plus toſt vn charge,
vn iointer ne poet eſte
fayt.

Alſo of a
villen, foꝛ he is an he-
reditament. And of al
theſe pꝛofit may come
to the woman.But of
thoſe things whereof
no pꝛofit will come,
but rather a charge,
a ioyntuꝛe cannot be
made.

¶Larceny.

LArceny eſt vn de-
ceiptfull priſell des
biens dun auter hõ,
mes nemye de ſon
perſon, oue vn ment
dʼ eux embleer encõ-
ter ſon volunt que bi-
ẽs ils fueront.

Et larcenye eſt en
deux ſortes , lun iſ-
ſint appelle ſimple-
ment, & lauter petite
larceny.

Le pꝛimer eſt lou
le choſe emblee ex-
cœda le value de xij.
dʼ . & ceo eſt felo-
nye.

Le auter (que eſt

¶Theft.

THeſt is a deceipt-
ful taking away of
an other mans gœds,
but not from his per-
ſon, wyth a minde to
ſteale them , agaynſt
his will whole gœds
they were.

And theft is in
two ſoꝛtes , the one
ſo called ſimple, and
the other pety oꝛ lit-
tie theft.

The firſt is where
the thynge ſtollen ex-
cœdeth the value of
xij. d. and that is fe-
lonpe.

The other)which is
cal-

called little oʒ petite theft) is ꟸhere the thing stollen doth not exceed the value of xij. d. & that is no felony.

appell petit larceny) est lou le chose emblee, ne exceda le value de xij.d. & cco né felony.

¶Lastage.

¶Lastage.

Lastage, that is to bee quite of a certeyne custome exacted in faires and markets foʒ carryinge of thinges ꟸhere a man ꟸill.

Lastage, hoc est qui etum esse de quadam cōsuetudine exacta in nundinis & mercatis pro rebus cariandis vbi homo vult.

¶Lessor and lessee.

¶Lessor & lessee.

Lessoʒ is hee that lesseth lands oʒ tenementes to an other foʒ terme of life, yeres oʒ at ꟸill, and hee to ꟸhome the lease is made, is called lessee.

Lessour est celuy que lessa terres, ou tenementes al auter pur terme de vie, ans, ou al volunte, & celuye a que le lease est fait, est appell lessee.

¶Leuant & couchant.

¶Leuant & couchant

Leuant, and Couchant is sayd, ꟸhen the beastes oʒ Cattell

Leuaunt & Couchant est dit, quant les beastes, ou Cattell

dun eſtraunger ſount venue en le terre dune auter home, & la ount remayne vn certeyne bone ſpace de temps, cye longe que ils ount byen maunger, & auxy eux meſines reſt.

of a ſtraunger are come into an other mans grounde, and there haue remayned a certeyne good ſpace of tyme, ſo long that they haue well fedde, and alſo reſted them ſelues.

¶Ley gager.

¶VVager of lawe.

LEy gager eſt quāt vn action eſt port vers vn ſauns eſpecyaltye monſtre, ou auter matter de recorde : come action de dette ſur vn contracte, ou detynue, donques le defendant puyt gage ſa ley ſil voyle. s. iurer ſur vn lyuer, & certeyne perſones oueſque luy, que il doyt ryens al playntife en le manner & fourme come il ad declare : Mes en action de det ſur vn leaſe pur terme dans, ou ſur arrerages

VVager of lawe, is when an action is brought agaynſt one wout eſpecialtye ſhewed, oʒ other matter of recoʒde, as an action of debt vpon contract, oʒ detinue, then the defendaunt may wage his lawe, that is to ſay, ſweare vppon a booke, and certaine perſons with him, that he oweth nothing to the plaintife in manner & fourme as hee hath declared. But in an action of debt vpon a leaſe foʒ terme of yeares, oʒ vpon the arrerages of

of accompt before au=
ditors assigned, a man
shal not wage his law
And when .one shall
wage his law, he shall
bring with him vj. vith
or rij. of his neighbors
as the court shall as=
signe him to sweare to
him. And if at that day
assigned he faile of his
lawe, then he shalbee
condempned.

de accompt deuaunt
audytours assygne ,
hom ne gagera sa ley.
Mes quaunt vn ga-
gera sa ley, il ameine-
ra ouesque luy vj. viij.
ou xij . de ces vicy-
nes, come le court luy
assignera de iurer o-
uesque luy, et si al iour
assigne , il faut de sa
ley , donques il sera
condempne.

¶ Liuery of seisin.

¶ Liuery de seisin.

Luery of seisin, is
a ceremony vsed in
conueyance of landes
or tenementes where
an estate in fee simple,
fee taile, or a freeholde
shal passe: and it is a
testimonial of the wil-
ling departinge from
al that which he who
makes the liuery hath
in the thinge whereof
liuerie is made: And
the receyuinge of the
liuery, is a willing ac=
ceptance by the other

Luery de seisin, é vn
ceremony vse en
coueiance de terres ou
tenements lou vn es-
tate en fe: simple , fee
tayle, ou vn frankte-
nement passera. Et il
est vn tesmoigne de
le voluntarie depar-
tinge de tout ceo que
il que fait le liuerye
ad en le chose de que
lyuerie est fayt : Et
le resceit del liuerie est
vn voluntary accep-
taunce per le auk .
S. iiij.   par-

partye , de tout ceo de que lauter ad luy dif-miffe. Et fuit inuent come vn ouert & notorious chofe , per meanes de que le cō-mon people · poyent auer intelligence de paffinge ou alterati-on de eftates de l.ome al home , que per ceo ils poient eftre le meliour able pur tri-er en que le droyt & poffeffyon de ter-res & tenementes fuerount , fils doyent eftre impannel & iures , ou auterment ount a faire concer-nant ceo.

Le common man-ner de lyuerie de fey-fin , eft en ceft forte fait : Si il foit en le ouert champe ou ne font edifices ou mea-fon , donques vne que poit lyer prift le fait en fon maine , fi leftate paffera p fayt , et declare al eux q̃ la fōt,

party , of al that wher of the other hath dif-miffed him felfe : And was inuented as an open and notozious thinge , by meanes whereof the common people might haue knowledge of y̆ paf-finge oz alteration of eftates from man to man , that thereby they might be the better able to trie in whom the right and poffeffi-on of lands and tene-ments were , if they fhould be impanneled in Juries , oz other-wife haue to doe con-cerning the fame.

The common maner of deliuery of feifin is after this fozt done : If it be in the open feeld where is no buil-dinge oz houfe , then one that can reade ta-keth the wzitinge in his hād , if y̆ eftate fhal paffe by deed , & decla-reth to y̆ ftanders by
the

the cause of their mee=
tinge there together
&c.and then openlye
readeth the deede in
English , and after y
it is sealed,the partye
who is to depart frō
the ground , taketh y
deed in his handes to=
gether with a clodde
of the earthe, and a
twigge or towe if a=
ny be there, and all
this he deliuereth to
the other party in the
name of possession or
seisin,accordinge to y
forme and effect of the
deed,which before thē
was there reade.But
if there be a dwelling
house or building vp=
on the land,then this
is done there at the
doore of the same,none
beeinge lefte at that
tyme with in the
House, and the par=
tye deliuereth all the
aforesaide toogether
with the ringe of the
doore in the name

le cause de lour ve-
ner la ensemble , &
donques ouertment
lya le fait en Englois,
& apres que il est seale
le partye que est a
departer oue le ter-
re , prist le fayt en
ses maynes ensem-
ble ouesque vn clod
del terre , & vne
twigge ou bowe, fil
y ad ascun la , &
tout ceo il deliuer al
auter partye , en le
nosme de possessyon
ou seisine accordant
al fourme & effecte
del fait , que deuant
eux fuit la lie. Mes
fil soit vn habitation
ou edifice sur le ter-
re, donques ceo est
fayt la a le doore del
ceo , nul esteant re-
linquishe a cest temps
deins le meason , &
le partye deliuer tout
les auauntdists en-
semble ouesq le annu-
el del doore en nosme

S.iiij.   de

de feifyn ou poffef-
fion , & il que re-
ceiua le lyuerye en-
tra primes fole &
fhotta le doore , &
prefentement ouert
ceo , & leffa eux eins
&c. Sil foit de vne
measona que eft nul
terre , le lyuerie eft
fayt & poffefsyon
prife per le delyue-
rye del annuel del
doore et fait folement.
Et ou il eft fauns fait
de terres ou tenements
la le partye declare
per parol deuaunt tes-
teftemoignes , leftate
que il entende de
departer oue , & don-
ques deliuer feifyne
ou poffeffyon , en
manner come eft a-
uauntdift. Et iffint
le terre ou tenement
paffera cybien lou il
nad fayt , come per
fait , & ceo per force
del lyuerye de fei=
fyne : Il fuit agree
en Grajes Inne, per

of feifine or poffeffion,
and he that receineth
the liuerie entreth in
firft alone and fhut=
teth to the doore, and
prefently openeth it
againe, and lettethe
them in &c. If it be of
a houfe whereto is no
land or ground, the li=
uerie is made and pof=
feffion taken by the
deliuerie of the ringe
of þ doore and deed one
ip. And where it is
without deed either of
lands, or tenementes,
there the party decla-
reth by word of mouth
before wittneffe, the
eftate that he meaneth
to depart with, and
the deliuereth feifine
or poffeffion in maner
as is before faid: so
the land or tenement
doth paffe as wel wher
there is no deede as by
deed, and that by force
of the lyuerye of fei=
fine: It was agreed
in Grayes Inne by
the

the right worſhipfull maſter Snagge, at his readinge there in ſommer an. 2574. that if a feoffour deliuer the rede in biew of the land, in name of ſeiſin that it is good, becauſe that he hath a poſſeſſion in him ſelfe. But otherwiſe it is of an atturney, for he muſt goe to the land, and take poſſeſſiō him ſelf before p hee can geue poſſeſſion to an other, accordinge to p words of his letter &c. And where lyuerye of ſeiſin is by biewe, if the feoffee we not enter after &c. nothinge paſſeth, for he ought to enter indeede.

le droit worſhipful M. Snagge, al ſon lecture la en ſommer Anno 1574. que ſi vn feſſour delyuer le fait en view del terre, en noſme de ſeiſine, que il eſt bone, pur ceo que il ad vne poſſeſſyon en luy m̄. Mes auterment eſt dun atturney, car il doit aler al terre, & priſe poſſeſſyon luy meſme, deuaunt que il poit doner poſſeſſiō al auter, accordant al parols de ſon letter &c. Et lou lyuereye de ſeiſin eſt per le viewe, ſi le feoffee ne entra pas puis &c. nul choſe paſſa, car il doiet enter en fait.

¶ Lotherwite.

¶ Lotherwite

L Otherwite, that is that you maye take amendes of him which with file your

L Otherwite, hoc eſt quod capiatis emendas ab ipſo qui corrumpit   veſtram
                nati-

nátiuam fine licentia veftra.

bondwoman without your licence.

¶Mahim ou Maime.

¶Mahim, or Maime.

MAhim eſt lou aſcun member eſt dampnifie ou toll, per que le partie iſſint dãnifie eſt fait imperfect a cõbatier. Cõe ſi vn oſſe ſoit priſe hors del teſt: ou vn oſſe ſoyt debruſe en aſcun auter part del corps , ou vn pee, ou maine , ou digit, ou ioint du pee, ou aſcun member ſoyt ſcyer : ou per aſcun plague, les nerues ſont fait deſhrinker, ou auter member, ou les digits fait curue, ou ſi vn oyle ſoyt myſe hors, ou les anterior dentes debruſe, ou aſcun auter choſe en le corps dũ home, p reaſon de que il eſt fait le meins able pur defender luy meſme.

Mes le ſcyer dun

MAhim, is where a= ny member is hurt oʒ taken away,where= by the partye ſo hurt is made vnperfecte to ſight : As if a bone bee taken out of the hedde : oʒ a bone bee bʒoken in any other part of the bodye: oʒ a foote , oʒ hande, oʒ finger, oʒ ioynte of a foote,oʒ any member te cut:oʒ by ſome wound the ſinewes be made to ſhʒinke , oʒ other member , oʒ the fin= gers made crooked , oʒ if an eye be put out, oʒ the foʒeteeth bʒoken, oʒ any other thinge hurt in a mans bodye by meanes wherof hee is made the leſſe able to defende hym ſelfe.

But the cutting oʒ of

of an eare, or hose, or breaking of the hinder teeth, or such like, is no maihim, because it is rather a deformity of the body, then diminishinge of strength. And if the Justices stande in doubt whether the hurt be a maihim or not, they vse, & will of their great discretion take the helpe and opinion of some skilfull Surgeon, to consider thereof, before they determine vppon the case.

¶Mainprise.

Mainprise is when a man is arrested by capias, then the Judges may deliuer his bodye to certeyne menne for to kæpe and to bringe him beefore them, at a certaine day, and these bæ called maynpernours, and if the par=

---

orial, ou nase, ou len-freind' del dents mo-liers, ou tiels féblables, nest afcun mayhem, pur ceo q̃ il é pluis vn deformity de le corps, q̃ vn defect del ftrégth Et fi les Iuftices fount en doubt fi le dam foit vn mayhem ou ne-my, ils vfe, & voylent de lour graunde dif-cretion prender le aide & opinion de afcun erudite Surgeon pur confid' de ceo deuant que ils determine fur le cafe.

¶Mainprife.

Maynprife eft q̃t vn home eft ar-reft per Capias, donques les Indges poient deliuer fó corps a certayne homes pur garder, & de luy a-mefne deuaunt eux a certaine iour, & ce-ux font appels main-pernours, & fi le par-tye

tye ne appeare al iour
alsygne , les mayn-
pernours serrount a-
mercies.

¶Mannour.

MAnnour , est vn
chose compound
de diuers choses, com
dun meason terre ar-
rable, pasture, pree,
boyes,rent, auowson,
court baron, & tyel
semblable fount vn
manor, & ceo doyt
este per auncient con-
tinuance de temps,cu-
ius contrarium memor
hominum non existit,
car a cest iour vn ma-
nor ne poet este fait
pur c' q vn court barō
ne poit eē fait a ore,et
vn mañ ne poet ēe sās
vn court bar et sutors,
ou frākē,deux al meins
car si touts les frankē
preter vn escheate al
le seignior, ou sil pur-
chase tout , preter vn,
la son mannor est ale,
pur ceo que il ne poit
este vn manour sauns

tye appeare not at the
day assigned,the main-
pernors shalbe amer-
ced.

¶Mannour.

MAnnour,is a thing
compounde of dy-
uers thinges, as of a
house , lande arrable,
pasture , meadowe,
woode, rent , auow-
son, court baron, and
such like make a man-
nor,and this ought to
be by long continuāce
of time, to the contra-
rie whereof mans me-
mory cannot tell, for
at this day a mannor
cānot be made,because
a court baron cannot
nowe be made , and a
mannor cannot be w-
out a court baron,and
suters,or freeholders,
two at the least, for if
all the freeholdes ex-
cept one eschete to the
lord , or if he purchase
al except one,there his
manor is gone,for þ it
cānot be a manor wout

a

a court Baron (as is aforesaid)? a court baron cannot be holden but before sutors, and not before one suter, & therefore where but one fræholde or fræholder is, there cannot be a mannor.

vn court baron (come auantdit) & vn court ne poit estetenus mes deuant suters,& nemy deuaunt vn suter , & ideo lou forsque vn frankeñ,ou tranktenãt est,la ne poit estre vn mannour.

¶Manumission

¶Manumission.

MAnumission is in ij. sorts, the one is a manumission expressed, the other a manumission implyed or secreate.

Manumission expressed is when þ lord maketh a dæde to hys villein to enfraunches him by this word(Manumittere)which is as much to say as to let me goe out of an other mans handes or power.

The manner of manumitting or infranchtinge in olde time moste vsuallye was

MAnumission est en deux sortes,le vn est vn manumission explicita , lauter vn manumission implicita.

Manumission explicita, est quaunt le seigniour fait vn fait al son villeine pur luy enfraunchiser per cest paroll manumittere, quod idem est quod extra manum, vel extra potestatem alterius ponere.

Le maner de Manumitting ou enfranchesing en temps passe plus vsualment fuyt issint

issint . Le seygniour (en presence de ses vicines) prist le villeine per le test disant, Ieo voyle que cest home soyt franke , & oue ceo il luy mise auāt hors de ses mains, & per ceo il fuit frank sauns ascun pluis fair. Manumission implicita sauns cest paroll (Manumittere) est quaunt le seignyour fait vn obligation a son villem a paiera luy money al vn certeine iour , ou luy sue ou il poic enter sans suit, ou graunt al son villeine vn annuitie , ou lessa terre a luy per fayt pur ans , ou pur vie, & dyuers tyels semblables cases : le villeyne per ceo est fait franke.

thus. The Lorde (in presence of his neighbors) toke the bonde man by the heade saying, I will that thys man be free, and therewith shewed him forward out of his hāds, & by this he was free without any moze ado. Manumission impryed without thys worde(Manumittere)is when the lord maketh an obligation to hys villein to pay him money at a certain day, oz sueth him where he might enter without sute, oz graunteth vnto his villein an annuitye, oz lesseth lande to hym by deede foz yeres oz foz life, and in diuers such like cases, the villein thereby is made free.

¶Maximes.

¶Maximes.

Maximes font les foundations del

Maximes bee the foundations of the law,

law, and the conclusi=
ons of reason, and are
causes efficient, & cer=
tein vniuersal propo=
sitions so sure and per=
fect that they may not
be at any time impea=
ched or impugned, but
ought alwayes to bee
obserued and holden
as strong principalles
and authorities of thē
selues although they
cannot be proued by
force of argument or
demonstrations logi=
cal, but are knowen by
enduction by the way
of sence and memory.
As for example, it is
a maxime that if a man
haue issue ij. sonnes
by dyuers women,
and the one of them
purchase landes in fee
and dyeth wythout
issue, the other bro=
ther shall neuer be his
heire &c.

Also it is an other
maxime that lāds shal
discēd from the father

ley, & les conclusions
de reason, & sont suf-
ficient , & certeyne
vniuersall propositi-
ons, cy sure & perfect
que ils ne poyent este
a ascun temps im-
peache, ou impugne,
mes doyēt toutes foits
este obserue & tenus
cōe fort principales &
avcthorityes de luy
mesme, nyent obstant
ils ne poyent ēe proue
per force de argu-
ment ou demonstra-
tions logicall , mes
sount conus per en-
duction per le voye
de sence & memory.
Come pur example
il est vn maxime que
si vn home ad issue ij.
sites per dyuers ven-
ters , & le vn de eux
purchase terres en fee
& morust sauns issue,
lauter sites ne vnques
serra son heire &c.

Item il est vn auter
maxyme que terres
dyscendra del pyer
al

al fits , mes nemy del fits al pere, car eft vn afcention &c. & dyuers tiels femblables il y ad.

to the fonne , but not from the fonne to the father for that is an afcention &c. & diuers fuch like there &.

¶Maynour.

¶Maynour.

MAynour eft quāt vn laron ad emble & eft purfue oue hue & cry,& prife, aiant ceo troue ouefque luy que il ad emble, ceo eft appel le main. Et iffint nous communement vfe pur dire quaunt nous trouomus vn fairans de vn ylloyall acte, que nous luy prift ouefque le maynor , ou manner.

MAynour is when a theefe hath ftolen , and is followed wyth hue and cye, and taken , hauinge that founde about him which he ftole, that is called the maynour. And to we commonlye vfe to faye when we finde one doing of an vnlawfull act, that wee toke him wyth the mainour, or manner.

¶Mifprifion.

¶Mifprifion.

MIfpifion eft quant afcun fceit que vn auter ad fait treafon, ou felony , & il ne voile luy difcouer al Roigne,ou fa Confell

MIfprifiō, is whē on knoweth ý another hath cōmitted treafon or felony, and wil not difcouer him to the Q or to her Councell o, to any Magistrate, but doth conceale the same.

A Chaplein had fixed an olde seale of a patent to a new patent of Non residence, and this was holden to be a Misprision of treason onelye, and no counterfapting of the Queenes seale.

Also if a man know money to be counterfait, & bring the same out of Ireland hither into England, & vtter it in payment, this is but misprision of treason, & no Treason, & so it is in dyuers such lyke cases.

And in all cases of misprision of Treason the party offendor shal forfait his goodes for euer, and the profites of his landes for terme of hys life, and hys bodie to pryson at the Queenes pleasure.

And for Misprision

ou a ascun Magystrate, eins concela son offence.

Vn Chaplein ad fixe vn auncient seale dun patent, a vn nouel patent de Non residence, & ceo fuit tenus deste Misprision de treason tantum, & nul counterfaiter del seale del Roigne.

Item si vn auter sciet money destre faux, & port ceo hors de Ireland en Engleterre, & vtter ceo en payment, ceo est forsque Misprision de Treason, & nemy Treason, & issint est en dyuers tiels semblable cases.

Et en touts cases de misprision de Treason le partie offendor forfeitera ses brens a touts iours, & les profits de ses terres pur terme de son vie, & son corps al prison, al pleasure del Roigne.

Et pur Mysprision

de felony ou trespas, le offendour serra commit al prison, tanque il ad troue suertyes ou pledges pur son fine, que serra assesse per le discretion de les Iustices deuant que il suit conuict,

Et nota que en chescun Treason ou Felonie est include Misprision, & lou ascun ad fait troason ou felonie, le Roigne poit causer luy deste indicte & arraygne forsque de Misprision solement sil voyle.

of ful nie or trespace, the offendour shal be committed to prison vntil hee haue founde suerties or pledges for his fine, whych shalbe assessed by y discretion of the Iustices before whom he was conuict.

And note that in euery Treason or felonie is included misprision. & where any hath committed treason or felony, the Q. may cause the same to be indicted & arrayned but of Misprision only it the w it
l.

¶Monstrance de faits, ou Recordes.

¶Shewing of deedes, ou Recordes.

MOnstrance de faits ou Recordes, est sicome pur example, vn accion de dette soit port enuers vn sur vn obligation, ou per executors &c. la apres que le plaintife ad declare,

SHewinge of deedes or recordes, is as if for example, an action of dette be brought against one vpon an obligatiō, or by executors &c. there after that the plaintif hath declared, he he ought to shew hys obligation, or the executor the testament to the court, and so it is of Recordes.

And the diuersitie betwene shewinge of deedes or Recordes, & hearing of deedes or recordes, is thus, he p pleads the deede or record, or declares vpon it. to him it doth appertaine to shew the same. And the other against whom such deede or record is pleaded or declared, & is thereby to be charged, may demaunde hearing of the same deede or recorde, which his aduersarie bringeth or pleadeth against him.

il doit monstr son obligation ou le executor le testament al court, & issint est de Recordes.

Et le diuersitie par enter Monstraunce de faits ou records, et cier de faits & recordes est issint, Il que plede le fait ou recorde, ou declare sur ceo, al luy il appertaine de monstre ceo. Et lauter vers que tiel fait ou recorde est plede ou declare, & est per ceo deste charge, poyt demaunde oyer de ceo fayt ou Recorde, que son aduersarye port, ou plede vers luy.

¶ Mortgage or Morgage. — ¶ Mortgage ou morg.

Mortgage or Morgage, is when a man maketh a feoffement to another on such condicion, that if the feffor

Mortgage ou morgage, est quant vn fait vn feoffement a vn auter sur tiel condicion, que si le feoffour

T.ij.   paya

paya al feoffee a cer-
taine iour xl. li. dar-
gent, que adonques la
feffor puit reenter &c.
en ceo cafe le feoffee
eft appell tenaunt en
Morgage. Et ficome
vn home puit faire fe-
offemét en fee en mor-
gage, ifsint il puit faire
done en le taile, ou leas
pur terme de vie, ou
pur term dans en mor-
gage. Et il femble que
la caufe pur que il eft
appell mortgage, eft
pur ceo que il eftoit en
awerouft fi le feoffour
voile payer al iour ly-
mit le argent ou non,
& fil ne paya paffe,
donq; la terre q il myt
en gage fur condition
de payment de le mo-
ney, eft ale de luy a
touts iours, & ifsint
mort a luy fur condi-
tion,& fil paya le mo-
ney, donques eft le
gage mort quant a le
tenant, ceftaffauoir, le
feffee,& pur ceft caufe

pay to the feoffee at a
certeine day xl. li. of
money, that then the
feoffor may reenter &c,
in this cafe the feoffee
is called tenát in mor-
gage. And as a man
may make a feoffemét
in fee in Mortgage, fo
he may make a gift in
taile, or a leafe for
terme of lyfe, or for
terme of peres in mor-
gage. And it feemeth
that the caufe why it
is called Mortgage, is
for that it ftandeth in
doubt, whether the
feoffor will pay p mo-
ney at the day appoin-
ted or not, & if he faile
to pay, then the lande
which he laied in gage
vpon condicion of pai-
ment of the money, is
gon from him for euer
& fo dead to him vpon
condicion: but if he pay
the money, then is the
gage dead as to p te-
nát, that is to fay, the
feoffee, & for this caufe
it

it is called in Latine
Mortuum vadium, as
master Littleton saieth,
or rather mortuum vas,
as I thinke.

il est appel en Latine
Mortuum vadium, côe
Master Littleton dit,
ou mortuum vas, come
ieo pense.

¶Mortmaine.

¶Mortmaine.

MOrtmayne was
when lands were
geeuen to a house of
religion, or to a com-
pany which be corpo-
rate by the kinges
graunt, then the land
is come into mortmain
that is to say in Eng-
lish a dead hand, & the
kinge or the Lorde of
whom the lande is
holden may enter into
them.

MOrtmayne fuyt
quant terres fue-
ront dones a vn mea-
son de religion, ou a
vn companie que sont
corporate per le graunt
le Roy, donques cest
terre est deuenus en
Mortmaine, cest adire
en Anglois a deade
hande, & le Roy ou
le seigniour de que le
terre est tenus poit en-
ter en eux.

¶Mulier.

¶Mulier.

MUlier, is a worde
vsed in our lawe,
but how aptly I can-
not tell, nor do well
know howe it should
come in that sense as
we there take it: For

MVlier est vn parol
vse en nostre ley,
mes come aptment ieo
ne voy dire ne scay bn,
cor il doit vener en
tiel sence come nous la
ceo prendromus: Car

T.iij.   2c-

accordaunt al proper
ſignification, Mulier
eſt fæmina corrupta,
ſicome il eſt vſe per
Vlpianus, en vn cer-
teine lieu en tiel man-
ner. Quod ſi ego me
virginem emere puta-
rem cum eſſet mulier,
emptio non valebit.
Per ceo poyes veyer,
que Mulier eſt vn feme
que ad ewe le compa-
nie dun home: Mes a
relinquiſher le droyt
ſignification. Mulier
eſt priſe en noſtre ley,
pur vn que eſt loyal-
n ent engender & nee:
& eſt tours dyts vſe en
comp ar.ſon oueſq; vn
baſtaid ſolement pur
monſtre vn difference
parenter eux come pur
example. Vn home
ad vn f.tes per vn feme
deuaunt mariage, ceſt
iſſue eſt appel vn baſ-
tarde, & i.loial. .a-
pres ils entermarie, &
ount vn auter fites,ceſt
feconde fites eſt appel

accoꝛding to the pꝛo=
per ſignification. Mu=
lier is a defiled woman
lyke as it is vſed by
Ulpianus, in a cer=
teine place after thys
ſoꝛt. If I thought y
I had bought a Uir=
gine, when it was a
defyled woman, the
bargain was not good.
Hereby you may ſee,
y Mulier is a woman y
hath had the companie
of a man. But to leaue
the right ſignification.
Mulier is taken in our
law foꝛ ene y is law=
fully begottē & boꝛne:
& is alwaies vſed in
compariſon iþ a baſ=
tarde, onely to ſhew
a difference beetwene
them, as thus foꝛ er=
ample. A man hath a
ſonne by a woman be=
foꝛe mariage, that is
called a baſtarde, and
vnlawfull. And after
they entermarie and
haue an other ſonne,
this ij. ſonne is called
Mu-

Mulier, that is to say lawfull, and shalbee heire to hys father: but that other cannot be heire to any man, because it is not knowen nor certein in the iudgement of the law, who was his father, and for that cause is saide to bee no manes sonne, or the soane of the people, and so without father, according to thys olde Verse.

¶To whom the people father is, to him is father none and all.

¶To whom the people father is, well fatherlesse wee may him call.

¶And alwayes you shall finde this addition to them, (Bastard eldest, & mulier yongest) when they bee compared together.

Mulier, cest a dire loyall, & serra heire al son pier, mes le auter ne poet este heire al ascun home, put cy que il nest conus ne certeyne, en le iudgement del ley, que fuit son pere, & pur cest cause est dit, deste nullius filius, ou filius populi, & issint sans pere accordaunt al cest vrcle verse.

Cui pater est populus, pater est sibi nullus & omnis.

Cui pater est populus, non habet ipse patrem.

Et toutes foys vous troues cest addision al eux, (Bastarde eigne & mulier puisne,) quant ils sount compare ensemble.

¶Murder.

¶Murder.
T.iiij.	Mur

MVRder eſt vne
voluntarye oc-
cyder dun hom̄
ſur malice prepenſe,
& ſemble de vener
de le Saxon paroll
Mordren que iſsint
ſignifie. Et Mordri-
dus eſt le murderer
tanque al ceſt iour
enter eux en Saxonie,
de que nous auomus
mults de noſtr parolx
come ad eſtre ſepe dit.

Murder is a wil-
ful killinge of a
man vpon ma-
lice forethought, and
ſeemeth to come of the
Saxon word Mordren
which ſo ſignifieth: &
Mordridus, is the mur-
derer euen vntil this
day amonge them in
Saxonie, from whe͠re
wee haue moſt of our
wordes as hath bene
often ſaid.

¶Negatiua preignans.

¶Negatiua preignans.

NEgatiua preignans
eſt quaunt vnę
action , ou informa-
tion , ou tiel ſembla-
ble eſt port enuers
vn , & le defendant
pleade en barre del
actyon , ou auter-
ment vne negatiue
plea, que neſt cy ſpe-
cyall aunſvvere al acc'
mes que il enclud auxi
vn affirmatiue. Come
pur example, ſi ceſtuy
en reuerſion enter ſur

NEgatiua pregnās
is when an acty-
on, or information, or
ſuch like is brought
againſt one, and the
defendant pleadeth in
barre of the action, or
otherwiſe, a negatiue
plea which is not ſo
ſpeciall an aunſwere
to the action, but that
it includeth alſo an
Affyrmatiue. As for
example : If hee in
reuerſion enter vppon
tenant

tenant for life suppo-
singe that hee hath a-
liened in fee (which
is a forfaiture of his
estate) and the te-
naunt for life sayeth
that hee hath not ali-
ened in fee , this is a
negatiue wherin is in-
cluded an affirmatiue:
for althoughe it bee
true, that he hath not
aliened in fee : yet it
may be that hee hath
made an estate in taile
(which is also a for-
faiture)and then the
entrie of him in the re-
uersion is lawfull &c.
Also in a Quare impe-
dit the Queene makes
tytle to present to a
Prebend for that the
Temporalties of the
Bishopricke were in
her hands by the deth
of W. late Bishop &c.
The defendant saieth
that it was not voide
bring the temporalties
in the queens hands by
the death of W. this is

tenaunt pur vie suppo-
saunt que il ad alien
en fee(que est vn for-
faiture de son estate)
& le tenaunt pur vye
dit que il nad alien en
fee, cest vne negatiue
en que est include. vn
affirmatiue. Car ny-
ent obstant il soit ve-
ray que il nad alyen
en fee, vncore il poys
estre que il ad fait vne
estate en taile(le quel
est auxi vn forfeitur)
& donques lentrie de
celuy en le reuersion
est loyall &c. Item en
vne Quare impedit
le Roigne fist tytle
de present a vne Pre-
bende ratione que
les Temporaltyes le-
uesque fuerount en sa
maynes , per le mort
de VV. nuper epis-
copi &c. Le defen-
daunt dist que ne voi-
da pas esteuines les
Temporaltyes en les
maynes del Royghe
p le mort de VV. cest

vn

vn negatiue preignans, car il poit estre en les maines del Roigne autrement que per le mort de VV. & il suffist al Roigne si soit en sa maines per ascun meanes &c. Issint est ou vne information suit port in scaccarie vers I. S. pur ceo que il achate laines enter sheringe temps & le Assumpteon tali anno de I. N. Le defendaunt dist quod non emit del. N. come il est alledge, &c. ceo est appell vne negatiue preignans, car sil ceo achate de auter, vncore il est culpable pur le achate.

a negatiue preignans, for it may bee in the queens hands otherwise then by p deathe of W. and it suffiseth the queene if it bee in her handes by anye meanes &c. So it is where an Information was brought in the escheker against I. Stile, for that hee bought wool tetwene shering time & the assumption, such a yeare of John N. The defendant saith that hee did not buy any of I. N. as it is alledged &c. this is called a negatiue preignans, for if he bought it of any other, yet he is culpable for the buyinge.

¶Niefe.

¶Niefe.

Niefe est vn feme q est bond ou vne villen feme, mes si el mary vn frank home,

Niefe is a woman that is bonde, or a billen woman, but if shee marrie a free man shee she as thereby made free for euer (although that her husband dye and she suruiue him) because that she and her husbād ar but one person in law, and she ought to be of the sāe nature and condition in lawe to al intents that her husbande is. But her husbande is free to al intents wiout any condition in lawe or otherwise, and so by consequens þ wife ought to be, and is free accordinge to the nature of her fre husbād & thē if she were one free and clerelye discharged of bondage to al entents, she can not be niese after without especiall acte done by her, as diuorce, or confession in court of record, and that is in fauor of liberty, & therefore a free woman shal not be bōud by taking of a villein to her husbād

el est per ceo fait frāke a touts iours (coment que le baron deuy, & el suruiue) pur ceo que el & son baron sount forsque vn person en ley, & el couient estre de mesme le nature & condicion en ley a touts intents come son baron est. Mes son baron est franke a touts intents sans ascun condition en ley, ou auterment, & issint per consequens le femme couient estre, & est franke accord' al natur de son frank baron, & donques si el soit vne foits frank & cleremt discharge de villenage a touts intents, el ne poit estre niefe apres sans especial act fait p luy, come diuorçe, ou conulas en court de record, et ceo est en fauour de liberty, et pur ceo vn frank feme ne serra villene per prisell del villen al son baron.

Mes

Mes lour issue serra villeins come lour pere fuit, que est contrarie a le ley ciuile, car la est dit , partus sequitur ventrem . Bondage ou villenage ad son commencement enter les Hebrewes, & son originall proceding de Chanaan le fites de Cham , que pur ceo que il derisee son pere Noe gysant dissolutement quaunt il fuit ebriee, fuit puny en son fites Chanaan ouesque penaltie de bondage.

But their issue shalbe billeines as their father was , which is contrary to the Ciuile law. for there it is said the birth followeth þ belly. Bondage or villenage had beginning among the Hebrewes & his original proceding of Canaan þ sōne of Cham, who because þ he had mocked his father Noe to scorne, lying desolutely when he was drunke , was punished in hys sonne Chanaan with penaltie of bondage.

¶Nihil dicit.

¶Nihil dicit.

Nihil dicit, est quāt vn action est port enuers vn home , & le defendant appeare, le plaintife declare , & le def. ne voile responder, ou plede al action , & ne maynteyne son plee, mes fait default , ore sur cest

Nihil dicit , is when an actiō is brought against a man, and the defendāt appeares, the plaintife declares, ānd the def. will not aunswere, or pledes to the actiō, & doth not maintain his ple, but makes defaut, now vpō this

de=

defaut, he shalbe con=
dempned , because hee
sayeth nothing.

default, il serra con-
dempne , quia nihil
dicit.

¶Nomination.

¶Nomination.

NOmination , ys
where one may in
right of his manor or
otherwise , nominate
and appoint a worthy
clerke or man to a par=
sonage , vicarage , or
suche like spirituall
promocion.

NOmination , est
ou vne poit en
droit de son manour
ou auterment nomi-
nate, & appoint vn a-
ble clerke, ou home al
vn parsonage , vyca-
rage, ou tiel spiritual
promocion.

¶Nonabilitie.

¶Nonabilitie.

NOnabilitie , ys
where an action is
brought against one, &
the defendaunt sayeth
that þ plaintife is not
able to sue any action
& demaundeth iudge=
ment if he shalbe aun=
swered. There are vj.
causes of nonabilitie
in the plaintife , as if
he be an outlaw, or an
alien borne , but that
disability is in actions

NOnabilitie, est lou
vn action est port
vers vn , & le defen-
dant dit que le playn-
tife est nonable de
suer ascun action &
demaunde iudgement
sil serra respond. Il y
ad vj . causes de no-
nabilitie en le plain-
tife , come sil soit vt-
lage , ou vne aljen
nee , mes cest dis-
abilitie est en actions
reals

reals & mixt ſolement
& non en actions per-
ſonalls , ſinon que il
ſoit vn alyen enemie,
ou condempne en pre-
munire , ou profeſſe
en religion , ceſtaſca-
uoir, le Romiſh Re-
ligion , ou excom-
mege, ou vn villeyn &
ſue ſon ſeigniour, mes
ceſt darreine neſt plee
pur autr̄ que neſt ſeig-
nioural villeine.

reales and mixt onely
and not in actyons
perſonalles , except
hee bee an alien ene-
mye , oz condempned
in pzemunire , oz pzo-
feſſed in religion, that
is to ſaye, the komiſh
religton , oz accurſed,
oz a villen and ſueth
hys Lozde , but this
laſt is noe ple foz an
other y is not lozd to
the villen .

¶Nude contract.

¶Bare, or naked contract.

NVde contract, ou
nude promiſe, eſt
lou vn home bargaine
ou vende ſes terres, ou
biens, ou promiſe pur
doner al auter money,
ou vn chiual, ou a ede-
fier vn meaſon, ou faire
tiel choſe a tiel iour, &
nul recompence ap-
point a luy pur le faire
de ceo. Come ſi vn dit
al auter , ieo vende ou
done al vous toutes
mes terres ou byens.

BAre Contract, oz
naked pzomiſe , is
whhere a man bargay-
neth oz ſelleth hys
lads, oz goods, oz pzo-
miſeth to geue to one
money, oz a hozſe, oz to
buylde a houſe, oz doe
ſuch a thing at ſuch a
day, & there is no recō-
pence appoynted to
him foz y doing therē-
of. As if one ſay to an
other I ſel oz geue to
you al my lads oz goods
And

And there is nothing appointed, assigned, or agreed vpon, what the other shal geue or pay for it, so that there is not one thing for another, this is a naked contract, and voyde in law, & for not performance therof no action lieth, for of a naked contract cometh no action.

Et la est nul chose appoint, assigne, ou agree, que lauter donera, ou payera pur ceo, issint que il nad quid pro quo, cest vn nude contract & void en ley; & pur non performaunce de ceo nul action gist, car ex nudo pacto non oritur actio.

¶ Oredelfe.

O Redelfe is where one claimes to haue the ore that is founde in his soile or ground.

¶ Oredelfe.

O Redelfe, est lou vn clayme de auer le ore que est troue é son soile ou terre.

¶ Outfangthiefe.

O Utfangthiefe, that is, that theues or felones of your lande, or fee, out of your land or fee taken with felonie or a stealinge, shalbe brought backe to your Court, and there iudged.

¶ Outfangthiefe.

O Vtfangthiefe, hoc est quod latrones de terra vestra vel feodo vestro extra terram vestram, vel feodum vestrum, capti cum latrocinio, ad curiam vestram reuertantur, & ibidem iudicentur.

¶ Owel-

¶Oweltie.　　　¶Oweltie.

OVVeltie, est quant il y ad seigniour, mesne, & tenant, & le tenant tient del mesne per mesne les seruices que le mesne tient ouster de le seigniour paramount. Come si le tenant tyent del mesne per homage, fealtie, & xx.s. de rent annuelment, & le mesne tyent ouster de le seygniour paramount per homage, fealtie, & xx. s. rent auxy, cest appell Oweltie de seruices.

OWeltie, is when there is Lord, mesne, and tenant, and the tenant holdeth of the meine by the same seruices, that the mesne holdeth ouer of þ lord aboue him. As if the tenant hold of the mesne by homage, fealtie & xx. s. of rent yerely, and the mesne holdeth ouer of the lord aboue by homage, fealtie, and xx shyllynges rent also, this is called Oweltye of seruices.

¶Oyer de recordes & faits &c.　　¶Hearing of Recordes and deedes &c.

OYer de Recordes & faits, est si pur example, vn action de Dette soit port enuers vn home sur vn obligation, & le defendant appeare al action, & donques prya que il

HEaring of records and deeds is, it for example, an action of det be brought against a man vpon an obligation, & the defendaunt appeares to the action. & then prayeth that he

may

may heare the obliga=
tion where with the
plaintif chargeth him.
So it is when as
executors bring an ac=
tion of det, & the defē=
dant demaundeth to
heare the testamēt, by=
pon this demaunde it
shalbee reade vnto the
defendaunt . But if
it bee in ann other
terme or after that
the defendaunt hath
imparied, then he shal
not heare it . And so
as is sayde of dœdes,
is to bee vnderstœde
of recordes that are
alleaged against him.

poet oyer lobligation
ouesque que le pleintif
charge luy.
Issint est quant ex=
ecutours port vn ac-
tion de dett, & le de-
fendaunt demaunde
oyer del testament: sur
cest demaunde il ser-
ra lectu al defendant,
Mes sil soyt en va
auter terme, ou a-
pres que le defendaunt
ad imparle, donques
il nauera le oyer. Et
issint come est dit de
faites est deste in-
tende de recordes que
sount alledge enuers
luy.

¶Pape.

¶Pape.

Pape is an auncyent
name falsely arro=
gated, or proudly v=
surped by the By=
shop of the onely Ci=
tis of Rœme in Ita=
lie , and is common=
ly Englished þ Pope,
a name truely much

Pape , est vn aunc'
nosme fauxement
arrogate, ou hautment
vsurpe per le Euesque
de le sole Cytie de
Rome en Italye, & est
communement appell
en Anglois le Pope, vn
nosme veramēt mult

V.j   .fic-

Frequent en noſtre aū-
cient annels liuers, ſpe-
cialment en les temps
de ceux Royes , queux
graundement aban-
donans lour imperi-
all aucthoritye , & a-
baſans eux meſmes,
mult debaſe lour eſ-
tate , ne fueront hont
de ſuffer vn alien &
outlandiſh Eueſque q̃
enhabite ouſter cinq;
diz cent miles de eux,
deſtre ſoueraigne de-
haut eux en lour dō-
minions demeſne , &
de toller de eux nõ
ſolement le diſpoc⁹ de
certeine petite trifles
de nul accompt , mes
auxy le nomination d'
Archieueſq̃s , eueſq̃s ,
Abbeis , deanes , pro-
uoſts , appropriations,
de benefices, preſenta-
tions al perſonages,
vicarages , & general-
ment de toutes ſpy-
rituall perſons a lour
prefermentes, aſc' tẽps
per laps , aſcun teinps

frequenteꝺ in our an-
cient yeare bꝛoks, ſpe-
cially in the times of
thoſe kinges, who to
much abaꝛoning their
impertall audhoꝛitye,
and abaſinge them
ſelues far bneth their
eſtate, were not aſha-
med to ſuffer an alyen
and outlandiſh Biſ-
ſhoppe, that dwelt a-
boue fiftene hundꝛeꝺe
miles from them, to be
ſoueraigne ouer them
in theyꝛ owne donyi-
nions, and to take frõ
them not onelye the
diſpoſition of certeine
ſmall trifles of none
accompte, but alſo the
nomination of Arch-
biſhoppes, Biſhoppes,
Abbots, Deanes, pꝛo-
uoſts, appꝛopꝛiations
of beneſices, pꝛeſenta-
tions to perſonages,
bicarages , and gene-
rally of all ſpirituall
perſõs to their pꝛefer-
ments ſometimes by
lapſe, and ſometymes
other-

otherwiſe wherebye
the kinges princelye
Prerogatiue was ve=
rye muche abridged
within their owne
Realmes.

auterment, per que le
prerogatiue del royes
fuit moult abridge
deins lour Realmes
demeſne.

¶Partition.

PArtition is a deuy=
dinge of landes diſ=
cended by the common
lawe, or by cuſtome
amonge coheires or
parceners wher there
be ij. at the leaſt whe=
ther they bee ſonnes,
daughters, ſiſters auts
or otherwiſe of kinne
to the aunceſtor from
whom the land diſcē=
ded to them.

And this particy=
on is made iiij. waies
for the moſt part,
whereof three are at
pleaſure and by agree=
ment amonge them,
the fourth is by com=
pulſion.

One partition by a=
greement is whē they
them ſelues deuide the

¶Partition.

PArtition eſt vne di-
uiſion de terres diſ-
cendus per le com-
mon ley, ou per cuſ-
tome ¦ perenter co-
heires, ou parceners, ou
ils ſount deux al meins
ſoyent ils fites, files,
ſoers, auntes, ou au-
terment de kynne al
aunceſtour de que
le terre diſcend al
eux.

Et ceſt partiticion
eſt fait quatuor voies
pur le plus part, de
que trois ſont al plea-
ſure & per agree-
ment perenter eux, le
quart eſt per com-
pulſion.

Vn particion per
agreement eſt quant
ils meſmes deuide le

V.ij.   terre

terre equalment en tants partes , come la font de eux copercens & chefcun de eflier vn fhare ou parte,le eigne primerment , & ifsint lun apres lauter,come ils font de age,fi non q̄ le eigne per confent fait le particion, donq̄s le election appertient al prochaine , & ifsint al eigne darreignemēt accordant come il est dit : Cuius est particio, alterius est electio.

Vn auter partition per agreemt est quant ils eflieu certeine de lour amies de faire diuifion pur eux.

Le tierce partition per agreemt est p trahēs de lotts ifsint : primermt de deuider le ſſ en tants des parts come la font parcens,dōq̄s a fcriuer chefc' parte feueralment in vn petit fcrolle ou peece de paper ou parchement

lande equally into fo many partes, as there bee of them coparce=ners, and each to chofe one fhare or parte, the eldest first, and fo the one after other , as they bee of age, except that the eldest by con=fent make the partici=on, then the choice be=longeth to the next, & fo to the eldest last, according as it is faid Who fo maketh the particion , the other must haue the choice.

An other partition by agreement is when they chofe certain of their frends to make diuifion for them.

The thirde partici=on by agreement is by drawing of lots thus: first to deuide the land into fo many parts as there bee parceners, then to writt euerye parte feuerrallye in a little fcrole, or peece of paper or parchment
and

and to put the same
scrolles vp close into
a hate, capp, oz other
such like thinge, and
then ech parcener, one
after an other as they
bee of age to dzawe
out thereof one peece
oz scrolle wherein is
wzitten a part of the
lande which by this
dzawinge is now se=
ueralye alotted vnto
them in fœ simple.

The fowerth par=
tition which is by cõ=
pulsion is when one
oz some of the copar=
ceners would haue
partition and other
some will not agree
thereto, then they that
so would haue parti=
cion may bzing a wzit
de particione facienda a=
gainst the others that
would not make par=
tition, by vertu wher
of they shalbe compel=
led to depart &c. Wee
in Kent (Bzother
Nicholas (where the

et de mitter ceux scrols
close en vn hat, cappe,
ou auter tiel sembla=
ble chose, & donques
chescun parcener vn a=
pres lauter come ils sõt
de age a traher hors
de ceo vne peece , ou
scrole en que est es=
cript vne parte del ter=
re que per cest tra=
hens est a ore seueral=
ment allott al eux en
fee simple.

Le quater partici-
on, que est per com-
pulsion , est lou vn
ou ascun de les co-
parceners voilent auer
particion et auters ne
voilent agree al ceo,
donqs ceux que issint
voilent auer particion
poient porter vn briefe
de particione facien-
da enuers les auters
queux ne voylent fair
partition , per vertue
de que ils serra com-
pell de departier &c.
Nous en Kent (Frere
Nicholas) ou les
                    ter-

V.iij,

terres ſount de Gauel-kinde nature, appello-mus a ceſt iour noſ-tre particyon , Shyf-ting , il meſme paroll que les Saxons vſe noſment Shyftan, que ſignifie pur faire par-ticyon perenter co-heires , & pur aſſig-nera a cheſcun de eux lour porcyon. En la-tin eſt appelle Her-ciſcere.

landes are of Gauel-kinde nature , cal at this day our particy-on Shifting euen the very ſame word that the Saxōs vſed nam-ly (Shiftan) which ſigni-ficth to make particiō betwene coheires, and to aſſigne to eache of them their portion, in latyn it is called Her-ciſcere.

¶Parties.

¶Parties.

PArties al fine, ou fayt , ſount ceux queux leuye le fine, & auxi ils a que le fine eſt leuie . Et ils que ſount vn fait de feof-fement, & ils a que il eſt fayt , ſount appels parties al fait, & iſſint en auters ſemblables caſes.

PArties to a fine , or dœde.are thoſe that leuy the ſame fine, and alſo they to whom the fine is leuied : And they that make a dœde of fcoffement, and they to whom it is made are called parties to the dœde, & ſo in any other like caſes.

¶Patron.

¶Patron.

PAtrō is he that hath a perſonage, vyca=rage, free chappell, oꝛ ſuch like ſpirituall pꝛo=motiōn belonging to his mannoꝛ. and may oꝛ ought to giue the ſame benefice when and as often as it fal=leth voyde. And thys being patron, oꝛ patro=nage had beginninge foꝛ the moſt part by one of theſe iij. waies, namely eyther by rea=ſon of the foundaty=on, foꝛ that the patron oꝛ hys aunceſtours, oꝛ thoſe from whom hee claymes were foun=ders oꝛ buylders of the Churche, oꝛ by reaſon of Dotation, foꝛ that they did en=dowe oꝛ geue landes to the ſame foꝛ main=tenaunce thereof, oꝛ els by reaſon of the grounde becauſe the Churche was ſet oꝛ builded vpō their ſoile oꝛ grounde: and many

PAtron eſt celuy que ad vn perſonage vycarage, franke chap=pell, ou tyels ſem=blable ſpirituall pro=motion appurtenaunt al ſon manor, & po=et ou doet doner cea benefice quaunt & cy toſt queil deuient voide. Et ceſt eſteant patron, ou patronage ad commencemēt pur le pluis parte per vn de ceux troys voyes, noſment, ou Ratione fundationis, pur ceo que le patron ou ſes aunceſtours, ou ce=ux de que il clayme fuerount foundours, ou edeſiers de le eſ=gliſe, ou Ratione dotationis, pur ceo que ils endovve ou done terres al ceo pur maintenaunce: ou au=terment Ratione fun=di, pur ceo que le Eſ=gliſe fuyt myſe, ou edefye ſur lour ſoyle ou terre, & dyuers

V.iiij.   tempꝛ

temps per reafon de ils troys.

times by reafon of the al thẛee.

¶Perquifites.

¶Perquifites.

PErquifites font ad-uauntages & pro-fittes queux vyent al vn mannor per ca-fualtye , & non an-nuelment , come ef-cheates, hariots, re-liefes, waiues eftraies, forfaitures , amercia-mentes en courtes, gardes , mariages, bi-ens & terres purchafe per villeines de mef-me le mannor , & di-uers femblables cho-fes queux ne fount certein mes happen p chance , afcun temps pluis often que a au-ter temps.

PErquifites are ad-uauntages and pʒo-fittes that come to a mannoʒ by cafualty,& not yearely : as Ef-cheates , Hariotes , Reлyefes , Waʏfes , ftrayes foʒfaʏtures, amẛrcemẛts in courts, wardes , maryages, goods and landes pur-chafed by villaines of the fame mannoʒ, and diuers fuch like thigs that are not certeine but happen by chaun-ce , fometymes moʒe often then at other tymes.

¶Plaintife.

¶Plaintife.

PLaintife eft celuy que fue ou com-playne en vn affife, ou en vn action per-

PLayntife is hee that fueth oʒ com-playneth in an affyfe oʒ in an actyon per-fonal.

sonall , as in an acti=
on of det,trespas,dis=
cept, detinue, and such
other.

fonal , come en vn ac-
tion de det, trespasse,
disceit, & detinue, &
tiels semblables.

℔Pleading.

¶Pleading.

Pleadinge is that
which cōmeth after
the count, namly that
which is contained in
the barre, replication,
and reioinder, and not
that contayned in the
count it selfe, & there=
foze defaultes in the
matter of the Count
are not compzifed win
mifpleading, oz infuf=
ficient pleadinge, noz
are remedied by p̄.sta=
tute of Jeofailes:But
only that mifpleading,
oz infufficyent plea=
ding.committed in the
barre,replication, and
reioinder , are there
pzouided foz.

Pleadinge est ceo
que vyent apres
le count, nosement
ceo que est contayne
en le barre, replica-
tion, & reioinder , &
non ceo contayne en
le count mesme , &
pur ceo defautes en le
matter del count, ne
fount comprise deyns
nispleading, ou insuf-
ficient pleading , ne
sont remedy per le sta-
tute de Ieofailes . Mes
solement ceo misplea-
ding ou insufficient
pleading, commit en
le barre,replication,&
reioynder , sount la
prouide.

¶Pound.

¶Pounde.

Poundes

POundes fount en deux fortes, lun poundes ouert, les auters pounds clofe.

Pounde ouert, eft chefcun lyeu en que vn diftreffe eft myfe, foit ceo common poũd tiels que font en chefcvn ville ou Seignyorie, ou foit ceo backfide, court, yarde, pafture, ou auterment quecunque, lou le owñ del diftreffe poit vener a doner eux viande fans offence pur lour efteant la, ou fon veñ la.

Pounde clofe, eft tiel lyeu, lou le owner del diftreffe ne poyt vener a doñ eux vyande fauns offence, com en vn clofe, meafon, ou quecunque auter lieu.

POundes are in two fortz, the one pounds open, the other pounds clofe.

Pounde open, is euery place wherein a diftreffe is put, whether it bee common pounde fuch as are in euery towne oz lozdefhip, oz whether it bee backfide, Court, yard, pafture, oz els whatfoeuer, whether the owner of the diftreffe may come to geue thẽ meate & dzinke without offence foz their being there, oz his cõming thither.

Pound Clofe is fuch a place, where the owner of the diftreffe may not come to geue them meat and dzinke, without offence, as in a clofe houfe, oz whatfoeuer els place.

¶Poffeffion.

¶Poffeffion.

Poffef=

POſſeſſiō is ſaid two wayes, eyther actuall poſſeſſion, oꝛ poſſeſſion in lawe.

Actuall poſſeſſion, is when a man entreth in deede into landes oꝛ tenements to him diſcended, oꝛ otherwiſe. Poſſeſſion in lawe is when landes oꝛ tenements are diſcended to a man, and he hath not as yet really, actually, and in deede entred into them. And it is called poſſeſſion in lawe, becauſe that in the eye, and conſideration of the lawe, hee is deemed to be in poſſeſſion, foꝛ aſmuch as he is tenaunt to euery mans action that will ſue concernynge the ſame landes, oꝛ tenements.

¶Preamble.

PReamble taketh his name of the ꝑrepoſi=

POſſeſſion eſt dit ij. voyes, ou actuall poſſeſſion, ou poſſeſſ. en ley.

Actuall poſſeſſion, eſt quaunt vn home enter en fayt en terres, ou tenementes, a luy diſcende, ou auterment. Poſſeſſion en ley eſt quaunt terres, ou tenementes ſount diſcende al vn home, & il nad vncore realment actualment, & en fayt enter en eux. Et il eſt appell poſſeſſion en ley, pur ceo que en le oile, & conſideration del ley, il eſt penſe deſte en poſſeſſion, entaunt que il eſt tenaunt a cheſcun action que voet ſuer concernāt meſmes les terres, ou teneu entes.

¶Preamble.

PReamble ad ſon noſm de le prepoſition

fition (pre) deuaunt, & le verbe (Ambulo) pur va, ifsint ioint enfembl᷑ , ils font vn compounde verbe de le primer coniugation (Preambulo) pur va- deuaunt, & de ceo le primer part ou commencement dun acte eft appell le preamble de act,le ql pamble, eft vn cliffe de ouert les ments del fefors del act, & les mifchiefes que ils intende de remedy per ceo, come pur example leftatute fait al VV . le primer le 37.ceo que done attaint, le preamble de que eft ifsint. Pur ceo que afcuns gents de la terre doutent meines faux ferement farie, que faire ne duiffent, per que multes des gentes fount difheri- tes & perdent lour droit, puruiewe eft &c.

tion(Pre) before, and the verbe (Ambulo)to goe, fo ioyned toge= ther,they make a com- pounde verbe of the firft coniugation (Pre- ambulo) to go before, & hereof the firft parte or beginning of an act, is called the preamble of the act, which pre= amble is a key to open the mindes of the ma- kers of the acte,& the mifchiefes that they intende to remedy by the fame,as for exam= ple the ftatute made at Weftminfter the firft, the 37. chapter which giueth an attaint,þ p̄= able of which is thus. For afmuch as certein people of the realme, dout very little to giue falfe verdicts or othes, which they ought not to do , whereby many people are difherited & lofe their right, it is prouided &c.

Pre-

¶Prescription .　　　¶Prescription.

Prescription is whē
one hath had oz v=
sed any thinges sithe
the time whereof no
minde is to the con=
trary.

Prescriptyon est
quaunt vn ad ewe
ou vse ascun chose de
puis le temps dount
nul memory al con-
tra.

¶Presentment.　　　¶Presentment.

Presentmēt is whē
a man which hath
right to gæue a bene=
fice spirituall nameth
the person to whome
he wil giue it,and ma=
keth a wziting to the
Bishop foz him, that
is a pzesentation oz
pzesentment.

Resentment , est
quaunt vn home
que ad droit a done
vn benefice spirituall
nosme le person a que
il voit le doner, & fait
vn letter al euesque
pur luy,ceo est vn pre-
sentation ou present-
ment.

¶Pretensed right or
Title.

¶Pretensed droit ou
Title.

Pretensed right oz
title is where one
is in possession of lāds,
oz tenementes, and an
other who is out of
possession,claimeth it,
oz sueth foz it. Nowe

Retensed droit ou
title , est lou vn est
en possession de ter-
res , ou tenementes,
& vn auter que ē hors
de possession , claime
ceo ou sue pur c'. Ore
le

The expoſition of

le pretenſed droit, ou title, eſt dyt en luy que iiſint ſue ou claim Et ſil puis vient a le poſſeſſion de meſme le terres, ou tenements, ſon droit ou tytle eſt extinct, ou ſuſpend en le terre.

the pꝛetenſed right oꝛ title is ſayde in him, whoe ſo doth ſue oꝛ claim. And if he after ward come to the poſſeſſió of the ſame lãds, oꝛ teneniĕts, his right oꝛ title is extincte, oꝛ ſuſpended in the land.

¶Priuie ou Priuite, & Priuities.

¶Priuie or Priuitie, and Priuies.

PRiuie, ou priuite, eſt lou vn leaſe eſt fait a tener a volunte, pur ans, pur vie, ou vn feoffement en fee, & en diuers auters caſes, ore pur ceo de ceo que ad paſſe perenter ceux parties ils ſount appell priuies, en reſpect de eſtraungers perenī queux nul tyel conueiaunces ad eſtre.

Auxy ſi ſoit Seygniour & tenaunt, & le tenaunt tient del ſeigniour per certeine ſeruyce, il y ad vn pri-

Priuie, oꝛ pꝛiuity is wher a leaſe is made to holde at will, foꝛ yeres, foꝛ life, oꝛ a feffement in fee, & in diuers other caſes, now becauſe of thys that hath paſſed betweene theſe parties, they are called pꝛiuies, in reſpect of ſtraungers betwene whom no ſuch dealings, oꝛ conueiances hath ben.

Alſo if there be loꝛd and tenaunt, and the tenaunt holdeth of the Loꝛde by certeyn ſeruyce, there is a pꝛiuitie

uitie betwene thē te=
cause of the tenure, & if
the tenaunt bee disse[=]
sed by a straũger, there
is no priuity betwene
the disseisor & the lord,
but the priuity stil re=
maineth betwene the
Lord and the tenaunt
that is disseysed, and
the Lord shall auowe
vpon him, for that hee
is his tenant in right
and in the iudgement
of the lawe. Priuies
are in diuers sorts, as
namely priuies in es=
tate, priuies in deede,
priuies in law, priuies
in right, and priuies in
bloode.

Priuies in estate is
where a lease is made
of the manor of Dale to
A. for life, the remain=
der to B. in fee, there
both A. and B. are pri
uies in estate, for their
estates were bothe
made at one time. And
so is it in the first case
heare where a lease is

uitie perēt eux per
cause de tenure, & si le
tenaunt soyt disseisie
per vn estraunger , il
ad nul priuitie perent
le disseisour & le seig-
niour , mes le priuitie
vncore demurt peren-
ter le seigniour et le tenaunt que est dissey-
fie , & le seigniour a-
uowera sur luy pur ceo
que il est son tenaunt
en droit,& en lē iudg-
ment del ley , Priuies
sount en dyuers sortes
cõe nosmēt, priuies en
estate, priuies en fait,
priuies en ley , priuies
en droit, & priuies en
sange.

Priuies en estate ,
est lou vn lease est fait
del mannor de Dale
al A. pur vie, le re-
maynder al B. en fee,
la & A. & B. sount
priuies en estate , car
lour estares fuerount
ambideux al vn tēps.
Et issint est en le pri-
mer case ou vn leas est
fait

fait al volunt, pur vie ou ans, ou vn feoffement en fee , les leſſees , ou feoffees, ſont appel priuies en eſtate, & iſsint ſont lour heires &c.

Priuies en fait, eſt lou vn leaſe eſt fayt pur vie, & apres per vn auter fayt, le reuerſion eſt graunt al vn eſtraunger en fee, ceſt grauntee del reuerſion eſt appell priuie en fait, pur ceo que il ad le reuerſion perfait.

Priuie en ley , eſt ou il ad ſeygniour & tenaunt , le tenaunt leſſa le tenauncy pur vie , & moruſt ſauns heire , & le reuerſion eſcheate al ſeignyour, il eſt dyt priuye en ley, pur ceo que il ad ſon eſtate ſolement per le ley ceſt adire per eſcheate.

Priuie en droit, eſt lou vn poſſeſſe dun

made at will, for life or yeares or a feoffement in fee, the leſſees or feffees , are called priuies in eſtate, and ſoe are their heires &c .

Priuies in deed is where a leaſe is made for life, and afterward by an other deede the reuerſion is graunted to a ſtraunger in fee, thys grauntee of the reuerſion is called priuate in deede, becauſe that he hath the reuerſion by deede.

Priuie in lawe is where there is Lord & tenant, the tenant leſſeth the tenauncy for life and dieth without heire, & the reuerſion eſcheates to the lorde, he is ſaid priup in law becauſe that he hath his eſtate onely by the lawe, that is to ſay by eſcheate.

Priuie in ryght, is whereon poſſeſſed of a terms

terme for yeres, grãts his estate to another vpon condicion, and maketh his executors & dyeth, now these executors are priuies in right, for if the condicion be broken, & they enter into the lande, they shal haue it in the right of their testator, & to his vse. Priuie of bloode is y heire of the feoffor or donor &c.

Also if a fine bee leuied, the heires of him that leuyeth the fine are called priuies.

terme pur ans graunt son estate al vn auter sur condition, et fayt ses executors et morust, ore ceux executors sont priuies en droit, car si le condicion soyt enfreint, et ils enter en le terre, ils auera ceo en le droyt de lour testatour, & a son vse. Priuie de sanke est le heire del feoffor ou donor &c.

Item si vn fine soyt leuie, les heires de celuy que leuie le fine sõt appell priuies.

¶Priuiledges.

Priuiledges are lyberties and fraunchises graunted to an Office, place, towne, or mannour, by the Queenes great charter, letters patentes, or acte of Parliament, as Tolle, sake, socke, Infangtheefe, Outfangtheefe, Turne

¶Priuiledges.

Priuiledges sont liberties & franchises graunt al vn office, lieu, ville, ou mannour, per le graunde charter del Roygne, letters patentes, ou acte de parliament, come tolle, sake, socke, Infangtheefe, Outfangtheefe, Turne tolle,

X.j.

tolle , Oredelfe , & dyuers tyels femblables, pur queux voyes en lour proper titles & lieus.

tolle , Oꝛedelfe , and dyuers fuch lyke, foꝛ which looke in theyr pꝛoper titles and places .

¶Procheine amy.

¶Next friende.

PRocheine amy , & gardein en focage eſt tout vn , et eſt lou vn home feiſie de terres tenus en focage moruſt fon iſſue deyns age de 14. ans, donques le prochein amy , ou procheyne de fanke a que les terres ne poyent vener ou difcende , auera le garde del heire , & del terre , al vfe folement del heire , tanque il vyent al age de xiiij. ans , & donques a tiel ans , il poit enter & luy ouſte , & port luy de accompter, mes en ceſt accompte il auera allowaunce, pur toutes reafonable coſtes & expenſes

NExt friende and wardeine in Socage is all one, and is where a manne feyfed of landes holden in Socage dyeth, hys iſſue within age of 14. yeares , then the next friende , oꝛ next of kynne to whom the lands cannot come oꝛ difcende , ſhall haue the keepynge of the heire,& of the land, to the onely vfe of the heire , vntyll he come to ẏ age of xiiij.yeres, & thē at that yeres he may enter & put hym out.& bꝛing him to accompt: but in that accompt he ſhalbe allowed foꝛ all reafonable coſtes & expences, be-

bestowed epther vpon
the heire oz his land.

And the next friend
oz next of kynne to
whom the inhery=
taunce cannot dys=
cende, is thus to bee
vnderstwde: If the
landes discende to the
heyre from hys fa=
ther, oz anye of the
kynne of hys fathers
syde: then the mother,
oz other of the mo=
thers syde, are called
the next of kynne to
whom the inheritance
cannot dyscende, foz
befoze that it shal so
dyscende, it shall ra=
ther Escheat to the
Lozde of whom it is
holden. And so it is
to bee vnderstwde,
where the landes
come to the Heyre
from hys Mother,
oz any of the kynne
of hys mothers syde:
Then the father oz o=
ther of the fathers
syde, are called the next

bestow ou sur le heire
ou son terre.

Et le prochein amy,
ou prochein de sanke
a que le inheritaunce
ne poet discender est
issint deste intende.
Si les terres discende
al heire de son pier,
ou ascun del sanke
del parte son pier,
donques le meere,
ou auter del part
le mere, sount ap=
pell le procheyne de
sanke a que le en=
heritaunce ne poyt
dyscender, car de=
uaunt que il issynt
dyscendera, il pluys
toste Escheatera al
Seigniour de que il
est tenus. Et issint
est deste entende,
ou les terres vyent al
Heire de sa mere,
ou ascune auter de
sanke del parte sa
Mere: Donques le
pere ou auter del
part son pere sount
appell le procheyne

X.ij.   de

de ſanke a que le en-
heritaunce ne poyt
diſcende , mes plus
toſt eſchetera al ſeig-
niour, de que il eſt
tenus.

of kynne to whom the
inheritaunce cannot
diſcende: but that ra-
ther eſcheat to the
Lozde of whome it is
holden.

¶Proteſtation.

¶Proteſtation.

℘Roteſtation eſt vn
ſaluation al partie
(que iſſint plede per
proteſtation,) deſte
conclude per aſcune
matter alledge ou ob-
iect encounter luy, ſur
que il ne poit ioyner
iſſue. Et i eſt auter
choſe que excluſion
del concluſion , car il
que priſt le proteſta-
tion exclude lauter
partie de cōcluder luy.
Et ceſt proteſtatyon
doit eſtoyer oue le
ſequele del plee, &
nemy deſte repug-
nant, ou auterment
contrarie.

℘Roteſtation is a ſa-
uinge to the partie
(that ſo pleadeth by
proteſtation) to bee
concluded by any mat-
ter alledged oz obiec-
ted againſt him, vpō
which he cannot ioin
iſſu: And is no other
thing but an excluſion
of the concluſion, foz
hee that taketh the
proteſtation excludes
the other party to cō-
clude hym. And this
proteſtatyon ought to
ſtande wyth the ſe-
quele of the plœ, e not
to be repugnaunt, oz
otherwiſe contrary.

¶Purchaſe.

¶Purchaſe.

Pur-

Purchase is the possession that a man hath in lands or tenements by his owne act meanes or agreement , and not by title of discent, from any of hys aunceftors.

Purchase eſt le poſ-ſeſſion q̃ vn home ad en terres ou tenements per ſon act de-meſne , means , ou a-greement , et nemy per tytle de diſcent, de aſc' de ſes aunceſtors.

¶ Quarentine.

¶ Quarentine.

Quarentine , ys where a man dy-eth seysed of a man-nour, place , and other landes whereof hys wife ought to bæ en-dowed , then the wo-man shal hold the ma-nour place xl. dayes, within whiche tyme her dower shalbee af-ſigned. But if shæ marrie within the xl. dayes, she shall loose her quarentine.

Quarentine , eſt lou vn home deuy ſci-ſie dun mannor place & auter terres , dount ſa femme doit eſte en-dowe , donques la feme tyendra le man-nour place per 40. iours , deyns quel temps ſon dower ſer-ra a luy aſſygne , mes ſi el marrie in-fra les 40. iours , el perdra ſon Qua-rentine.

¶ Fifteene.

¶ Quinzime.

Fifteene, is a pay-ment graunted in Parliament to the

Vinzime. eſt vne payment graunt en Parlyament al X.iiij.   Roigne

Roigne, per les layes, ceftafcauoir le quin-zime part de lour by-ens . Et fuit vfe en auncient temps defte leuie fur lour auers efteants en lour terres que fuit mult trou-blous , & pur ceo a ore pur le plus part , ceft voy eft alter , & ils vfe de leuie ceo per les Verges, ou Acre ou auter meafure de terre . Per reafon de que il eft a ore meins troublous , & plus certeine que deuaunt il fuit . Et chefcune ville & pays fcient, quel fumme eft defte pay parenter eux , & coment ceo ferra raife. Nous legimus que Moyfes fuit le primer que number le people, car il number les If-raelites , & pur ceo le prymer Taxe , Sub-fidye , Tribute , ou Quinzyme fuit in-nent per luy enter les

Queene , by the tem-pozaltie , namely the 15. part of their goods: And was vfed in aun-cient time to be leuied vppon their cattel go-yng in their grounds, which thynge was very troublefome, and therefoze nowe foz the moft part , that way is alltered , and they vfe to leuy the fame by the yarde, oz Acre oz other meafuf of lad By meanes where of it is now leffe trouble-fome, and moze certen, then befoze it was. And euery towne and countrey doe knowe , what fumme is to bee paied amonge them, e how the fame fhalbee raifed. we read that Moyfes was the firft that did number y peo-ple, foz he numbzed the Ifraelits, e therefoze the firft taxe, fubfidye, tribute, oz fiftene was inuēted by him among
the

the Hebꝛewes, as Po-
lidoꝛ Virgill dothe
thinke.

Hebrewes, come Po-
lidore Virgill sup-
pose.

¶ Regrator.

REgratoꝛ is he that
hath coꝛne, vitails
oꝛ other things suffi-
cient foꝛ hys owne
necessarie neede, occu-
pation, oꝛ spending, ⁊
doth neuerthelesse en-
grosse and buy vp in-
to his handes moꝛe
Coꝛne, vittailes, oꝛ o-
ther such thinges, to
the intent to sell the
same again at a higher
and deerer pꝛice, in
Faires, Markets, oꝛ
such like places.

¶ Regrator.

REgrator est celuy
que ad blees, vit-
tailes, ou auters choses
sufficient pur son ne-
cessarie oeps, occu-
pation, ou expences,
& nyent obstant en-
grosse & achate en ses
mains plus blees, vit-
tailes, ou auters tiels
choses, al entent de
vender ceo arrere al
vn plus haut & chare
price, en Faires, Mar-
kets, ou tiels sembla-
bles lieus.

¶ Reioynder.

REioynder, is when
the defendant ma-
keth aunswere to the
Replication of the
plaintife.

And euery reioinder
ought to haue these

¶ Reioynder.

REioynder, est
quaunt le defen-
dant fayt respons al
Replication del plain-
tyfe.

Et chescun Reioin-
der doyt auer ceux
deux

X.iiij.

deux propertyes ſpe-
cyalment ceſtatcauoir
il doit eſtre vne ſuf-
ficient reſpons al re-
plycation , & auxy
de ſubſequer & en-
forcer le matter del
barre.

two properties ſpeci-
ally,that is to ſay,it
ought to be a iuſticy-
ent aunſwere to the
Replication and alſo
to follow and enforce
the matter of the
barre.

¶Reliefe.

¶Relyfe.

R Eliefe eſt aſcun
foits vne vncer-
taine ſome de mo-
ney que le heire pai-
era al ſeigniour de
que ceux terres ſont
tenus,queux aƥs le diſ-
ceaſe deſon aunceſtor
ſont a luy diſcend cõe
pchein heire,aſc' foits
il eſt paiment dun au-
ter choſe,& nemy mo-
ny.Et pur ceo reliefe
neſt certein & ſemble
pur touts tenures,mes
cheſcun ſundry tenure
ad(pur le plus part)
ſon ſpecial reliefe cer-
tain en luy meſme.
Neque eſt ceo deſtre
pay touts foits al vne

R Elife is ſometime
a certein ſome of
money that the yeire
ſhal pay to the lord of
whom thoſe lands are
holden , which after
the deceaſe of his aun-
ceſtour are to him diſ-
cented as next heire:
ſometimes it is the
paiement of an other
thinge,and not mony:
And therefore reliefe
is not certaine,and a-
like for all tenures,
but euery ſundry te-
nure hath(for þ moſt
part (hys ſpecyall
Reliefe certaine in it
ſelfe. Neyther is it to
be paied alwaies at a
cer-

certaine age, but vari=
eth therein also accoz-
dinge to the tenure.
As if the tenant had
lands holde by knights
seruice (except great
Sergeancy) and dye
his heire being of full
age, and helde his lāde
by þ seruice of a whole
knightes fæ, the lorde
of whom that landes
are so holden shal haue
of the heire C.s. in
the name of reliefe, &
if he hold by lesse then
a knightes fæ, he shall
pay lesse, & if moze thē
moze, hauinge respect
alwaies to the rate
for eue ry knightes fæ
an hunozed shillings.
And if hæ helde by
Graunde Serieancye
(which is alwayes
if the Quæne, and is
also knyghtes ser=
uice) then the reliefe
shall bæ the value of
the lande by the yere,
bæsides all charges is-
suing out of the same.

certaine age, mes il va-
rye en ceo auxy ac-
cordaunt al tenure.
Come si le tenaunt ad
terres tenus per ser-
uice de chiualer (fore-
prise graund sergean-
cy) & morust son
heire esteant de pleine
age, & tyent ses ter-
res per le seruice dun
entier fee de chiual-
ler, le seigniour de que
ceux terres sount is-
sint tenus, auera del hr
C.s. nomine releuij, et
si il tient p meins que
vn fee de chiualer, il
paiera meins, et si plus
donq; plus, aiant res-
pect touts foits al rate
pur chescun fee de
Chiualler vne cent
souze. Et sil tient per
graund serieancy (que
est touts foits del roigñ
& est auxy seruice de
chiualer) donques le
reliefe serra le value
del terre per an, preter
touts charges issuaunt
hors de ceo.

Re-

Reliefe que le feig-
niour auera' pur terres
tenus en focage,eft tãt
plus come le rent que
le tenant tient .fon ter-
re en focage per,come
fil tient per vn denier
rent,& moruft,le feig-
nior auera ceft denier
rent,& vn denier ouft
pur reliefe,de quecun-
que age le tenant foit,
al mort de fon auncef-
tor.Et nota que en af-
cun cafes le feigniour
auera fon reliefe main-
tenant.apres le mort
de fon tenant,fi il foit
iffint que le temps del
an voit fuffre ceo defte
ew,come money,blees
carne,pifhe,fpices,ou
afcun tiel femblable,
& pur defaut de pay-
ment,le feigniour po-
et pur ceo de common
droyt prefentment dif-
traigner.

Mes en afcun cafes
le feigniour doit de-
murre pur fo relief cer-
tain temps qñt necef-

Reliefe that the lord
fhall haue for landes
holden in Socage,is
fo much more as the
rent that the tenaunt
holdeth his lande in
Socage by,as if hee
holde by a penny rent
and dye,the lorde fhal
haue that penny rent,
and a penny ouer for
relife,of what age fo-
euer the tenant was
the death of his aun-
ceftour.And note that
in fome cafes the lord
fhall haue his reliere
immediatly after the
death of his tenant,if
it fo be,that the time
of þ yere wil fuffre the
fame to be gotten,as
mony,corne,flefh,fifh,
fpices,or any fuch like
& for default of pay-
ment,the lorde maye
therefore of common
right prefetly diftrein

But in fome ca-
fes the lord muft ftay
for hys reliefe a cer-
taine time whë necef-
fit

sitye so constraineth.
As if the tenant helde
by a rose, a cherry, a
stawberry, or such like
and dye in winter, he
shal not haue reliefe
til roses, cherries, and
strawberries are na=
turally fresh and ripe,
which is about Mid-
somer, and then he shall
haue one for rent, and
an other for reliefe.

There is an other
kinde of reliefe that is
paied after the death
change, or alienation
of freholders that hold
in auncient demesne,
and otherwise, and is
paied as a knowledge
of the tenure betwen
the lord and the tenãt.
The same is not cer=
taine how much, but
doth varye accordinge
to the custome of the
mannor, or tenure and
is to be presented by
the Homage or Su-
tors at the next court
day of the same manor

sitye issint constraint.
Come si le tenant ty-
ent per vn rose, vn che-
rye, vn strawbery, ou
tiel semblable, & de-
uie en winter, il naue-
ra reliefe tanq; roses,
cheryes, & strawberies
sont maturalmẽt fresh,
et ripe, que est al temps
de midsomer, et donqs
il aña vn pur rent, et vn
auter pur reliefe.

Il y ad vne auter
kinde de reliefe que est
paye apres le mort,
change, ou alienacy-
on de fraunketenantes
que tyent en auncy-
ent demesne, & auter-
ment, & est paie come
vn cognusans del te-
nure perenter le seig-
niour et le tenant, ceo
nest certein quãt: mes
il vary accordaunt al
custome del mannor,
ou tenure, et est destre
presẽt per le ho-
mage, ou sutours, al
procheine court iour
de m̃ le manor.

Et

Et nota que toutes
foits quant le relyefe
est due,il doit este pay
al vn entier payment,
& nemy per partes,
nient obstant que le
rent soit deste pay al
seueral feastes.

And note that al=
waies when the relief
is due,it must be paid
at one whole payment
and not by partes,al=
though that the rent
be to be paied at seue=
ral feastes.

¶Remainder.

REmainder de terre
est le terre que re-
maynera apres le par-
ticuler estate deter-
mine : Come si vne
graunt terre pur terme
de ans, ou pur vie, le
remainder al I.S. cest
adire que quant le les-
see pur vie est mort,
que donques le terre
remaynera, serra, ou
abyde oue, al, ou en
I.S.

REmainder of lande
is the lãd that shal
remaine after the par=
ticuler estate determi=
ned : As if one graunt
land for terme of yeres
or for lyfe , the re=
mainder to J.S.that
is to say, ꝑ when the
lease for yeres is deter
mined,or lesse for life
is dead, ꝑ then ꝑ land
shal remain, shalbe, or
abide,ẃ,to,or in J.S

¶Replication.

REplication est quãt
le defendant en as-
cun action fait res-
pons, & le playntife

REplication is when
the defendant in a=
ny action maketh an
aunswere,& ꝑ plaintif
ma=

maketh an aunswere to that, that is called the Replication of the plaintife.

fait vn respons al ceo, ceo est appell le Replication del playntife.

¶Reprises.

¶Reprises.

REprises, are deduc= tions, paymentes, and duities that goe yearely and are payed out of a mannor. As rent charge, rent secke, pencions, co= rodies, annuities, and such lyke.

REprises, sount de- ductions, paiments, & duities, que va an- nuelment & sont pay hors dun mannor. Come rent charge, rēt secke, pencions, coro- dies, annuities, & tiels semblables.

¶Resceipt.

¶Resceipt.

REsceipt, is when an actiō is brought against the tenant for terme of life, or tenāt for terme of yeares, and he in the reuersion commeth in and pray= eth to be receyued to defende the land, and to pleade with the de= maundant. And when he commeth it beho= ueth that he be alway

REsceipt, est quant vn action est port vers tenaunt pur terme de vie, ou tenaunt a terme dans, & cesty en la reuersion vy- ent eyns & prya de este resceiue pur de- fender le terre, & pur pleder ouesque le de- maundant. Et quant il vient, il couyent que il soit routs foits prist prift a pleder oue le demaundant.

readie to plede wyth the demaundant.

¶ Referuation.

¶ Referuation.

REferuation eft pris diuers voyes , & ad diuers natures, com afcun foits per'voy de exception de referue ceo que vn home ad deuant en luy Come fi vn leas foit fait pur ans de terre referuant les grañd arbors cref- fants fur ceo . Ore le leffee ne poit meddle ouefque eux, ne ouef- que afcun chofe que vient per reafon de eux cy longe come il demurt en , ou fur les arbors , come maft de Oke, cheftnut, pomes, ou tyels femblables . Mes fils chient del ar- bors al terre, donques ils font en droit le lef- fees , car le terre eft leffee a luy , & tout fur ceo nient referue &c.

Afcun foits vn refer-

REferuation, is ta= ken diuers waies, and hath diuers na= tures , as fometimes by way of exception to kepe that whych a man had before in him , as if a leafe bee made for yeares of ground referuing the great trees growyng vpon the fame, now p leffee may not medle with them, noz wyth any thinge that com= meth by reafon of th̄e fo long as it abydeth in, oz vpon the trees, as maft of Oke, chek= nutt, apples, oz fuch like, but if they fal fr̄o the trees to the groūd, then they are in right the leffes, foz p groūd is let to him, & al there vpon not referued &c.

Sometimes a refer= uation

uation doth get and bring forth an other thing which was not before. As if a man lease his lands, reserving yerely for ŷ same rr. li. &c. And dyuers other such reseruations there be.

And note that in aunciẽt tyme, theyr reseruations were as wel (or for the more part) in bittaills, whether flesh, fishe, corne, bread, drinke, or what els, as in money bntil at the last,& that chefely in the Raigne of king H. the first by agreement, the reseruation of bittals was chaunged into ready money, as it hath hytherto since cõtinued.

uation obtayneth & port hors vn aut'chofe que ne fuit deraure, Come fi vn home lefse ses terres reseruant annualment pur ceo xx. li. &c. Et diuers auter tiels reseruations y sount.

Et nota que en auncient temps, lour reseruations fueront libien, (ou pur le ius part) en victuals, soyt ceo, carne, piffie, blees, pane, boyer, ou auterment, come en money, tanque al darrein, & especialment en le temps del Roy Henry le primer per agreement, le reseruation de victuals fuit change en prift mony, come il ad tanque cy continue.

¶Retraxit.

REtraxit, is the preterperfectence of retraho, compound of Re and traho, which make Retraho, to pull

¶Retraxit.

REtraxit, est le preterperfectence de Retraho, compounde de Re et traho, q̃ signifie retraho pur euulser
arrere

arrere . Et eſt quaunt
le partie plaintife, ou
demaundant vient en
proper perſon en le
Court ou ſon ſuit eſt,
& dit que il ne voyt
vlterius proſequi in
placito illo &c . Ore
ceo ſerra vn barre al
action a touts iours.

backe . And is when
the partie plaintife oʒ
demaundant commeth
in pʒoper perſon into
the Court where hys
plœ is, and ſayth that
he wil not pʒocœd any
farder in the ſame ꝛc.
now this ſhalbe a barr
to the action foʒ euer.

¶Reeue.

¶Reeue.

REeue eſt vn officer,
mes plus conus en
auncient temps que a
ceſt iour . Car cheſ-
cun manour ad don-
ques vn Reeue , &
vncore en diuers Co-
pyholde manours(ou
le viele cuſtome aſ-
cun choſe preuayle ,)
le noſme & office neſt
en tout obliue . Et eſt
en effect ceo que a ore
cheſcun Baylife dun
mannor practiſe : ni-
ent obſtaunt le noſme
de Bailife ne fuit don-
ques en vre enter nous
eſteaunt puys porte

REeue is an officer,
but moʒe knowen
in auncient tyme then
at this day . Foʒ al-
moſt euerie manoʒ had
then a Rœue , and yet
ſtill in many Coppe
holde manoʒs (where
the olde cuſtome any
thing pʒeuayleth) the
name and office is not
altogether foʒgotten.
And is in effect that
which now euery bai-
life of a mannoʒ pʒac-
tiſeth : although the
name of Bailife was
not then in vʒe among
vs being ſince bʒought

in

in by the Normans:
But þ name of Reeue,
auncyently called Ge=
reue, (which particle
(Ge)in continuance of
time was altogether
left out and lost) came
from þ Saxon word
Geresa, which signyfi=
eth a ruler: And so in
dede his rule & autho=
ritie was large with=
in the compas of hys
Lordes mannour and
amonge his men and
tenauntes as well in
matters of gouerne=
ment in peace & warre,
as in the skilfull vse
and trade of husban=
dry: For as hee did ga=
ther his Lords rents,
pay Reprises, or due=
tyes issuinge out of
the mannor: set the
seruauntes to worke,
fell and cut downe
Trees to repaire the
buildinges, and en=
closures, with dy=
uers such like for his
Lordes commod'tye:

ens per les Normans:
Mes le nosm de Reeue
auncientment app ll
Gereue, (quel parti-
cle (Ge) en continu-
aunce de temps fuit
oustrement omise &
parde) vyent del Sax-
on paroll Geresa, que
signifie vn ruler. Et
isint veramēt son rule
& aucthoritye fuyt
large deins le compas
del mannor son seyg-
nior & enter ses homes
& tenauntes q bien
en choses de gouerne-
ment en peace de gu-
erre, come en le skil-
full vse & trade de
husbandrye. Car si-
cōe il collect les rentes
del snr, payer reprises,
ou duities issiūts hors
del manner, appoynt
les seruaunts de vior-
ker, succide & decoupr
arbres pur repayres
les edefices, & enclo-
sures, vutque diuers
tiels semblables pur le
cōmodity del seignior.

Y.j.　　Isint

Iffint auxi il ad actho-
ritie de gouerner., &
feruer les tenauntes en
peax (fil befoigne, de
conducter eux en gu-
erre.

¶Reuerfion.

REuerfion de terre,
eft vn certein eftate
remainant en le leffor
ou donour, apres le
pertyculer eftate &
poffeffion conuey al
vn auter.

Et eft appelle vn
Reuerfion en refpecte
del poffeffion feperate
de ceo, Iffint que
il que ad le vn, nad
lauter a mefme lo
temps, car efteaunt
en vn fimul, la ne
poet efte dir vn re-
uerfion., pur ceo que
perole vnitinge, lun
eft merge en lauter,
Et iffint le reuerfion
del terre, eft le terre
mefine quaunt il ef-
chuft.

So alfo hee had auc-
thoritie to gouerne &
keepe the tenaunts in
peace,& if næde reqim-
red, to leade the forth
in warre.

¶Reuerfion.

REuerfion of lande.
is a certeine eftate
remaininge in the lef-
for or donor, after the
particuler eftate & pof-
feffion conueyed to an
other.

And it is called a re-
uerfion in refpecte of
the poffeffion fepera-
ted from it: fo that hee
that hath the one hath
not the other at the
fame time, for being in
one bodye together,
there cannot be faid a
reuerfion, becaufe by y
vniting, the one of thē
is drowned in the o-
ther: And fo the re-
uerfion of land, is the
lande it felfe when it
foureth.

¶Riot.

¶Riot.

¶Riot.

RIot is where thre (at ẏ least) or more do some vnlawful act: as to beate a manne, Enter vppon the possession of an other, or such like.

RIot est lou troys (al meynes) ou plures font ascun illoyall act come de bater vn hõe, Enter sur le possesion dun auter, vel huiusmodi.

¶Robbery.

¶Robberie.

RObbery is when a mã taketh any thing from the parson of an other feloniously, although the thinge so taken be not to the balue but of a peny, yet it is felony, for which the offendour shal suffer death.

RObbery est quaunt vn home prent ascun chose del person dun auter felonisment, coment que la chose prise ne soit al value forsque dun denyer, vncore il est felony pur quel le offendour suffera mort.

¶Rout.

¶Rout.

ROut, is when people to assemble them selues together and after do proceede, or ride, or go foorth, or to moue by the instigation of one, or more,

ROut est quant people assemble eux mesmes, & puis procedunt, ou chiuauchant, ou allant auãt, ou mouent per instigation dun ou plures

Y.ij.   que

que eſt conductor de eux : Ceſt appelle vn rout, pur ceo que ils mouent, & pro-ceed en routs & nũ-bers.

Item ou plures af-ſemble eux ſur lour quarelles & braules demeſne, come ſi les inhabitauntes dun ville voyle aſſembler eux pur debruſer huis mures, foſſes, pales, ou tye.s ſemblables, dauer commen la, ou de bater vn auter que ad fait al eux vn com-mon diſpleaſure, vel huiuſmodi, ceſt vn rout & encounter le ley, coment que ils nount fayt, ou miſe en execution lour male entent.

whoe is their lea-der: Thys is called Rout, beecauſe they doo moue, and proceede in Routes and num-bers.

Also where many af-ſemble thē ſelues to-gether vpõ their owne quarrels & braules, as if the inhabitants of a towne wil gather thē ſelues together, to breake hedges, wales, ditches pales, or ſuch like to haue common there, or to beate ano-ther that hath done to them a cõmon diſplea-ſure or ſuch like, that is a Rout & againſt ẏ lawe although they haue not done or put in execution their miſ-cheuous entent.

¶Sake.   ¶Sake.

SAke, hoc eſt pla-citum & emenda de transgꝛ hominum in cuꝛ veſtra,quia (Sake)

Sak, this is a plee and coꝛredyon of treſ-pas of men in your court, becauſe (Sak) in

in English is Achelō
in french, and Sak is
put for Sik, as to say
for sik sak , also for
what hurt , & Sak is
put for forfait.

Anglicæ, est Acheson
Galice & dicitur pur
sick sack idem quod
pur quel acheson , &
sack dicitur pro for-
fayt.

¶Scot.

¶Scot.

SCot, that is to bee
quite of a certeine
custome, as of commen
tallage made to the
vse of the Sherife or
Bailife.

SCot, hoc est quietū
esse de quadam con-
suetudine, sicut de cō-
muni tallagio facto
ad opus vic vel balli-
uorum eius

¶Shewinge.

¶Shewing.

SHewing that is to
bee quite wyth at-
tachment in any court
and before whomsoe-
uer in plaints shewed
& not auowed.

SHewing hoc ē qui-
etū esse cū attachia-
ment' in aliqua cur, &
corā quibuscunq in q-
relis ostēsis & nō ad-
uocaī.

¶Sok.

¶Sok.

SOk this is suite
of menne in your
court according to
the custome of the Re-
alme.

SOk hoc est secta
de hominibus in
Curia vestra secun-
dum consuetudinem
regni.

¶Sok-

The exposition of

¶Sokmans. ¶Sokmans.

SOkmans sount les
tenauntes en aun-
cient demesne que-
ux tyent lour terres
per socage, cest adire,
per seruice del carue,
& pur ceo ils sount
appell Sokmans, que
est taunt adire come
tenants ou homes qux
tyent per seruice del
carue, ou homes del
carue. Car sok sighifie
vn carue.

Et ceux Sokmans
ou tenauntes en aun-
cyent demesne, ount
plusours & dyuers li-
berties done & graunt
a eux per le ley. Cy-
bien ceux tenauntes
queux tient dun com-
mon person en aun-
cient demesne, come
ceux queux tient del
Roygne en auucyent
demesne, come nos-
ment deste quite de
paier tolle en chescun
market, faire, ville, &

SOkmans, are the te-
nants in aūcient de-
mesne, that hold their
lands in Socage, that
is by seruice with the
plough, and therefore
they are called Sok-
mans, which is as
much to saye, as te-
nauntes or men that
hold by seruice of the
plough, or plowmen.
For Sok signifieth a
plough.

And these Sokmās
or tenaunts in aunci-
ent demesne, haue ma-
ny and dyuers liber-
ties giuen & graunted
to them by the lawe,
as wel these tenaunts
that holde of a com-
mon person in auncy-
ent demesne, as those
that hold of ꝑ Queene
in auncient demesne,
as namely to bee free
from payinge tolle
in euerye Market,
Faire, Towne, and
City

City throughout the whole Realme, aswel for their goods & catteis p̄ they sell to others, as for those things that they buy for their prouiṡiō. of other. And thereupō euery of thē may sue to haue letters patents vnder p̄ Quēens seale directed to her officers, & to the Maires, Bailifes & other officers in the realme to suffer thē to be tolle free. Also to be quite of pontage, murage & passage, as also of taxes and tallages grāūted by parliamēt, except that the Quēen taxe auncient demeſne as she may at her pleasure for some great cause. Also to be free frō paimentstowards the expenses of the knightes of the shire p̄ come to p̄ parliament.

And if the sherif wil distreine them or any of them to bee cons-

City p̄ tout le realme, cybn̄ pur lour byens & chattels que ils véde as auters, come put. ceux choses que ils achaí pur lour prouiſion, de auters. Et sur ceo cheſcī de eux poet suer dauer letters patents de south le seal le Roygne a ses officers, & al Maìres, Bailifes, & auters officers en le realm̄ de suffer eux deſte quite de tolle. Item deſte quite de Pontage, murage, & passage, & auxy de taxes & tallage grāūt per Parliament sinon que le Roygne taxe auncyent demeſne, cō el poet al sa pleaſure pur graund cauſe. Auxy deste quite de paiments as les expenſes del chvualers del shire queux vient al parliament.

Et si le vicont veile distreigñ eux ou aſcun de eux distī con-

Y.iiij.   trī-

tributorye pur lour
terre en auhcient de-
mefne, donques lun
de eux ou toutes co-
me le cafe requyre
poit fuer vne briefe
direct al vicount luy
commaundaunt que
il ne compel eux deftr
contributoryes al ex-
pences de chiualers. Et
celuy briefe luy com-
maund auxy , que fil
ad diftrein eux pur ceo
que il redeliuer mefme
ceft diftreffe.

Item que ils ne de-
ueront eftre impan-
nell , ne mife en Iu-
ryes & enqueftes en
payes hors de lour
manor ou feigniorye
de auncyent demefne,
pur les terres queux
ils teigne la (finon
que ils ount auters
terres al common ley
pur queux ils deue-
rount eftre charge)
& fil le vifcount re-
tourne eux enpan-
nells , donques ils

tributory for their
landes in aunctient de-
mefn, the one of them
or al as the cafe require-
reth may fue a write
directed to the sherif co-
manding him that he be
not compel them to bee
contributories to the ex-
penses of the knights, &
the fame writ with co-
maund him also, that
if he haue already dif-
trained them therfore
that he receiuer the
fame diftreffe.

Also that they
ought not to bee im-
panneled , nor put in
in Iuries and enquests
in the countrye out
of their manner or
lordeshippe of auncy-
ent demefne, for the
landes that they hold
there(except that they
haue other landes at
the common lawe, for
which they ought to
be charged)and if the
sherife to return them
in panells , then they
may

may haue a writte against him de non ponendis in assisis & iuratis. And if he to the contrary, then lyeth an attachement vpon that against him. And so it is also, if the bailifes of franchiles that haue returne of writtes will returne any of the tenaunts which hold in auncyent demesne in assises or iuries.

And also to be exempt from leets, and the shirifs turne, with diuers other such like lyberties.

¶Spoliation

SPoliation is a suit for the fruites of a church or for the church it selfe, and it is to bee sued in the spirytuall Court, and not in our courts. And this suit lieth for one incumbent against an other in-

---

poyent auer vn brief enuers luy de non ponendis in assisis & iuratis. Et sil face al contrary, donques gist vne attachement sur ceo enuers luy. Et issint est auxy si les bailifes des franchises queux ount retournes de briefes voil returne ascun del tenants quevx teigne en auncient demesne en assise ou iuries.

Et auxi deste exépts del leets, et de turnes del vicont, ouesq; diuers auters semblables liberties.

¶Spoliation.

SPoliation est vne suit pur les fruites dñ esglis, ou pur lesglis mesme, & est deste sue en le spirituall Court, & nemy en nostre courtes. Et cest suite gist pur vne encumbent enûs vn auter encumbent

cumbent , ou ils ambideux clayme per vn patron , & lou le droit del patronage ne vient in queſtion ou debate. Come ſi vne perſon ſoyt cree en Eueſque & ad diſpenſation de tener ſon rectorye , & puis le patron preſent auter encumbent que eſt inſtitute & induct : Ore leueſque poet auer enuers ceſtuy encumbent vne Spoliation en le ſpirytuall Court , pur ceo que ils ambydeux claime per vne patron , & le droit del patronage ne vyent en debate , & pur ceo que lauter entumbent vient al poſſion del benefice per le courſe del ley ſpiritual, ceſtaſcauoir per inſtitution et induction iſſint que il ad colour de auer ceo,& deite perſon per le eſ-

cumbnt , where they both claime by one patron,and where the right of the patronage doth not not come in queſtion oʒ debate. As if a perſon be created a biſhoppe , and hath diſpenſation to keepe his benefice ſtill , and afterward the patron pʒeſents an other incumbent which is inſtituted,and inducted: Nowe the Biſhoppe may haue againſt that incumbent a Spoliation in the ſpirituall Court , becauſe they claime both by one patron,and the right of the patronage doth not come in debate,& becauſe that the other incumbent came to the poſſeſſion of the benefice by þ courſe of the ſpiritual law, that is to ſay by inſtitutis & induction,ſo that hee hath colour to haue it & be perſon by the eſ-

ſyl-

spiritual lawe, for other wise if he be not instituted and inducted &c. Spoliation lieth not against him, but rather a writt of Trespas, or an assise of novel disseisin &c.

So it is also where a personne doth accept an other benefite, by reason whereof the patrone presentes an other clerke who is instituted & inducted, now the one of them may haue Spoliation against the other, and then shal come in debate if he haue plurality or not. And so it is of depriuation &c.

The same lawe, is where one saieth to þ patron, þ his clerke is dead, where vppon he presentes an other: There the first incumbent which was supposed to bee dead may haue a spoliatiõ against the other, & so

spirituall ley. Car au terment sil ne soit institute & inducte &c. Spoliaryon ne gist enuers luy, mes vn briefe de Trespas, ou vne asise de nouel disseisin &c.

Issint est auxy lou vne person accept auter benefice per reason de que le patron present vn auter clerk, que est institute & induct, ore lun de eux poit auer Spoliation enuers le auter, & donques viendra en debate si il ad pluralytye ou non. Et issint est de depriuation &c.

Mesme le ley, est lou vne dist al patron, que son clerke est mort sur que il present vne auter. La le primor incumbent que fuit surmise de estre mort poit auer vne Spoliation enuers lauter. Et issint en

en diuers auters ſem-blable caſes.	in dyuers other ſuch like caſes.

¶ Stallage. — **¶ Stallage.**

S Tallage hoc eſt qui-etum eſſe de quadã cõſuetudine exact' pro platea capta vel aſsig-nata in nundinis & mercatis.

S Tallage that is to bee quite of a cer-teine cuſtome exacte for the ſtreat taken or aſſigned in faires and markets.

¶ Suit couenant. — **¶ Suit couenant.**

S Vit couenaunt eſt quaunt voſter aun-ceſtors ont couenaunt oue mes aunceſtours de ſuer a le court mes aunceſtours.

S Uit couenaunt is when your aunceſ-tors haue couenanted with my aunceſtours to ſue to the court of my aunceſtors.

¶ Suit cuſtome. — **¶ Suit cuſtome.**

S Vite cuſtome eſt quaunt ieo & mes aunceſtours ount eſ-tre ſeyſies de veſter ſuit demeſne & voſ-tre annceſtoures de temps &c.

S Uit cuſtome is whē I and my aunceſ-tours haue bẽne ſei-ſed of your owne ſuite and your aun-ceſtours, time out of minde &c.

¶ Suit

¶Suit riall.   ¶Suit riall.

SVit riall is when men come to the shirifes tourne or læte, to which court al mē shal be cōpelled to come to know the lawes, so ẏ they shal not be ignorant of the things that shalbe declared there howe they shalbe governed. And it is called rial suit because of their allegeance, & this appeareth by common experyence when one is sworne, his othe is that hée shalbe a loyall and faithfull man to the Quæne. And this suit is not for the land which he holdeth wtin the Countie, but by reason of hys person, and his abode there, and ought to bée done twise a yeare, for defaut whereof, he shall be amerced & not dystrained.

SVit rial est quaunt homes vient al turne de viscount ou leete, a que courtes toutes homes serra compell de vener a conuster le leies, issint que ils ne serra ignoraunt de les choses queux serra monstres la coment ils serra gouernes. Et est appell riall suit per cause de lour allegeaunce, & ceo appiert per common experience quaunt vn est iure son othe est que il serra loyall & foial home al Roigne. Et ceo suit nest pur le terre que il tient deins le countie, nes per reason de son person, & pur son rest la & doyt estre fayt deux fortes per an, pur defaut de que, il serra amerce & non distreigne.

¶Suit

¶ Suit ſeruice

SVit ſeruice , ē de ſu-
er al turne del viſ-
count ou leete , ou al
court del ſeigniour dē
troys ſemaynes en
troys ſemaynes per
lentier an: Et pur de-
faut de ceo, vn home
ſerra diſtreigne & non
amerce . Et ceſt ſuit
ſeruice eſt per reaſon
del tenure del terres
dun home.

¶ Taxe & Tallage.

TAxe & Tallage ſot
paiments,come diſ-
mes quinzimes, ſubſi-
dyes , ou tiels ſembla-
bles graunt al roygne
per parliament.

   Les tenauts en aun-
cyen demeſne ſount
quites de ceux taxes, et
tallages grauntes per
parliament , ſinon que
le Roygne taxe aun-
cyen demeſne , come
el poet quaunt a luy

¶ Suit ſeruice.

SUit ſeruice , is to
ſue to the Sherites
tourne oꝛ leete, oꝛ to
the Loꝛds court from
thꝛee weekes to thꝛe
weekes by the whole
yeare, and foꝛ default
thereof , a man ſhalbe
diſtrayned and not a-
merced And this ſuit
ſeruice is by reaſon of
the tenure of a mans
landes.

¶ Taxe and Tallage.

TAxe & Tallage, are
paimēts as tethes,
fifteenthes , ſubſidyes,
oꝛ ſuch like graunted
to the Queene by par-
liament.

   The tenants in aun-
cien demeane are quite
of theſe taxes & talla-
ges graunted by par-
liamēt except that the
Queene to taxe aun-
cient demeſne, as ſhe
may whē ſhe thinkes
good

good for some great
cause. See auncient
demesne.

pleast pur graunde
cause. Voyes auncient
demesne.

¶ Tenure in capite.

¶ Tenure en capite.

TEnure in Capite
is where any hold
of the Queene as of
her personne bæinge
Queene, and of her
Crowne as of a Lord-
shippe by it selfe in
grosse, and in chyefe
aboue al other Lord-
shippes. And not
where they hold of her
as of any mannor, ho-
nor or castell, excepte
certeine auncient ho-
nors, which awete in
the Eschequer.

TEnure in capite est
lou ascun tient del
Roigne come de sa p-
son esteant roigne, &
de sa Corone; come
dun seygniourie per
luy mesme en grosse,
& en chyefe de suys
toutes auters seygnio-
ries. Et nemy lou ils
tient de luy come de
ascun mannor, honor,
ou Castell, sinon cer-
teyne auncyent ho-
nors, vt patet in Scac-
cano.

¶ Testament.

¶ Testament.

TEstament is thus
defined or expoun-
ded in master Plow-
dens comentaries, a
testament is the wit-
nes of the minde, and
is compound of these

TEstament est issint
define ou expound
en Mounsier Plowe-
dens commentaryes,
Testamentum est tes-
tatio mentis & est
compounde de ceulx
deux

deux parolx. Testatio & mentis que issint signifie veraye il est, que vn testament est testatio mentis, mes que il est vn compounde paroll, Aulus Gellius en son vj. lyuer cap. 12. deny ceo al vn excellent Lawier vn Seruius Sulpitius & dit que il est vn simple paroll, come sount ceux, Calciamentum, Paludamentum, Pauimentum,& diuers tyels semblables. Et mult meynes est agreamentum vn compounde paroll de aggregatio, & mentium, come est dit en mesme title, car il ny ad nul tiel latin paroll simple ou compounde, mes il poet nient obstaunt serue bien pur vn ley latyn paroll.

Et pur ceo il poet issint este meliour define. Testamentum

two wordes. Testatio & mentis, which so signifieth, trueth is, that a Testament is a witnes of the minde, but that it is a compounde worde, Aulus Gellius in his vj. booke cap. 12. doth deny the same to an excellent Lawyer one Sernius Sulpicius, and sayeth that it is a simple worde, as are these: Calciamentum, Paludamentum pauimentum, and dyuers such like: And much lesse is agreamentum a compounde worde of aggregatio, and mentium as is sayde before in that tytle, for there is noe suche latyne worde simple or compounde, but it may neuer the lesse serue well for a lawe latyn worde.

And therefore thus it may bee better defined. A Testament is

is the true declara=
tion of our laſt wyll,
of that we would to
be don after our death
&c. And of Teſtamēts
there be ij.ſoꝛts, name
lye a Teſtament in
wꝛiting, & a Teſta=
mēt by woꝛds which
is called a Nuncupa=
tiue teſtament .

The firſt is alwayes
in wꝛiting as is ſayd.

The other is when
a man beeing ſicke,and
foꝛ feare leaſt death oꝛ
want of memoꝛie, oꝛ
of ſpeach, ſhould come
ſo ſuddenly and haſte=
ly vpon him that hee
ſhould be pꝛeuented if
he ſtayed the wꝛiting
of his teſtament, de=
ſireth his neyghbours
and friendes to beare
witneſſe of his laſte
will ,and then decla=
reth the ſame preſent=
ly by woꝛdes befoꝛe
them , which after his
deceaſe is pꝛoued by
wytneſſes , and put

eſt vltimę voluntatis
iuſta ſententia de eo
quod quis poſt mor-
tem ſuam fieri vult
&c. Et de Teſtaments
il y ad deux ſortes, ceſ-
taſcauoir, vn teſtamēt
en eſcript, & vn teſta-
ment per parolx, que
eſt appell vn Nuncu-
patiue Teſtament.

Le prim eſt touts foits
en eſcript cõe eſt dit.

Le auter eſt quant vn
home eſteant malady,
& pur pauor ne mort
ou faut de memorie,
ou de parler, voit ve-
ner cy ſuddeinment et
haſtiuement ſur luy,
que il ſerra preuent, ſil
demurt le ſcripture de
ſon teſtament, requeſt
ſes vicines & amyes,
de porter teſtmoygne
de ſon darreine vo-
lunt , & donques de-
clare ceo preſent ment
per parollx deuaunt
eux, que apres ſon de-
ceaſe eſt proue per teſ-
moygnes , & myſt

en

en eſcript per le Ordi-
narie , & donques il
eſt en cy bone force,
(ſinon pur terres) ſi-
come il ad al prymer
en le vie del teſtatour
eſte miſe en eſcript.

in wꝛiting by the Oꝛ-
dinarie, & then ſtan-
deth in as good foꝛce,
(except foꝛ landſ) as
if it had at the firſt in
the life of the teſtatoꝛ
ben put in wꝛiting.

¶Them.

¶Them.

Hem,hoc eſt quod
habeatis totā ge-
nerationem villano-
rum veſtrorum , cum
eorum ſectis & car-
tallis vbicūquᵉ in
Anglia fuerūt inuen-
ta, excepto quod ſi a-
liquis natiuus quieᵗ p
vnum annum & diem
in aliqua villa priui-
legia manſerit , ita
quod in eorum com-
muniam vel gildam
tanquam vnus illarum
repertus fuerit,eo ipſo
a villenagio liberatus
eſt.

Hem, that is that
you ſhall haue all
ẏ generationſ of your
billaines wyth theyr
ſuites & cattel where
ſoeuer they ſhall bee
found in England ex-
cept that if any bond-
man ſhal remain quite
one yere and a day in
any pꝛiuiledged town
ſo that he ſhalbe recei-
ued into theyr Com-
minaltie oꝛ guild, as
one of them , by that
meanes hee ẏſ deiy-
nered from billenage.

¶Theſbote.

¶Theſbote.

Heſbote,eſt quant
home priſt aſcun

Heſbote, is when
a man taketh any
gꝏdeſ

goodes of a theefe to fauour and mainteine him. And not when a man taketh his owne goodes that were stolen from him &c. The punishment in auncyent time of theefebote was of lyfe and member. But now at this day Master Stamforde sayeth, it is punished by raunsome, and imprisonment. But enquire farther, for I thinke it be felonie.

byens dun larone de luy fauourer et mainteyner. Et nemy quât home prist ses byens demesne, que fueront emblees de luy &c. Le punishmt en auncient temps de Thefebote, fuit de vie & de member. Mes a ore Master Stamforde dit, que il est punishe per raunsome & imprysonment. Sed Quære car ieo pense ceo este felonie.

¶ Title.

Title, is where a lawfull cause ys come vppon a man to haue a thinge whych an other hath, and he hath no action for the same, as title of mortmaine, or to enter for breach of a condicion.

¶ Title.

Title, est lou loyall cause est veygne a vn home de auer chose que auter ad & il nad ascun action pur ceo, come title de Mortmayne, ou de entrie pur condicion enfreynt.

¶ Title of entrie.

Title of entrie, is when one seised of

¶ Title dentrie

Title dentrie, est quaunt vn seisi de terre

Z.ij.

terre en fee fait feoffe-
ment de ceo sur con-
dicion, & le condicion
est enfreint: Ore apres
le condicion issint en-
freint, le feoffor ad ti-
tle dentrie en le terre,
& issint poit quant a
luy pleist, & per son
entrie le franktenemt
serra dit en luy main-
tenaunt. Et est appel
title dentre, pur ceo
que il ne poit auer
briefe de Droit enuers
son feoffee sur condi-
cion, car son droit
fuit hors de luy per
le feoffement, le quel
ne poit este reduce
sauns entrie, & le
entrie doit este pur
le enfreinder del con-
dicion.

lande in fee maketh a
feoffement therof vp-
pon condicion, & the
condicion is broken:
Now after the condi-
cion thus broken, the
feoffour hath title to
enter into the land, &
may so do at his plea-
sure, and by his entry
the freeholde shal bee
saide to be in him pre-
sently. And it is cal-
led title of entrie, be-
cause that hee cannot
haue a writ of Ryght
against his feoffee vp-
pon condicion, for hys
right was out of him
by the feffemet, which
cannot be reduced w-
out entrie, & the entrie
must be for the breach
of the condicion

¶Tolle, ou Tolne.

¶Tolle, or Tolne.

TOlle ou Tolne, est
plus properment
vn payment vse en ci-
ties, villes, marketts,
& fayres, pur biens &

TOlle or Tolne, is
most properlye a
payment vsed in Ci-
ties, townes, markets
& faires for goods and
cat-

cattel brought thither
to bee bought & solde.
And is alwaies to bee
paied by the buyer, &
not by the seller, ex=
cept there be some cus=
tome otherwise.

There are diuers o=
ther tolles, as Turne
tolle, & that is where
toll is paied for beasts
that are driuen to bee
solde, although that
they bee not solde in
dæde.

Also Tolle trauers,
that is where one clai=
meth to haue a halfe=
peny, or such like toll
of euery beast that is
driuen ouer his groũd

Through tolle, is
where a Towne pre=
scribes to haue tol for
euery beast that goeth
through their towne
a certein: or for euery
score of 100. a certein,
which seemeth not to
bee so vnreasonable a
prescription or custõe
as some haue thought

cattel port la destre a=
chate & vende. Et est
toutes dits destre pay
per le achatour, et ne=
my per le vendour, si=
non q̃ soit ascun cus=
tome al contrarie.

Il y ad diuers auters
tolles, come Turne
tolle, & ceo est lou
tolle est pay pur auers
queux sount dryues
deste vendus, coment
que ils ne sount ven=
dus.

Item Tolle trauers,
ceo est ou vn clayme
dauer vn ob. ou tyel
semblable tolle, de
chescun beast que est
driue sur son terre.

Through toll, est lou
vn ville prescribe de
auer tolle pur chescun
beaste que ale tho=
rough lour ville vn
certein, ou pur chescun
vint ou cent, vn certen
que ne appert deste cy
vnreasonable prescrip=
tion ou custome, come
ascuns ount suppose,

Z.iij,   nient

nient obftant il foyt per le haut chimin del Roigne (come il ceo appel)ou chefcun poit loyalment paffe : fil y ad quid pro quo,come fi la foit vn pont ou tiel femblable commoditie puruiew al coftes & charges del ville, pur le eafe de trauaylers que chafe mefine voy,per q̃ lour iourney eft ou abridge ou fait le meliour, pur que donques ne poyt tolle efte demaunde loyalment,& oue bon reafon de eux &c.Mes dyuers Citizens & Burgeffes font quyte de pay tolle p le grant del Roigne, ou fa aunceftors, ou claime ceo per prefcription ou cuftome . Iffint auxy efpirituall perfons & religious homes(come ils fueront appels) fueront quyte de tolle pur lour byens & marchaundifes achate

although it be through the Quænes hyghe way(as they call it,) where euery man may lawfully go , if that there be one thing for another,as if there be a bridge or fuch lyke commoditie proupded at the coftes & charges of the Towne, for the eafe of trauaplers y̆ driue that way,where by theyr iourney ys either fhortned or bettered, why then may not tolle be lawfully and with good reafon demaunded of them &c. But diuers Citizẽs & Townes men are free from paying tolle by graunt of the Quæne or her aunceftors, or do claime the fame by prefcription or cuftome. So alfo fpirytual perfons & religious men(as they call thẽ)were quit of paying tol for their goods & marchãdifes bought

and

and fold, but now the Statute of king H. 8. will that they shall not marchandise. But enquyre whether the intent of the statute be obserued among them at this day oz not, some say it is not.

Also tenants in auncient demesne ought to be quite thozough the whole Realme of paying tolle, as appeareth befoze in the title Sokemans. And in al these cases where toll is demaůded where it ought not to be paied of the that should go, buy, & sell tolle free there ỹ partie oz parties greued may haue a wzit, De essendi quietum de tolonio, against him oz them that so demaunded tolle contrarie to the Queene oz her progenitours graunt, oz contrarie to custome oz pzescription.

& vendus &c. Mes a ore le Statute del Roy H. 8. voit que ils ne marchaundiser. Sed Quære si le entent de cest estatute soit obserue enter eux al cest iour ou nemy, ascuns diont que non.

Item tenants en auncient demesne doyent este quite per tout le Realme de paier tolle, come appiert deuaunt en le title Sokemans. Et en touts ceux cases ou tolle est deste demaunde, ou il ne doit este pay de eux que doyent a!er, achate, & vende, quite de tolle, la le partie ou parties greeue poyent auer vn briefe, De essendi quietum de tolonio, enuers luy, ou ceux que issint demaunde tolle contra al graunt le Roygne ou sa progenitours, ou contra al custome ou prescription.

Z.iiij, Tourne

¶ Tourne del vifcont.

Tourne del vifcont eſt vne Court de record en touts choſes que pertaine al tourne Et eſt le leete le roigñ per touz le county,& le viſcount eſt iudge, Et quecunque ad vne leete ad meſme le aucthority deins le precinct,ſicome le vicont ad deins le torune.

¶ Sheriffes tourne.

Sherifes tourne is a court of record in al things that pertaine to the tourn. And it is the quæenes lœte thorough al the countye, and the ſherif is iudg. And whoſoeuer hath a lœte, hath the ſame aucthozity within the pzecinct, as the ſherife hath win the tourne.

¶ Treaſure troue.

Treaſure troue eſt quaunt aſcun money, ore, argent, plate, ou bolion, eſt troue en aſcun lyeu, & nul conuſt a que le propertye eſt, donques le propertye de ceo appertyent al Roigne, & ceo eſt dit treaſure troue. Mes ſi aſcun mineral de mettall ſoit troue en aſcun terre, ceo touts foites appertyent al

¶ Treaſure found.

Treaſure founde is when any money, gold, oz ſiluer, plate, oz wlion, is found in any place, e no man knoweth to whom the pzoperty is, then the pzoperty thereof wlõgeth to the quæene, and that is called treaſure troue, that is to ſay treaſure found. But if a myne of mettal be foũd in any ground that alway pertaineth to the
lozd

Lorde of the ſoile, ex=
cept it bee a myne of
golde, oꝛ ſiluer which
ſhall bee to the quæn
in whoſe grounde ſo
euer it be found.

ſeignior del ſoile, forſ
que que il ſoet mine-
ral de ore ou de argét
queux ſerrount toutes
foits al roigne ⁊en que-
cunque ſoile que ils
ſont troues.

¶ Viewe

¶ Viewe.

*V*Iewe is when a=
nye acyon real is
bꝛought and the te=
naunt knoweth not
well what lande it is,
that the demaundant
aſketh, then the tenãt
ſhal pꝛaye the viewe,
that is to ſay, that he
may ſe the land which
hee claimeth. But if
the tenant hath had
the viewe in one wꝛit
and after the wꝛitt is
abated by miſnaming
of the towne, oꝛ by
iointure, and after the
demaundaunt bꝛin=
geth an other wꝛitte
againſt the tenaunt,
then the tenant ſhall

*V*Iewe eſt quant aſ-
cun acyon reall
eſt port & le tenaunt
ne ſcauoit byen quel
terre il eſt que le
demaundant demãde
donques le tenaunt
priera le viewe ceſt
aſcauore que il puit
veier le terre que il
claima. Mes ſi le te-
nant ad ewe le view
en vne briefe, & pu-
is le briefe eſt aba-
tus per miſnoſmer
del ville, ou per
iointenure, & pu-
is le demaundaunt
port vn auter briefe
vers le Tenaunt,
donques le tenaunt
nauera

nauera le viewe en le
fecond briefe.

not haue the biew in
the fecond writ.

¶Vifcount.

¶Vifcount.

Vifcount eft vne
magiftrate et of-
ficer del graunde auc-
thorytye que nous
communement ap-
pellomus (Sheriffe)
ou de parler plus ve-
rayment (fhire reue)
& fuit al primes appel
(Shire gereue) ceft a
dire cuftos comitatus,
ou le reue ou ruler del
countye, car (gereue)
efteaunt deriue d' Sax-
on parol (Gereccan)
pur rule, fuit al primes
appel (Gerecfa) &
donques(Gerefa)que
betoken vn ruler. Et
de ceo vient (Port-
reue ou Portgereue)
vne nofme que en viel
temps fuit done al
chiefe officer dun ville,
& fignifie le gouernor
del ville pur ceo que
(Port) veniens de le

Vifcount is a ma-
giftrate , and offi-
cer, of grat authozpty
whom wee commonly
call (Sherife) oz to
fpeake moze truelye
(Shire reue) and
was at the firft called
(Shiregereue) that
is to fay the keeper of
of the Shire, oz the
reue oz ruler of the
Shire, foz (Gereue) be-
ing deriued of the fax-
on wozde (Gereccan)
to rule, was firft cal-
led (Gerecfa) & then
(Gerefa)which teto-
keneth a ruler. And
hereof commeth(Poz-
treue oz rather Poзt-
greue)a name that in
olde tyme was geuen
to the head officer of a
town, & fignifieth the
ruler of þ town foz þ
(Poзt) cominge of the
latine

latine worde Portus, signifieth a port town and (Gereue) bringe deriued as is aforesaid signifieth a ruler, soe ye portgereue or as we now shorter speake it (Portreue) is the ruler of the towne.

And thus was the heade Officer or Gouernour of the Citye of London long since (before they had the name of Maior or Baylifes) called, as it doth appeare in diuers olde monuments But chiefelye in the Saxon Charter of Willyam Bastard the conqueror, which thus beginneth. Willyam the kynge greeteth Willyam the bishope, and Godfreye the Portreue, and also the Citizens that in London &c.

So also they of Germany from whom wee and our language

latine parol portus, signify vn port ville, & (Gereue)esteat deriue coe est auantdit signify vn ruler, issint que Portgreue ou coe nous a ore briefement parle ceo(Portreue) est le gouernor del ville.

Et issint fuit le chief Officer ou Gouernour del Cytje de Londres longe temps past(deuaunt que ils ad le nosme del Maior ou Bailyfes)appel, come il appiert en diuers viel monumentes, mes principalment en le Saxons Charter de Guillyam Bastarde le conquerour, que issint commence. VVilliam Cyng greit VVillam Bisceop, and Godfrey Ges port Geretan, & dalle tha Burwarren the on Loundon beon &c.

Issint ils de Germany (de que nous & nostre language ca-enfemble primerment vient)appel enter eux vn gouernour Bur-greue, vn auter Mar-greue , & vne auter Landfgreue, oue tiels femblables &c.

Ceft taunt eft dyt tantfolemt pur vfe le droit Etymon & an-tiquitie del parol (Shi-rife,) a quel officer noftre common ley ad toutes foits accor-daunt done graunde confidence et auctho-ritie , come deftre vn fpeciall preferuer del peace: et pur ceo tours obligatiõs que il prift a mefme le purpofe , font come Recogny-fances en ley . Il auxy eft vn Iudge de record quant il tient les leetes ou Tournes, lefqueux font courts de record.

Item il ad le returne des briefes , & impa-nelling des Iuryes , & tyels femblables &c.

together firft came,) call among them one gouernoʒ Burgræue, and other Margreue, and an other Landf-greue, with fuch like &c.

Thus much is fayde onely to fhew þ right Etymon and antiqui-tie of the woozd (fhi-rife)to which Officer our common law hath alwayes accozdinglie gæuen great truft and authozitie, as to be a fpecial preferuer of þ peace. And therefoze all obligations that he takes to the fame end, are as Recogny-fances in law. He alfo is a Iudge of Recoʒd when hee holdes the Læetes oʒ Courtes, whych are Courts of recoʒde.

Alfo hee hath the retourne of wʒittes, and impannellyng of Iuries, and fuch like &c.

¶ Vou-

¶Voucher.

V Oucher, is when
a Precipe quod red-
dat of land is brought
against a man, & an o=
ther ought to warrāt
the land to the tenāt:
then the tenant shall
bouch him to warran-
tie, and thereupon he
shal haue a writ called
Summonias ad warran-
tizandum, & if the Shi=
rife returne that hee
hath nothinge by the
which he may be sum-
moned, then ther shal
go forth a writ called
Sequar sub suo periculo,
and when he commeth
he shal plede with the
demaundant, and if he
come not, or if he come
and cannot barre the
demaundant, then the
demaundant shall re=
couer the land against
the tenant, & the te=
nant shall recouer as
much lande in balue
against the bouchee,

¶Voucher.

V Oucher, est quant
vn Precipe quod
reddat de terr est port
vers vn home, & vn
auter doit garraunter
le terre al tenaunt,
donques le tenaunt
luy vouchera a gar-
rauntie, & sur ceo
il auera vne briefe
appell, Summoneas
ad warrantizandum,
& si le Vycount re-
tourne que il nad ry-
ens que il puyt este
summon, donques il
sera briefe appel, Se-
quatur sub suo peri-
culo, & quaunt il vi-
ent il pledera ouesque
le demaundant, & si
il vyent & ne puyt
barre le demaun-
daunt, donques le
demaundaunt reco-
uera la terre vers le
tenaunt, & le te-
naunt recouera taunt
de le terre en value
vers le Vouchee,
&

& ſur ceo il auera vn briefe appell Capias ad valentiam vers le vouche.

and thereupon he ſhal haue a wꝛit called Capias ad valētiam againſt the vouche.

¶ Vſes.

¶ Vſes.

_V_ Ses de terre ad ſon commencemēt a- pres que le cuſtome de propertie commence enter homes . Come ou vn eſteant ſeiſie de terres en fee ſimple, fait vn feffement al vn auter ſans aſcuñ con- ſideration, mes ſolemt meaning que le auter ſerroit ſeiſie al ſon vſe, & que il meſme voile prender le commodi- tie & profites de les terres, & que le feffee doit auer le poſſeſſion & frankrenement de ceo al meſme le vſe &c. Ore apres ceo, ſur bone conſiderati- ons, & pur auoyder diuers myſchiefes & inconueniences, fuit le ſtatute de Anno 27.

_V_ Ses of lande had beginning after ꝑ the cuſtome of ꝓꝑer- tie began among men. Is where one bæyng ſeiſed of landes in ſe ſimple, made a feoffe- ment to another with out any conſideration, but onely meaninge that the other ſhould bee ſeiſed to his vſe, and that hee him ſelfe would take the com- moditie and pꝛofits of the landes, & that the feoffæ ſhould haue the poſſeſſion and frank- tenement thereof to ꝑ ſame vſe &c. Now af- ter this vpon good cō- ſiderations, & to auoid diuers miſchiefes and inconuentences, was the ſtatute of Ꭺꞏ 27. ꞏH. 8.

H.8 cap.10.prouided, which vniteth the vse & possession together, so that who hath the vse of lands, the same hath p̃ possession therof. by vertue of that estatute.

¶ Vsurie.

Vsurie, is a gayne of any thing aboue the principal, or that which was lent, exacted onely in consideration of the loane, whether it be of corn, meat, apparel, wares, or such like, as of money. And here much myght be saied, and many cases might bee putt concernynge Vsurie, whiche of purpose I omytte, onely I wyshe, that they who accompte the selues religious & good christians, would not deceiue the selues

H.8.ca.10.puruiew, quel vnite le vse et possession ensemble, issint que il qus ad le vse de terre, il mesme ad le possession de ceo, per vertue de cest estatute.

¶ Vsurie.

Vsurie est vn gaine de ascun chose ouster le principal, ou ceo que fuit lent, exact solement en consideration de le loane, soit il de corne, viand, apparel, wares, ou tiels semblables, come de money. Et icy mult puit estre dyt, & dyuers cases poyent estre mise concernant Vsurie, le quel de purpose ico omit, solemet ico pria, que ceux que accompt eux mesmes religious et bon christians, ne voyllent deceiue eux mesines, per

per colour de le fta-
tute de Vfurie, pur ceo
que il dit, que il ne
ferra loyal pur afcun
de prender oufter x.li.
en le C. li. pur vn an
&c. per que ils collect
(mes fauxment) que
ils poient per ceo pre-
der x.li. pur le loane
dun C.li. oue vn bon
confcience, pur ceo q
le ftatute folonque vn
maner difpence oue
ceo, (pur ceo que il
ne punifhe tiels pren-
dors) quel chofe il ne
poit faire oue les leyes
& ordinances de dieu,
car Dieu voile auer fes
decrees obferue inuio-
lable, que dit, lende
expectens pur nul
chofe pur ceo &c. Per
quex parollx eft ex-
clude, le prifel de x.li.
v.li. ou de vn der yer
oufter le principall.
Mes plus penfant tiels
que ceft ftatute fuyt
fait fur tyel caufe
que moua Moyfes

by colour of the fta-
tute of vfurie, becaufe
it fayeth that it fhall
not be lawful for any
to take aboue x. li. in
the C .li. for a yere &c.
Whereby they gather
(although falfly)that
they may therefore
take x. li. for the loane
of an C .li. with a good
confcience, becaufe the
Statute doth after a
fort difpence withal,
(for that it doth not
punifh fuch taking,)
which thing it cannot
do with the lawes &
ordinaces of God, for
God will haue his de-
crees to be kept inuio-
lable, who fayth, lende
looking for nothynge
thereby &c. By which
woordes is excluded,
eyther the taking of
x. li. v. li. yea, or one
penny aboue the prin-
cipall. But rather let
fuch think, y that fta-
tute was made vppon
like caufe, that moued
Moyfes

Moyſes to gyue a bill of dyuozce to the Iſralites, as name= lye to auoyde a grea= ter miſchiefe, and foz the hardneſſe of their hartes.

Moyſes de doner vn bill de diuorce al les Iſralites, come noſ= ment, pur auoider vn greinder miſchiefe, & pur le durytie de lour ceurs.

¶ Vtlawrie.

¶ Vtlagarie.

Vtlawzy is whē an exigent goeth fozth againſt any mā, & pzo= clamation made at v. coūties, then at the v. countye if the deſ. ap= pere not, the cozoner ſhal giue iudgement ỹ he ſhalbe out of ỹ pzo= tection of the Queene, & out of the aide of the lawe, and by ſuch an vtlary in actions per= ſonals, the party out= lawed ſhall fozfayt al his goodes and cattels to the Queene. And by an vtlary in felony, hee ſhall fozfait aſwel all his landes, and tene= ments that he hath in fee ſimple, oz foz terme

Vtlagarie eſt quant exigent iſsiſt vers aſcun home & pro= clamatyon fait al v. counties donques a le v. countie ſi le defen= daunt nappiert, le co= roner donera iudge- ment que il ſerra hors de protection de roi- gne, & hors del eide le ley, & per tyel vt- lagary in actions per- ſonels le partye vt- lage forfetera toutes ſes byens & chateux al Roigne. Et per vt- lagary in felonye il forfetera auxibiē touts ſes terres & tene- ments que il ad in fee ſimple, ou pur terme

A a.j.   de

de sa vie, come ses biens & chateux. Et si vne home soit vtlage vncore si ascun discontinuance ou error soit en la suit del proces le partye de ceo auera la aduauntage, & pur tyel cause le vtlagarye serra reuers & adnul. Ou si le partye defendant soit oustr la mere al temps de vtlagarie pronouce ceo est bone cause de reuersal del vtlagarv.

Sy vn exigent soit agarde vers vne home en vne countye lou il ne demurre pas, vncore vn exigent oue proclamation issera al county lou il demurre ou auterment sil soit sur ceo vtlage, le vtlagarie puit estre reuerse come appiert per lestatute fait an quarto H. octaui. Et si vn soyt vtlage in action personal al suit dun auter, & il puis pur-ter ,

of his life, as his goods & catttals. And though a man be outlawed, yet if any error or discontinuance be in the suit of the proces the party thereof shal haue aduantage, & for such cause the vtlary shalbe reueried & adnulied. Or if the partye defendant be over the sea at the time of the vtlary pronouced that is a good cause of the reuersal of the vtlary.

If an exigent be awarded against a man in one couty where he dwelleth not, yet an exiget in proclamatio shal go forth to the couty where he dwelleth: or els if he be therupon vtlased ed, the vtlary may be reuersed as it appeereth by the statute made the 4 yere of King H. 8. And if a man be outlawed in an actio personal at the suit of another, and after he pur-chase

chafe his charter of
pardon of the Queen,
fuch charter fhal ne-
uer be allowed, til hœ
hath fued a wꝛitte of
Scire facias to warne
the partye plaintife,
and if he appeare,then
the defendant fhal an-
fwere him, and barre
him of his action, oꝛ
els make agreement
with him.

chafa fon charter de
pardon de Roigne, ti-
el charter ne ferꝛ iam-
mais allow tanque il
ad fue vne briefe de
Scire facias de garni le
partye plaintife, & fi
il appeare, donques le
defendaunt refponder
a luy,& luy barrer de
fa action,ou autermēt
ferra agreement ouel-
que luy.

¶ VVaife.

VVayfe is when a
thœfe hath felo-
nioufly ftolne gœdes,
and winge nœrelye
followed with hue,
and crye,oꝛ els ouer-
charged with the bur-
ten oꝛ trouble of the
gœdes, foꝛ his eafe
fake and moꝛe fpœdye
trauailinge, without
hue and cry, flieth a-
way and leaueth the
gœds oꝛ any part of
them behind him,then
the quœnes officer oꝛ

¶ VVaife.

VVAife eft quaunt
vn laron ad fe-
lonioufemēt ē-
blee biens,& efteaunt
neerement purfue o-
ue hue & erie, ou au-
termēt furcharge oue
le burden ou trouble
des byens, pur fon
eafe & plus fpeedye
trauaile fauns hue &
erye fua, & waiua
les byens ou afcun
part de eux arrere
luy &c. donques le
officer del roigne, ou

Aa ij.   le

le Reeue ou Bayliffe al Seigniour del mannour (deyns que iurifdiction ou circuit ils fuerount wayfe) que per prefcriptyon, ou graunt del Roigne ad le fraunchyfe de wayfe, poyent feyfer les biens iffint wayfe al vfe de lour feygniour, que poet retayne eux come fes proper byens finon qu le owner vient ouefque fresh fuit apres le felon, & fue vn appell, ou done en euidence enuers luy al fon arraynment fur lendictment, & il attaint de ceo &c. En queux cafes le primer owner auera reftitution de fes biens iffint emblee & wayfe.

Mes nient obftaunt côe ad efte dit, waife eft properment de biens emblees, vncore wayfe poet efte auxy de biens nient embles,

the Reeue, or Bailiffe to the Lord of the manour (within whofe Jurifdiction or circuit they were left) that by prefcriptyon, or graut frô the Queene hath the fraunchife of waife, may feyfe the goodes fo wayued to their lordes vfe, who may keepe them as his owne proper goods: except that the owner come with fresh fuite after the felon, & fue an appeale, or giue in euidence againft him at his arrainemêt vpô the indictment, and be attainted thereof &c. In which cafes ý firft owner fhall haue reftitution of his goodes fo ftollen and wayued.

But although as hath byn fayd wayfe is properly of goodes ftollen, yet wayfe may bee alfo the goodes that are not ftolne.
As

Is if a man bee pur=
sued wyth hue , and
crye , as a felon, and
hee flyeth, and leaueth
his owne goodes &c.
these shalbe taken as
goodes wayued, & for=
fait as if they had bin
Coine.

qVVaiue.

VVaiue is a woman
that is autlawed,
& she is called waiue,
as left out or forsaken
of the law, and not an
vtlawe as a man is.
For women are not
sworne in leetes to the
Queene , nor to the
lawe, as menn are,
whoe therefore are
within ý law, where=
as women are not,
and for that cause
they cannot bee sayd
out of the lawe in so
much as they neuer
were within it. But a
man is called vtlawe,
bæcause that hæ was

Come si vn home soit
pursue ouesque hue
et crie, come vn felon,
et il fue et relinquish
ses biens demesñ &c.
ils serra prise come bi=
ens waife, et forfayt
come sils ad este em=
blees.

VVaiue.

VVaiue est vn
feme q̃ est vt-
lage, et est ap-
peal waiue, quasi re-
licta a lege , et non
vtlage come home
est, car femes ne sount
iures en leetes al
Roigne , ne al ley
come homes sount,
queux pur ceo sount
deyns le ley ou fem-
mes ne sount, et pur
cest cause ils ne po-
ent cite dyt hors del
ley entauot que ils
ne vnques fuerount
deynes ceo . Mes vn
home est dyt vtlage,
pur ceo que il fuit

vn foites iure al ley,
& a ore pur contempt
il est mys hors del
ley , & dictus vtla-
gatus quasi extta le-
gem positus.

once sworne to þ law:
& now for contempt he
is put out of the law,
& is called vtlawe, as
one shoulde say wout
benefite of the law.

¶VVarwite.

VVArwyte (ou
wardwite come
ascuns copies ad ceo)
hoc est quietum esse
de denarijs dandis pro
wardis faciendis.

¶VVarwite.

VVArwite (or ward
wite as some co-
pies haue it) that is
to bee quite of giuing
of money for keping
of watches.

¶VVrecke.

VVRecke ou varech
come les Nor-
mans de que il vyent
appellant ceo, est quar
vn niefe est perish sur
la mere, & nul home
escape viue hors de
niefe & le niefe ou
parte del niefe issint
perishe ou les biens en
la nyefe vyent al ter-
re dascun seygniour,
le seygniour les aue-
ra come vn wrecke
de mere, mes si vn

¶VVrecke.

VVRecke or barech
as the Normans
from whom it came
call it, is where a ship
is perished on the sea,
and no man escapeth
a liue out of the same,
and the shippe, or part
of the ship is perished,
or the goods of the ship
come to the lande of a-
ny Lorde , the Lorde
shall haue that as a
wreck of þ sea, but if a
man,

man, oz a dogg, oz cat,
escape a liue, so that ẏ
partye to whom the
goods belong come wi-
in a yere and a day and
pzoue the goods to bee
his, he shal haue thē a
gaine, by pzouision of
the statute of west. ẏ
1. cap. 4. made in king
Ed. 1. daies, who there
in followed the decre
of Henry the first, be-
foze whose daies, if a
shippe had ben cast on
shoze, tozne with tem-
pest, and were not re-
paired by such as es-
caped a lyue within a
certeyne tyme, that
then this was taken
foz wzecke.

home ou vn chȳen
ou chate escape viue
issint que la partie a
que les byens sount
veigne deyns lan &
iour, & prouc les bi-
ens distī ses, il auer eux
arr, per prouision del
statute de VV. le pri-
mer cap. 4. fayten les
iours del Roy Ed. le
1. que en ceo follo-
wed le decre de H. 1.
deuaunt que iours, si
vn niefe ad estre mise
sur le shore, torne oue
tempest, & nemy re-
paier per eux que esca-
pont en vie deins vn
certen temps, que don-
ques ceo fuit prise cōe
wrecke.

FINIS.

TEnir per ser-
uice de chiua-
ler est a tener
per homage
fealtie, & es-
cuage, & treit a luy
garde mariage & re-
liefe. Et nota que ser-
uice de Chiualer est
seruice de terre ou de
tenementes pur armes
port en guerre en de-
fence de Royalme . Et
doit gard & mariage p
la reason que nul est
able ne de power &
ne poit auer conu-
saunce darmes por-
ter auaunt que il soit
dage de xxj . ans . Et
purtaunt que le seig-
niour ne perdera ceo,
que de droit il doit an,
& que la power de la
royalme de ryen ne
soit enfeeble : La ley
voet per cause de son
tender age que le
seigniour luy auera en
sa gard tanque al plein

TO holde by
knightes ser-
uice,is to holde
by homage, fe-
alty, & escuage,
and it draweth to it
warde, mariage, & re-
liefe,and knowe thou
that knightes seruice
is seruice of landes or
tenementes to bere
armes in warre in the
defence of the Realme,
& it oweth warde and
mariage by reaso that
none is able nor of
power, nor may haue
knowledge to bere
armes,before p he be of
the age of 2 1 . yeres.
And for so much p the
lord shal not lese that
that of right he ought
to haue,& that p power
of the realme, nothing
be made weake . The
law wil because of his
tender age , that the
Lord him shal haue in
his warde till the full

a ge

age of him, that is to
say xxj.yeres.

age de luy cestassauoir
xxj.ans.

¶Graunde serieantie.

¶Graund serieantie.

TO hold by graund
serieanty is as if a
man hold certein lāds
oz tenementes of the
king to go with him
in his host,oz to beare
his banner with him
in his warres, oz to
leade his host, oz such
like, and thereto bae=
longeth warde mary=
age and relyefe, as it
appeareth in the trea=
tise of wards and re=
liefes in þ statute made
the 28. of Edwarde
the 1.

2 Tenir per graunde
Serieauntye, est si-
come vn home tyent
certeyne terres ou te-
nementes de Roy dal'
oue luy en son host,ou
de porter son banner
oue luy en ses guerres,
ou amesner son hoste,
ou tyel semblable, &
a ceo appent garde
maryage & relyefe,si-
come il appiert en la
treatise de gardes &
relyefe enter lesta-
tutes 28. Edwardi
primi.

¶Petit Serieantie.

¶Petit serieantie.

TO holde by petit
serieantie is as if a
man hold of the kinge
landes oz tenementes,
yelding to him a knife.
a buckler,an Arrowe,
a Bow wout stringe,

3 Tenir per petit' ser-
ieauntye est sicome
vn home tient de roy
terres ou tenements,
rendaunt a luy vn cot-
tel vn escue, vn sete,
vn arc sauns corde,
ou

on auter seruice sem-
blables, a la volunt le
primer feoffour . Et
la nappent, garde, ma-
riage ne reliefe. Et no-
ta que home ne puit
tener per graunde fer-
ieantie, ne per petite
ferieauntie , finon del
Roy.

oz other like seruice at
the will of the firſt
feoffour, and there be-
longeth not warde
marpage ne reipefe.
And marke well that
a man may not holde
by graunde noz petit
ferieantie , but of the
King.

¶Efcuage.

¶Efcuage.

4 ¶Tener per efcu-
age eſt a tener per fer-
uice de chiualer . Et
la appent garde, ma-
riage, & reliefe . Et
nota que home ne
puit tener per efcu-
age, finon que il tey-
gne per homage, pur
ceo que efcuage de
common droit treyt
a luy homage come
il fuit aiudge in Ter-
mino H. 21. E. 3. ca.
42. fol. 52. Auowrye
115. Et nota que ef-
cuage eſt vn certeine
fumme de argent , &

To hold by efcuage is
by knightes seruice, ¶
there belongeth ward,
mariage , and reliefe.
And marke well that
a man may not holde
by efcuage , but that
hæ holde by homage,
foz that efcuage of
common ryght dza-
weth to him homage,
as it was Judged
Termino H . 21. E.
3 . cap. 42. fol. 52.
Auowzye 115. And
note well , that ef-
cuage is a certeyne
fumme of money, and
it

it ought to bee leuyed by the Lord of his tenant after the quantitie of his tenure. when efcuage runneth by al Englande. And it is ordeined by al the coũfell of England how much euery tenaunt fhal geue to his Lord, and that is properlye for to maintayne the warres betwene England, & them of Scotlande or of Wales, and not beetwene other landes; for that, ϸ thofe forefayd lands fhould be of ryght belonginge to the Realme of England.

doit eftr leuy per le feygnior de fon tenant folonques le quantitie de fon tenure quant le efcuage courge per tout Engleterre . Et ordeyne eft per tout le counfell Dengleterre, quaunt tenaunt donera a fon feignyour, & ceo eft properment pur fuftener la guerre perenter Engleterre & ceux de Efcoce ou de Galeys , & non pas perenter auters terres, pur ceo que les auauntdits terres ferront de droit appendant a la royalm Dengleterre.

¶Homage aunceftrel.

¶Homage aunceftrel.

TO holde by homage aunceftrel is where I or my aunceftours haue holdẽ of you & of your auncestors from time out of mind wher of no minde runneth),

5 Tener per homage aunceftrell eft lou ieo & mon auncestours ont tenus de vous & de voftre Auncestours de temps dount memorye ne courge,
per

per homage , fealty, & certaine rent. Et nest pas a tener per seruice de chiualer, & la nap- pent garde , mariage, ne reliefe. Et nota que homage poit estre dit in deux maners cestas- cauoire, homage aun- cestrel, & homage de fait. Homage aun- cestrel est la ou vous & voster auncestours ount tenus de moy & mes auncestours puis le temps de que non memory, per homage, fealtye, & certain rent Homage de fait est la ou ieo enfeoffe vous mesmes auenes d' moy por homage, & rent, & entant que cest ho- mage commence per mon fait, il est ho- mage de fait.

Et nota que homage auncestrel trie a luy voucher, cest ascauoire garranty des ancestors, mes non pas homage de fait,

by homage, fealty, and certaine rent. And it is not to holde by knightes seruice, and there belongeth not ward, mariage, nor reliefe. And note well that homage may be said in ij. maners, þ is to say, homage ance- trel, & homage de fait Homage auncestrel is where you or your aun- cestors haue holden of me and mine auncest- tors during the time of mans remembrance, by homage, fealty, and rent. Homage de fait is where I enfeoffe your selfe, to hold of me by homage and rent, and in so much that this homage beginneth by my deede, it is called homage de fait.

And note wel that Homage auncestrell draweth to him vou- cher, þ is to say, war- ranty of auncestors, but not homage de fait

C

¶ Curtesy of England. ¶ Curtesie dangliterr.

To hold by the cur-
tesy of Englande
is there where a man
taketh a wife inheri-
trix, & they haue issue
a sonne or daughter, &
the wife dieth, whe-
ther the issue be deade
or aliue, þ husbãd shal
hold this lãd for term
of his life by the cur-
tesy of England, & by
the law. And in this
case the fee & the right
remaineth in þ person
of him of whom he hol
deth: and for that, this
tenant may not alyen
in fee, nor for terme of
anothers life, & if he w
it is lawful to him in þ
reuersion to enter.

6 Tener per la Cur-
tesye de Angly-
terre est la ou vne
home prent feme en-
heritrix, & ount issue
fits ou file, & la feme
deuy soit la issu mort
ou en vye , le baron
tyendra cest terre a
terme de son vye per
la curtesie de Angly-
terre, & per le ley. Et
en cest case le fee & le
droit remaine en le
person celuy de que
il tyent: et pur ceo cest
tenaunt ne puyt alyen
en fee ne a terme dau-
ter vye, & sil face byen
lyst a celuy en le re-
uercion dentre.

¶ Fee simple. ¶ Fee simple.

To hold in fee sim-
ple is to hold to a-
ny man or woman, to
him & to his heirs and
his assignes for euer.

7 Tener in fee simple
est a tener a ascũ home
ou feme, a luy et a ses
heires & a ses assignes
pur touts iours.
¶ Franke

¶Franke tenure.

¶Franke tenure.

8 Tener en franke tenure eſt a tener a terme de ſa vye demeſne, ou a terme de auter vye. Et en ceſt caſe le fee & le droit remaynt en la perſon celuy de, que il tient. Et puꝛ ceo cel tenaunt ne puyt pas alier en fee ne a terme de auter vie : Et ſil face, byen lyſt a celuy in quel le fee & le droyt demourt, dentrer.

TO hold in free hold is to hold foꝛ terme of his owne lyfe, oꝛ foꝛ terme of anothes mans life. And in this caſe the fee & the right remaineth in the perſon of him, of whome he holdeth. And foꝛ y this tenaunt may not alien in fee noꝛ foꝛ terme of life: And if he do, it is well lawfull to him in whom the fee & the right abideth to enter.

¶Dower.

¶Dower.

9 Tenure in dower eſt, lou home inherite prent femme & deuye, lheire entra & endowera la femme de la tierce part de tout ceo que fuit a ſon baron en ſa vie, en fee ſimple ou fee tayle, & el tyendra cels terres pur terme de

TO hold in dower is where a man inherite taketh a wife and dieth, the heire ſhal enter, & endow the wyfe of the third part of al that y was to her huſband in his life, in fee ſimple oꝛ fee taile, and ſhee ſhall holde theſe landes foꝛ terme of
her

her lyfe as her free holde.

sa vie come son frank-tenement.

¶Terme dans.

TO hold for terme of yeares is not but chattel in effect, for no action is maintenable against the termour, for the recouering of the freehold. for no free hold is in him. A leas for terme of yeares is a chattell reall, and the other chattel per=sonall, and all goods whych are remoua=ble are chattelles per=sonals.

¶Terme dans.

10 Tener a terme dans nest forsque chat-tell en effecte, car nul action est mayntena-ble enuers le termor quaunt a recouerer de franketenement , car nul franketenement est a luy . Leale a terme dans est chat-tell reall . Et lauter chattell est personall, & toutes biens mo-uables sont chattelles personals.

¶Mortgage.

TO hold in mortgage is to hold for a cer=taine terme vpon con=dition, that if the les=for pay so much mony at such a day, that hee may enter, and if not, that þ other shal haue a fee simple or fee taile, or free holde. And in

¶Mortgage.

11 Tener in morgage est a tener a cert terme sur condition , que si le lessour paya taunts deniers a tiel iour, que il puit enter , & sinon que lauter eyt fee sim-ple ou fee tayle , ou franktenement. Et en chescun

chefcun cafe lou ter-
res ou tenements font
dones a home a cer-
teyne terme fur con-
dicion de part le lef-
four pur faire le lef-
fee auoyr plus longe
temps ou terme , fi
lauter ne face ficome
la condicion eft , les
terres & tenementes
tanque le iour que la
condicyon ferroyt fait,
fount 'enus in mor-
gage , quafi in mort-
gage.

Et nota que fi ter-
re foyt leffe a vn hom
en morgage en fee
fimple , ou in fee taile
fur condicion, que fi le
primer leffour come
deuaunt eft dyt, pay
tauntes des deniers a
tiel iour , que il puit
enter , & finon que le
leffee eyt mefme lef-
tate en les terres , que
le leffour luy graunt
adeprimes . Et fi de-
uaunt le iour afsigne,
le leffee foyt difseyfie,

euery cafe where lãds
oʒ tenements be geuen
to a man foʒ a certeine
terme vpon condition
of the part of the leſſoʒ
foʒ to make the leſſee
to haue moʒe lõg time
oʒ terme, if the other w
not as the condition
is , the landes and te=
nementes vntyll the
daye that the con=
dityon ſhoulde bee
done , bee holden in
moʒgage, as in a dead
gage.

And note well that
if land be let to a man
in moʒgage in fee ſim=
ple oʒ in fee taile vpon
condition , that if the
firſt leſſoʒ, as is befoʒe
ſaid, pay ſo much mo=
ney at ſuch a day that
he may enter, & if not,
that the leſſee haue the
ſame eſtate in ẏ lands,
that the leſſour vpõ
him graunt at the be=
ginninge . And if be=
foʒe the day aſſigned,
the leſſee bee diſſeiſed,
he

he shall haue assise of
nouel disseisin. And in
case that if the lessee
take a wife & dye sey=
sed before the day as=
signed, the woman shal
be endowed.

And note well, that
if the lessor after the
death of the lessee pay
not the money, at the
day assigned, then the
woman shall hold her
dower, and the issue
his heritage. And in
case the lessour at the
day assigned pay the
money to the heire of
the lessee, then he may
put out the woman &
the heire also of al the
land first let. And if a
man geue lands to an
other in the taile, yel=
ding to him a certaine
rent by the yere, & one
enter for default of
payment, the done ta=
keth a wife and dyeth
seised, the woman shal
be endowed. And in
case that after the rent

il auera assise de No-
uel disseilin. Et en case
que si le lessee prent
feme & deuie seisi de-
uaunt le iour assygne,
sa femme serra en-
dowe.

Et nota que si le les-
sour apres le mort le
lessee ne pay les de-
niers a le iour assesse
adonques la feme ty-
endra sa dower, &
lyssue son heritage. Et
en cas que le lessour
a le iour assesse paya
les denyers al heire de
le lessee, donques il
puit ouster le femme,
& le heire auxy de
tout le terre pryment
ment lesse. Et si yne
home done terres a vn
auter en le taile, ren-
dant a luy certein rent
per an, & vn enter
pur default de pay-
ment, le donce prent
femme & deuye sey-
sie, la femme serra
endowe. Et en case
que apres le rent soit

B b.j.

soit aderere, le donour puit enter & ousta le feme & lheire auxy. Et nota que si terres soyent lesses a vn hom en Mortgage en fee sur certeine condicions, le lessee alyen, le lessour serra charge de paier les denyers al alienee, & non pas a son feoffee, come il est dit. 17. Ass. 2.

be behind, the donour may enter & put out the woman & the heire also. And note well, that if landes be let to a man in Mortgage in fee vpon condicion, the lessee doth alien, the lessour shal bee charged to pay the money to the alienee, and not to the feoffee, as it is saide.

¶Burgage.

¶Burgage.

12 Tener en Burgage est a tener sicome les burgeis teignēt de Roy, ou de auter seigniour terres ou tenements rendant a luy vn certeine rent per an, ou aurermēt la ou vn auter home que burgeis tient dascun seigniour terres ou tenements en Burgage rendant a luy vn certein rent per an.

TO holde in Burgage, is to holde as if the Burgeis holde of the king, or of another Lord landes or tenements, yelding to him a certeine rent by the yeare, or els there where another man Then burge is holdeth of any Lord landes or tenemēts in burgage, yelding to him a certein rent by yeare.

¶Socage.

¶Socage.

To

TO hold in Socage
is to holde of any
Lord landes or tene=
ments, yelding to him
a certeine rent by the
yere for al maner ser=
uices. And note wel,
that to holde by So=
cage is not to holde by
knightes seruice, nor
there belongeth ward,
mariage, nor relyefe,
but they shall double
once their rent after y
death of their auncef=
tors according to that
that they be wont to
pay to their lord. And
they shall not be ouer
measure greued, as it
appereth in y treatise
of wardes & relietes.
And note wel, y So=
cage may be said in iij.
maners, that is to say,
socage in frœ tenure,
Socage in auncient
tenure, and Socage in
base tenure. Socage
in frœ tenue is to hold
frely by certein rẽt for
all maner of seruices,

13 Tener en Socage
est a tener dascun seig-
niour terres ou tene-
ments rendãt a luy vn
certein rent per an pur
touts maners des ser-
uices. Et nota que te-
ner per socage nest pas
tener per seruice de
chiualer ne la appen-
garde, mariage, ne re-
liefe, mes ils double-
ront vn foits lour rent
apres le mort lour ãce-
stor, solonque eeo q̃
soleynt paier a lour
seigniour. Et ils ne
serrount ouster mea-
sure greues, come il
appiert en le treatise
de gardes & de Re-
liefes. Et nota que so-
cage puit estre dit en
iij. maners, cestascauoi r, Socage en frank
tenure, Socage en
auncient tenure, et fo-
cage in base tenure,
Socage en franke te-
nure, est a teñ frãkmẽt
per certeine rent puer
touts mañ des seruices
　　B b.ij.　　　co.u:

come deuant eſt dyt,
& de ceo le procheine
amy auera le garde a
que lheritage ne purra
my diſcender, tanque
al age lheire de xiiij.
ans, ceſtaſcauoir ſi le
heritage veygne per
le part le pere, ceux
del part le mere a-
uerount le garde &
econtra.

Et nota que ſi gar-
deine en Socage fayt
waſte, il ne ſerra my
empech de waſt, mes
rendra accompt al
heire quant il viendra
al pleine age de xxj.
ans. Et vide leſtatute
de Marlebridge ca-
pitulo 17. pur ceſt
matter.

Socage de auncient
tenure eſt ceo ou gēts
en auncient demeſne
tenoyent, que ne ſoy-
lent auter briefe auoir
que le briefe de Droit
cloſe, que ſerra deter-
mine ſecundum con-
ſuetudinem manerij,

as is before ſaid, and
of that the next kyns
bodie ſhall haue the
warde to whom the
heritage may not diſ-
cend, til the age of xiiij
yeares, that is to ſay,
if the heritage come
by ꝑ part of the father
they of the part of the
mother ſhall haue the
ward, & contrarywiſe

And note wel that if
the gardein in So-
cage do make waſt, he
ſhall not be impeched
of waſt, but he ſhall
yelde accompt to the
heire when he ſhal cōe
to his full age of xxj.
yeares. And looke the
ſtatute of Marlebridge
ca. 17. for this matter.
Socage in auncient te-
nure is ꝑ where the
people in auncient de-
meſne helde, whych
vſe no other wryt to
haue then the wryt of
right cloſe, which ſhal
be determined accor-
ding to the cuſtome of
the

the manoz, & the Monstrauerunt foz to dyscharge them whē their Lozd distraypneth thē foz to do other seruice p̃ they ought not to do And this wzit of Mōstrauerunt ought to bee bzought agaynst the Loed, & those tenants hold al by one certain seruice, & these be free tenaunts of auncient demesne.

Socage in base tenure is where a man holdeth in auncyent demesne, that may not haue the Monstrauerūt, and foz that it is called the base Tenure.

¶ Fee ferme.

To hold in fee ferme is to hold in fee simple, yelding to p̃ Loed the value, oz at p̃ least the fourth part by the yeare, & he ought to do no other thing, but as it is conteined in the feffement, and he that

& le Monstrauerunt pur eux dyscharger quaunt lour seigniour eux distraine pur faire auters seruyces que faire ne duissent. Et cest briefe de Monstrauerunt doit estre port enuers lour seigniour, & ceux tenants teygnent touts per vn certeine seruice. Et ils sont franktenants de auncient demesne.

Socage en base tenure, est lou home tient en auncient demesne. que ne puit auer le Monstrauerunt & pur ceo il est appel le base Tenure.

¶ Fee ferme.

14. Tener en fee ferm est a tenīt en fee simple, rendant a le seigniour le value ou la moitie, ou al meins le iiij. part per an, & ne doyt auter chose faire, mes sicōe est conteign en le feffemt, & il que

tient en fee ferme, doit faire fealtie & nyent reliefe.

¶Franke fee.

15 Tener en frank-fee, eſt a tener en fee ſimple terres pledable a la common ley.

¶Baſe fee.

16 Tener en fee baſe eſt a tener a la volunt le ſeigniour.

¶Villenage.

17 Tenure en pure villenage eſt a faire tout ceo q̃ le ſñior luy voit commaunder.

La diffinition de vil-lenage eſt villeine de ſank, & de tenure. Et il eſt de q̃ ſon ſeignior prent redemption de ſa file marier, ou ſoy meſme enfraunchiſe. Et le ſeigniour puit luy ouſter de ſes

holdeth in fœ ferme ought to do fealtie & not reliefe.

¶Franke fee.

TO holde in franke fee, is to hold in fee ſimple lands pledable at the common law.

¶Baſe fee.

TO hold in fee baſe, is to holde at the will of the Lord.

¶Villenage.

TO hold in pure vil-lenage, is to doe all that, that the Lorde wil him cõmaund.

The diffinition of villenage is villein of bloud, and of tenure. And it is he of whom ý Lord taketh redep-tion to marie his dau-ghter, & to make hym free, & it is he whom ý Lord may put out of his

his landes oz tene=
mentes at his will, ¢
also of all his goods ¢
cattel. And note wel,
that a sokeman is no
pure villein, noz a vil=
lein oweth not ward,
mariage, noz reliefe,
noz to do any other
seruices reall. And
note well, that the te=
nure in villenage shal
make no free man vil=
lein, if it be not conti=
nued sith time out of
minde, noz villein land
shal make no free man
villein, noz free lande
shal make no villeine
free, except þ the tenãt
haue cõtinued free sith
the time of no minde,
but a villein shal make
free lãd villein by sei=
sin oz claime of þ lozd.
And note wel, that if
a villein purchase cer=
teine landz, and take a
wife ¢ alyen, and dy=
eth befoze the clayme
oz seisin of the lozd, þ
wife shalbe endowed,

terres ou tenementes
a sa volunt , & auxy
de touts ses biens &
chateux . Et note que
Sokeman nest pas
pure villeine , ne
villeyne doit pas
garde marriage ne
reliefe , ne faire auter
seruices reals. Et nota
que tenure en Ville-
nage ne ferra nul frãk
home villeine , sil ne
soit continue puys le
temps de non memo-
rie , ne villeine terre
ne ferra franke home
villein , ne frank terre
ne ferra villein frank,
sinon que le tenaunt
soit continue frankmẽt
puis le temps de non
memorie , mes villein
ferra frank terre vil-
lein per seisin ou per
claim de son seignior.
Et nota q̃ si vill pur-
chase certein terre &
prent feme & alien &
deuie deuãt le claime,
ou seisin de son snior,
la feme serra endow.

B b,iiij.　　　Et

Et nota que en cest
case que le seigniout
port Precipe quod red
dat enuers lasien son
villein le quel vouche
a garrauntye le issue
la villein que est vil-
leihe a la seigniour ,il
auera le voucher. Et
per protestatiõ le seig-
nior puit sauer (que
non obstaunt que il
pled oue son villeine)
vncore son villeine ne
serra mye enfranchise.
Et nota que bastarde
ne serra iammaies ad-
iudge villeine sinon
per conusaunce en
court de recorde. Et
nota que si dett soit
due per vn seigniora
vn home et il face ij.
homes ses executours
les queux sount vil-
leins al dit seignior &
deuy les villeins aue-
rount actyon de dette
enuers lun seigniour,
nient obstaunt que il
pled ouesque eux. Et
sil face protestation

And note wel, that in
case that þ lord bringe
a Precipe quod reddat a-
gainst the alien which
voucheth to warrant
the issue of the villein
which is villein to þ
lord,he shal haue the
voucher,& by protes-
tation the lorde may
say þ(notwithstãding
that he pled with his
villein) yet his villein
shal not be enfranchi-
sed. And note wel þ
a bastard shall neuer
be iudged villeine, but
by knowledg in court
of recorde. And note
well that if bet be due
by a Lorde to a fre
man, and hee maketh
two men his execu-
tours the which bee
villeines to the saide
Lorde and dyeth, the
villeines shal haue an
actyon of bet against
their Lorde not with
standinge that hee
plead with them.And
if be make protestatio
they

they ſhal not be foz ſo
much enfranchiſed,foz
that that they be to
recouer the vett afoze
ſaid to the vſe of an o=
ther perſon that is to
ſay to the vſe of their
teſtatour, and not to
their owne vſe. And
if the tenant in tower
haue a villeine which
purchaſeth certaine
lande in fee,and after
the tenaunt in tower
entreth,ſhe ſhal haue
the land to her and to
her heires foz euer=
moze,& the ſame lawe
is of tenant foz terme
of yeares of a villein.

And note wel that
the lozd may robb his
villein,bete & chaſtice
at his wil,ſaue onely
that he may not maim
him foz then he ſhall
haue appel of maime a
gainſt him.

And note wel,that
a villein may haue iij.
actiōs againſt his lozd
that is to ſay,appeale

ils ne ſerrount pur
taunt enfraunchiſe ,
pur ceo que ils ſount
a recouer le dette a-
uauntdiſt al vſe dun
auter perſon , ceſtaſ-
cauoire al vſe lour
teſtatour & nyent a
lour vſe demeſne. Et
ſi le tenaunt en dow-
er eyt vne villayne le
quel purchaſe cer-
taine terre en fee &
puis le tenaunt en
dower enter , il auera
la terre a luy & a ſes
heires a touts jours,
& meſme le ley eſt de
tenaunt a terme dans
de vne villeine.

Et nota que le ſeig-
neor poit robber ſon
villen nauſrer & cha-
ſtiſer a ſa volunt ,ſalue
ꝙ il ne puit luy maime,
car donques, il auera
appeal de mahim en-
uers luy,

Et nota que villeine
poit auer iii. actions
enuers ſa ſeigniour,
ceſtaſcauoire appeale
de

á mort sō anceft, appel derope fait a sa fée & appel de maihim. Et nota si ij parceners port briefe de neiftye, & lun de eux soit non suite, le nonfuit de luy serra adiudge la nonsuie de ambydeux, issint que si le nonfuite soit apres apparance, ils serront oustes de cē action a tours ioures car la ley est ciel in fauorem libertatis. Et nota si deux cunt vne vylieme in commone, & lun de eux fayt a luy vne manumission, il ne serra my enfraunchise ouuers amdeux. Et nota que en briefe de Natiuo habendo, il couyent que le seignyour monstre coment il a vsigna prouy de sanke a celuy villeine de que il est seigniour &c. Et sil ne nul de ses auncestours ne soyt seisye de nul de son

..eth of his ancestor, appel of rape done to his wife, and appel of maime. And note wel if ij. parceners bringe a writ of niefe, and one of them be nonsuit, the nonsuit of him shal be iudged the nonsuit of them both, so that if ȳ nonsuit be after apperance, they shal be put out from that accion for euer, for the lawe is such in fauour of lybertye. And note wel, if two haue a bōdrine in common, and one of them make to him a manumission, he shal not be made fra against both, And note weil, that in a writ de Natiuo habendo, it behoueth that the lorde shew how he cōmeth priup of the bloode of the billeine of whom he is lord &c. And if he not none of his auncestours were not seised of none of his bloode blood, he shal not winn by his action, if the villeine haue not kno= wledged in court of record him selfe to bee his villein. And note wel that in a writt of Niefe may not be put more Niefes then two and this was first brought in in the ha= tred of bondage. But in a writt de libertate probanda, may be put as many niefes as the plaintife wil.

And note wel that if þ villein of a lord be in auncien demesne of þ king, or other town priuiledged, within a yeare & a day, the lord may seise him, & if hee dwel in þ same towne or other place franchi= sed vp a yere & a daye without seisin of the lord, he hath no pow= er to seise him after, if he go not in estrey out of þ forsaid frauchis.
¶Taile.

sanke, il ne gainera per son action si le villeine nad pas conus é court de record luy estre son villein. Et nota que en briefe de niefe ne pur= ront estre mis plusours niefes que deux tant= solement, & hoc in= troductum fuit prius in odium seruitutis. Mes en briefe de Ly= bertate probanda, pur= rount estre mese tants Nifes come le plain= tife voudra.

Et nota que si le nief de seigneor soit sue en auncient demesne de roy ou auter villein pri uilegie, deins lan & iour, le seignior poit luy seiser, & sil demurt en la dit ville ou lyeu fraunchise per vne an & vn iour sansle seisin de son seigniour. il nad my povver de luy sei= ser apres, sil ne va en estraye dehors le suis= dit fraunchise.
¶Taile.

18 Tener en le taile,
eſt lou home tiēt cer-
teine terres ou tene-
ments a luy & a ſes
heires de ſon corps en-
gendres. Et nota que
ſi la terre ſoit done a
vn home & a ſes hſes
males, et il ad iſſu male
il ad fee ſimple, & ceo
fuit aiudge en le Par-
liament noſtre ſeigni-
our le Roy . Mes lou
terres ou renementes
ſont oones a vn home
& a ſes heires males
de ſon corps engen-
dres, il ad fee taile, &
liſſue female ne ſerra
my inherite, vt patet
Anno 14. Edwardi
3 . en vn Aſſiſe 18 .
Ed. 3. 45.

TO hold in the taile
is where a manne
holdeth certain landſ
oʒ tenements to hym
e to his heires of hys
bodie begotten . And
note wel, that if þ lād
be geuen to a mā e to
his heires males, e he
hath iſſu male, he hath
fee ſimple, e that was
adiudged in the Parli-
ament of our loʒd the
king. But where lādſ
oʒ tenemētſ be geuen
to a mā e to his heires
males of his bodie be-
gotten , then hee hath
fee taile, e the iſſue female ſhal not be enhe-
ritable , as it appea-
reth the xiiii. yeare of
Ed. the iij. in aſſiſe.

¶Taile aʃʃ poſſibility

¶Taile after poſſibilitie.

19 Tener en le taile
aptes poſſibilitie d iſ-
ſue extinct. eſt lou fre
eſt done a vn home &
ſa feme, & a les heires
de lour deux corps

TO hold in the taile
after poſſibilitie of
iſſue extinct, is where
land is geuen to a mā
e to his wife, e to the
heirz of their ij bodies
in-

ingendzed, and one of them ouerlyueth the other wythout issue betwene them begot= ten, he shall holde the land for terme of hys owne life, as tenant in the taile after possibi= litie of issue extinct. And notwithstanding that hee do wast, hee shal neuer bee impea= ched of that waste. And note that if he a= lien, he in ꝑ reuersion shall not haue a wꝛit of entrie in consimili casu. But he may en= ter, & his entre is law= full, per Rob. Thorpe chiefe Iustice.

engendres, lun de eux suruiue lauter sans is= sue enter eux issuant, il tiendra sa terre a term̄ de sa vie demesn̄, come tenaunt en le taile a= pres possibilitie dissue extinct. Et non ob= stant que il face wast, il ne serra iammays empeche de cel wast. Et nota sil alyen , ec= luy en la reuersion ne auera briefe dentre in consimili casu. Mes il puit entrer, & son entre est congeable, per Rober̄ Thorpe chiefe Iustice. 28.Ed. 3. 96. & 49.Ed.3. 25.

¶Free Mariage.

¶Frankmariage.

TO holde in frank= mariage, is to hold in the second taile ly= mitted in the statute of Westminst. ij. cap. 1 And the feoffor shall acquite the feoffee of all maner of seruices

20 Tener en frank= mariage est a tener en le seconde taile limyt en lestatute de West= minster ij. cap. 1. Et le feoffour quytera le feoffee de toutes manner de seruyces
tan=

tanque le quart de-
gree soyt passe, & le
feoffour ferra toutes
les seruyces & suites
duraunt la dit terme.
Et puis les heires le
feoffee le ferrount, pur
ceo que le priuitie de
sanke est passe. Et sil
soit distreine pur ser-
uice, il auera briefe de
mesne enuers luy sup-
posaunt que il tyent
les terres de luy, mes
il nauera pas le fore
iudgement sil ne soyt
en auauntage de ses
issues.

Et nota que apres
le quart degree soyt
pas il serra attendant
des tauntes des ser-
uyces a le donour,
come le donour est
attendaunt al seyg-
nyour paramount. Et
sil face felonye pur
quoy il est attaynt,
le Roy auera sa terre
pur terme de sa vye
naturall. Et apres sa
mort, son issue serr in-

vntil the 4. degree be
past, & the feffor shal do
al the seruice & suites
during the said terme.
And after the heires
of the feoffee shal do it,
for that that the priu-
itie of bloud is past.
And if he be distrained
for seruice, he shal haue
a writt of Mesne a-
gainst him supposinge
that hee held the lands
of him, but hee shall
not haue the fore-
iudgement if it bee not
in aduauntage of his
issues.

And note wel, that
after the fowerth de-
gree bee past, he shalbe
attendant of as much
seruice to the donour,
as the donor is atten-
dant to the Lorde pa-
ramount. And if hee do
felony for which hee
is attaint, the kinge
shal haue his lands for
terme of his lyfe na-
turall. And after hys
death, his issue shal in-
herite

herite, as by force of the taile. And in this case, none shall haue his landes by way of escheate, no more then in any other taile. And in case that the tenant die without heire of his body begotten, the lande shall reuert to the donor as it should in the common taile. And if a man let hys lande to another in in franke mariage yeldinge to him a certayne rent by yeare, hee shal hold this land in the common tayle, and not in frankemariage for by the rent reserued, these words (in liberum maritagium) bee al vtterly voyd, so that the tenure shalbe intended after the tenure in the common taile.

And note well that the gift in franke mariage hath a condicion annexed to it, notw-

herite come per force de la tayle. Et en cest case, nul avera sa terre per voye descheate, nyent puis que en auter tayle. Et en case que le tenaunt devie sauns heire de son corps engenders, la terre reuertera a le donour come serroit en le common tayle. Et si home leisa sa terre a vn auter en franke maryage, rendaunt a luy vn certayne rent per an, il tyendra cest terre en le commen taile, & nient en franke maryage, car per le rent reserue, ceux parolx, (in liberum mariragium)sont tout oustrement voydes, issynt que la tenure serra entendus solonque la tenure en le common taile.

Et nota que le done en franke maryage ad condicyon annexe a luy non obstaut stant que il nest pas expressement declare en la charter del done, vt patet per Statutum VVestminst. ij. cap. 1 de Donis condicionalibus

Et nota que home ne donera pas terres ou tenementz en frankmariage, forsque lou le feme est priuie de sanke a le donor. Car auterment naueroyt home ne feme afcun estate per tiel feoffement forsque a terme de vie.

standing that it be not openly declared in the deede of the gift, as it appeareth by the statute of VVestminst. ij. cap. 1. De donis condicionalibus.

And note well that a man shall not geue landes nor tenementes in frankmariage, but where the woman is priuie of blood to the donor, for els the man nor the woman shall haue no other estate by the feoffement but for terme of lyfe.

¶Frankalmoigne.

¶Free almes.

11 Tener en franke almoigne est a tener terres ou tenementes pur Dieu seruer & faint Esglise dower sans faire afcun auter maner de seruice. Et nota que en cest case, le donour est mesne, & luy doit acquyter frankement enuers

7 To holde in franke almoigne, is to hold landes or tenementes for to serue God and holy church to endow without doing any other maner of seruice. And note wel, that in this case the donor is mesne, & ought to acquit him freely against the

the chiefe Lorde, & also they that hold in frāk almoigne ſhal doe no fealtie, but they that holde in tranke mariage, ſhal do fealtie.

¶Elegit.

TO holde by Elegit is where a mō hath recouered debt or dāmage by a writte against another or by confeſſion or in other manner, he ſhall haue within the yeare against him a writ Iudiciall called Elegyt to haue execution of the halfe of al his lāds and cattelles, (except Oxen and beastes of the plowe) tyll the debt or dammages bee vtterly leuied or paied to him, & during the terme he is tenaunt by Elegit. And note wel if he be put out within the terme hee ſhall haue aſſiſe of nouell

le chiefe ſeigñ, & auxi ceux q̃ teignēt en frākalmoigne ne ferroyent fealtie, mes ceux que teignont en frankmariage, ferront fealtie.

¶Elegit.

22 Tener per Elegit eſt lou home ad recouer det ou dammage per briefe deuers vn auter, ou per conuſaunce ou in auter manner, il auera deyns le an deuers luy vn briefe iudiciall noſme Elegit, dauer execution del moytie de toutes ſes terres & chattels (exceptes beofes, & affers a ſa carues) tanque le det ou les dammages ſoyent ouſtrement leues ou payes a luy, & duraunt ceſt terme il eſt tenant per Elegit. Et nota ſil ſoyt ouſte deins le tīe il auera aſſiſe de nouel

disseisin, & apres vn
redisseisin si besoigné
soit, & cest done per
lestatute de VVest-
monaster 2. cap. 18. &
auxy per equitye de
mesme lestatute celuy
que ad son estate sil
soit ouste auera assise
& redisseysin si be-
soigne soit. Et auxy
sil face ses executours
& deuye, & ses ex-
ecutours entrount &
puys soyent oustes,
ils auerount per le-
quitie de mesme les-
tatute actyon come
luy mesme suisdit, mes
sil soyt ouste & puis
face ses executours &
deuye, ses executours
purront entrer & sils
soyent estoppes de
lour entre ils aue-
rount vn brief de tres-
pas sur lour matter
& case.

Et nota sil face
wast en tout la terre,
ou en parcell, lauter
auera enuers luy main-

disseisin, and after a redisseisin if neede be, and
this is geuen by ý sta-
tute of westminster 2
cap. 18. & also by the
equity of the same sta-
tute, he that hath his
estate if hee be put out
shal haue assise and a
redisseisin if neede bee,
and also if hee make
his executors and die,
and his executors en-
ter and after bee put
put, they shall haue by
the equity of the same
statute such action as
hee him selfe before-
sayde, but if hee bee
put out, and after
make his executors
and dye, his executors
may enter, and if they
bee stopped of their
entre, they shall haue
a writte of trespasse
vppon their matter
and case.

And note wel if hee
to wast in al the lande
or parcel, the other shal
haue against him im-
medi-

mediately a writ Iu=
diciall out of the first
recorde called a veni=
re facias ad computan-
dum, by which it shal
bee inquired if he haue
leuyed all the money,
or parcell, and if hee
haue not leuyed the
money, then it shalbee
inquired to how much
the wast amounteth,
and if the waste a=
mount but to parcell,
then as much of the
money, as the wast
amounteth shalbee a=
bridged of the fore=
sayde money which
was to be leuied. But
if hee haue done more
wast then the foresaid
summe of mony which
was to bee leuyed a=
mounteth, the other
shall be discharged by
and by of all the sayd
money, and shall re=
couer the lande, and
for the superfluity of
the wast made aboue
that that amounteth

tenaunt vn briefe Iu-
diciall hors de la pri-
mer resorde nosme
venire facias ad com-
putandum, per force
de quel serra enquyse
sil ad leue toutes les
denyers ou parcell,
& sil nad leue les
denyers, donques se-
ra enquise a quaunt
le waste amount, Et
si le waste amount si
non a parcell, don-
ques tauntes des de-
nyers que le wast a-
mount serra abridge
de les suisdits denyers
queux fueront estre
leues. Mes sil ad fait
pluis waste que le a-
uauntdit summe dar-
gent que fuit a estre
leue amount, lau-
ter serra dyscharge
mayntenaunt de touts
les denyers suisdytes
& recouera sa ter-
re. Et pur la super-
fluitie de waste fayt
ouster ceo que amount

C c.ij.   a le

a le dist summe il re-
couera ses dammages
singles , & mesine le
ley est de ses execu-
tours , & auxy de
cestuy que ad son es-
tate , & nota sil alien
en fee , ou a terme
de vye , ou en tayle,
tout la terre ou par-
cel de la terre que il
tient per Elegit , si le
alienation soit fayt
deins le terme ou a-
prés , cestuy qne ad
droit auera vers luy
vne assise de nouel dis-
seisin. Et cottient que
ils soient mise en sas-
sise ambideux , auxy-
bien le alienee come
le alienor, & non ob-
staunt que laliene de-
uy maintenaunt vn-
core cestuy que ad dst
auera vers laliene sole
assise, come sil vst estre
son simple tenaunt a
terme de ans. Et ceo
est per lequity del sta-
tute de VVestmister 2
capitulo 25. pur ceo

to the saide summe, he
shall recouer hys da-
mages single, and the
same lawe is of hys
executours , and also
of him that hath his
estate. And note that
if hee alyen in fee, for
terme of lyfe , or in
taile all or parcell of
the land which he hol-
deth by Elegit, if the
alienation be made wi-
in the terme or after,
hee which hath right
shall haue against him
one assise of nouel dis-
seisin. And they both
must be put in the as-
sise the alyenour & the
alyenee, and notwith-
standinge that the a-
lienor by preseptip, yet
he which hath right
shall haue an assise a-
gainst the alienee alone
as if the alienor had ben
a plain tenant for term
of yeres, & that is by
the equity of the statute
of W. 2. ca. 25. for that
that

that he hath not but a chattel in effect, and þ same law is of his executours and of him which hath his estate as is aforesaid.

And note wel that in an Elegit, if the sherife returne that he had nothinge the daye of þ reconizance made but that he purchased lands after the time, then the party plaintife shal haue a newe writte to haue execution thereof, the same lawe is of a statute marchant. And note wel that after a fyery facyas a man may haue the Elegit, but not contrarie wise, for so much that the elegit is of more higher nature then the fiery facias. And note wel þ if a man recouer by a writt of debt and sueth a fiery facyas, and the sherife return that the partye hath no-

que il nad sinon chattell en effecte & mesme le ley est de ses executours & de cestuy que ad son estate come est suisdit.

Et nota que en elegit si le viscount returne que il auoit riens iour de la reconizaunce fayt, mes que il purchase terre puis le temps, adonques la partye plaintife auera nouel brief de auer execution de ceo, mesme le ley est de vne estatute marchaunt. Et nota que apres le fiery facyas vne home puit auer le Elegit, mes non econtra, entaunt que le Elegyt est de plus haut nature que le Fiery facyas. Et nota que si home recouer per briefe de dett, & sue vne fiery facias & le vicount retourne que le partye nad ry-

C c.iij. ens

ens dont il puit faire gree a la party, donques le pleyntife aura vn Elegyt ou vn capias sicut alias & plures . Et si le vycount retourne a le capias mytto vobis corpus & il nad ryens dount il puit fayre gree a la partye, rsserra maunde al gayle de Fleete , & illonques demourra tanque il ad fait gree al partye, & si le vycount retourne non est inuentus , adonques iss ra lexigent enuers luy . Et nota que en biefe de dette port deuers persson de saynt Esglise que nad ryen de lay sée, & le vicount retourne que il nad ryens per que il puit estf summós, adonques suera le pleyntife briefe al Euesque que il face vener son clerke & Leuesque luy ferra

thing whereof he may make grœ with þ party, then þ plaintiff shall haue a capias sicut alias. & a pluries , and if the sherife returne at the capias mitto vobis corpus, & he haue nothing whereof he may make grœ to þ partye, he shall be sent to the prison of the Fleete. & there shal abide till he haue made agrœment wt the party, & if þ sherife returne non est inuentus then there shall go forth an exigent against him . And note wel þ in a writ of debt brought against a person of holy Church, which hath nothinge of lay fée, & the sherife returneth, þ hee hath nought by which hée may be summoned, thē shal the plaintife sue a writ to the Bishoppe that he make his clerk to come, and the Bishop shall make him to

come

come by sequeſtration
of the Church . And
note well, that if a mā
bꝛing a wꝛit of debte
⁊ recouer, ⁊ make hys
executoꝛs ⁊ dieth, they
ſhall haue execution
notwithſtanding that
it be within the peare
by a fieri facias.

vener per ſequeſtrati-
on del Eſgliſe. Et no-
ta que ſi home porte
briefe de dette & re-
couer, & face ſes exe-
cutors & deuie , ils a-
ueront execution non
obſtaunt que il ſoyt
deins lan per vn fieri
facias.

¶ Statute merchant.

¶ Statute merchant.

T'O holde by Sta-
tute merchaunt, is
where a man knowle-
geth to paye certayne
money to another at a
certaine day befoꝛe the
maioꝛ, bailife, oꝛ other
warden of any towne
ꝑ hath power to make
execution of the ſame
ſtatute, ⁊ if the obligæ
pay not the debt at the
day, ⁊ nothing of hys
gꝍds. landes, oꝛ tene-
mentes may be founde
within the warde of
the maioꝛ oꝛ warden
befoꝛeſaide, but in o-
ther places wythout,

23   Tener per leſta-
tute merchaunt . eſt
lou home conuſt a
paier certaine denyers
a vn auter a certayne
iour deuaunt le maire,
bailye , ou auter gar-
deine daſcun ville que
ad poyar de faire exe-
cution de meſme leſ-
tatute , & ſi le obligee
ne paya le dette a le
iour aſſes & ṙie de ſes
biens, terres, ou tene-
ments ne purront eſtre
troues deins la garde
le maire ou gardeine
auauntdyt , mes en
auters lyeus dehors,
    C c.iiij. don-

donques le reconisee
suef le recognisaunce
& obligation oue vn
certification al chaun-
cerve desouth le seale
le Roy , & il auera
hors de la chaunce-
cerie vn capias al vi-
count de quel coun-
tye il est de luy ap-
prender & metter en
prison sil ne soyte
clerke , tanque il ad
fait gree de la dette.
Et vn quarter de san
apres ceo que il ser-
ra pris , il auera sa
terre liuere a luy mes-
me pur faire igree a
le party de dette . Et
il puit vender tan-
que il est enprison
& sa vende serra bon
& loyall . Et sil ne
face gree deyns le
quarter dun an , ou
il soit returne que il
nest troue , & sil ne
soit clerke , adonques
le reconisee puit auer
briefe de la chaunce-
rye que est appelle

then ꝑ recognisee shall
sue the recognisaunce
and obligation with
a certification to the
Chauncery vnder the
kinges seale, and hee
shall haue out of the
chauncery a capias to
the sherife of the coun-
tie where he is to run
him and to put him in
prison, if hee bee not a
clarke, tyil hee haue
made greement of the
debt. And one quar-
ter of the yeare after
that, that hee shall bee
taken, hee shall haue
his lande delyuered
to himselfe to make
gree to the partye of
the debt, and hee may
sel it while hee is in
prison, and his sale
shalbee good and law-
full. And if he doo not
gree win a quarter of a
yere, or if it be retur-
ned ꝑ he be not founde,
then the reconisee may
haue a writt of ꝑ chas-
cery which is called
Ex-

Extendi facias, directe to al sherifes, where he hath landes, to extend his landes and goods, & to deliuer the goods to him, and to seyse him in his landes, to holde them to him and to his heires and his assignes, till that the debtes bee leuyed or payed, & for that time he is tenaunt by Statute merchaunt. And note well, that in a statute merchaunt the reconisee shal haue execution of al the lands which the reconisour had the day of the recognisaunce made, and any time after by force of the same statute.

And note well, that when any wast or destruction is made by the reconisee, his executors, or by him that hath estate, the reconisour or hys executours shall haue the same law as is before-

Extendi facias, direct al toutes vicount lou il ad terres dextender ses terres & biens, & ses byens a luy deliuer, & luy seiser en ses terres, pur les tener a luy & a ses heires & a ses assignes tanque le dette soyt leue on paye, & per cel temps il est tenannt per statute merchant. Et nota que en lestatute merchaunt, le reconisee auera execution de toutes les terres que le reconysour auoyt iour de la reconysaunce fayt, & vnques puis per force de mesme lestatute.

Et nota que quaunt ascun waste ou destruction est fait per le reconisee, ses executours, ou per celuy que ad son estate, le reconysour & ses executours aueront mesme la ley com est suisdyt

dit de le tenant per e-
legit.

Et nota si tenaunt
per lestatute marchant
tyent ouster son terme
cestuy que ad droyt
poyt suer enuers luy
Venire facias ad cō-
putandum , ou en-
trer tantost sicome
sur le tenant p Elegit.

¶Rent seruice.

24 Trois maners de
rentes y sount cest
afcauoire rent seruice
rent charge , & rent
secke. Rent seruice
est lou vne home ti-
ent dun auter per se-
alte , & pur fayre
suit a son court , &
rendaunt a luy vne
certaine rent per an
pur touts maners de
seruices.

Et nota que si le
seigniour soyt seisie
des seruices & rens
auauntdists , & ils
soient aderere , & il
distreine , & le te-
naunt rescue le distres

saide of the tenant by
Elegit.

And note wel, if the
tenaunt by statute
marchant holde ouer
his terme , hee that
hath right maye sue
against him a Venire
facias ad computandum
or els enter by & by as
vpō tenar by Elegit.

¶Rent seruice

There be three ma-
ners of rentes , that
is to saye, Rent ser-
uice Rent charge, and
Rent secke. Rent ser-
uice is , where a man
holdeth of an other
by Fealtye , and for
to do suit to his court
and yeldinge to him
a certaine rent by the
yeare for al manner
of seruices.

And note wel that
if the Lorde be seised
of the seruice and rent
beforesaid, and they be
behinde , and hee dis-
traine, and the tenant
rescueth the distresse

he

hee may haue aſſiſe, oȝ a wȝitte of reſcous, but it is moȝe neceſſa=rye foȝ him to haue aſſiſe then a wȝitt of reſcous, foȝ that by aſſiſe he ſhal recouer his rent and his da-mages, but by a wȝitt of reſcous he ſhal not recouer but the thing and the dammages.

And note wel, that if the loȝde be not ſei-ſed of the rent and ſeruice and they be be-hinde, and he diſtreine foȝ them, and the te=nant take againe the diſtreſſe, he ſhall not haue aſſiſe, but a wȝit of reſcous, and ſhall not neede to ſhewe hys right.

And note well that if the Loȝde diſtreyne hys tenaunt in ſocage foȝ Knightes ſeruice whi he is not deny=ed hym, and auowe foȝ the ſame ſeruice in courte of Recoȝde

il puit auer aſſiſe, ou briefe de reſcous. Mes il eſt plus neceſſarye pur luy de auer aſſiſe. que briefe de Rescous pur taunt que per Aſſiſe il recouera ſon rent & ſes dammages, mes per ceſt briefe de Reſcous il ne reconera mes les repriſes & les dammages.

Et nota que ſi le ſeigniour ne ſoit my ſeiſie del rent & ſer-uice , & ils ſount a-derere,& il diſtrayne pur eux ,& le tenaunt reprent le diſtreſſe,il ne puit my auer aſ-ſiſe , mes briefe de reſ-cous,& ne couient my al ſeignior de monſtre ſon droit.

Et nota que ſi le ſeigniour diſtreine ſon tenaunt en ſocage pur ſeruice de chiualer q̄ il ſuppoſe deſtre te-nus de luy,& auowe pur meſmes les ſeruic en court de Recorde

il

A ferra charge per tiels feruices , per Fynch. termino Hillarij Anno xlvj.

Et nota que fi le feygniour ne puit mye trouer dyftreffe per deux ans, il auera vers le tenaunt briefe de Ceffauit per biennium, vt patet per leftatute de VVeftminfter 2. cap. 21. Et fi le tenaunt denie en le meane temps & fon iffue entre , le feygniour auera vers liffue briefe dentre fur Ceffauit, ou fi le tenaunt alien, le feigniour auera vers lalyenee lauauntdit briefe. Mes fi le feygniour ad iffue & deuie, & le tenaunt foyt en arrerage de dyt rent & feruices de le temps le pyer del iffue & nemye en temps del iffue, il ne puyt mye diftreyne pur arrerages en temps fon pier,

he fhalbe charged by the fame feruyce by Finch.term Hillarij Anno xlvj.

And note wel that if the lord may not finde a diftreffe by twe yere, he fhall haue againft þ tenaunt a wrìt of Ceffuit per biennium as it appeareth by the ftatute of Weft.2.ca.21. And if the tenant die in the meane time and his iffue enter, the lord fhall haue againft the iffue a wrìt of entre vpon the Ceffauit, or if the tenant alien, the lord fhall haue againft the alienæ the forefaid wrìt. But if the Lord haue iffue and die, and the tenaunt bee in arrerages of the faid rent and feruice in the time of the father of the iffue, & not in the time of the iffue, he may not diftrain for þ arrerages in þ time of his father, and

and he shall haue none
other recouery againſt
the tenaunt oꝛ any o=
ther.foꝛ that that ſuch
aduantage is geuen by
the law to the tenant.
And note wel that rēt
ſeruice is that to the
which belongeth feal=
tie.but to rent charge
and rent ſecke belon=
geth not fealtie, but
it belongeth to rent
ſeruyce of common
right.

& il nauera aſcun au=
ter recouere vers le
tenaunt ou aſcun au=
ter , pur ceo que ti=
el aduantage eſt done
pur le ley al tenaunt.
Et nota que rent ſer=
uics eſt , a quel ap=
pent fealtie, mes a rent
charge & rent ſecke
ne appent pas fealtie
mes il appent a rent
ſeruice de common
droit.

¶Rent charge.

¶Rent charge.

Rēt charge is where
a man graunteth cer=
taine rent goinge out
of his laudes oꝛ tene=
mentes to another in
fee ſimple , oꝛ in fee
taile , oꝛ foꝛ terme of
life by dede vpon cō=
dition, that at what
time the rent bee bee=
hinde, it ſhall be well
and lawful to ꝑ graſi=
tee to his heires oꝛ aſ=
ſignes to diſtrayne in

25 Rent charge eſt
lou home graunt cer=
teyne rent iſſant de
ſes terres ou tene=
mentes a vn auter
en fee ſimple ou in
fee tayle, ou a terme
de vye per fayt ſur
condicyon, que a
quel heure que le rent
ſoyt aderere , byen
lyrra a le grauntee
ou a ſes heires ou aſ=
fignes a diſtrayne en
meſmes

mesmes les terres ou tenements. Et nota que si le rent soit adererè, bien list a le grauntee per election dauer briefe dannuitie, ou il puit distraynet, & si le distres soit rescue de luy, & il ne fuit my seisie adeuant, il nad my recouerie torsue per briefe de Rescous, car le distres primerment fait, ne done a luy seisin, forsque sil happe le rent adeuaunt, car sil fuit seisie del rent adeuaunt, & puis le rent soit aderere, & il distrayne, & rescous a luy soyt fait, il auera Assise, ou briefe de Rescous.

Et nota, que en chescune Assise de rent charge, & de annuel rent, & en briefe de Annuitie, couyent a celuy que port le briefe de

the same landes or tenements. And note well, that if the rent bee behinde, it is well lawfull to the grauntee at his election to haue a writ of Annuitie, or els he may distrain, & if the distres bee taken against his will from him, and he was neuer seised before, hee hath no recouery but by writ of Rescous, for the distres first taken geueth not to him seisin, onely if he happ the rent before, for if he were seised of the rent before, & after the rent be behid, & he distrain, & rescous to him bee made, he shal haue ass. or a writ of rescous,

And note well, that in euerie Assise of rent charge and annuell rent, or in a writ of Annuitie, it behoueth to hym that bringeth the writ to shewe

ſhewe foorth an eſpe=
cyaltye , oz els hee
ſhall not mayntayne
the Aſſiſe , but in a
Moztdaunceſtour oz
Foʒmedone in the diſ-
cender oz other wʒits
(in the which title
is gꝯuen oʒ compʒi=
ſed) bʒought of rent
charge , oʒ annuell
Rente , it needeth
nòt to ſhewe eſpecy=
altye.

And note well that
if a man graunt a rent
charge to an other, ⁊
the grauntꝯ purchaſe
the halfe of the lande
whereof the rent is
going out, al the rēt is
extinct, and if the grā=
tꝯ releaſe to the grā=
tour parcell of the
rent, yet al the rent is
not extincte.

But in rent ſeruice
the law is otherwiſe,
foʒ notwithſtandinge
that the Loʒde hath
purchaſed the halfe of
the lande whereof the

monſtre auaunt eſpe-
cyaltye , ou auter-
ment il ne mainte-
nera aſſiſe , mes en
mort de aunceſtour
ou Formedone en le
diſcender , & auters
briefes (en les queux
tytle eſt done ou
compriſe) port de
rent charge , ou de
annuel rent , neſt my
beſoigne de monſtre
eſpecialtye.

Et nota que ſi hom
graunta rent charge
a vne auter , & le
grauntee purchaſe le
moytye de la terre
dount le rent eſt iſ-
ſuant , tout le rent
eſt extincte. Et ſi le
grauntee releaſſe a le
grauntour parcell de
le rent , vncore tout
le rent neſt extincte.

Mes en rent ſer-
uice , le ley eſt au-
terment ,car non ob-
ſtaunt que le ſeigni-
or ad la moity purchs
de la terre , dount le
rent

rent eſt iſſuant, vncore
le rent neſt pas extinct
forſque a le moitie, &
la cauſe de diuerſitie
eſt , pur ceo que rent
ſeruice puit eſtre ſeuer
a vn porcion, mes ne-
my rent charge.

Et nota que ſi rent
charge ſoit graunt a
deux ioyntment, &
lun releas. vncore lau-
ter auera la moitie del
rent , Et auxy ſi lun
purchaſe le moitie de
le terre dount le rent
eſt iſſuant , lauter a-
uera le moitie del
rent dr ſon compaig-
nion. Et ſile diſſeiſor
charge la terre a vn eſ-
traunge, & le diſſeiſee
port laſſiſe & recoñ, le
charge eſt defeat. Mes
ſi celuy que ad droit,
charge la terre, & vn
eſtraunge fayne vne
faux action enuers luy
que nad droit et reco-
uera per default , le
charge demurra. Et
nota que en caſe que

rent is going out, yet
the rent is not extinct
but for the halfe, & the
cauſe of the diuerſitie
is , that rent ſeruice
may be ſeuered to one
porcion, but not rent
charge.

And note well, that
if rent charge be gran-
ted to two iointly, &
the one releaſe, yet the
other ſhall haue the
halfe of the rent. And
alſo if one purchaſe y
halfe of y land where-
of the rent is goinge
out , the other ſhall
haue y half of the rent
of his compainion: &
if y diſſeiſor charge y
land to ſtranger, & the
diſſeiſie bring an aſſiſe
& recouer , the charge
is defeated. But if hee
y hath right charge y
land, & a ſtranger faine
a falſe action againſt
him, and recouer by
defaut . the charge a-
bydeth . And note
well, that in caſe that
pur-

purpartie be betwene
ꝑ.parceners, and moꝛe
land be allotted to one
then to the other, and
ſhæ that hath moꝛe of
the land, chargeth her
land to the other, and
ſhe happeth the rent,
ſhe ſhal maintein Aſ-
ſiſe without eſpecial-
tie. And if the graſitee
haue in fæ ſimple, oꝛ in
fæ taile, ꝯ hath iſſue ꝯ
dyeth, if the iſſue bꝛing
a Foꝛmedon, oꝛ aſſiſe
of Moꝛtdaunceſter, he
ſhall neuer be charged
to ſhew an eſpecialty.

vn purpartie ſoit per-
enter deux parceners,
& pluis terre ſoit allot
a luñ que a lauter &
celuy que ad pluis de
terre, charge ſa terre
a lauter, & el happe
le rent, el maintey-
nera aſſiſe ſans eſpe-
cialtie. Et ſi le graun-
tee auoit in fee ſim-
ple, ou en fee tayle, &
ad iſſue & deuie, ſi liſ-
ſue port vn Forme-
done, ou Aſſiſe dē
Mortdauncester, il ne
ſerra iãmes charge dē
monſtre eſpecialtie.

¶Rent ſecke.

¶Rent ſecke.

REnt ſeck, is where
a man holdeth of me
by homage, fealtie, ꝯ
other ſeruice, yelding
to me a certeine rent
by the yeare, and I
graunt this rent to an
other, reſeruing to me
the ſeruice.

And note well, that
in rēt ſeck, if a man be

26 Rent ſecke eſt lou
home tient de moy per
homage, fealtie, & au-
ters ſeruices, rendaht a
moy vn certeine rent
per an, & ieo graunt
ceſt rent a vñ auter,
reſeruant a moy le
ſeruice.

Et nota que en rent
ſecke, ſi home ſoyt

D d.j. ſeiſie

feifie del rent , & le
rent foit aderere , il
ne puit my diftreine
mes il auera Affife de
nouel diffeifine.

Et nota que fi rent
fecke foit graunt a
vne home & a fes
heires , & le rent foit
aderere , & le graun-
tour deuye , le heire
ne purra mye diftrei-
ner , ne recouera les
arrerages de tempes
fon piere , ficome eft
auauntdit de rent fer-
uice.

. Et en mefme le ma-
ner eft adire en rent
charge ou annuel rent
Mes en toutes les rêtes
auantdits lheire pur-
roit auer pur arrerages
en fon temps demefne
tiel auauntage come
auoit fon piere en fa
vie. Vide ftatutum 32.
H, 8. 37.

Et nota que in rent
feck fi home ne foit
feifie del rent, & il foit
adderere, il eft faums

feifed of the rent, and
the rent be behind, hee
may not diftreine, but
he fhall haue affife of
nouel diffeifine.

And note wel that if
rent feck be grãted to
man and to his heirs
and the rent bee bee-
hinde, and the grãu-
tour dye, the heire
may not diftrein, nor
fhall recouer the ar-
rereges of the tyme
of his father, as it
is beefoze faide of rent
feruice.

And in the fame
manner it is to faye
of Bent charge, oz
annuell rent. But
in all thefe rentes
beefoze faide the heire
maye haue foz the
arrerages in his own
tyme fuch aduaun-
tage as his father had
in his life.

And note well, that
in rêt feck if a man be
not feifed of the rent, &
it be behind he is wout
st=

recouery, foz that that it was his own folly at þ beginninge when the rent was graūted to him, oz reserued, þ he toke not seisin of þ rent as a pennye oz two pence. And note wel that a man maye not haue a Cessauit per biennium, oz an other writte of entrye sur Cessauit foz no rent seck behinde by two yeares, but onely foz rent seruice, as it appeareth in the statute.

And note wel that in rent secke it behoueth hym that sueth foz the rent secke foz to shewe a deede to the tenaunt, oz els the tenaunt shall not bee charged with the rent but · where the rent secke was rent seruice befoze, as in this case lozd, mesne, and tenaunt, and euerye of them holdeth of other by homage and fealty

recouery, pur ceo que il fuit son folly demesñe adeprimes quant le rent fuist graunt a luy ou reserue, que il ne prist my seisin del rent sicome vne denier ou deux. Et nota que home ne puit my auer Cessauit per biennium ou auter briefe dentre sur Cessauit pur nul rent seck aderere per 2 ans, mes ils purrount tant solement pur rent seruice vt patet in statuē w. 2. ca. xxj

Et nota que en rent secke il couyent pur luy que sue pur le rent secke pur monstre fait al tenaūt, ou auterment le tenāt ne serra mye chargē del rent forsque lou le rent secke fuist rent seruice adeuaant come en cest case, seigniour, mesne & tenaunt, et chescun de eux tyent de auter per homage et fealty,

& le tenant del mesr̄e x.s. de rent, le seigniour paramount purchase les terres ou tenements de le tenant, tout le seigniorie del mesne, forsprise le rent est extinct. Et pur cest cause cest rent est deuenus rent secke, & le rent seruice chaunge, car il ne puit distreine pur cest rent. Et en cest case celuy que demād le rent ne serra iammes charge de monstre fait. Auxy en briefe de Mordauncester, Ayle, ou Besaile de rent secke, il ne besoigne de monstre especialtie, pur ceo que ceux briefes de possession comprehendont vn title deins eux mesmes, cestascauoir, que launcestor fuit seisi de mesme le rent, & continua son possession, per cause de quel seisin le ley suppose que est auxy auerrable per

and the tenant of the Mesne x. s. of rent, the Lorde paramont purchaseth the landes or tenemēts of the tenant, all the seigniory of the Mesne but the rent is extinct. And for this cause this rēt is become rent secke, & the rent seruice chaūged, for hee may not distrain for this rent, & in this case hee that demādeth the rent shal neuer bee charged to shew a deede. Also in a writ of Mordauncester, Ayle, or besaile of rent seck, it needeth not to shew a specialtie, for þ these writtes of possession do comprehend a title within them selues, that ys to say, that the auncestour was ieised of the same rent, & continued his possessyon, because of which seisin the law supposeth þ it is also auerrable by the

the Countrey. Yet
learne, for some sup=
pose that it behoueth
of necessitie to shewe
forth a deede, for that
that rent secke ys a
thing against common
right, aswell as rent
charge. But in Assise
of Nouel disseisin, & in
a writ of Entre sur dis-
seisin brought of rent
secke, it behoueth of
necessity to shew forth
a deede, for that that
rent seck is a thing a=
gainst a comon right,
except in the case be=
fore saide, where it
was rent seruice be=
fore. And Assise of
Nouel disseisin, & a writ
of entre sur disseisin, con=
teine within them no
title, but suppose a
disseisin to be done to
ÿ plaintif, & of the en=
tendement of the law,
the disseisin geueth no
cause of auerrement a-
gainst common right,
but of necessitie it be=

le pais. Tamen quere
car ascuns supposont
que il couient a fine
force a monstre, a-
uant fait, pur ceo que
rent secke est vn chose
encounter common
droit, auxybien come
rent charge. Mes en
assise de Nouel dis-
seisin, & en briefe de
Entre sur disseisine
port de rent secke, il
couient de fine force
de mostr auat fait, pur
ceo que rent secke est
vn chose enconter co-
mon droit, sinon en le
case suisdit, ou il fuit
rent seruice adeuant.
Et Assise de Nouel
disseisin, & briefe den-
tre sur disseisine ne
conteygne deins eux
nul title, mes suppo-
sant vn disseisin destre
fait a le plaintife, et de
entendement del ley,
le disseisin ne done
nul cause dauerremet
encouter comon droit,
mes de fine force il
mon-

monstre auaunt espe-
cialtie.

hooueth to shew forth
a deede.

¶Suit seruice.

¶Suit seruice.

27 Suit seruice est a
vener a la Court, de
iij. semaignes en trois
semaignes per an en-
tier , & pur ceo serra
home distraine & ni-
ent amerce.

Suit seruice is to
come to the Court
from iij. weekes to iij.
weekes by the whole
peare , and for that a
man shalbe distrayned
& not amerced.

Suit real est a vener
a la Court del Leete,
& ceo nest forsque ij.
foits en an, & pur ceo
home serra amerce,
& non pas dis-
trayne.

Suit real is to come
to the Court of leete,
and that is not but ij.
times in the pere.& for
that a man shalbe a-
merced , and not
distrayned.

¶FINIS

¶Imprinted at Lon-
don , in Fleetestrete within
Temple Barre, at the Signe of
the Hand and Starre
by Richarde
Tottell.
1579.